THE CONTEMPORARY HOUSE OF LORDS

The Contemporary House of Lords

Westminster Bicameralism Revived

MEG RUSSELL

Reader in British and Comparative Politics
Constitution Unit, School of Public Policy
University College London

OXFORD
UNIVERSITY PRESS

OXFORD
UNIVERSITY PRESS

Great Clarendon Street, Oxford, OX2 6DP,
United Kingdom

Oxford University Press is a department of the University of Oxford.
It furthers the University's objective of excellence in research, scholarship,
and education by publishing worldwide. Oxford is a registered trade mark of
Oxford University Press in the UK and in certain other countries

First Edition published in 2013

Published in the United States of America by Oxford University Press
198 Madison Avenue, New York, NY 10016, United States of America

British Library Cataloguing in Publication Data
Data available

Library of Congress Control Number: 2013938732

ISBN 978–0–19–967156–4

To Philip

Acknowledgements

This is a single-authored book, but was only made possible by the help and support of many people over a long period of time.

My research on the House of Lords has been funded principally through two grants from the Economic and Social Research Council (ESRC). The first (RES-000-23-0597) ran from 2004–07, and supported creation of a database of Lords membership and divisions since 1999, and study of the effects of the 1999 reform. Further funding was provided during 2008–11 as part of a Fellowship (RES-063-27-0163), which allowed maintenance of the database and preparation of additional publications. Since the Fellowship ended, this work has been supported at a lower level by a group of donors to the Constitution Unit, for whose generosity I am very grateful. In addition, the research reported in Chapter 7 on the legislative process was funded by the Nuffield Foundation. My thanks to the Nuffield trustees, and particularly to the Foundation's Director, Sharon Witherspoon.

The ability to conduct this research was also dependent on the cooperation of key staff in the House of Lords, and numerous peers. The initial data on membership and divisions during 1999–2004 had been gathered by David Beamish, now Clerk of the Parliaments, who kindly shared it with me. Since then David has offered much advice and practical help. Mark Simpson and his team in the House of Lords Information Office have also supplied essential information and guidance regularly over the years, as have Alex Brocklehurst and his colleagues in the House of Lords Library.

Large numbers of peers have taken time to respond to my surveys, which are quoted throughout the book: 396 in 2005, 381 in 2007 (including some replying for the second time), plus 79 newly appointed peers since 2009. In addition, well over 100 peers have kindly agreed to be interviewed in connection with the research, as have numerous MPs, parliamentary staff, civil servants and others. It would not be practical to mention all of them by name, but backbenchers and frontbenchers from all of the chamber's groups have helped me build up an understanding of its changing dynamics. I am particularly grateful to those with busy central roles in the organization of the chamber and its groups for giving up their time. These have included group leaders and convenors Cathy Ashton, Tom McNally, Margaret Jay, Herbert Laming, Bill Rodgers, Jan Royall, Tom Strathclyde, Shirley Williams, David Williamson and the late Bernard Weatherill; likewise chief whips Joyce Anelay, Steve Bassam, John Cope, Bruce Grocott, John Roper, David

Shutt and the late Denis Carter; and also group staff including Philip Bassett, Julian Dee, Margaret Ounsley, Carolyn Rampton and Celia Thomas. The first two Lord Speakers—Helene Hayman and Frances D'Souza—have been particularly supportive and kind.

At the Constitution Unit at UCL, my work on the Lords has been assisted by some very able researchers. Maria Sciara maintained the database and worked with me on data analysis for three years from 2004, and Meghan Benton did the same for three years from 2008. Both shaped the work in important ways, as well as being a great pleasure to work with. Meghan also contributed to the legislative analysis reported in Chapter 7, but most of this painstaking work of coding and analysing legislative amendments was conducted by Daniel Gover and Kristina Wollter. From 2011, Eimear O'Casey maintained the database, and contributed significantly to the media analysis in Chapter 9. Tom Semlyen provided essential fact checking and work on the tables and bibliography. Simon Kaye and Ashley Palmer also helped at the early stages, particularly with historical research for Chapter 2. The Constitution Unit in general forms a mutually supportive team environment. Various other Unit colleagues provided useful ideas and help, including Robert Hazell, James Melton, Vicki Spence, Ben Webb, Ben Yong and numerous dedicated research interns. Staff and students in the Department of Political Science/School of Public Policy in turn contribute to a beneficial wider environment. Beyond UCL, fellow members of the Study of Parliament Group—crucially including Donald Shell—have over the years offered much encouragement and help.

While writing the book I have plagued many officials in the Lords for material of various kinds, and their efficiency and kindness has been invaluable. They include Simon Burton and his team in the Public Bill Office, Benet Hiscock and his colleagues working in public outreach, Christopher Johnson and his team in the Journal Office, Kate Lawrence, Ed Ollard, Michael Torrance, Philippa Tudor, Jake Vaughan and Rhodri Walters. Several of these same people—and also David Beamish, Ruth Paley and Paul Seaward—made time to look over chapters, or parts of chapters, for me in draft. My partner, Philip Carter, then nobly spent a week's 'holiday' reading through the entire draft with me, with both an editor's eye and that of an incisive critic. This helped me to iron out numerous weaknesses, and for this alone (never mind much else) he has earned the dedication. Nonetheless, remaining errors of fact or judgement are of course my own. Last, my thanks to John Louth, Alex Flach, Natasha Flemming, Olof Eyjolfsdottir and others at Oxford University Press for efficiently turning the text into an actual published book, and to those who have said such nice things about it on the back cover.

Contents

THE FUTURE

List of Tables, Figures and Boxes

Tables

Figures

Boxes

List of Abbreviations

ACP	Association of Conservative Peers
APPG	All-Party Parliamentary Group
BMA	British Medical Association
BNP	British National Party
CCLA	Commons consideration of Lords amendments
CRAG	Constitutional Reform and Governance
DCMS	Department of Culture, Media and Sport
DPRRC	Delegated Powers and Regulatory Reform Committee
DUP	Democratic Unionist Party
FCO	Foreign and Commonwealth Office
HMRC	Her Majesty's Revenue & Customs
JCHR	Joint Committee on Human Rights
JCSI	Joint Committee on Statutory Instruments
LCCA	Lords consideration of Commons amendments
LegCo	Legislation Committee
LP	Legislative Programme Committee
MPC	Monetary Policy Committee
Nacro	National Association for the Care and Resettlement of Offenders
NSPCC	National Society for the Prevention of Cruelty to Children
OBR	Office of Budget Responsibility
PAC	Public Accounts Committee
PASC	Public Administration Committee
PBL	Parliamentary Business and Legislation Committee
PMB	Private Member's Bill
PR	Proportional representation
SDP	Social Democratic Party
SLSC	Secondary Legislation Scrutiny Committee
SNP	Scottish Nationalist Party
UKIP	United Kingdom Independence Party
UUP	Ulster Unionist Party

1
Introduction

'We already suffer from an overmighty executive. Removing the hereditary peers will make that much worse'
(*Daily Telegraph* editorial, 29 March 1999).

'People have faffed around but it has never been committed to. Now 100 years after the whole thing started, it is going to happen. We will have at least an 80 per cent elected second house, starting this parliament'
(Simon Hughes, Liberal Democrat Deputy Leader, 19 September 2010).[1]

'...the real challenge to completing reform is that the interim arrangements have resulted in a second chamber that has become reasonably effective at causing the government to pause and reconsider... Meanwhile, democratisation leads directly into the political minefield of electoral systems, the role of parties and how best to protect independents'
(*Guardian* editorial, 31 August 2009).

'So, after a long process - almost two and a half years - we do not have the Commons majority needed to ensure this bill progresses through parliament.... I can confirm today that we do not intend to proceed with the bill in this parliament'
(Nick Clegg, Liberal Democrat Leader, 6 August 2012).[2]

'It is striking that the unelected House of Lords now holds government to account better than the Commons'
(*Financial Times* editorial, 20 August 2009).

The House of Lords, as the second chamber of the Westminster parliament, lies at the heart of the British system of government. Yet it is at once both highly controversial and relatively little understood. As an unelected chamber, few members of the public have contact with its members, and its work rarely reaches the news. For the majority of people, if the Lords enters their consciousness at all, this is probably only ever in connection to its proposed reform. Yet the chamber now plays a significant role in policy-making at Westminster. To understand the power dynamics of British politics today, this book argues, it is increasingly important to understand the House of Lords.

The popular image of the Lords—not only in Britain, but for many around the world who recognize its famous architecture and ceremonies—is as a historic but by now outdated institution. However, the reality is far more complex. If they looked inside the chamber today, many would probably be surprised by what they found. Several important reforms took place during the 20th century; the most recent, by Tony Blair's Labour government in 1999, removing hundreds of hereditary peers who had inherited their seats by accident of birth. This transformed the Lords from a chamber of privilege into one predominantly based on merit, and from a body dominated by the Conservative Party into one where no party has a majority. Indeed, with a certain irony, the balance between the parties in the Lords now reflects general election votes more proportionally than does that in the House of Commons. Its members also include a large group of non-party-aligned 'Crossbenchers'—which seems to reflect the public mood in 21st-century Britain, where declining numbers of citizens strongly support any political party, in a curiously modern way.

The 1999 reform was presented by Labour as the first stage of a process, to be followed by a second stage to make the Lords 'more democratic and representative'.[3] But despite numerous reform schemes (described later in the book), no such second stage was ever reached. In 2010 the new coalition government took up the cause of Lords reform, which was a particular demand of the Liberal Democrats, and the coalition agreement included a commitment to pursue 'a wholly or mainly elected upper chamber on the basis of proportional representation' (HM Government 2010: 27). The policy was led by the Liberal Democrat Deputy Prime Minister Nick Clegg, and a bill to create an 80% elected chamber was introduced into the Commons in 2012. But the bill was later abruptly dropped, following resistance from Conservative MPs. At this point Lords reform briefly reached centre stage, threatening to sour relations between Conservative Prime Minister David Cameron and his deputy, and to destabilize the coalition government itself.

Given the failure of repeated reform schemes, and the level of controversy that has surrounded them, it is no wonder that the Lords is so widely associated with the need for reform. But this is now off the government's agenda until at least 2015, and the obstacles to large-scale change remain daunting. In the meantime the Lords gets on with its daily business of scrutinizing and amending government legislation, questioning ministers, and conducting debates and committee work—all of which largely goes on away from the public gaze.

The impact of the 1999 change has been hotly disputed, as illustrated by the quotations at the start of this chapter. Labour's removal of the hereditaries evicted a large group of Conservative (i.e. opposition) legislators, and appeared at least partly self-interested. Hence some feared that it would strengthen government with respect to parliament. In retrospect, however, it seems clear that reform had the opposite effect. That is, the change from a Conservative-dominated to a 'no overall control' chamber strengthened the Lords against the government. This happened partly because the remaining peers felt that the chamber was more 'legitimate', and partly because the removal of so many Conservatives gave new groups of members the potential to affect its decisions. From 1999–2010, under the Blair and Brown governments, the Liberal Democrats in particular benefited from this position. The Lords inflicted over 450 government defeats, and commentators from both left and right began increasingly to praise the chamber's interventions, most notably on civil liberties matters. The Liberal Democrats' entry into coalition government with the Conservatives in 2010 might then have been expected to undermine the Lords. But the Labour opposition has still been able to inflict defeats if supported by sufficient Crossbenchers, which gives this group of independents a newly important role. Since 1999 ministers have thus been forced to negotiate frequently with non-government peers, which sits awkwardly with Westminster's reputation for executive dominance.

In a poll of the British public in 2006, only 5% claimed to understand the House of Lords 'very well'.[4] Even MPs and political experts frequently either applaud what the chamber does, or call vigorously for its reform, while knowing relatively little about how it actually works. On a day-to-day basis most journalists simply ignore the Lords, while few academics have troubled to study it in detail. But there is a danger that, by viewing the chamber as constantly being on the brink of reform, we overlook what it does now and its influence on the policy process. Following the failure of the Clegg proposals, and with major reform looking a long way off, this book seeks to enhance understanding of the second chamber that we have actually got.

Six key questions about the House of Lords

Given the dearth of information about the Lords, there are many issues that a book on the chamber could usefully answer. This book defines its scope quite broadly, but could never do justice to them all. Its most basic purpose is to describe, and explain, the post-1999 House of Lords. But in doing so it considers some of the questions most often asked by educated observers of the Westminster parliament, and seeks to answer them in as objective a manner as possible. Of the many detailed questions addressed throughout the book, the six most important are as follows:

1. To what extent and how has the House of Lords changed, particularly following its reform in 1999? Despite many attempts, the Lords has never been subject to what might be described as a 'big bang' reform, fundamentally shaking up its composition and powers. Instead it has adapted through many incremental or 'piecemeal' changes, particularly during the 20th century. The eviction of the hereditary peers in 1999 was one of the biggest of these, and removed approximately half of the chamber's membership. What effect did this have on the behaviour and culture of the Lords? Can it really still be seen as an 'unreformed' body? What further developments have there been since 1999, during Labour's time in office and under the coalition government of 2010? How does today's chamber differ from its predecessors?

2. In what ways do the culture and membership of the Lords differ from those in the House of Commons? At one level the difference between the Commons and the Lords is obvious: one is elected, while the other is not. But other claims are frequently made about the Lords, which are based on subjective judgements and are therefore harder to assess. For example, it is often said that the chamber is 'more expert', or 'less political' than the Commons. What these terms mean, and how they manifest themselves in practice, is important but complex. The party make-up of the two chambers is also very different, with no party enjoying an overall majority in the Lords, and the presence of many non-party-aligned members. All of these factors have important implications for the chamber's political dynamics, and its wider effects on the system at Westminster.

3. What impact does the contemporary House of Lords have on policy outcomes and on the culture of British politics? The pre-1999 House of Lords was seen as very weak. The respected constitutional scholar Vernon Bogdanor (1997: 119) described Britain as having 'in effect a unicameral system of government but with two chambers of parliament'. Well-known comparativist Giovanni Sartori (1994: 188) likewise characterized British bicameralism as 'extremely feeble'. The Lords was thus frequently dismissed as neither influential nor important (which helps to explain why it was so little studied). Since 1999, however, the chamber has become more active, as seen most visibly through regular government defeats. But how influential are these in practice, and what other impact does the chamber have on the policy process? If it does have influence (as this book suggests), which groups within it have the greatest potential to affect decisions? What does this mean for the power balance in British politics, and the way that policy is made? Of the six main questions considered in the book, this one is probably the most important.

4. Is the House of Lords 'legitimate'? A connected question, however, is whether the unelected chamber's role can be considered 'legitimate'. Prior to

1999 it was widely felt that the Lords, a majority of whose members had inherited their seats, lacked the necessary legitimacy to participate in the policy process. This led the chamber to act with caution, and made it in practice weak. The 1999 reform changed the chamber's composition, and it has become more active, which gives questions about legitimacy a new importance. But while this term is often used in public debates about the Lords, its meaning is often unclear, and among political scientists it is a contested concept.

5. What lessons does the Lords hold for comparative bicameralism, and what can comparative bicameralism teach the UK? The Lords is often seen as unique, but it actually shares many common features with other second chambers. Considering the composition and role of these chambers outside the UK, and how they are perceived, can therefore help us to understand the Lords better. But the House of Lords pre-1999 also had a significant impact on theories of bicameralism. If it has changed, do these theories perhaps now need to be revised?

6. What are the future prospects for the House of Lords? Although this is very emphatically not a book about Lords reform, it would be strange to reflect on the chamber's present situation without also considering its future. When thinking about future reform there are two quite distinct questions. First, what *should* happen? And second, what *will* happen? A connected question is why, given the many failed attempts at Lords reform, this has proved so elusive. Hence Lords reform is the final major issue addressed by the book.

What do we already know?

Like any scholarly work, this book seeks to learn from and build on the prior research of others. Despite the relative neglect of the House of Lords, there is much in the existing literature that can help to guide our analysis.

Detailed studies of the Lords and its work have been few and far between. Exceptions with respect to the pre-1999 chamber are Donald Shell's (1992) very useful general book, and the detailed edited collection produced by himself and David Beamish (now Clerk of the Parliaments) which focused on the 1988–89 session (Shell and Beamish 1993). Much in these books has now been superseded by the 1999 reform, but they provide a useful framework against which change can be assessed. Other analysis of the chamber in the period immediately pre-1999 is also largely found in the work of Shell (e.g. 1985, 1999) and of limited others such as Nicholas

Baldwin (e.g. 1985, 1995). These scholars built in turn on preceding works, most notably those by Peter Bromhead (1958) and Janet Morgan (1975), which now most definitely describe the chamber's history, and thus join the fine body of research on the Lords in earlier periods (as referenced in Chapter 2). In more recent years Emma Crewe (2005) provided an interesting anthropological study of the chamber on the cusp of the 1999 reform, while the only post-reform volume—again by Shell (2007)—was far less detailed than his earlier works. Most book-length studies on the work of the Lords therefore predate the 1999 reform, though a number of more recent articles have been published (e.g. Russell 2010; Russell and Sciara 2007, 2008, 2009). The post-1999 catalogue on Lords reform, meanwhile, has been considerably larger (e.g. Ballinger 2012; Dorey 2006, 2008; Dorey and Kelso 2011; Kelso 2006, 2009, 2011; McLean, Spirling and Russell 2003; Richard and Welfare 1999; Russell 2000, 2009).

Earlier scholarship about the chamber can help inform our analysis. In terms of conclusions, one focus by Shell and others was how (as further discussed in Chapter 2) the Lords was reinvigorated to some extent by a previous incremental membership change: the introduction of life peerages in 1958. Rather than stage one of an incomplete process by Labour, the eviction of the hereditaries in 1999 could perhaps better be seen as 'stage two' of this earlier reform (albeit one which left some distinctly loose ends). A key question for this book is whether it too resulted in a strengthening of the chamber. In terms of methods, earlier authors drew on a range of official data about peers' membership, attendance and voting, and traced the Lords' impact on legislation through case studies and analysis of government defeats. Similar methods are deployed in this book, but benefit from the advantages of both modern computing power and better developed data collection by the Lords authorities themselves. The book also draws on methods of analysis developed by more recent authors in other legislative settings (as referenced in Chapters 6–8).

Despite some revival post-1958, Shell concluded that the Lords was 'reasonably diligent and generally dull, with a whiff of expertise but no real boldness' (1993a: 334). This was consistent with the claim that the UK, despite possessing a second chamber of parliament, was little more than unicameral in practice. And such views were crucial to how the whole British system of government was understood. The central feature of the old 'Westminster model' was that Britain's political executive—generally bolstered by a single-party majority in the House of Commons—faced few obstacles in getting its policy agreed (Lijphart 1984, 1999). The Lords' *de facto* weakness, despite its considerable formal powers, was thus important to wider perceptions of British politics.

The Westminster model has long been questioned, with various proposals that the distribution of power in Britain is more diffuse than it suggests. However, these alternative conceptions generally claim that there is less, rather than more, power residing in Westminster itself. Richardson and Jordan (1979) went so far as to suggest that Britain was a 'post-parliamentary' democracy, where the key site of policy-making was negotiation between government and external interest groups. In response to this 'pluralist' turn (of which other examples include Rhodes 1988; Rhodes and Marsh 1992), David Judge (1993) argued that Britain remained a 'parliamentary state', with Westminster acting as the ultimate arbiter of policy. But even in his analysis 'parliament' was interpreted for practical purposes as the Commons only.

More recently, the distribution of power in British politics has been reconsidered in the light of Labour's constitutional reform programme 1997–2010, of which Lords reform was only one of many parts. Some have concluded that these reforms moved Britain away from the 'majoritarianism' of the old Westminster model (Flinders 2005, 2009; Hazell 2008), towards what Lijphart (1984, 1999) termed 'consensus' democracy. But again scholars' primary focus has been on change outside of Westminster. Some have particularly emphasized the shift towards a greater judicialization (or 'juridification') of politics following the Human Rights Act and establishment of the Supreme Court (e.g. Bevir 2008), while others assert that the devolution of power to new institutions in Scotland and Wales was the key reform (Flinders 2005, 2009). One whole-system characterization has proposed that Britain is now 'bi-constitutional', with consensus democracy operating at the periphery (where the devolved areas have multi-party systems, and elect bodies by proportional representation) but majoritarianism enduring at the centre (Flinders 2009; Flinders and Curry 2007). Some do acknowledge that Lords reform had important effects (e.g. Bogdanor 2009; King 2007), but these views have not yet led to widespread reappraisal—perhaps because of the dominant rhetoric that the chamber remains 'unreformed'. One recent textbook on British politics suggested that the Lords remained part of 'the living dead' of the constitution (Kingdom 2003: 347), while other scholars suggest that '[t]he Lords still lacks any democratic legitimacy (in 2009), and plays little role in policy-making' (Dryzek and Dunleavy 2009: 174).

The analysis in this book, in contrast, suggests that the Lords is now increasingly influential on policy. A key reason is the chamber's 'no overall control' character, where neither government nor opposition has a majority, and policy must be carefully negotiated with non-government peers. This change has brought a significant degree of consensus politics to the heart of Westminster itself, which has thus far been largely overlooked. Such a claim, if it is true, has important implications for how British politics is understood. But it is an empirical claim, which must be backed up by evidence. This is provided in the central chapters of the book.

There are other bodies of literature which inform the book's analysis, and in turn may be informed by it. One important perspective is on the Lords as an unelected institution, lacking the obvious 'democratic legitimacy' that applies to the Commons and other elected bodies. As a second chamber, the Lords has the potential to act as an anti-majoritarian institution or, to use a term coined by Tsebelis (2002), a 'veto player'. But the ability for an unelected institution to do so is fundamentally controversial. The discussion of this issue in Chapter 9 draws on a well-developed literature about the legitimacy of other unelected institutions. There is a live debate about the role that such bodies play in an increasingly complex policy world, and about the phenomenon of 'depoliticization'—whereby policy makers delegate power to unelected 'experts' in response to citizens' growing scepticism about political parties and politicians (Flinders 2012; Hay 2007; Stoker 2006; Vibert 2007). Developments surrounding the unelected House of Lords have clear relevance to this debate.

Sources, methods and style

This book is based on almost 15 years of research about the House of Lords, bicameralism and bicameral reform, and draws from a wide range of both qualitative and quantitative data sources. One of the most important is a database of Lords membership and divisions (i.e. votes) since 1999, first constructed by the author under a grant running from 2004–07 (for this and other work described here I owe thanks to funders and numerous others: see Acknowledgements). The database is updated almost daily using *Hansard*, with records checked periodically against those of the chamber's authorities. In late 2012 it contained records of all 1,113 members who had served in the chamber since the 1999 reform, and all 1695 divisions (as this included how every peer voted in every division, it comprised over 1.5 million records). The database provides information used throughout the book, alongside data drawn from parliament's website and official publications, and made available to the author by the parliamentary authorities. Much of this covers the whole period 1999–2012. Where only illustrative periods are covered, data is drawn from the 2008–09 and 2010–12 parliamentary sessions. The second of these was the most recently completed session at the time of writing, but was unusually long. The 2009–10 session was only five months long, so 2008–09 illustrates a more 'normal' one-year session. Where one-off recent figures are quoted throughout the book, these are usually either for October 2012 or May 2013.

Another key source is information drawn from questionnaires and interviews, mostly with peers. Two main postal questionnaires were circulated to all members of the Lords, in February 2005 and April 2007. The first received 396 replies (57% of eligible members) and the second received 381 (52%). In both cases responses were broadly representative, for example in terms of party group, pre- and post-1999 entrants to the chamber and more versus less active peers. Results are quoted throughout the book. An adapted questionnaire was also sent to all new peers appointed after July 2009, and 79 responses (52%) had been received by October 2012. In addition, interviews were carried out between 2004 and 2012 with more than 120 peers, and others with MPs, parliamentary staff, civil servants and outside groups. Some of these formed part of a research project on parliament's impact on legislation, which included a detailed amendment analysis of 12 case study bills, reported in Chapter 7. Chapter 9 also draws on questions included in a survey of MPs, and commissioned by the author in two surveys of the general public, and includes an analysis of newspaper editorials.

One quirk of this book, which I hope will not irritate too many people, is the naming convention that has been adopted when referring to peers. Elsewhere, the formal means of referring to a peer is normally by their title and surname (often with a suffix for their territorial designation): for example 'Baroness Chapman' or 'Lord Jenkins of Hillhead'. First names do not form part of the official title. But these titles can be unwieldy, and many peers are better known by their pre-peerage name, for example, in the earlier cases 'Nicky Chapman' or 'Roy Jenkins'. Increasing numbers of peers prefer to style themselves using their first name instead of, or as well as, their title. The book therefore uses ordinary first and last names to refer to peers in most cases, since many will be more recognizable to readers that way. Use of ordinary names also better reflects the Lords' status as an increasingly normal, modern parliamentary institution. Exceptions to this rule include references to peers in the pre-1999 chamber, bishops, and some hereditary peers. In all cases, peers' full titles can be found in the index.

Structure, and how to use this book

The remainder of the book is structured in 10 chapters. These are intended to form a natural sequence, but it is recognized that many readers (in particular university teachers or students) may wish to focus on just one or two particular topics. As far as possible, therefore, each chapter is designed also to stand alone. The book is intended for use by both general readers and scholars with an interest in the British parliament and British politics. It also presents findings that may interest some comparative scholars of legislative studies. The approach is intended to be academically rigorous, but driven by real-world concerns, with evidence presented in a clear and accessible way.

The next two chapters provide two different kinds of context for the Lords: historical in Chapter 2 and comparative in Chapter 3. Chapter 2 explains key developments during the chamber's past, from the emergence of the English parliament to the present day, focusing on aspects with most resonance in contemporary debates: the chamber's composition, its powers with respect to the Commons, and proposals for its reform. This analysis shows that much has changed during the chamber's long history, but also that some contemporary debates have very long roots. Chapter 3 looks at bicameralism around the world, considering the composition and powers of all national second chambers, and drawing out some general lessons. This demonstrates that the Lords is not quite as unique as some people might assume. Both chapters provide important indications of why ambitious proposals to reform the Lords have so often failed.

Chapter 4 introduces the contemporary House of Lords, and is where some readers may choose to start. It sketches out the chamber's current membership, functions, powers and organization, explaining how members reach the chamber, and broadly what they do when they get there. This provides necessary context for subsequent chapters. It may also be used as a stand-alone introduction to how the Lords currently works, but does not summarize the material in later chapters—for example, on the chamber's policy contribution.

Chapters 5–8 look in detail at how the Lords works now. Chapter 5 starts with analysis of the main groups in the chamber (i.e. the three main political parties, the independent Crossbenchers and the bishops). In each case it explores the kinds of people who sit in these groups and how they behave, including peers' attendance, the cohesion of party groups, and voting patterns of non-party members. It then considers the extent to which each group influences the outcome of divisions. This demonstrates how important the Liberal Democrats were under Labour, and the growing importance of the Crossbenchers post-2010.

Chapters 6 and 7 concentrate on the chamber's treatment of legislation, which takes up the majority of its time. Chapter 6 starts with a brief description of the legislative process, then focuses on government defeats in the House of Lords. The more than 500 defeats since 1999 are analysed, in terms of the topics on which government is vulnerable, the extent to which defeats are overturned, and which factors are associated with whether a defeat goes on to be accepted by the government and House of Commons. Some examples of notable defeats are also given. Chapter 7 instead looks at negotiated outcomes between government and the Lords, where thousands of amendments are agreed far more consensually each year. It describes how government prepares legislation for passage through the chamber, and the various strategies that peers employ to have influence. These two chapters (though each can be read separately) are closely linked, since the non-conflictual influence of the Lords depends in part on the constant threat of defeat. Chapter 8 then considers non-legislative policy-making, including through questions, debates and committees, reflecting on how these differ from arrangements in the Commons, and what contributions they make to the policy process.

Chapter 9 looks at attitudes towards the chamber, and the difficult but important question of legitimacy. It analyses uses of this term in debates about the Lords and its reform, and how it has been defined by political science scholars. It then draws on survey evidence from peers, MPs and members of the public, and from newspaper coverage, to explore how much the chamber's role is accepted. The chapter concludes that legitimacy is multifaceted, and that while the Lords lacks 'democratic legitimacy' its ethos and its contributions to the policy process are nonetheless quite widely valued.

Chapter 10 is the final main chapter of the book, and focuses on Lords reform. It looks at the many failed attempts at reform since 1999, and why this has proved so difficult, pointing out that the years since 1999 were spent almost exclusively debating the chamber's *composition*, but that concerns about its *powers* are fundamental to the lack of progress. It also considers reform prospects, and whether there are smaller-scale changes that might prove both feasible and effective.

The conclusion to the book—Chapter 11—returns to the six key questions already posed. It suggests that the Lords should be considered significantly reformed, despite the chamber's composition remaining problematic. The Lords is very different to the Commons, in both mechanistic and cultural terms. The post-1999 chamber has had an important impact on policy, and has helped to change the culture at Westminster away from single-party dominance, even before the arrival of the 2010 coalition. Not only has bicameralism in Britain revived, but Westminster now has a relatively proportional 'consensus'-style institution at its heart. This requires us, at least to some extent, to rethink our understanding of how British politics works. It also teaches us important things about bicameralism. In particular, a key conclusion from the book is that a stronger House of Lords has not resulted in a weaker House of Commons. Instead, the ability of both chambers to challenge the executive has been enhanced. The revival of bicameralism has strengthened the Westminster parliament as a whole.

Notes

1. Interview for the *Independent*: <http://www.independent.co.uk/news/uk/politics/simon-hughes-the-party-animal-with-a-taste-for-grass-roots-2083302.html>.
2. Full statement available here: <http://www.bbc.co.uk/news/uk-politics-19146853> (accessed 15 December 2012).
3. The words are from Labour's 1997 general election manifesto.
4. Hansard Society poll conducted by YouGov, 17–18 October, 1,980 respondents.

2

A Brief History of the House of Lords

The focus of this book is the contemporary House of Lords. But one cannot fully understand today's chamber without some grasp of its history. The same could be said of all institutions to some extent, but it is rarely more true than in this case. The Lords has an extremely long history, and continues to be governed partly by conventions and traditions that have settled over centuries. A better understanding of the chamber's past can therefore help to explain what it is today. But a historical perspective is equally important to understanding what the chamber is not. Because of its longevity, we may be tempted to assume that certain aspects of the Lords' composition and behaviour are long-established, but this is not always true. The chamber has also changed substantially throughout its existence, and particularly in the 20th century.

This chapter therefore provides some context by summarizing the Lords' historical development, focusing in particular on aspects that have most resonance today. As the chamber's roots can be traced back over 1,000 years, a single-chapter account must necessarily be somewhat superficial: those wanting a more detailed history are encouraged to pursue the many specialist volumes cited later. But without claiming to be comprehensive, the chapter highlights various key moments in the Lords' evolution as an institution, pointing out some features that are well established, and others which are relatively new. The focus is primarily the two most controversial elements in contemporary debates: the chamber's composition, and its political power.[1] In terms of composition, the chapter summarizes who sat in the House of Lords historically, how they got there, and what implications this had for how the chamber behaved. In terms of political power, it sketches the Lords' changing relationship with the House of Commons and the political executive—i.e. initially the monarch and latterly ministers. The chapter also, almost by necessity, discusses reform. Throughout the centuries there have been various reforms that succeeded, and many others (particularly in later years) which failed. Indeed, there is little in contemporary debates about reform of the Lords, and what its appropriate role and membership should be, that has not been said many times before.

The structure of the chapter is chronological, providing relatively more material on the later periods, since these are both better documented and have more obvious contemporary political resonance. But it is notable that some familiar themes emerge extremely early on. The extent to which contemporary controversies were rehearsed in earlier centuries is something that many readers may find surprising. The conclusion of the chapter draws together some of the most important threads regarding continuity and change in the Lords. This provides material relevant to the first question at the start of the book, regarding the extent to which today's chamber is different to its predecessors. But it also suggests important lessons about the chamber's future, and the prospects for its reform.

In the beginning

> It would be half true to say that William the Conqueror founded the House of Lords. Only half true, because what William founded was not the House of Lords itself, but the institution from which that House is descended, and also because what William founded was not wholly new, but was at least partly based on the old Saxon *Witenagemot*, the Meeting of Wise Men which was already some four centuries old at the Conquest of 1066 (Perceval 1953: 33).

This quotation conveys how the Lords has long-established roots, and it is indeed not straightforward even to say when the chamber first came into existence. While parliamentary bodies in many other states have clear-cut founding moments, the English parliament emerged gradually, and evolved over centuries into the UK parliament that exists today.

What is clear, however, is that while the Lords is now referred to as the 'second chamber', it evolved from what was chronologically the first and only body of the English parliament. The precursors of today's MPs then joined centuries later, creating an eventual split into a bicameral arrangement. The original unicameral assembly was made up of powerful figures drawn together to advise the king. These 'magnates' were the forerunners of the nobility, but positions were not always hereditary, initially being connected to the holding of land. Titles used in the later House of Lords hence have distant origins. These include—in order of decreasing rank—Duke (based on the Latin *Dux*, the first English Duke being created in 1337), Marquess (the earliest dating to 1385), Earl (derived from ealdorman, an ancient English title), Viscount (derived from the French, first used in 1440) and Baron (the most junior title, used to denote tenants-in-chief) (Powell and Wallis 1968). Earls and barons were called to the earliest assemblies, alongside clerical figures including archbishops, bishops and abbots. The assembly that met in 1295, for example, included nine earls, 41 barons, two archbishops, 18 bishops and 67 abbots (St George 1953). Initially attendees were called by name, with no necessary expectation that a summons to one meeting would be followed by one for the next.

The first examples of other groups being called to the assembly have been traced as far back as the 12th century (Maddicott 2010). In the 1230s the term 'parliament' was used in the official record for the first time. Thereafter parliaments, which were themselves intermittent, included knights of the shires and burgesses from the boroughs only when the king called them—in particular in order to request revenue. This was done via local sheriffs, rather than by name—for example, in 1258 four knights were chosen from each county to attend (Holt 1981). To deliberate, 'parliament divided into groups, barons, clergy, knights and burgesses sometimes meeting separately or in changing combinations', but joining together in what was 'parliament' (Harriss 1981: 38). There are records of regular sittings in two distinct chambers from the early 14th century, but also of joint meetings as late as the reign of Henry V (1413–22). Over this period the nobility developed from an 'undifferentiated group of landholders' to 'a structured class of earls and barons constituting the peerage, which excluded the knights and lesser landholders'(Harriss 1981: 36). At the same time it became increasingly established that a person once summoned to one assembly would be summoned to the next, and that this entitlement would pass to his heir on his death. In other words, both the hereditary peerage and the House of Lords were beginning to appear in recognizable form.

The Lords and the origins of parliamentary government

It took centuries more until the powers and privileges of parliament were established with respect to the monarch. The key moment came in the 17th century, but controversies began far earlier. In 1258 a crisis culminated in King Henry III agreeing to hold three parliaments per year, and giving up significant authority to a council composed of barons. His reign was followed by that of Edward I (1272–1307) who held regular parliaments, and enjoyed 'a harmony of purpose with his magnates' (Harriss 1981: 30). But relations worsened under Edward II (1307–27), who was ultimately forced from the throne with parliament's assent. This was a turning point, between the institution being simply a 'royal tool' and instead assuming 'a political momentum of its own' (Harriss 1981: 29).

One of parliament's primary roles was the consent to taxation, particularly to fund successive foreign wars. Here the lower house's right to initiate taxes was established by the 14th century. The role of the two chambers also differed in other ways in these early years. Initially members of what became the Commons were primarily petitioners, while decision-making power lay with the monarch and upper house. But the Commons gradually attained a coequal role in lawmaking, which became firmly established during the 15th century (Graves 1990). As a consequence, the use of joint conference committees, comprising members of both chambers, was established for the resolution of disagreements between them. This practice fell into abeyance only in the 19th century.

In this early period the organization of the two chambers also took on some familiar features. The chamber that became the Lords was generally presided over by the king's chief minister, the Lord Chancellor. The House of Commons established its own Speaker in 1376. The most senior clerk initially served both chambers, until the Commons gained its own clerk in 1388. But despite their increasing procedural separation, the chambers were less distinct in social terms. The status and wealth of upper house members enabled them to significantly influence who was chosen to serve in the Commons. This was to be an enduring feature, highly controversial in future centuries.

The Tudor period brought an important change in the upper house's composition, following Henry VIII's break from Roman Catholicism and the dissolution of the monasteries in 1536–39. This removed the abbots, leaving bishops and archbishops as the only 'Lords spiritual', establishing the so-called 'Lords temporal' clearly in the majority. It made an already small chamber smaller still, and the bishops initially held about a third of seats. But numbers soon revived, following Henry's 'lavish creation of new peers' (MacCaffrey 1965: 55). It is notable that even the old largely hereditary chamber depended to a significant extent on new peerage creations to refresh its membership.[2] The monarch gradually lost discretion over which existing peers could be issued writs to attend, but the ability to create new peers has existed since at least the 1430s (Powell and Wallis 1968). This was necessary even to maintain the chamber in a steady state, following extension of family lines in the absence of heirs.

The late 16th century is seen by some historians as the age when the importance of the Commons overtook that of the Lords. In pure membership terms the Commons was certainly growing: having had fewer than 300 members in the early 16th century it reached 462 in 1586. In contrast, Elizabeth I (1558–1603) was reluctant to create new peers, which led to a

Table 2.1. Eligible membership of the House of Lords (and its predecessors) to 1906

Year	Total members	Spiritual	Temporal	Source
1295*	140	90	50	St George (1953: 61)
1377*	106	46	60	Harriss (1981: 38)
1510	85	48	37	Miller (1982: 13)
1603	81	26	55	Graves (1987: 25)
1661	158	26	132	Swatland (1996: 29)
1719	220	26	194	Turberville (1927: 171)
1783	238	26	212	Turberville (1958: 42)
1801	344	30	314	Turberville (1958: 478)
1837	433	30	403	Turberville (1958: 42–3)
1906**	613	26	587	Walters (2003: 201)

* Note that in these very early years the number called by the monarch could fluctuate considerably. Figures relate to those called to one particular meeting in the given year.

** For a party breakdown, see Table 2.2.

slight decline in their number. Parliamentary attendance had always been officially compulsory, and fines for non-attendance at the upper house were introduced in the 15th century. Nonetheless, just 33 Lords attended the final day of Elizabeth's parliament of 1598 (Graves 1985)—which demonstrates how total eligible membership (see Table 2.1) could often be a poor indicator of the size of the actual 'working' House. But despite peers' relative numerical decline, Graves (1985, 1990) argues that the chamber's political importance remained substantial under Elizabeth. She was 'no lover of parliaments', and called only 13 during her 45 year reign (Graves 1985: 147). However, one of her few appointments to the Lords was her chief minister, William Cecil (created Lord Burghley in 1571). He had sat in the Commons from 1542 and went on to have a controlling role in the Lords until 1598. This, and the fact that peers dominated Elizabeth's privy council, ensured that the chamber remained a central forum. In any case, the dwindling number of peers retained significant influence over the Commons' constituencies.

Controversies, abolition and a new settlement: the Lords in the 17th century

While the late 16th century is generally seen as a time of relative harmony between the chambers, and between parliament and monarch, the 17th century is well known as the most turbulent period in English constitutional history.

The start of this century also witnessed a controversy of a more mundane and familiar kind.

On taking the throne in 1603, James I faced considerable pressure for the creation of new peerages after the long period of restraint under Elizabeth. The chamber was no doubt in need of renewal, but the number of peerage creations that followed was extensive. Together, James and his successor Charles I (1625–49) created over 120 peers, which (once extinctions are accounted for) resulted in a net increase of 83 Lords members. But more notably, James provides the first well-documented case of peerage creations being used as a source of revenue. In the period 1615–28 it is believed that around £200,000 changed hands in return for titles (Beckett and Jones 1989), with the going rate for a barony being around £10,000 (Mayes 1957). These dealings caused consternation in the Lords, and damaged the reputation of both chamber and monarch.

It was of course under Charles that relations between king and parliament entered their worst crisis, leading to civil war and ultimately his execution in 1649. Charles always had more supporters in the Lords than in the Commons, and following his death the Commons declared the abolition of the second chamber on the basis that it was 'useless and dangerous' (quoted in Peacey 2012: 48). England under Oliver Cromwell therefore became not only a republic, but at least initially a unicameral one. However, this settlement did not prove stable, and in 1657 the Humble Petition and Advice proposed the re-creation of a bicameral parliament, which Cromwell welcomed (Paley and Seaward 2010). The new chamber, which was known as the 'other house', was to comprise 40–70 members chosen by Cromwell. He issued 63 writs of summons, some to peers and many to his own relatives. But while a number of meetings of the 'other house' were held, the new arrangement was never accepted by the House of Commons. In contrast, when the monarchy was restored in 1660, the Commons readily accepted the restoration of the House of Lords (Swatland 1996). The bishops, who had been removed from membership in 1642 under the Bishops Exclusion Act, regained membership under the Clergy Act of 1661.

Some familiar features are clearly documented in the restoration period. For example, no fewer than 30% of members of the reconstituted House of Lords of 1660 had previously served in the Commons (Swatland 1996). This was for two reasons. First, many Commons seats were—as long remained the case—held by the eldest sons of peers, who would later inherit their fathers' seats. In addition, when new peerages were created they were often given to former MPs, many of whom were peers' younger sons or other relatives. Thus for many, membership of the Commons acted as an apprenticeship for membership of the Lords. A further familiar feature under Charles II

(1660–85) was that new peerage creations 'were normally determined by political considerations', being used both to reward favourites and to boost the king's support in parliament (Swatland 1996: 30). Charles created 64 new peers, and the chamber was often well attended. When the throne passed to William III (1689–1702), he likewise used the Lords to appoint various political favourites, including several from his native Netherlands.[3]

In the late 17th century the Commons asserted its financial privilege, and this was established more firmly. In 1671, in response to what it considered inappropriate action by the Lords, the Commons passed a resolution stating that 'in all aids given the King by the Commons the rate of tax ought not to be altered by the Lords'. When in 1678 the Lords sought to amend a financial bill, this resulted in a more strongly worded resolution. As Bromhead (1958: 10) indicates, these actions meant that 'something like a constitutional rule had been written down to express a disability of the House of Lords that had already been inherent in the origins of the bicameral Parliament'.

An increasingly political House: the 18th century

In the 18th century there were further familiar controversies, particularly around Lords membership. The first of these occurred at the start of the century, beginning under Queen Anne (1702–14). By this time the roots of the modern party system were becoming established, following the sharp splits in parliament around the civil war and subsequent succession crisis of 1688. A general election in 1710 was won by the Tories, while the Whigs enjoyed a narrow majority in the House of Lords. This made relations between the two chambers difficult. In similar circumstances in 1703 ministers had convinced the queen to create four new Tory peers. In 1711 she agreed to 12 further such appointments to strengthen the ministry's position in the Lords. But this proved hugely contentious, including amongst the existing peers (Turberville 1927). Then when George I (1714–27) took the throne he favoured the Whigs, and created 15 new peers within four years (Paley and Seaward 2010). These developments helped provoke one of the first attempts to regulate the membership of the House in statute.

The Peerage Bill of 1719 was introduced by the Duke of Somerset, and sought to limit the monarch's freedom to create peers, by capping the size of the peerage at 235. This would therefore only permit new creations in order to fill vacancies, when existing lines died out. The purpose was to 'preserve the dignity of the peerage', and avoid a growing politicization of the chamber (Turberville 1927: 170). But while the bill was supported by ministers, the Lords, and even the king, it was dropped after repeated rejection by the House of Commons. Had it become law, the reform would have had important consequences. In the words of Marriott (1910: 18), the peerage would have become 'an exclusive and oligarchical caste' (which many might today assume it was), 'instead of being constantly recruited from the best brains of the country'. This comment underlines the extent to which the hereditary peerage—and thus membership of the Lords—was always porous and dependent on renewal. In addition, as Turberville (1927: 170) points out, placing such limits on the monarch's power would have completely changed the dynamics of later crises in 1832 and 1911.

An important membership reform that did occur in this period, and further boosted the chamber's political nature, was the addition of Scottish representative peers after the union with Scotland in 1707. At that point there were 134 Scottish peers, and only 157 English peers (Smith 1992). Had all Scottish peers gained seats, they clearly would have swamped the Lords. The Act of Union therefore allowed them to elect 16 of their number to membership. But although these were hereditary peers, elected to a hereditary chamber, the seats fell vacant after each general election. This allowed for significant politicking, with parties promoting rival lists. Generally the government's list was able to prevail, and Scottish peers were seen as loyal government supporters (then latterly as loyal Tory voters).

Likewise the role of the bishops in this period was surprisingly political by modern terms. Indeed, 'in the 18th century the nomination of a bishop was largely decided by the part he was likely to play in the House of Lords' (Archbishop of York 1953: 96). The bishops had for centuries been important political figures, and continued as such in the early years of the party system. They could largely be relied upon to support the government of the day, and promises of promotion by the Crown up the church hierarchy were used to induce individual bishops to be loyal (Beckett and Jones 1989). Turberville's description of the 'violent partisanship' of the Bishop of Salisbury Gilbert Burnet (1927: 40) under Queen Anne seems quite alien in the context of the bishops' careful party neutrality today.

In the subsequent years relations between the two chambers became more settled, during what is commonly described as the 'Whig oligarchy'. Under George I the Lords was very influential, as the incoming foreign monarch 'was quite willing to allow the English aristocracy to control the country' (Turberville 1927: 480). But the century as a whole is seen as one in which power shifted further from the monarch to the government in parliament, and from the Lords to the Commons. Notably Robert Walpole, generally seen as Britain's first prime minister, served his entire office (1730–42) from the Commons, and the expectation of ministerial responsibility to that chamber became increasingly established. Nonetheless, the Lords remained extremely important, for several reasons. First, peers tightened their grip on elections to the first chamber, through the 'pocket' or 'rotten' boroughs, where cash, lavish entertainment or other payments in kind could be used to garner the votes of a small electorate for a chosen candidate. Second, most ministers continued to be drawn from the Lords rather than the Commons, with the Chancellor of the Exchequer often being the only senior Commons minister. Notably, the dismissal by George III (1760–1820) of the Fox-North government in 1783, and his appointment of the younger Pitt as Prime Minister, was sparked by the rejection of a bill by the Lords rather than the Commons.[4] Pitt went on to form a cabinet in which all members but himself were peers, and initially governed with no Commons majority. The 'Commons continued to pass one motion after another in calling for the dismissal of a Ministry which did not command their confidence' (McCahill 1978; Turberville 1958: 61), but it was three months before a general election was held. Although this was clearly highly controversial at the time, it demonstrates how the seniority of the Commons in the making and breaking of governments—over that of the monarchy and the Lords—was not yet unequivocally established.

The century ended as it had begun, with a controversy about the creation of new peers and the ever-growing size of the chamber. It was at this point that political control over appointments effectively shifted, to the monarch only creating new peers on prime ministerial advice. Although George III had refused creations requested by Fox-North, he was keen to support Pitt and 'completely changed his policy with regard to the bestowal of peerages' (Turberville 1958: 44). Pitt requested an unprecedented number of new creations, adding 87 peers during his first administration alone, which greatly strengthened the Tories in the Lords. In 1790 the king wrote to the prime minister warning that 'the House of Peers is certainly becoming too numerous' (quoted in Turberville 1958: 44), but by now seemed powerless to stop the flood. In all, the size of the Lords under Pitt increased by almost half between 1783 and 1801 (see Table 2.1). He was also alleged—most notably by Disraeli in his novel *Sybil*—to have changed the nature of the peerage, bringing in entrants from 'new money' and with backgrounds in trade. However, these claims are generally seen as greatly exaggerated (Richards 1928; Turberville 1958).

The growth of democracy: the Lords in the 19th century

By the 19th century the House of Lords had thus reached a very recognizable form. Parliament's policy-making role was well established, clear political party blocs had formed, and regular appointments to the chamber were made, with patronage largely in the Prime Minister's hands. It was also in this century, with the gradual extension of the franchise for House of Commons elections, that the Lords' power came to be severely questioned.

Pitt's creations meant that the Tories started the century with a large numerical advantage in the Lords, which they maintained for most of the subsequent 200 years. This generally included the Scottish representative peers, and was boosted by 28 Irish representative peers who joined following the 1800 Act of Union with Ireland (Large 1986: 246). Unlike their Scottish counterparts, Irish representative peers were elected to the chamber for life, and there were also four Irish Lords spiritual. Election for life meant that by-elections were necessary to fill occasional vacancies. This provided a precedent for the later arrangements under the 1999 House of Lords Act.

When the Whigs returned to power in 1830, with Lord Grey as prime minister, they faced a serious political disadvantage in the Lords. Recalling this period, Lord John Russell (himself later prime minister) reported that the 'Tory element was so predominant that Lord Grey and his cabinet advised the creation of 50 peers at once' (quoted in Pumphrey 1959: 5). In the event, Grey created 40 new peers, most of them in 1831 (Turberville 1958). By now loyalty to party was entrenched, and it was no longer possible to rely on a bloc of peers simply being loyal to the 'ministry'. The Tories, upon finding themselves out of power, established a system of opposition whips in the Lords, which from then on became the norm (Large 1986).

This prepared the ground for one of the most bitter political showdowns ever between the chambers, over the 1832 'Great Reform Act'.[5] The bill was the first of several measures in the 19th and early 20th centuries to widen the franchise. But more importantly in this context it also abolished many 'rotten boroughs', where MPs were chosen by a tiny number of voters. As already indicated, these were often controlled by peers. Estimates vary as to how extensive the peers' patronage was, but it has been suggested that immediately before the Act they controlled the election of as many as 354 MPs, or 54% of the Commons (Smith 1992). There were therefore strong reasons of both a partisan and pragmatic kind for the peers to resist reform.

The bill was introduced following a resounding Whig majority in a general election in 1831, during which the reform had been much debated. The government therefore claimed a strong electoral mandate for its proposals, which passed by a comfortable Commons majority in September 1831. But at second reading in the Lords on 8 October the bill was defeated by 41 votes, which immediately provoked a crisis.[6] It was later reintroduced, and a combination of persuasion, plus threats that sufficient new peers would be created to force it through, proved enough to secure its second reading in the chamber in April 1832. But a month later the bill was subject to a wrecking amendment in Lords committee. The 'country erupted in fury', and a written agreement to create peers was provided reluctantly by the king (Smith 1992: 135). In the end no such creations were necessary, as this very concrete threat was enough to persuade many of the bill's opponents to abstain, and it successfully completed its passage through the Lords (Turberville 1958).

More than any previous episode, this fuelled demands for reform of the chamber, which was to become a regular preoccupation for the rest of the century, and into the next. The general rallying cry by radicals became that the Lords must be 'mended or ended' (Smith 1992: 169). But the episode also attracted criticism of specific groups of peers. Perhaps unsurprisingly, in October 1831 the Scottish representative peers had divided 12:4 against the bill. But more controversially, the bishops divided 21:2 against, which was enough to deprive the government of a majority. Bishops remained partisan figures at this time, and some even formally took the Conservative whip (Smith 1992). Their role in the government's defeat provoked rage, and some (including *The Times* newspaper) demanded their removal from the chamber. Several subsequent initiatives to eject the bishops were made by members of the Commons, all of which failed (Pike 1894; Turberville 1958). But a reform in 1847 capped the number of English and Welsh bishops at 26. The four Irish bishops departed following church disestablishment in 1869, and the Welsh bishops likewise in 1920, but the 26 member limit remains today.

Another growing difficulty for the chamber's composition related to its judicial role. Since its earliest years the House of Lords had served as the nation's highest court of appeal (Jones 2009). But the law was becoming more complex, and hearing appeals required specialist legal expertise. Although peers with no legal qualification could in theory still participate in judicial business, this ceased by convention in the 1840s. There was instead 'increasing differentiation between those who came to be known as "Law Lords"...and the majority of the peers' (Smith 1992: 31). However, few peers had appropriate legal qualifications to carry the burden of this work, which led an innovation to be attempted. The monarch conferred a life peerage in 1856 on the senior judge James Parke, creating him Baron Wensleydale, specifically in order that he could serve as a Law Lord. Yet this decision was resisted by many of the peers, and referred to the chamber's Privileges Committee. The fear was that accepting a precedent of life peerages would facilitate future political 'packing' of the chamber. The Privileges Committee ruled that no prerogative power existed to allow a life peer to sit (claiming that the only possible precedent was by now 400 years out of date, since when all peerages had been hereditary). The immediate problem was resolved through conferring an ordinary hereditary peerage on Parke, but an opportunity for incremental reform without legislation had been missed.

Life peerages were not an entirely new idea. In 1849 Lord John Russell as prime minister had proposed reform to introduce a limited number for 'distinguished men', but his cabinet was 'unreceptive' (Smith 1992: 138). In 1869, after he had been appointed to the Lords himself, Russell took up the cause again through a private peer's bill, which was defeated in the Lords.[7] This would have allowed the creation of four life peerages a year for those with certain qualifications, to include judges but also other public servants and eminent former MPs. The problem of legal expertise was subsequently resolved by the Appellate Jurisdictions Act 1876, which allowed a limited number of life peerages to be conferred specifically on senior lawyers to sit as Lords of Appeal.[8] Further attempts at reform were made, including a proposal by (future Liberal prime minister) Rosebery in 1888 to both introduce life peerages and limit the rights of hereditary peers to sit (Smith 1992). In response Prime Minister Lord Salisbury, promised a government bill. This was published, and would have allowed the creation of 50 life peerages, but was withdrawn following opposition in the Commons (Bailey 1953). The introduction of life peerages was thus to wait a further 70 years.

Following the 1832 confrontation, relations between the chambers became much calmer. The Lords in the mid-19th century is generally considered to have acted with relative moderation, even when faced with governments of a political complexion opposed by the majority of peers. This resulted in part from caution by governments, but also from caution by the peers in overreaching themselves in challenging the elected Commons. In 1867 Walter Bagehot suggested that, despite its continued formal veto power, the Lords had effectively 'become a revising and suspending House' (2001 [1867]: 79). That year, the second Reform Act, which further widened the franchise, passed the chamber easily. However, it was a Conservative measure, which the Liberals also supported. The later years of the century, and the early years of the next, were to prove far less consensual.

Some procedural aspects are worth noting in this period (Smith 1992). Members could still be fined for non-attendance at the Lords, and on one occasion in 1820 a fine of £500 per peer was applied. But proxy votes could also be cast on behalf of absent members. This system had been in place since the early years of bicameralism (Snow 1963), but became increasingly controversial (not least following the events of 1832). Proxies were eventually abolished in 1868. The conference committee for resolution of disputes, also centuries-old, was by now in disuse; the last conference was reputedly held in 1836.[9] The role of Leader of the House of Lords was effectively established in its own right in 1846, when Lord John Russell became prime minister in the House of Commons. Historically, Prime Ministers had more often been drawn from the Lords, at which time they were also Leader of the House, but now the need for separate Lords leadership was recognized.[10] Throughout the 19th century the cabinet still included many peers, though their numbers eroded gradually from a majority to a minority. The last British prime minister to serve wholly from the House of Lords was Lord Salisbury in 1895–1902.[11] At the start of his time in office Salisbury led a cabinet of 20, in which nine were peers.

As already indicated, the late 19th century was again marked by conflict between the chambers. One notable problem occurred in 1860, when the Liberals were again in power, and Gladstone was Chancellor of the Exchequer. He proposed to abolish paper duties (i.e. excise duties which affected the costs of newspapers and other publications), but the Lords rejected his bill. This was highly controversial as it was seen as a 'money bill', so it could be claimed that the Lords was challenging the Commons' financial privilege. The policy had split the cabinet, so some peers hoped that by rejecting it they would persuade the government to think again. But instead Gladstone combined the measure with numerous others in the Finance Bill of the following year, and challenged the Lords to reject this. The peers promptly backed down.

There were also many tensions over non-financial legislation. Several of these concerned Irish matters. In 1868 Gladstone (by then opposition leader in the Commons) proposed a paving measure in preparation for the disestablishment of the church in Ireland. This passed the Commons but was rejected by the Lords. Following a general election late that year, won by the Liberals, a full disestablishment bill was introduced. Conservative leader Lord Salisbury successfully urged the peers to support it, on the basis that the public's views had been clearly expressed at the recent election (Smith 1992). This marks the birth of Salisbury's so-called 'mandate doctrine' or 'referendal theory', which sought to establish a new defence for the Lords in a more democratic age (Weston 1986, 1995). He claimed that the chamber's role should be 'to acknowledge that the nation is our Master, though the House of Commons is not, and to yield our opinion only when the judgement of the nation has been challenged at the polls and decidedly expressed' (quoted in Smith 2004).

Numerous clashes followed in the subsequent years, when Gladstone was prime minister (Rowse 1933; Smith 1992). One concerned the third Reform Act of 1884, which further widened the franchise: proponents of reform presented this conflict as one of 'peers versus people' (Adelman 1985). But the most bitter dispute was over the question of 'home rule' for Ireland.

Gladstone's first home rule bill never reached the Lords, having been defeated in the Commons in 1886. This triggered a general election, which was won by the Conservatives. But when the Liberals regained power in 1892, home rule returned to the agenda. A new bill passed the Commons in 1893, but was rejected by the Lords. Here Salisbury's referendal theory came into play: *The Times* urged the peers to defeat the bill in order that the voters could decide the matter (Weston 1986). But no general election was held for two years, during which time 'Salisbury used the Tory majority in the Lords ... significantly to alter or reject almost every major Liberal bill' (Matthew 2004). Harmony between the chambers was restored only after the Conservatives won the general election of 1895.

A final key development worth noting in this period is the change to the nature of the peerage. While some claimed that Pitt had brought industrialists into the chamber, this does not appear to be supported by the facts. At the beginning of the 19th century practice had still been that those ennobled should possess significant income and acreage of land. But both Gladstone and Salisbury wished to make the Lords more representative: the former for party political reasons, and the latter to enhance the chamber's authority and power.[12] Salisbury's first premiership is seen as the 'turning point', after which industrialists made up around one third of new creations (Pumphrey 1959: 8). Peerages were also extended to former diplomats and military personnel, ex-civil servants, and various others at the top of their fields, such as artist Frederic Leighton, surgeon Joseph Lister, and former House of Commons clerk Thomas Erskine May. But 'the largest single field of recruitment for the Lords remained, as it had always been, the Commons'; in the period 1885–1914, two thirds of new peers had previously been MPs (Cannadine 1992: 196).

Pressures for reform: the Lords in the 20th century

The 20th century began with another major showdown between the chambers, to rival that of 1832. This followed the election of a Liberal government in 1906. As shown in Table 2.2, the Conservatives (recently boosted by the breakaway Liberal Unionists over home rule) were hugely numerically dominant in the House of Lords. The new government faced various difficulties with its legislation, and during 1906–10 was defeated in the chamber 113 times (Jennings 1957). The Education Bill was lost completely, and a bill to end plural voting (i.e. certain electors having multiple votes) was rejected at second reading. The real crisis, however, arose over the Finance

Bill of 1909 (commonly known as Lloyd George's 'people's budget'), which sought to fund new social provisions such as pensions through increased taxes, particularly on the wealthy. Despite the long-established convention of Commons' financial primacy, the Lords defeated the bill at second reading by 350 votes to 75 (Jenkins 1999). Parliament was immediately dissolved as a consequence and an election held in January 1910, which the Liberals narrowly won. After the election the budget was passed by the Lords, largely without debate, in line with the referendal theory.

Disagreements between the chambers were far from over, however. The Liberals were now intent on limiting the Lords' power, their January 1910 manifesto having suggested that 'the possession of an unlimited veto by a partisan Second Chamber is an insuperable obstacle to democratic legislation . . . The limitation of the veto is the first and most urgent step to be taken' (quoted in Dorey and Kelso 2011: 16). Hence the Parliament Bill was introduced in April 1910. This contained two key provisions. First, to end the Lords' absolute veto on legislation starting in the Commons, and replace it with a 'suspensive veto'. Under this provision a bill that passed the Commons in three successive sessions, with at least two years between its initial debate and its third approval, could be sent for royal assent notwithstanding objections from the Lords. The second key provision defined 'money bills' and allowed these to be passed without the Lords' consent after a delay of only one month.[13]

Unsurprisingly, this bill was hugely controversial amongst peers, and was expected to face enormous resistance. Prime Minister Asquith, therefore asked King Edward VII to consider creating sufficient new peers to allow it to pass the Lords. But the monarch was resistant, at least until the public's opinion had been explicitly tested (Jenkins 1999). Matters were then complicated further by Edward's sudden death within a month of the bill's publication. His successor, George V, was similarly reluctant to rush into such a plan. Cross-party talks were held on options for Lords reform, but broke down without agreement. The new king was then forced to consent to the creation of peers if needed to get the bill through, on the basis that another election would first be held to test public opinion. Hence, a second 1910 'peers versus people' election followed, in December. Afterwards, members of the Lords faced the same difficult choice as in 1832: between letting the bill through, or resisting it and risking the chamber's 'swamping' with possibly hundreds of Liberal peers. Ultimately, while some Conservative peers (the so-called 'ditchers') were prepared to risk the latter path, sufficient numbers abstained or voted with the government to allow the bill to pass. It thus became the Parliament Act 1911.

The passage of the Parliament Act has been described as 'a source of very great demoralisation of the upper House', ending as it did the historic veto (Walters 2003: 192). In subsequent years the chamber became more timid, although this did not occur immediately. Most notably, a further home rule measure, the Government of Ireland Bill, was overwhelmingly rejected in 1913—which left the Irish question unresolved at the outbreak of World War I in 1914. The chamber likewise repeatedly rejected a bill to disestablish the Church of Wales. Both measures were passed using the new Parliament Act, but enactment was delayed until after the war (with the Irish problem in the meantime descending into armed conflict). These were the first, and only, occasions that the 1911 Act was used to enact ordinary legislation, until the passage of its successor Act of 1949.

The early 20th century saw the repeat of another kind of familiar controversy, regarding 'cash for peerages'. It is suggested that this practice had been going on in a discreet way since the late 19th century, partly as a result of the growing cost of party politics, and partly thanks to the widening pool of potential peers (Cannadine 1992). A Commons debate was held on the question in 1894, and there was suspicion over some of Balfour's appointments in 1905. But the great scandal came in the 1920s, when Lloyd George was prime minister. Some 26 ennoblements were involved, in an operation run by the notorious Maundy Gregory from offices in Parliament Square. Lord Selborne, who vociferously protested against this practice, memorably claimed that peerages were 'being bought and sold over the counter like packets of tea' (quoted in Cannadine 1992: 319). Both MPs and peers raised objections, and Lloyd George was forced to establish a Royal Commission into the process for awarding honours. This resulted in the creation of a Political Honours Scrutiny Committee to vet nominations for peerages, and the Honours (Prevention of Abuses) Act 1925.

Another argument over membership, which was not resolved for decades, concerned the admission of women as members of the chamber. The 1918 Representation of the People Act gave women the right to vote, and to stand for election to the House of Commons. The Sex Disqualification (Removal) Act of 1919 then opened the professions, including the civil service, to women, stating that 'a person shall not be disqualified by sex or marriage from the exercise of any public function, or from being appointed to or holding any civil or judicial office or post'. Until this point the small number of women inheriting peerages (which mostly passed only through the male line) had not been considered eligible for membership of the Lords. But now Lady Rhondda, who had inherited her father's title the previous year, claimed her right to sit. As with the earlier Wensleydale case, this claim was referred to the chamber's Privileges Committee, which ruled her ineligible (Takayanagi 2008). Legislative attempts to admit hereditary peeresses to the Lords were made throughout the 1920s, but all failed, and this question was not resolved until 1963.

In the early part of the century the options for reforming the chamber's membership were much discussed. In 1907 a Conservative peer, Lord Newton, proposed another bill to allow life peers, and to restrict the number of hereditary peers allowed to sit. This was withdrawn, and referred to a select committee which reported in favour of life peerages, but no further action was taken (Bailey 1953). Discussions on the Liberal side at this time were more focused on powers (where options to recreate a joint 'conference committee' or use some kind of joint sitting to resolve disputes were ultimately rejected in favour of the suspensive veto). The preamble of the 1911 Act famously stated that 'it is intended to substitute for the House of Lords as it at present exists a Second Chamber constituted on a popular instead of hereditary basis, but such substitution cannot be immediately brought into operation'. However, nothing further happened until 1917, when a cross-party commission was set up under the Liberal constitutionalist Lord Bryce. It produced a definitive statement on the role of the chamber (Bryce 1918), but failed to reach agreement on composition. Various options were floated, with the majority favouring a mixed chamber, in which 75% of members would be elected by MPs and the remainder drawn from among existing peers (Dorey and Kelso 2011). A cabinet committee established in 1921 noted the Bryce report, but failed to reach agreement on a way forward. Lord Salisbury (son of the former prime minister), then proposed a private peer's bill in 1934 to create a 300-member chamber: half hereditary and half appointed, with members serving 12-year terms. But like so many other such proposals, this made no progress.

Throughout the 20th century the membership of the House continued to grow rapidly, as shown in Table 2.2. Increasing numbers of appointments were given to financiers, industrialists, lawyers and other professionals, including those from the armed services and civil service. But while the peerage grew, the proportion of those receiving honours who actually attended the Lords was shrinking. For example, Walters (2003) reports that in 1912 the chamber's formal membership was 642, but average daily attendance was just 69. The Lords could by now be seen to be in decline, and was to remain so until 1958. It offered some resistance to the 1924 and 1929 Labour governments, but more muted than its earlier rebellions (Bromhead 1958; Rowse 1933).

Table 2.2. House of Lords membership in the 20th century, by party

	1906	1952	1968	1986	1999	2000
Conservative	461*	490	351	416	484	233
Liberal/SDP/Lib Dem	98	44	41	86	72	63
Labour	–	63	116	119	193	201
Crossbench**	–	–	–	244	355	163
Bishops	26	26	26	26	26	26
Independent/other	44	203	255	56	80	8
Total	629	826	789	947	1,210	694

Source: Adonis (1993: 20) for 1906, Walters (2003: 201) for all other figures.

* Includes 107 Liberal Unionists.

** Although the Crossbench group became established in the 1960s, official figures were not kept by the House of Lords authorities until after 1968. Morgan (1975: 25) notes that 125 members received the Crossbench 'non-whip' in 1964.

The post-war period, 1945–63

A major question arose over how the Lords would treat the post-World War II Labour government, elected by a landslide in 1945. The new government had ambitious plans, including for the nationalization of industry and the development of the welfare state. It also had a clear electoral mandate. Yet Labour had just 16 peers, in a chamber of over 700. It was in this environment that the so-called 'Salisbury-Addison' convention was established, taking its name from the Conservative leader in the chamber (now the grandson of Prime Minister Salisbury) and the new Leader of the House of Lords, Labour's Lord Addison. This can be understood 'as a *post facto* reworking of the old doctrine of the mandate' as espoused by the earlier Salisbury (Walters 2003: 194). The agreement was that the Lords should not obstruct bills which sought to implement clear manifesto policies, though it reserved the right to amend them. This convention continued to govern relations between the chambers for the remainder of the century (see Joint Committee on Conventions 2006a).

Most agree that 'Conservative peers showed that they had learned the lesson of 1909–11, and conducted themselves with great moderation' during Labour's period in office 1945–51 (Bromhead 1958: 140). The government suffered 113 defeats (Jennings 1957), and there was much need for negotiation; but no bills were thrown out in their entirety. Yet there were concerns on the Labour side that the Lords' two-year delay power could cause difficulty towards the end of a parliament. Hence a plan was developed to further limit this power. Historically, Labour had favoured abolition of the House of Lords; this commitment appeared in its 1910 manifesto, and again in 1935. But senior Labour figures were divided and somewhat ambivalent in their attitudes towards the chamber, some acknowledging that it could serve a useful legislative function (Dorey 2006). The 1945 manifesto stated only that 'we give clear notice that we will not tolerate obstruction of the people's will by the House of Lords' (quoted in Dorey 2006: 600). Yet in 1948 a new Parliament Bill was introduced, to amend the delaying power in the 1911 Act from two years to one. Not having been in the manifesto, this became the first and only of the government's bills to be rejected outright by the Lords (at its second reading, by 177 votes to 81). It also became only the third measure to reach the statute book via the 1911 Act.

Membership reform was again firmly on the agenda in the run-up to the 1949 Parliament Act. Further cross-party talks were held, on both composition and powers, but these broke down. By this point the Conservatives had warmed to the idea of membership reform, in order to protect the chamber and enhance its status. But Labour figures were split, many being wary of strengthening the Lords against the Commons. Former Leader of the Commons Herbert Morrison, for example, suggested that the 'very irrationality of the composition of the House of Lords and its quaintness are safeguards for our modern British democracy'(1964: 205). In the end, therefore, the 1945 government acted only on the chamber's powers.

Actual membership reform did not occur until 1958, under a Conservative government. The Life Peerages Act finally introduced the change that had been called for for over 100 years, being a simple measure just to allow life peers to be created and to sit. Although further measures such as restricting the number of hereditary members were discussed, these were excluded in favour of a narrow bill. Some 44 Labour peers had been appointed 1945–51, but one of the arguments made for the change was a need to create more, since many on the left objected on principle to becoming hereditary peers (Bromhead 1958). Labour nonetheless opposed the bill. As well as resolving the life peer issue, the reform finally admitted women into the Lords, as they were explicitly made eligible for this new form of peerage. Five years later another small measure, the Peerage Act 1963, allowed women hereditaries to take their seats. It also enabled hereditaries to renounce their titles and thereby stand for the House of Commons, which Lord Home did later that year in order to serve as prime minister.[14] Since the 1911 Act it had been considered increasingly inappropriate that a prime minister might serve from the Lords, and this effectively cemented the convention, further affirming the seniority of the elected chamber.[15]

The post-1958 chamber

The 1958 Act, in particular, helped to revive an institution which, in the words of Conservative Party chairman Lord Woolton in 1955, had 'the atmosphere of a Chamber that is slowly dying' (quoted in Dorey and Kelso 2011: 94). In general, life peerages of course increased the turnover amongst members, though it is clear that this had always been significant. Even in 1957 half of members owed their (hereditary) peerages to 20th-century creations, while more than half of new peers created 1916–45 were former MPs. Indeed, even when Bromhead (1958: 20–1) asked immediately before the Life Peerages Act 'how aristocratic is the House of Lords?', he concluded that 'if an aristocrat is a person of ancient noble lineage it seems... legitimate to deny that the composition of the House as a whole is essentially aristocratic'.

Under the new Act Shell (1992: 44) notes that 'the vast majority of life peers [were] the same kind of people as might have been offered hereditary peerages in the past'. But the reform brought in more Labour members (see Table 2.2) and also further accelerated the by now well-established practice of appointing various members of 'the great and the good' as peers. This contributed to a significant growth in the number of independent members who took no party whip. Strikingly, in the late 19th century 'most crossbenchers were men disaffected with their former party rather than true independents' (Smith 1992: 157). In 1887 only 10 peers out of 511 (excluding bishops) had no party allegiance (Adonis 1993).[16] But the appointment of more peers from outside the world of politics gradually changed this, and helped to build the Lords' reputation as an 'expert' chamber. The Crossbench group took on its own organization in the 1960s, as further discussed in Chapter 5.

The revived chamber also became somewhat more confident, and its assertiveness was boosted by the return of Labour to power in 1964. Harold Wilson's governments suffered some familiar problems, though well short of those faced by the Liberals earlier in the century (Morgan 1975; Walters 2003). The 1966 Wilson government then became the first to propose a bill for wholesale reform of the chamber's composition and powers.[17] The project again began with the now-familiar pattern of interparty talks, which ultimately failed. The breaking point came in June 1968 when the Lords rejected—for the first time—a piece of 'delegated' legislation, relating to sanctions against Rhodesia.[18] The Parliament Acts did not cover such legislation, so the chamber retained a veto, which by convention had never been used. Following this provocation, Labour ended the talks. But the government nonetheless pressed ahead with a bill, which would have created a

Table 2.3. Peerage creations 1958–2007, by prime minister and party of peer at appointment

	Conservative	Labour	Liberal/ SDP/Lib Dem	Crossbench/ other	Total	Average per year
Macmillan (Con) 1958–63	29	20	–	41	90	16
Douglas-Home (Con) 1963–64	11	9	–	9	29	26
Wilson (Lab) 1964–70	20	62	6	55	143	25
Heath (Con) 1970–74	8	9	2	29	48	12
Wilson (Lab) 1974–76	22	39	6	16	83	38
Callaghan (Lab) 1976–79	5	29	1	25	60	19
Thatcher (Con) 1979–90	98	56	10	52	216	18
Major (Con) 1990–97	75	40	17	39	171	25
Blair (Lab) 1997–2007	62	163	53	108	386	38
Total	330	427	95	374	1,226	25

Source: Brocklehurst (2008). Figures include Law Lords (52 over the period, classified as 'Crossbench/ other'), but exclude bishops. For 2007–12 figures, see Chapter 4.

chamber with a mixed membership of life peers, bishops, and existing hereditaries (the latter on a non-voting basis), and with a reduced delaying power of six months. The Lords approved the proposals in principle, but the bill faced opposition from all sides in the Commons. After 88 hours in committee on the floor of the House, and only five of the bill's 18 clauses yet considered, the government cut its losses and dropped the proposals. Opposition had famously united Labour left-winger Michael Foot (who favoured abolition of the Lords), and Conservative right-winger Enoch Powell (who sought to preserve the chamber).

The failure of the 1968 reform again added incrementally to the chamber's confidence. After all 'it was, many members felt, not their Lordships' fault that they still went unreformed' (Walters 2003: 232). The Conservative government of Edward Heath (1970–74) was not seriously threatened by the chamber, but Labour peers forced significantly more divisions than previously, and there were 26 defeats (Shell 2007). The Labour governments of 1974–79 then suffered many more defeats (see Chapter 6), some of which ultimately proved fatal to bills. But most were simply overturned in the House of Commons, with the Lords not insisting on its amendments (Baldwin 1995).

In the 1980s Margaret Thatcher's Conservative governments enjoyed large House of Commons majorities. This in a way also fed the Lords' boldness, as some sensed that legislation would pass too readily without careful scrutiny by the chamber. However (as seen in Table 2.2), Conservative peers remained predominant. Even so, Thatcher's own appointments were greatly skewed to her own party (see Table 2.3). There was resistance from the Lords on some legislation, notably regarding the abolition of the Greater London Council and the introduction of the so-called 'poll tax' (Richard and Welfare 1999; Shell 1985, 1992). But if necessary the government could generally call on sufficient loyal troops (the so-called 'backwoodsmen') to get itself out of difficulty. The longest running clash was over the War Crimes Bill, introduced in 1990, which sought retrospectively to allow prosecutions against those who had perpetrated crimes in Nazi-occupied Europe. The bill (which had not been in the party's manifesto) was twice rejected by the chamber at second reading, and reached the statute book under the 1949 Parliament Act. Ironically, it was the first time that the new Act had run its full course, never having been needed under a Labour government.

In 1997 Labour returned to office with a commitment to reform the House of Lords. The party continued to have fundamental objections to both the principle and practice of the chamber's composition. But Lords reform was always a divisive issue for Labour (Dorey 2006). In the 1970s the party had officially returned to an abolitionist policy, but the refusal by party leader James Callaghan to put this in the 1979 manifesto fed bitterness and splits (Minkin 1980; Seyd 1987). The 1983 manifesto included a commitment to abolition, but thereafter the party shifted to a more moderate position of reform. Initially, this focused on options for election, but by 1997 a more pragmatic 'two-stage' approach had been agreed. The manifesto promised that '[a]s an initial, self-contained reform, not dependent on further reform in the future, the right of hereditary peers to sit and vote in the House of Lords will be ended by statute'. There would then be a second stage of reform, 'to make the House of Lords more democratic and representative'. 'Stage 1' was enacted in the House of Lords Act 1999. This started as a simple measure to remove all hereditary peers, but a compromise was brokered between Tony Blair and the Conservative leader in the Lords, Viscount Cranborne (great-great-grandson of Prime Minister Lord Salisbury), to retain 92 of their number. This led rather spectacularly to Cranborne's sacking by his party leader, who had allegedly not been informed of the discussions (Crewe 2005; Kelso 2009; Shell 2000). The compromise amendment was moved by Lord Weatherill, convenor of the Crossbench peers, and accepted by the government. But although 92 hereditary peers remained, over 650 departed the chamber in November 1999, leaving it smaller, far more balanced in terms of party, and arguably more legitimate. The promised 'stage two' of reform has yet to be reached.

Reform in the 21st century

The focus of the remainder of this book is the contemporary House of Lords, which is essentially that left by the reform of 1999. Debates on further reform have continued unabated, with numerous government proposals published, and most recently a coalition government bill in 2012. In addition, a Royal Commission was established in 1998 to consider options for the next stage of reform, and many other groups have also made proposals. These developments are summarized in Chapter 10.

This chapter has concentrated largely on those reforms that actually took place, which since 1999 have been limited. However, one further important statutory change did occur. The Constitutional Reform Act 2005 transferred the chamber's judicial role to a new Supreme Court, which was established in 2009.[19] The initial members of the Court were the existing 'Law Lords' who had previously fulfilled their function from within the House of Lords. But under the Act, Supreme Court Justices are now appointed without being members of the chamber, and the remaining Law Lords lost their right to sit and vote while serving as members of the Court. This ended long-running controversies about the lack of 'separation of powers' between parliament (the maker of legislation) and the judiciary (responsible for its interpretation).

An additional consequence of the Act was a change to the historic position of Lord Chancellor, who until then had remained the head of the judiciary in England and Wales, presiding officer in the House of Lords and a member of the cabinet. The Constitutional Reform Act split these functions, with the judicial elements passing to the Lord Chief Justice, and the creation of a new Lord Speaker to act as the chamber's presiding officer. The first Lord Speaker was elected in 2006, as discussed in Chapter 4. The Lord Chancellor remains a member of the cabinet, currently responsible for the Ministry of Justice, but this post is now most likely to be held by an MP.

Conclusion: Continuity and change in the Lords

An understanding of the House of Lords' long history can help to clarify many aspects of its current composition and political role, and also demonstrates that contemporary controversies have deep roots. Meanwhile, certain other aspects of the chamber now seen as 'traditional' turn out to be relatively recent innovations.

Controversy about how members reach the Lords is particularly long established. This applies most obviously with respect to the periodic allegations of 'cash for peerages': most recently heard in the early 21st century, but clearly audible 400 years earlier, and more famously under Lloyd George. These scandals are fairly unusual, but more everyday concerns have long existed with respect to the extent of monarchical or (later) Prime Ministerial patronage power. The ability to 'pack' the House of Lords with political supporters of the executive has been discussed at times of crisis (notably 1832 and 1911), but also more routinely when incumbent ministers have sought to gain a numeric advantage in the second chamber. These complaints were particularly notable under Queen Anne and later under Pitt. More recently a convention of greater political balance in appointments has been established, whereby Prime Ministers also create some new peers to sit for the opposition parties (and on the Crossbenches). But as Table 2.3 demonstrates, recent governments have nonetheless primarily favoured their own supporters. This patronage power has resulted in constant upward pressure on the size of the House, which has likewise been a frequent cause of concern.

The current chamber is also often criticized for the number of former MPs among its members. For example, in February 2012 Deputy Prime Minister Nick Clegg suggested that the 'House of Lords . . . is far more populated these days than [before 1958] by people who . . . have been recycled from the House of Commons'.[20] In fact, history shows that there has long been a tradition of career progression from the Commons to the Lords. This previously occurred because many eldest sons of hereditary peers served an 'apprenticeship' in the Commons before inheriting their fathers' seats, but also because the Commons always provided the largest pool from which candidates for new hereditary peerages were drawn. This pattern simply continued with respect to life peerages after the 1958 Act. Indeed, the 37% of new peers created in 1958–2008 who were former MPs or MEPs (Brocklehurst 2008) represented a significant drop compared to earlier periods. There have thus always been stronger links between the two chambers than most people might appreciate.

Connected to this are two other important points. First, membership of the Lords has throughout its history been far from static. The pre-1999 chamber is often seen as one where seats were handed down by generation upon generation. While this was certainly true in some families (most clearly illustrated here by the Cecil/Salisbury family), renewal of the peerage always occurred. Pre-1958 the only way to create a member of the chamber was through granting a new hereditary peerage; in the late 19th and early 20th centuries numerous such honours were bestowed on former political statesmen, military leaders and other public figures. Hence, as Bromhead (1958) pointed out, the old House of Lords was not quite as 'aristocratic' as it might have appeared.

Second, complaints about former MPs' dominance of the Lords often go alongside suggestions that the chamber has become more 'political' or less 'independent'. These claims are similarly misguided. It was in fact only in the later 20th century that a clearly identifiable group of Crossbench independents emerged, and that the Lords cemented its reputation as a chamber of 'experts'. From the earliest emergence of the party system, it had been a highly political House, with party allegiance even extending to the bishops. Peers may have claimed that they were somehow above the political fray, but for 200 years the chamber was dominated by the Tory (latterly Conservative) Party. The independent, expert House is thus in important senses a relatively modern phenomenon.

The balance of power between the two chambers has varied a great deal over time. Undoubtedly in the early years of bicameralism the Commons was junior, but gradually became co-equal and eventually gained a status as the 'primary' chamber. But when exactly this came about is a matter much disputed by historians. As late as the 1780s a government (briefly) survived on the confidence of the monarch and the Lords, but not the Commons. The second chamber continued to be one from which many senior ministers—and even Prime Ministers—were drawn until the early 20th century. But the establishment of greater democracy for the Commons challenged the status of the unelected House, as well as its members' control over the constituencies. At key points—most obviously in 1832 and 1911—the Lords asserted its strength, but in doing so pushed government further than public opinion would bear, and risked being severely punished. In the later 20th century, peers were far more careful not to take their opposition too far. Ironically, the chamber's unelected basis, and the threat of reform hanging over it, has made it quite sensitive to public (and media) opinion, as further discussed in subsequent chapters.

Nonetheless, the Lords has long been controversial, and calls for reform have been widespread. But there has rarely been agreement on what shape such reform should take. The 20th century was littered with failed reform schemes (for a full account see Ballinger 2012; Dorey and Kelso 2011), although attempts started far earlier than that. Actual successful reform has been significantly rarer. Almost without exception, those reforms which succeeded had been under debate for many decades. The 'suspensive veto' was implemented in 1911, but was first suggested in the early 19th century. Life peerages were introduced in 1958, having been debated for over a hundred years. The 1999 Act followed a similar period of discussion about the need to end the hereditary route into the legislature. Cross-party talks on reform have repeatedly been convened, then failed, and there has been significant division within the parties (particularly Labour) as well. One reason is the long-standing concern that making the Lords' membership more defensible would strengthen the chamber, and thus compromise the Commons' primacy. These concerns have continued to animate recent debates, as further explored in Chapter 10. Both history and recent events thus show that Lords reform is difficult, and that those reform measures that succeed tend to be relatively small, simple, and well-rehearsed. The coalition's ambitious proposals in 2012 sought to buck that trend, but were ultimately dropped—partly for fear of entering a similar quagmire to that encountered by the last such ambitious government bill, in 1968.

One of the key questions in the previous chapter was whether Britain still has the 'same old' House of Lords, which is regularly characterized as 'unreformed'. The remainder of the book addresses this in particular with respect to the effect of the 1999 reform. But looking at the chamber's longer history it is clear that today's House of Lords is very different to that which existed in the past. Despite elements of continuity the chamber has undergone many changes in its history, and particularly during the 20th century. Collectively these add up to a transformation, but the evolutionary process of change has resulted in an exaggerated sense of stability. The 1999 reform (supplemented in 2005) was therefore the latest in a long chain of events. How important it was in practice, to the culture, behaviour and political impact of the Lords, is addressed in the remainder of the book.

Notes

1. This is a large amount of material to fit into a single chapter, and inevitably requires some matters to be left to one side. In particular, as the contemporary House of Lords no longer has a judicial function, discussion of how this function developed historically is largely omitted.
2. Hence, MacCaffrey (1965) notes that among 61 peerages existing in 1559, almost half (26) had been created in the preceding 30 years. Miller (1982) points out that the majority of new peers created by Henry post-1529 were former MPs.
3. Turberville (1927: 10) lists amongst these Keppel, created Earl of Albermarle, Zuylestein, created Earl of Rochford, and Auverqeuerque, created Earl of Grantham.
4. This was the India Bill, rejected by peers after the king had indicated his displeasure.
5. More properly, the Representation of the People Act 1832.

6. In fact the bill was not explicitly rejected outright but (as has occurred in recent instances: see Chapter 6) subject to a procedural amendment that the second reading should be delayed for six months, which effectively killed it (Turberville 1958: 273).
7. Russell was, like many members of the Commons at the time, the younger son of a hereditary peer. He did not inherit his father's peerage, but was appointed an Earl in his own right in 1861. Having first served as prime minister from the Commons (1846–52), he also served a short second term in office from the Lords (1865–66).
8. The original Act allowed for creation of four such positions, which were extended to six in 1913, seven in 1945, nine in 1947, 11 in 1968 and 12 in 1994 (Dymond 2009). Notably, there had first been an attempt to end the House of Lords' judicial role, through the Supreme Court of Judicature Act 1873. This was agreed and reached the statute book, but was rescinded in 1875 before taking effect (Goodman 1953). The reform finally happened in 2005, as discussed later in the chapter.
9. *House of Lords Hansard*, 15 July 1930, column 443.
10. Likewise, MPs who were prime minister were usually also Leader of the House of Commons. From Walpole onwards there had been nine Prime Ministers in the Commons, and 15 in the Lords before Russell.
11. Robert Cecil, third Marquess of Salisbury, who was a direct descendant of Elizabeth I's minister William Cecil.
12. On 20 February 1874 (reprinted 20 February 2009) *The Guardian* newspaper noted that 110 Liberal peers had been created since 1831, while only 32 had been created 'on the other side', but considered this justified given the Tories' former strength. See <http://www.guardian.co.uk/theguardian/2009/feb/20/house-of-lords-gladstone-peerages>.
13. For a fuller explanation of the Parliament Act, including money bills, see Chapter 4. The bill also limited the length of parliaments to five years, and allowed the House of Lords to keep its veto on any future bill seeking to extend the life of a parliament.
14. Home was, it should be noted, one of those many hereditary peers who had sat in the Commons (1931–45 and 1950–51) before inheriting his title. The 1963 Act is also closely associated with Tony Benn, who helped force the reform having inherited a peerage while sitting as an MP. See Ballinger (2012: 101–23) and Shell (1992: 18–19).
15. The decision by the Conservatives to choose Stanley Baldwin over Lord Curzon as leader in 1923 is generally seen as a watershed in this regard; though the decision was seemingly not based solely on the latter being a peer (see Cooper 2012).
16. Even among bishops, only six of the 26 were non-aligned.
17. For detailed accounts of the 1968 reform project see Dorey and Kelso (2011) and Morgan (1975).

18. For a definition of this term see Chapter 4. For discussion of the Lords' treatment of delegated legislation see Chapters 6 and 8.
19. Another reform that took place over 100 years after it was first proposed: see note 8.
20. Oral evidence to the House of Lords Constitution Committee, 1 February 2012, question 13.

3

Bicameralism in Theory and Comparative Perspective

The previous chapter set today's House of Lords in its historical context, and in so doing exploded some common myths. It demonstrated how there has been both significant continuity and significant change in the chamber's development. Understanding the Lords' history thus provides useful context for how it works today. This chapter provides a different kind of context, by surveying the existence and nature of bicameralism in other legislatures, drawing on an analysis of national constitutions worldwide. Such an exercise shows that the Lords is not quite as exceptional as some casual observers might assume. Many of today's second chambers are now elected; but the Lords is far from unusual in containing members not directly chosen by the people. Similarly, the Lords is often presented as comparatively weak, but in fact many other second chambers have formal powers nowhere near as great. In addition, British reformers are far from alone in feeling dissatisfied with their second chamber; reform debates are common in other bicameral states. Indeed, second chambers—including those that are elected—tend by their nature to be fundamentally controversial.

The chapter begins with a brief review of the origins of bicameralism, and then turns to the closely connected issue of the justifications for two-chamber parliaments. The heart of the chapter comprises a survey of the 76 national second chambers currently in existence, in terms of both their composition and their powers. This feeds the final sections, which reflect on the commonalities and differences between modern second chambers, and the factors that enable them to function most effectively. The chapter's conclusion draws lessons from this comparative survey both for bicameralism and for the House of Lords.

In terms of the questions at the start of the book, this material is clearly relevant when we consider how recent developments in the Lords relate to perceptions of bicameralism more broadly. It is also useful when considering recent schemes for Lords reform in Chapter 10. Although the current chapter's main role is to contextualize the Lords, it has also been designed to stand alone. As such, it may be useful to scholars of comparative politics as well as those seeking a better understanding of the British system.

The history of bicameralism internationally

The earliest known examples of multi-chamber arrangements were in ancient Greece and Rome. The body that first held the name now used by most of today's second chambers[1] was the Roman Senate: originally a body of elders appointed to advise the early kings. The term Senate literally meant 'council of old men', derived from the Latin *senex* (which provides the root for other modern terms such as 'senior').[2] Over time the Senate became the dominant governing body in the Roman Republic, despite later coexisting alongside assemblies more representative of the wider citizenry. Likewise in parts of ancient Greece, bodies of the wise or wealthy sat alongside more democratic assemblies (Shell 2001; Tsebelis and Money 1997). Such systems of 'mixed government' were celebrated by early scholars, most notably Aristotle. He famously expressed concern that each 'pure' form of government (rule by the one—monarchy, the few—aristocracy, or the many—polity) could develop into a corrupt variant (respectively tyranny, oligarchy or democracy) where the ruling group would serve its own ends. The representation of diverse interests, he believed, allowed each group's interest to act as a check upon the other.[3]

The next early example of bicameralism was possibly the emergence of separate chambers at Westminster in the 14th century, as described in the previous chapter. As in the classical arrangements, the two chambers were understood to represent different 'estates': the Lords being the chamber of the aristocracy and clergy, and the Commons of less privileged groups (on an increasingly wide franchise from the early 19th century). Few obvious vestiges of such arrangements exist today outside the UK, but they were common in early Europe. Some parliaments used three, or even more, chambers to represent different estates. For example, the Spanish *Cortes* was originally tricameral, with the nobility, commoners and clerics meeting separately. Ireland also had three chambers, with a House of Commons, House of Lords and separate chamber of clerical proctors. Sweden had four chambers, representing the aristocracy, clergy, towns and peasantry respectively. In a survey shortly before the 1911 Parliament Act Marriott (1910) reported that the late 19th-century second chambers of Austria, Hungary, Italy and Portugal all included both hereditary members and representatives of the church. Some similar arrangements also existed outside Europe: for example, Japan established a House of Peers in 1889. Hence one early form of bicameralism can most straightforwardly be described as an *elite model*, where the second chamber represents society's traditionally powerful groups.

Equally important, and with many more examples extant today, is the *territorial model* of bicameralism. The classic early example is the US Senate. As Tsebelis and Money describe, '[b]y 1776, the American colonies had a well-established tradition of bicameralism' (1997: 27). Most states joining the federation had bicameral legislatures, with first chambers representing the people and elected second chambers (in the absence of an aristocracy) with high property qualifications restricting eligibility of members, voters, or both (Shell 2001). Although some proposed a unicameral arrangement for the new federal assembly, the 'great compromise' agreed at the 1787 Philadelphia convention created a powerful model of bicameralism. The first chamber was to represent the people on a population basis, while the second chamber gave equal representation to each of the states. This was intended to protect the interests of the smaller states as—combined with the coequal powers enjoyed by the two chambers—it ensured that they could not be outvoted by their larger counterparts. Hence, federal legislation required the consent of representatives of at least half of the states, as well as at least half of the population. This was an alternative form of 'mixed' government to that based on elite representation, but offered some of the same benefits.

The US settlement provides the best known example of a federal, strongly territorial, second chamber; but it was not without precedent. The States General that governed the Netherlands from the late 16th century had comprised equal representation from each of the component provinces, with representatives chosen by provincial assemblies (Israel 1998). (The US Senate was initially chosen on a similar basis, with members elected by state legislatures, but this was changed to a system of direct election in 1913.) Federal second chambers composed of ambassadors from the component territories likewise existed in Switzerland and Germany in the 19th century. The US model went on to influence other bicameral arrangements, including in some former British colonies such as Australia, Canada and India. All of these incorporated some Westminster features as well.

The original elite chambers in Europe, Britain excepted, gradually disappeared. In France, repeated constitutional upheavals after the revolution of 1789 saw the country experiment with periods of unicameral, bicameral and tricameral rule, and second chambers including variously appointed, hereditary and elected members. A precursor of today's indirectly elected *Sénat* was established in 1875 (Smith 2009). Other countries, including the

Netherlands, Belgium, Denmark and Sweden (which became bicameral in 1866), adopted various forms of elected second chamber from the mid-19th century (Marriott 1910). Post-World War II constitutions created another wave of elected chambers, including in Japan (1946), Italy (1948) and Spain (1978). In other places, such as Denmark (1953), Sweden (1970) and Portugal (1974), the second chamber was abolished altogether. The Lords was thus unusual in continuing to evolve, rather than facing sudden radical change.

Modern justifications of bicameralism

The theory of the merits of bicameralism cannot be disentangled from its practical development. The early two-chamber parliaments, as we have seen with respect to the House of Lords, evolved rather than being consciously designed. Writers such as Machiavelli (1469–1527) and Montesquieu (1689–1755) extolled the virtues of 'mixed government' and therefore bicameralism but, as Shell points out, it would 'be a mistake to think that this theory was in some way responsible for the creation of the [initial] institutions which it sought to explain and justify' (2001: 7). Nonetheless, these thinkers' ideas were influential on the establishment of later bicameral institutions, including in the US. The *Federalist Papers,* in turn, then set out many articulate arguments for bicameralism which are still frequently cited today.[4]

In the contemporary context, numerous justifications can be presented for bicameralism (just as many arguments can be made against it, as discussed later in the chapter). The potential benefits offered to a system of government, given the diversity of both bicameral arrangements and bicameral states, are hard to generalize completely. Here we follow a recent account that usefully characterizes bicameralism's two primary functions as being 'representation' and 'redundancy' (Patterson and Mughan 1999).

The nature of the 'representation' function should already be clear. Second chambers offer opportunities for different groups to be represented, which may benefit those who are absent from, or disadvantaged by, arrangements in the first chamber. This applies in particular to minority groups, who may fear the effects of majority rule in a unicameral system. The elite model of bicameralism favoured class minorities, while the territorial model favours geographic minorities. Second chambers can likewise be constructed to guarantee representation to linguistic minorities (as in the contemporary Senate of Belgium) or religious minorities (as in the *Dom Naroda* of Bosnia and Herzegovina, and the Senate of the Irish Free State pre-1935).

But the alternative form of representation in a second chamber need not always benefit minority groups. In many systems it simply incorporates an alternative logic of representation to that in the first chamber. Thus, some second chambers have sought to provide 'functional' or vocational representation, in contrast to the party political representation in the first chamber. Vestiges of this *vocational model* may be found in contemporary Ireland and Morocco, as discussed later. Here, second chamber members formally represent professional groups such as medics, business people or farmers. A more common alternative form of representation can be found through use of different electoral systems for the first and second chambers. In Australia, elections to the first chamber use a majoritarian system which generally results in single party government, while the Senate is elected by a proportional representation system that tends to result in small parties and independents holding the balance of power. A similar system has been suggested in the UK by proponents of an elected replacement for House of Lords (as discussed in Chapter 10). Indeed, although it is not elected, the Lords already follows this logic to some extent, as the pattern of recent appointments leaves no single party holding a majority. Such a system could be described as a *partisan model* of bicameralism: whereby the design of the two chambers explicitly ensures different party majorities. However, the UK case clearly also bears remnants of the elite model, and the Australian Senate formally follows the territorial model.

All of these examples demonstrate that there may be controversy about the most appropriate means to compose a legislature. The existence of a second chamber can thus allow some kind of compromise to be reached between alternative models. As Riker points out, '[i]n a unicameral system there is no test of whether or not an apparent (that is, parliamentary) majority is in fact a real (that is, electoral or society) majority' (1992: 115). Indeed, in systems such as the UK and Canada, it is common for the majority in the first chamber to have been elected on less than 50% of the popular vote. Bicameral arrangements may therefore make it more likely that decisions reflect the interests of a real electoral majority.

The second proposed function of bicameralism, 'redundancy', refers to the duplication which is inherent in a two chamber parliament. Legislation is looked at not once, but twice, which has potential advantages for what Tsebelis and Money straightforwardly refer to as 'quality control' (1997: 40). Patterson and Mughan (1999) suggest that there are two primary arguments for institutionalizing redundancy. First, a revising role simply allows for policy questions to be looked at for a second time and with (ideally) a different perspective, so that obvious errors of judgement may be avoided. This capacity for 'sober second thought' is one of the classic functions of second chambers. In addition, the process of delay introduced by a second round of legislative consideration allows issues to be aired more widely—including in modern democracies, through the media—which provides a greater opportunity for the public to reach a view. The Bryce report of 1918 made a widely cited virtue of this function, proposing that one of the central functions of the Lords should be the 'interposition of so much delay (and no more) in the passing of a Bill into law as may be needed to enable the opinion of the nation to be adequately expressed upon it' (Bryce 1918: para 6). Early proponents of bicameralism saw it as guarding against the dangers not only of the 'tyranny of the majority' but also of over-hasty or ill-considered decision-making.

Thus, bicameralism exists to extend the range of actors involved in political decision-making, and necessarily at the same time slows the process down. For the well-known comparativist Arend Lijphart (1984, 1999), it is hence one of the 10 features that distinguish 'consensus' from 'majoritarian' democracies: consensus democracies being those which require a wider degree of consent for political decisions. Likewise, second chambers are important 'institutional veto players' for George Tsebelis (2002), who characterizes different political systems by the number of actors who may stand in the way of policy change (other such examples being supreme courts or elected presidents). Whether the inclusion of such 'checks and balances' in the system of political decision-making is desirable can be questioned, as further discussed later in the chapter.

The extent of bicameralism today

Despite its ancient origins, bicameralism remains a common legislative arrangement. In October 2011 the Inter-Parliamentary Union (IPU) recognized 190 national parliaments; of these, 76 (40%) were bicameral and 114 unicameral.[5] This represented a growth of bicameralism compared to 12 years earlier; in May 1999 the equivalent figures were 66 and 112 respectively (Russell 2000). Bicameralism thus appears if anything to be increasing in popularity in the 21st century.

The geographic distribution of today's bicameral states is heavily influenced by history. Two chamber parliaments remain common in Western Europe, the Americas and the Commonwealth, but—as shown in Table 3.1—can also be found in the Far East (e.g. Malaysia and the Philippines), Middle East (e.g. Morocco and Sudan), and Eastern Europe (e.g. Poland, Romania, the Russian Federation, and Tajikistan). As some of these examples demonstrate, bicameralism has formed part of the institutional settlement in many new democracies. Their arrangements have drawn on a mixture of experience in more established bicameral systems.

Bicameralism tends to be adopted by larger and more populous states, where it can help to capture diversity. Within the 27-member European Union, the largest unicameral state is Portugal, with a population of 11 million. Various smaller EU states (e.g. Greece, Denmark, Sweden) are unicameral, while all the largest states are bicameral. Similarly, of the 10 most populous countries in the Americas, only two (Ecuador and Peru) are unicameral. Nonetheless, smaller bicameral states do also exist. These include Ireland (population 4.4 million) and Slovenia (2 million) in the EU, and several Caribbean 'micro' states such as Barbados (285,000), Saint Lucia (173,000) and Antigua and Barbuda (86,000).

In terms of regime types, bicameralism is associated both with parliamentarism (i.e. where the political executive depends on the confidence of parliament, as in the UK) and presidentialism (where government is directed by a single figurehead elected independently of the legislature, as in the US).[6] The parliamentary model is widespread in Europe, and the presidential model in the Americas. This has implications for the composition of second chambers in these two regions, as discussed later. Unsurprisingly, two chamber parliaments are particularly common in federal states (i.e. where there is a level of subnational government with some distinct constitutional autonomy, as in the US and Germany), with the territorial model of bicameralism used to reflect regional diversity.[7] Of the 25 federal states recognized by the Forum of Federations in December 2011, 20 were bicameral.[8] In some federal countries, subnational legislatures are also bicameral: in both the US and Australia this applies to every state legislature except one. At subnational level in the British Isles, the Isle of Man (population 80,000) is bicameral, but both the Scottish Parliament and National Assembly for Wales are unicameral.

The composition of second chambers

The modes of selecting second chamber members are extremely diverse. In modern democracies first chambers are generally elected on a universal franchise, with seats distributed between territorial areas broadly in line with population. In contrast, modern second chambers often include members who are not elected directly, or not elected at all, and territories may have a larger or smaller share of seats than their populations would imply. Table 3.1 summarizes the composition of all national second chambers in existence in October 2011, split between parliamentary and presidential states.

Direct election

As the table shows, only 21 national second chambers, most of them in presidential democracies, are wholly directly elected. Where this is the case there is obviously a risk that the membership of the two chambers could be too similar to achieve the kind of creative tension or friction that makes bicameralism work. But there are various means by which distinctiveness between two elected chambers can be achieved.

As already indicated, the most obvious is the use of different electoral systems, with Australia as an example. Here, the House of Representatives is elected using a single member constituency system (the Alternative Vote), while the Senate uses a system of proportional representation (PR). Conversely, in Poland and the Czech Republic the lower house is elected by PR in multi-member constituencies and the Senate uses a majoritarian single-member constituency system. Such arrangements can result in the party balance in the two chambers being very different. In some cases, however, there is far more similarity between the electoral systems for first and second chamber. For example, in Chile elections to both chambers use a similar semi-majoritarian system, but differently sized constituencies.[9]

But differences between the chambers can also be created in other ways. In many cases only a portion of second chamber members are elected at any one time, in contrast to first chamber members who are all chosen on a single day. Thus, the second chamber may be elected in halves (as in Australia, Chile and Japan) or thirds (as in the US and Argentina), with these members serving longer terms than their counterparts in the first chamber. In federal states, and others using the territorial model, less populous areas also tend to be over-represented. The classic example is the US, where each state has just two senators, despite widely differing populations. But similar arrangements exist in various other countries.

In addition, there may be differing membership restrictions for the two chambers. Most notably, the age qualification for second chamber members is often higher, reflecting continued linkage between second chambers and notions of wisdom or maturity. According to the Comparative Constitutions project, of those 56 bicameral states setting age qualifications in their constitution, 36 (not all of them elected) use a higher qualifying age for the second chamber.[10] For example, in Italy the two chambers are elected using very similar voting systems, but members of the Senate must be at least 40 years of age, while members of the Chamber of Deputies need only be 25. The franchise for these two chambers also differs by age: those voting for the

Senate must be 25, while lower house voters need only to have reached 18. Ten countries require members of the second chamber to be at least 40, an additional 11 set an age of 35 (including, for example, Chile, where deputies need only be 21), and a further 18 require members to be at least 30.

Indirect election

Some of these same features also apply in systems of 'indirect election', where second chamber members are chosen by a body or bodies whose members have themselves been elected. This mechanism is often used in systems based on the territorial model, but applies in some others as well. In total, as the table shows, 15 second chambers are wholly indirectly elected, and an additional 19 include some indirectly elected members.

The commonest form of indirect election is that used for the original US Senate, whereby second chamber members are chosen by members of subnational legislatures. This is seen, for example, in Austria, India, South Africa, and several former parts of the USSR including the Russian Federation and Belarus. An alternative to representation of subnational *legislatures* is representation of subnational *governments*. This system continues to be used in Germany, where members of the second chamber are ministers from state governments, who in practice delegate much of their detailed policy work in the *Bundesrat* to state civil servants (Patzelt 1999; Russell 2000).

An alternative is to involve local government councillors in electing members of the second chamber: a mechanism used in several non-federal states. For example, in France senators are chosen by an electoral college including both councillors and MPs. This is organized territorially, but in Ireland councillors and MPs combine to elect the majority of senators in notionally vocational categories.[11] Vocational representation also forms part of the system in Morocco, where three-fifths of second chamber members are elected by local councillors, and the remainder by members of professional chambers (e.g. representing agriculture and industry) and trade unions (Ketterer 2001).

Appointment

Although direct and indirect election are both common, the House of Lords is not alone in including members who are not elected at all. Of the 74 national second chambers shown in the table, 16 contain no elected members, and a further 20 have some unelected members. Among these, the commonest route into the chamber is appointment.

Appointed chambers include several directly influenced by the legacy of the House of Lords, particularly in the Commonwealth. The most notable example is the Senate of Canada, where members are appointed by the prime minister, notionally to represent the provinces. When the federation was formed in 1867 this was the closest approximation that could be found to British arrangements. Likewise, several second chambers in the Caribbean are wholly appointed, as are some in the Middle East.

In some states small numbers of members are appointed explicitly to bring seniority and expertise to the second chamber. Thus, the Indian constitution specifies that the president will appoint 12 'distinguished' people to the second chamber, drawn from the fields of 'literature, science, art and social service'. In other cases appointment is automatic on an *ex officio* basis. For example, in Italy, where most senators are directly elected, the president can appoint a small number of members, in addition to which former presidents of the republic also sit automatically as of right.

Heredity

Where the House of Lords is more unusual is in the inclusion of hereditary members, though even here it is not wholly alone. As Table 3.1 shows, four second chambers still include some hereditary members. In two cases in Africa—Lesotho and Zimbabwe—seats are reserved for tribal chiefs. In Belgium children of the monarch (of whom there are currently three) can automatically sit in the Senate once they reach the age of 18. However, their role is now in practice only ceremonial (Deschouwer 2009: 172).

Mixed composition

As should by now be clear, it is common for second chambers to include a mixture of members entering via different routes. Wholly directly elected, indirectly elected or appointed chambers account for only 50 of the 74 second chambers for which information was available. The remainder include some combination of these different types, with the presence of some unelected members alongside elected members being particularly common. However, mixed membership is more widespread even than these categories suggest. For example, while the Moroccan second chamber is wholly indirectly elected, it contains a mix of members chosen by a combination of territorial and vocational groups, as indicated earlier. A similar mix applies in the wholly indirectly elected second chamber of Slovenia.

Table 3.1. Existing national second chambers, by composition and regime type (October 2011)

	Parliamentary (33)	**Presidential (41)**
Wholly directly elected (21)	Australia, Czech Republic, Japan, Romania, Switzerland (5)	Argentina, Bolivia, Brazil, Chile, Colombia, Dominican Republic, Haiti, Liberia, Mexico, Nigeria, Palau, Paraguay, Philippines, Poland, USA, Uruguay (16)
Wholly indirectly elected (15)	Austria, Bosnia and Herzegovina, France, Germany, Netherlands, Pakistan, Slovenia, South Africa (8)	Congo, Gabon, Mauritania, Morocco, Namibia, Russian Federation, Sudan (7)
Majority directly elected, minority indirectly elected (2)	Spain, Thailand (2)	
Majority directly elected, minority appointed (3)	Italy (1)	Bhutan, Burma (2)
Majority directly elected, plus indirectly elected, appointed and hereditary (2)	Belgium, Zimbabwe (2)	
Majority indirectly elected, minority appointed (11)	Cambodia, India (2)	Afghanistan, Algeria, Belarus, Burundi, Democratic Republic of Congo, Kazakhstan, Rwanda, Tajikistan, Uzbekistan (9)
Majority indirectly elected, plus directly elected and appointed (1)	Ireland (1)	
Wholly appointed (14)	Antigua and Barbuda, Bahamas, Barbados, Belize, Canada, Grenada, Jamaica, Saint Lucia, Trinidad and Tobago (9)	Bahrain, Jordan, Madagascar, Oman, South Sudan (5)
Majority appointed, minority indirectly elected (3)	Malaysia (1)	Senegal, Swaziland (2)
Majority appointed, minority hereditary (1)	United Kingdom (1)	
Majority hereditary, minority appointed (1)	Lesotho (1)	

Source: Adapted from Russell (2012a), largely based on IPU data.[12] Egypt and Tunisia, whose parliaments and constitutions were suspended at the time when this was researched, are excluded from the table.

The powers of second chambers

In the late 20th century the House of Lords was generally considered a relatively weak second chamber. For example, Lijphart (1999), in his well-known classification of 36 democracies (not all of them bicameral), judged the balance of powers between the Lords and Commons to be 'extremely asymmetrical'. He thus concluded that British bicameralism pre-1999 was 'between medium-strength and weak'.[13] As already noted, Sartori went further, claiming that Britain had 'extremely feeble bicameralism . . . [that] shades into unicameralism' (1994: 188).

One of the key claims in this book is that reform in 1999 strengthened the House of Lords. This was not because the chamber's formal powers changed: they did not. Instead, a strengthening resulted from the change to the chamber's membership, which made it more confident and willing to use the powers that it already possessed. This section focuses on other second chambers' formal powers: that is, those written down in constitutions and other documents. It shows that the House of Lords' *formal* powers are relatively strong in comparative terms. Judging a second chamber's *de facto* powers (i.e. the extent to which its formal powers are actually used) is however far more difficult. This issue is discussed later in the chapter.

A legislative body may have various kinds of formal powers. Key among them is obviously the power to agree, amend or reject legislation. But legislatures may also hold various powers over political executives (including the ability to remove them from office), and also over matters such as public appointments or the signing of international treaties. Second chambers' powers can differ from those of their respective first chambers on any of these matters, and frequently do. With respect to legislation, a second chamber's power can also differ substantially between different kinds of bills.

Making and breaking governments

A fundamental power held by the legislature in parliamentary systems is the ability to remove government from office through a no-confidence vote. The presence of this power is one of the key features distinguishing parliamentary from presidential systems. But it is also one of the key features that distinguishes between first and second chambers in almost all parliamentary states. That is, while first chambers in parliamentary systems may sack political executives, second chambers generally cannot. Thus, a British government may be brought down by a no-confidence vote in the House of Commons (as occurred, for example, in 1979), but there is no such concept in the contemporary House of Lords. The same is true of most other parliamentary states, even where the second chamber is elected: for example, in Australia, India and Spain. An exception is Italy, where governments may be brought down by no-confidence votes in either chamber. Each new government must also be formally approved by both chambers. In some other cases, such as Switzerland (and even the US), approval by the second chamber is needed for the appointment of ministers, but the chamber has no power to remove the executive from office after such appointments have been made.

'Ordinary' legislation

The next most basic power of parliaments is over legislation, particularly that emanating from government. While the consent of first chambers is invariably needed for such legislation to pass, this is often not the case for second chambers. As with the House of Lords post-1911, the government may be able to pass legislation without the second chamber's consent. Table 3.2 sums up as far as possible the powers of second chambers over ordinary legislation, based on a reading of bicameral countries' constitutions between October 2011 and January 2012. It shows that these powers vary widely, and that there is a clear relationship between powers and mode of composition. Elected chambers dominate the more powerful top rows of the table, while unelected chambers are mostly concentrated at the bottom.

The first row contains countries where the second chamber has an absolute veto over legislation. Without its approval a bill cannot become law. This arrangement is particularly common in presidential systems based on the US model, such as those in Argentina, Brazil, Chile, and Mexico. Like the US, these countries have powerful directly elected Senates. Some second chambers in parliamentary systems enjoy a similar power, though this is far less common. Amongst them is the House of Lords, on those (roughly one third of) government bills which start their passage in the chamber. The limitations on the Lords' powers in the 1911 and 1949 Parliament Acts were drafted to apply only to bills starting in the House of Commons.

This draws attention to a relatively common feature, which is that second chambers often have more power over some forms of legislation than others. Another classic example is found in Germany. Here, because of its special representative function with respect to the states, the *Bundesrat* has an absolute veto over the roughly 50% of bills which affect state policies, but not over other bills. A similar arrangement exists in South Africa. In cases such as these there is clearly no such thing as an 'ordinary' bill, so these countries' position in Table 3.2 reflects their second chamber's *maximum*

Table 3.2. The world's national second chambers, by composition and lower house override powers

	Wholly or largely elected (55)	Wholly or largely unelected (19)
No override power (25)	*Algeria**, Argentina$^{\Psi}$, Bosnia and Herzegovina*, Brazil, Chile*$^{\Psi}$, Colombia*, Dominican Republic, *Germany**, Haiti*, Italy, *Kazakhstan,* Liberia, Mexico, *Netherlands*‡, Nigeria, Palau, Philippines*, *Rwanda**, Sudan$^{\Psi}$, Switzerland*, USA*, Zimbabwe (22)	Canada, UK (Lords bills only), South Sudan$^{\Psi}$ (3)
Joint sitting (A = by absolute majority, 2/3 = by 2/3 supermajority) (11)	Australia (A)†, Bhutan, Bolivia (A), Burma, *India, Pakistan,* Romania*, Uruguay (2/3) (8)	Bahrain, Jordan, Swaziland (3)
Supermajority (all 2/3 except where stated) (9)	*Belarus**, *Burundi**‡, Japan, *Namibia*$^{\Psi}$, Paraguay$^{\Psi}$, *Russian Federation**, *South Africa**, *Tajikistan, Uzbekistan**(9)	
Absolute majority (10)	*Afghanistan**, *Austria, Cambodia,* Czech Republic, *Morocco**, Poland, *Slovenia,* Spain, Thailand*(9)	Madagascar*(1)
Normal majority (18)	Belgium‡, *Congo**, *Democratic Republic of Congo**, *France**, *Gabon**, *Ireland, Mauritania** (7)	Antigua and Barbuda, Bahamas, Barbados, Belize, Grenada, Jamaica, Lesotho, Malaysia, Saint Lucia, Senegal, Trinidad and Tobago (11), plus UK (Commons bills only)
Legislative power not specified in constitution (1)		Oman (1)

Source: Largely IPU for composition (but see Table 3.1 for exceptions and exclusions), individual country constitutions for powers (read October 2011–January 2012).

Italics denote wholly or mostly *indirectly* elected, others wholly or mostly directly elected.

* Conciliation process between the chambers includes use of a joint committee.

$^{\Psi}$ Argentina: Rejection of a bill cannot be overridden. On amendments, 2/3 upper house majority may only be overridden by 2/3 lower house majority. Chile: A 2/3 upper house majority cannot be overridden. Namibia: Ordinary lower house majority overrides, except where second chamber vetoes a bill completely and by 2/3 majority, when 2/3 lower house majority required to override. Paraguay: If the originating chamber re-passes its bill with an absolute majority, it may only be overridden by the revising chamber with a 2/3 supermajority. Sudan and South Sudan: Chamber only sees legislation affecting the states, which if approved by 2/3 majority goes straight for enactment.

† Australia: Joint sitting can only be held after an emergency general election caused by the dispute.

‡ Netherlands: Cannot amend bills, can only vote to reject or approve. Rejection used rarely. Belgium, Burundi: Can amend only, not reject bills.

powers, with some particular special cases listed in the notes. In Sudan and South Sudan the second chamber only sees bills affecting the states, and enjoys an absolute veto over these.

As the table shows, the majority of second chambers do not possess an absolute veto, and instead can be overruled in some way. In 11 cases disputes must be resolved by a joint sitting of both chambers together, often by an absolute or supermajority. This normally favours the first chamber, since it generally has the greater number of members. In the remainder of cases the second chamber may be overridden by a vote in the first chamber. In nine countries this requires some kind of supermajority, usually by two-thirds of MPs, and in a further 10 an absolute majority is required. In the remaining cases—including the Lords with respect to House of Commons bills—a simple majority in the first chamber is enough to override the second chamber.

On this analysis, the Lords' position with respect to Commons bills looks comparatively weak (despite being clearly strong with respect to Lords bills). But another important dimension is not shown in the table. A second chamber's formal power comes not only from how it can be overridden, but also when: i.e. the degree of delay that it may cause before an override can take place. Here, the House of Lords' delay power of roughly a year over Commons bills is relatively long (for a fuller discussion, see Russell 2012a). In some systems where the second chamber lacks a veto (such as the Czech Republic and France) there is no limit on how quickly the first chamber can override its concerns. In others only a very brief delay period is specified in the constitution: for example, 30 days in Poland, 60 days in Japan, and 90 days in Ireland. In only a few cases do second chambers enjoy a power of delay close to that of the House of Lords. One example is Thailand, where the chamber can delay for 180 days, and another is India, where it can delay for six months (after which a joint sitting is required). The actual terms of the 1949 Parliament Act (described in more detail in Chapter 4) require a disputed bill to be delayed until the next parliamentary session, as well as a period of one year between the two House of Commons considerations. Almost identically-worded provisions are included in the constitutions of several states which based bicameralism on the British model, but generally with a reduced period required between readings in the first chamber. These include Antigua and Barbuda (three months), Grenada (six months), Barbados (seven months) and the Bahamas (nine months).

Before the ultimate resolution of a legislative dispute between two chambers, various mechanisms may be used to try to reach agreement. The 'navette' system (more colloquially known as 'ping-pong' in the UK) is common, whereby a bill simply shuttles back and forth between the chambers. In some cases the number of rounds is fixed at as few as one or two, and at the other extreme is potentially unlimited (Tsebelis and Money 1997: 56–62). An example of the latter is Italy, where one bill shuttled for 17 years between the chambers before being finally agreed in 1995.[14]

A particularly common means of resolving intercameral disputes is the use of joint committees, whereby a number of representatives of each chamber meet to negotiate a compromise. As indicated in Chapter 2, this system operated in the UK from the earliest years of bicameralism through to the mid-19th century. The countries which currently use such a system are indicated in the table by an asterisk. In some cases a joint committee will be created automatically after a number of rounds of navette, while in others it must be requested by one of the chambers, or by the government (Russell 2012a). Depending on the detailed design of the system, this arrangement may be more or less advantageous to the second chamber (Russell 1999, 2000: 141–4).

Financial legislation

It has already been noted that a second chamber's power may vary over different kinds of bills. This is probably most common with respect to financial legislation. Here, second chambers not only often have less power than first chambers, but also less power compared to that enjoyed over ordinary legislation. The UK is again an example: as indicated in the previous chapter, the Commons' financial privilege is an ancient convention. This was formalized (at least in part) by the 1911 Parliament Act, which reduced the Lords' delay power over 'money bills' to just one month.

Such a notion of financial supremacy for the directly elected first chamber is quite common in other states, particularly those modelled on Westminster. For example, in Australia, where the elected Senate has an absolute veto over legislation, financial bills must nonetheless be introduced in the first chamber and cannot be amended by the Senate (though it can 'request' amendments). A survey in 1999 of the powers of 20 second chambers, mostly in established democracies, found that in 11 cases their power over financial legislation was more restricted than that over ordinary bills (Russell 2000: 34–8).[15]

Constitutional amendments

Similarly, constitutional legislation is often treated differently, but here the second chamber tends to enjoy greater, rather than lesser, power than that over ordinary legislation (Russell 2001a). This is consistent with the principle that constitutional change should require a broad consensus, going beyond that required for changes to normal statute law. In countries with written constitutions there will often be special extra-parliamentary mechanisms such as referendums required in order to agree such changes; but in many the second chamber also plays a special role. In Germany and Japan, for instance, constitutional amendments require a majority of two-thirds in both chambers. And even some otherwise weak second chambers have significant power over constitutional change. In the Czech Republic, where the Senate has only 30 days to review ordinary bills and can be overruled by an absolute majority in the first chamber, a three-fifths majority is required in both chambers on constitutional amendments. Likewise, in France, the second chamber can normally be easily overruled by the first, but constitutional changes require a three-fifths majority in a joint sitting, or else they must pass a referendum.

Other powers

Finally, second chambers may have various other kinds of power: for example, to call and question ministers or to approve public appointments. In parliamentary systems in particular it is common for ministers to face regular questioning in both chambers, even though most ministers may be drawn from the lower house (Russell 2000: 196–202). In some systems the two chambers share responsibility for key appointments: in Austria, India, Italy and Switzerland this applies with respect to electing the head of state. In France, Germany and Italy the chambers likewise share a role in appointing members of the highest courts. In other countries, such as the Russian Federation and the US, the second chamber alone is responsible for such appointments. This reinforces these chambers' status as constitutional guardians.

Some general lessons about bicameralism

This brief survey of the world's second chambers begins to demonstrate some of their key similarities and differences. But not all such features are captured in a straightforward description of composition and powers. This section begins by summarizing some of the key similarities and differences between second chambers before asking—given their diversity—which form(s) of bicameralism is considered most effective or 'best'. It ends by reflecting on one particularly important common feature of this form of government: that is, the extent to which second chambers are innately controversial.

Key similarities and differences between second chambers

Certain similarities between second chambers should by now be clear from the preceding discussion. In particular:

- In compositional terms, despite the decline of the elite model of bicameralism, many second chambers remain more loosely connected to citizens than are their respective first chambers. Even those that are elected are often chosen by 'indirect' means, and may include some appointed members. Additionally, their members often serve longer terms of office than those in first chambers, because the second chamber is, for example, renewed in halves or thirds.
- With respect to powers, second chambers often have significantly less formal power than first chambers—lacking the ability to sack political executives (even in parliamentary systems), and often having no final veto over legislation.

The combined effect of second chambers' distance from the electoral process and relative lack of power is that they frequently attract less media attention than first chambers, and are less visible to the public. They are also, for similar reasons, generally less well studied by academics. This low profile is complementary to certain other common features, including:

- A tendency to longer-term thinking, resulting from members' extended terms of office. The classic case here remains the House of Lords, with appointment for life. But many other less extreme examples exist. Canadian senators are appointed until age 75, Brazilian and Chilean senators are elected for eight-year terms, and until 2004 the term of office for French senators was nine years. According to data from the Comparative Constitutions project, almost half of second chambers use longer terms than their respective first chambers.
- A greater sense of continuity and stability can also flow from the fact that many second chambers are (e.g. because of election in halves or thirds) never wholly dissolved. This is a clear contrast to first chambers.
- In addition, second chambers are, everywhere but the UK, smaller than their respective first chambers. In Italy the first chamber has 630 members and the Senate 315; similarly, in India the respective figures are 545 and 245, and in Poland 460 and 100. This can contribute to a culture where members know each other better, and behave more courteously, than their first chamber counterparts.

- Finally, there remains association between second chambers and age or 'seniority'. Appointment may result in older members—as in India where appointees are chosen on the basis of their achievements. But as indicated previously, many elected second chambers also retain a formal age qualification for membership that is higher than the first chamber. Additionally, these institutions' lower profile can make them less attractive to young, ambitious politicians, and instead more likely to include members at the end of their careers. An analysis by Michael Rush (2001) of membership in five elected second chambers found that all had a higher age profile than their respective first chamber. The most extreme case was France, where more than half of senators were aged over 60, compared to fewer than a fifth of French MPs.

It would nonetheless be mistaken to suggest that all second chambers fit a single profile, as it is also clear that there is great diversity among them. Some contain no elected members, while others are entirely elected by the people. Some are relatively powerless, while others enjoy a veto over all legislation. Hence, while many second chambers may be sleepier, more mature and more polite institutions when compared to first chambers, some are nonetheless noisy, combative and highly partisan. In several countries where the second chamber has a real potential to block government policy—such as Australia and Japan—it is rarely out of the media spotlight.

The extent of this diversity clearly makes it difficult to speak in generalities about the benefits of bicameralism. Its effects depend very much on the detailed design of the legislative system. Various scholars have sought to model the effects of generic, stylized second chambers on the policy process (e.g. Buchanan and Tullock 1962; Heller 1997; Levmore 1992; Miller, Hammond and Kile 1996; Riker 1992; Rogers 2001). But while these models can be mathematically elegant, often make instinctive sense, and even improve our understanding in some respects, they require such simplifying assumptions that they rarely have application to more than a handful of real-world cases. For example, most such models (being influenced by US arrangements) assume that the second chamber possesses a final legislative veto, when the majority in fact do not. It should be clear from the previous discussions that there is no such thing as a 'typical' second chamber.

What makes bicameralism work?

The diversity among bicameral systems leads to an obvious question: which model is the most effective or desirable? The answer will to a large extent be culturally specific: it depends on the benefits that a country seeks from its bicameral arrangements, as well as the way in which these arrangements work in practice. This in turn is fundamentally connected to factors such as history and tradition, the territorial structure, and the party system. For example, the kind of diversity important in the second chamber will differ significantly state-by-state. Nonetheless, various scholars have sought to draw some general conclusions about what makes bicameralism work, or at least under which conditions second chambers are most likely to meaningfully influence the policy process. Such accounts tend to focus on the same two dimensions used to structure the survey of second chambers: these bodies' composition and their formal powers.

Perhaps the best-known comparative treatment of bicameralism is that of Lijphart (1984, 1999), who terms these two dimensions *incongruence* (of membership) and *symmetry* (of formal powers). On the first dimension, he stresses that second chambers whose memberships differ significantly from that of their respective first chamber are more likely to make an impact. This is wholly consistent with the 'mixed government' ideal, and the core representation function of bicameralism. Lijphart gives particular emphasis to territorial incongruence, and whether the second chamber over-represents certain geographic areas (as in the US and Australia). Other authors have instead emphasized the importance of partisan incongruence: i.e. the extent to which the party balance in the two chambers differs. Sartori (1994: 184–5) based his 'similar or dissimilar' composition purely on 'the extent to which a government obtains consonant majorities in both Houses'. Tsebelis (2002), in his treatment of second chambers as 'veto players', even suggests that when two chambers have the same partisan majority the second chamber may effectively be 'absorbed', and have minimal impact on the policy process. Empirical studies indicate that it is indeed partisan incongruence that is most important, with governments facing greater resistance from second chambers in which they lack a partisan majority (Druckman, Martin and Thies 2005; Druckman and Thies 2002; Hiroi 2008). In modern legislatures territorial representation among second chamber members will often be overshadowed in practice by their partisan allegiances (Russell 2001b). But while congruence between the two chambers' membership may render the second chamber weaker, it need not be wholly ineffective. 'Strong' bicameralism will not necessarily suit all countries, and could even be destabilizing. Even two chambers with identical memberships will sometimes make different decisions, and may still bring some of the benefit of 'second thought' and delay (Rogers 2001; Tsebelis and Money 1997). But such chambers do always risk, as discussed in the next section, appearing superfluous.

The importance of Lijphart's 'symmetry' dimension should be even more obvious: a second chamber that lacks the power to force the first chamber to think again seems (all other things being equal) less likely to make an impact on policy than one which has an absolute legislative veto or can delay bills for a lengthy period. Again, however, it should be noted that even second chambers with relatively weak formal powers can at times be influential: for example, by drawing public and media attention to controversial policies. The case of the House of Lords (as seen in Chapters 6 and 7) certainly demonstrates that a veto power is not essential for significant influence to occur.

There is also a third crucial dimension when considering second chambers' effectiveness, which is less immediately obvious than the previous two, but has been very important in the British case. That is, that chambers not perceived as 'legitimate' may hesitate to use their formal powers, even when their membership is distinct from that of the first chamber. As the previous chapter showed, the Lords in the 20th century became increasingly timid—despite its significant formal powers—as hereditary peers' right to block the decisions of elected MPs was questioned. By the 1990s Shell suggested that the chamber had 'embraced a voluntary impotence' (1999: 203). The importance of legitimacy to bicameralism has been noted by some scholars (Lijphart 1984, 1999; Money and Tsebelis 1992), but has not been well developed. There are various reasons why second chambers' legitimacy may be questioned: relating to their often less obviously 'democratic' composition when compared to first chambers, but also their fundamental role in questioning these chambers' decisions. This is further discussed with respect to the House of Lords in Chapter 9. To be effective, a second chamber must therefore normally have three qualities: a distinct composition from the first chamber, adequate formal powers to make that chamber think again, and sufficient legitimacy in the eyes of the public to exercise its powers (Russell 2013). To an extent, weakness on one dimension might, however, be compensated by strength on another: in particular, a chamber considered strongly legitimate could be persuasive with government, even if formally weak.

Second chambers are fundamentally controversial

This brings us to the last feature which unites a great many second chambers: the extent to which their role, and even their existence, is controversial. Mughan and Patterson (1999: 338) refer to second chambers as 'essentially contested institutions', adding that 'many countries choose not to have one, others have them but then do away with them, and still others keep them but are engaged in an apparently incessant dialogue about how they should be reformed'.

These controversies arise, as just indicated, both because of second chambers' core function of questioning first chambers, and because many are either unelected or over-represent certain sections of society (or both). In other words, ironically, the very features that ensure bicameral 'incongruence' may also lead to claims that a chamber is 'unrepresentative' or even 'illegitimate'. Hence, arguments in countries such as the UK and Canada focus on the second chamber's lack of democratic input, while in others such as France and Australia critics complain about its over-representation of certain groups (respectively, rural areas and smaller states). Yet where the second chamber has a membership too similar to that of the first (as in Italy) this very similarity leads its worth to be questioned. Likewise, powerful second chambers (as in Japan and Germany) are often viewed as overly disruptive, while those that are weak (as in Ireland) are criticized as well. One of the most well-worn quotations about bicameralism comes from the Abbé Siéyès, drafter of several constitutions for the French Republic after 1789, who suggested that 'if a second chamber dissents from the first, it is mischievous; if it agrees, it is superfluous'. This remains a fundamental tension in bicameralism.

Consequently, legislative history is littered with examples not only of the creation of new second chambers, but the abolition of existing ones (Longley and Olson 1991). Many old elite second chambers were swept away in the first half of the 20th century. More recently, New Zealand's second chamber was abolished in 1950, Iceland's in 1991 and Senegal's in 2001. A survey by Massicotte (2001) found that between 1950 and 1999, 25 countries had abolished their second chambers, but over the same period, 42 national second chambers were restored or created. In some cases both changes occurred: for example, South Africa and Liberia switched from bicameralism to unicameralism and back again. In 2007 the Senegalese Senate was re-established, and in recent years New Zealand has debated doing the same. A 2009 referendum in Romania decided in principle to abolish the new chamber re-established in 1991. At the time of writing, a referendum on Senate abolition had been promised in Ireland, but still not held.

As this last example illustrates, pressure for second chamber reform may be common but does not always result in action. A classic case is Canada, where the first parliamentary debate on Senate reform took place in 1874. Since then there have been numerous initiatives to rebalance seats between provinces, move from an appointed to an elected Senate, or at least give provinces the power to appoint their own senators—who are currently chosen by the federal prime minister (Franks 1999, 2003; Russell 2000). Similar territorial tensions have dominated debates in Spain, where indirectly elected members notionally provide a voice for regional parliaments at the centre, but instead the Senate is seen as party-dominated and weak (Juberias

1999; Russell 2000). In Italy, where the two chambers are largely indistinguishable both in terms of membership and powers, there have been numerous proposals for reform, to make them more distinct on one or both dimensions. In Japan debates focus on how the powerful and disruptive second chamber might be tamed. Nonetheless, while debates about bicameral reform are widespread, its implementation faces various obstacles (Russell and Sandford 2002). Most obviously, outside the UK, reform to the structures of parliament usually requires amendment of a written constitution, which may face a referendum, supermajority or other hurdle. But the barriers are political, as well as legal. While citizens can be dissatisfied with weak second chambers and want them to be stronger, political executives will often be resistant, because a stronger legislature would threaten their own powers. In contrast, strong second chambers that cause problems for executives are often popular with citizens, who may resist attempts to weaken them. At the root there is seemingly no model of bicameralism that pleases everybody. This is unsurprising, and indeed even appropriate, since second chambers fundamentally exist to reflect and articulate tensions within the political system.

Conclusion: The Lords in comparative perspective

This chapter has shown that bicameral arrangements are widespread, and remarkably diverse. A brief survey of such arrangements in national legislatures helps to put the Lords, and indeed debates about Lords reform, into clearer perspective. One of the key conclusions is that the Lords is not quite as anomalous as many people might assume. This can be summarized in terms of the three key dimensions of bicameralism: composition, powers and legitimacy.

In compositional terms the Lords is unusual for retaining strong elements of the *elite model* of bicameralism that used to dominate Europe. Centuries ago, many states had unelected chambers that included members drawn from the nobility and the church. These were mostly swept away, while the Lords remains—albeit (as Chapter 2 made clear) with a membership that has changed quite fundamentally over time. The previously dominant *elite model* has since been replaced in many states by a *territorial model* (and in a few cases by a *vocational model*) of bicameralism, usually based on election. Today, the Lords is in a minority as a wholly unelected chamber, but a common feature of second chambers remains their relative distance from the electoral process. Election to such chambers is often 'indirect' rather than direct by the people, and many otherwise elected chambers include at least some unelected members. Additionally, long terms of office, and renewal of membership only in parts, further distance many second chambers from the voters, while senators are often required to be older than MPs. The Lords, with its appointment for life, may therefore be seen as being merely at the extreme end of a spectrum. The expectations for membership of the two chambers commonly differ, and indeed this is essential to making bicameralism work. Today the Lords can be understood, at least in part, as fitting a *partisan model* of bicameralism, whereby two chambers are purposefully designed to have different party majorities. A close comparator here is the Senate of Australia. Recent proposals for Lords reform, which have all based membership on a proportional principle (mostly through election), would likewise have adhered to this model.

In terms of powers, the House of Lords is often presented as being weak in international terms. However, this is not entirely the case. Many second chambers do enjoy an absolute veto over legislation, but these are mostly concentrated in presidential systems. Only around a third of all national second chambers have this kind of veto power, so—particularly in parliamentary systems—the second chamber tends to be weaker than the first. Different countries employ various mechanisms to enable the first chamber to get its own way, such as joint sittings, the use of supermajorities, or simply a repeat vote by an ordinary majority. In some cases the second chamber is far more easily overridden than the Lords. Its delay power of one year (and absolute veto over Lords bills and delegated legislation) is relatively great when compared to other parliamentary democracies.

But this leads to the third key dimension: legitimacy. In the 20th century the Lords was in practice weak not primarily because of its formal powers, but because of its relative caution over using them in practice. This resulted from concerns, which grew increasingly post-1832 (as seen in Chapter 2), that it was inappropriate for a largely hereditary chamber to challenge an elected one. Had the Lords not held back, its powers were sufficient to prove very disruptive. With respect to legitimacy, the comparative survey in this chapter again holds interesting lessons. In particular, it would be wrong to assume that concerns about the Lords' place in British politics stem only from its peculiar composition. Second chambers are fundamentally controversial institutions, not least because of their core role questioning the decisions of elected first chambers. There is also a tension between the need to compose two chambers with distinctive memberships, and both being seen as legitimate. If a second chamber's membership differs from that of the first this may lead its legitimacy to be questioned, even if its members are elected. Thus, while reform of the Lords might reduce the criticisms of the chamber's membership and role, it is unlikely to eliminate them. We return to these issues in Chapters 9 and 10.

Notes

1. According to the Comparative Constitutions Project (see note 10), 51 of the world's second chambers are called 'Senate', and a further three are called 'Chamber of Senators'.
2. *Oxford English Dictionary.*
3. See Aristotle (1995 [*c.*330BC]).
4. For a summary, see Shell (2001).
5. The Inter-Parliamentary Union's Parline database is an excellent source of information about the composition of both first and second chambers: see <http://www.ipu.org>. However, on closer inspection when researching this chapter it became clear that the IPU's figure of 78 was incorrect, as Yemen was listed as bicameral and this was not in fact the case (my thanks to Philip Norton for pointing this out). Yemen has a 'Consultative Council' which has no formal role in the legislative process. Close reading of the constitution of Ethiopia likewise found that the House of Federation (listed by the IPU as a second chamber) has no legislative power, being limited to interpreting the constitution. As these examples demonstrate, it is not always clear where the boundary between unicameralism and bicameralism lies, as Norton (2004) himself has discussed elsewhere.
6. For a discussion of presidentialism and parliamentarism, and more detailed definitions, see, for example, Lijphart (1992) and Shugart (2006).
7. For a discussion of federalism, see Anderson (2007).
8. <http://www.forumfed.org/en/> (accessed 16 December 2011).
9. Elections for the lower house use 60 two-member constituencies, while the Senate uses only 13 constituencies, with either two or four members elected in each. A party gaining two-thirds of the vote may take both seats in the constituency, otherwise the second placed party takes the second seat. See IPU Parline Database, <http://www.ipu.org>.
10. See <http://www.comparativeconstitutionsproject.org> (accessed 20 November 2012). My thanks to James Melton for providing this data, and that quoted elsewhere in the chapter.
11. In practice these elections are dominated by the political parties, and vocational representation is largely symbolic (Russell 2000).
12. Information on the composition of second chambers was taken from IPU Parline database, <http://www.ipu.org>, accessed October 5, 2011, but with exceptions where this was known (or found) to be wrong. As indicated previously, Yemen and Ethiopia were excluded. Russia was coded as indirectly elected, despite IPU description as 'appointed', as members in the Russian upper house are indirectly elected by regional councils: see, for example, Henderson (2011). Bosnia and Herzegovina's constitution clarifies that the second chamber is likewise indirectly elected (not appointed as IPU suggests). Ireland is also classified on its own, rather than as mixed indirectly elected/

appointed as IPU suggests, since six members are directly elected by university graduates. Classification as presidential or parliamentary based on World Bank dataset, described in Beck et al (2001): data was from version updated December 2010, available at <http://go.worldbank.org/2EAGGLRZ40>, with the following exceptions. Palau and Antigua and Barbuda were missing from this dataset, Pakistan and South Africa were placed in a third category on the basis that they have an assembly-elected president; all four were therefore classified instead on the basis of their constitutions, and, specifically, presence or absence of a confidence vote.

13. Earlier, Lijphart (1984) had used three categories: 'strong', 'weak' and 'insignificant' bicameralism, with Britain considered 'weak'. In 1999 the 'insignificant' category was removed.
14. My thanks to Gianfranco Pasquino for this example.
15. The countries with these restrictions were Australia, Austria, Canada, France, India, Ireland, Japan, Mexico, South Africa, UK and USA. Those treating financial legislation effectively equally to other bills (or with differences not disadvantaging the second chamber in any way, such as simultaneous introduction of the budget in both chambers) were Belgium, Czech Republic, Germany, Italy, Netherlands, Poland, Russian Federation, Spain and Switzerland.

4

A Brief Introduction to the Contemporary House of Lords

The core purpose of this book is to explain the role of the contemporary House of Lords in British politics. This chapter sets the scene by summarizing some of the chamber's most basic features. In doing so it starts to address three of the key questions set out in the opening chapter, regarding how the Lords has changed since its reform in 1999, the ways in which its membership and culture differ from those in the House of Commons, and how the chamber influences the policy process. Although intended to lead in to the rest of the book, which explores these questions in greater detail, readers seeking only a sketch of what the current House of Lords is and what it does may want to use the chapter as a standalone introduction.[1] But they should note that it does not attempt to summarize the chamber's policy contribution, or its political dynamics, as addressed later in the book.

The discussion begins with issues of composition, setting out who sits in the contemporary House of Lords, and how they got there. This includes a brief introduction to the different groups of members that make up the chamber, whose composition and behaviour are discussed in greater detail in Chapter 5. The chapter also outlines the various processes by which members arrive in the Lords, and current controversies over these, including the chamber's growing size since 1999. It then provides a summary of the demographic and professional mix among members of the Lords, which in turn helps determine whether the chamber can really be considered 'expert', 'party political' or full- versus part-time.

The second half of the chapter outlines the chamber's contemporary functions, powers and organization. The core functions—of executive accountability, legislative scrutiny and debate—are further elaborated in Chapters 6–8. The framework within which these operate includes the chamber's powers, which are most obviously set out in the Parliament Acts, but are also reliant on established conventions. The chapter summarizes how these are understood, and how their interpretation changed following the

1999 reform and subsequent establishment of the 2010 coalition government. The next sections deal with another key part of the framework, in terms of the House of Lords' organization. This extends to both organization of business in the chamber (where the concept of 'self-regulation' is key), and the forms of support available to its members. The chapter then touches briefly on the House of Lords' image, and recent attempts at 'outreach'. It ends with some brief conclusions about the post-1999 chamber's role in contemporary politics, and reflections on the questions at the start of the book.

Membership of the contemporary House of Lords

In May 2013 the House of Lords was a chamber of 762 members, as shown in Table 4.1. The great majority of members are life peers, either chosen to represent a political party or to sit as independent 'Crossbenchers'. In addition, the chamber includes two smaller groups of members, of more ancient origin: the 26 Church of England bishops and archbishops, and the remaining 92 hereditary peers. These groups' presence in the Lords date back many centuries, as discussed in Chapter 2. In contrast, the current system of life peerages was established only in 1958.

In 1999 the House of Lords Act, which removed the great majority of hereditary peers, changed the chamber's membership in three fundamental ways. First, and most obviously, it created a chamber where life peers predominate. Second, it significantly reduced the size of the chamber, though this has since crept upwards again (as discussed later). Third, and crucially, the reform also changed the chamber's party balance. Since the late 18th century the Lords had been dominated by Tory/Conservative peers, and

Table 4.1. Breakdown of membership of the House of Lords, May 2013

Affiliation	Life Peers	Hereditary Peers	Bishops	Total	% of House
Labour	218	4	–	222	29%
Conservative	163	49	–	212	28%
Lib Dem	85	4	–	89	12%
Crossbench	150	31	–	181	24%
Bishops	–	–	25*	25*	3%
Other	32	1	–	33	4%
Total	648	89*	25*	762	100%

Source: House of Lords website. Excludes 38 members on leave of absence and 11 otherwise temporarily absent from active membership. Total potential membership is therefore 811.

* Three of the 92 hereditary peers were on leave of absence, so are excluded from these figures. One of the 26 seats for bishops was vacant, due to a recent retirement.

consequently represented a far larger potential obstacle to governments of the left than of the right. But the 1999 reform ended this, and subsequently Conservative and Labour peers have held broadly similar numbers of seats. The balance is now held by the relatively less numerous Liberal Democrat peers, the large group of Crossbenchers, and the far smaller groupings of bishops and other peers aligned to none of the main three parties.

The characteristics of these various different groups—including their demographic mix, their rates of attendance and voting, and their impact on policy outcomes—are explored in detail in Chapter 5. Here only a few general features are noted.

The basics of the three party groups are relatively straightforward to explain, as the same three main parties—Labour, Conservatives and Liberal Democrats—dominate the House of Commons. There are also a small number of representatives of other parties, in May 2013 comprising seven Northern Irish peers—three from the Ulster Unionist Party (UUP) and four from the Democratic Unionist Party (DUP)—two United Kingdom Independence Party (UKIP) peers and two from Plaid Cymru (the Welsh nationalist party). Other small parties had no representation. The Scottish Nationalist Party (SNP) notably has a policy against accepting seats in the Lords, while other parties (most obviously the Greens and British National Party (BNP)) would take seats if offered, but have not been given the opportunity.[2]

Among those parties which have representation in both the Commons and the Lords, the profile of members in the two chambers tends to be quite different. Peers are on average older than MPs, and many have been drawn from walks of life outside professional politics, often relatively late in their careers. But many peers have also served previously in the House of Commons, and joined the Lords following either their retirement from the first chamber or their forced exit having lost their seat in a general election. After the 2010 general election, for example, 15 former Labour MPs were given seats in the Lords, two of whom had stood for the Commons and been defeated. Of the 762 peers in May 2013, 182 were former MPs, representing 24% of the chamber as a whole. In total 31% of party peers were former MPs. A number of peers have also formerly served as local government councillors, or members of the European Parliament or the devolved assemblies in Scotland, Northern Ireland and Wales.

The greatest overall contrast between the members serving in the Commons and the Lords comes through the presence of large numbers of non-party peers. The largest group amongst them are the Crossbenchers, so called because they sit on the benches spanning those occupied by government and opposition. This group has a broadly similar number of members to the two main parties and has developed significantly in recent years, as further explored in Chapter 5. While Crossbench membership used to be more haphazard, criteria have now become relatively strict, with members required to show clear distance from the political parties. This is formalized, in particular, through appointment by the independent House of Lords Appointments Commission (described later), which is now responsible for choosing most Crossbenchers.

The bishops have their own separate organization from the Crossbenchers, and likewise distance themselves from any association with partisan politics. These 'Lords spiritual' (the other peers being 'Lords temporal') are the only members of the chamber who do not sit for life. Instead, they vacate their seats on retirement from the church, normally aged 70. Like the Crossbenchers, the bishops select one of their number to act as a 'convenor' in the Lords. Unlike the organization of the parties the convenors cannot be seen as 'leaders' of their respective groups, and neither group supports a collective policy line.

The growth in overall size of the House of Lords since 1999 is illustrated in Figure 4.1. This shows that the chamber's membership has swollen significantly over 13 years. Several factors have contributed to this change. The biggest is the constant temptation for party leaders to reward supporters by appointment to the Lords, and to bring in new talent to serve on their benches. As Chapter 2 demonstrated, gradual growth in the size of the chamber is nothing new: it contained around 300 members in the early 19th century, growing to 600 a century later, and eventually over 1,200 by the time of the 1999 Act. A major difficulty is that (with limited exceptions) there is no means to permanently retire from membership, and there is certainly no system of forced retirement. Peers appointed to the Supreme Court or elected to the European Parliament are now automatically disqualified from membership, but only on a temporary basis while holding these positions. In addition, since 1958 members have been able to take 'leave of absence'—thereby indicating that they do not wish to attend for a period, and since 2011 members have been encouraged to use this to indicate their intention to permanently 'retire'. But as members are 'life peers' they always retain the right to return. Those disqualified and on leave of absence account for the difference between 'actual eligible membership' and 'potential eligible membership' in Figure 4.1. A third factor is that there has been a shift since 1999 from seeing appointment as an 'honour' to regarding it as a job, with an expectation of active attendance. Thus more members are being appointed relatively earlier in their careers.[3] Since peers serve for life, this means that each will on average hold their seat for longer than in the past, unless a more formalized retirement scheme is introduced.

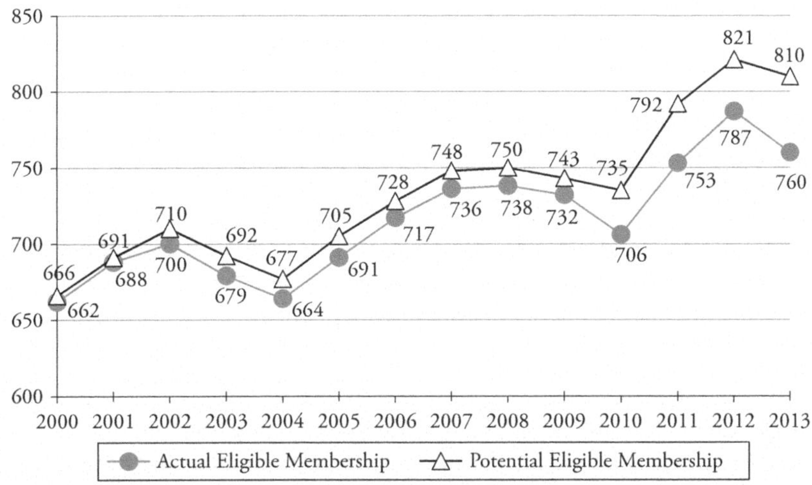

Figure 4.1. Change in size of the House of Lords, January 2000–January 2013

Source: Constructed from figures provided by House of Lords Information Office. All figures are for January.

* The drop from 732 to 706 between 2009 and 2010 is explained largely by one-off changes: the introduction of disqualification for serving 'Law Lords' and MEPs, and two suspensions. The similar drops 2002–04 and 2012–13 are accounted for simply by lack of appointments (see also Table 4.2).

It has already been noted that party representation in the House of Lords is now far more proportional between the parties than it was in the past. Perhaps ironically, it is also far more proportional to the way that people vote in general elections than is the elected House of Commons. For example, in 2010 the Conservatives won 47% of Commons seats on 36% of the vote; in contrast they hold only 39% of party seats in the House of Lords (and 28% of seats overall). In the Commons the Liberal Democrats are consistently under-represented; they won only 9% of seats in 2010 on 23% of the vote, but hold 17% of party political seats in the Lords (and 12% overall). These discrepancies were even more stark after the 2005 election, when Labour won 55% of Commons seats on just 35% of the vote; in the Lords the parties were much more evenly matched. This led to increased claims (particularly by Liberal Democrats: as discussed later) that the Lords had become more 'legitimate', and entitled to stand up to the Commons. Over recent years all three main political parties have agreed that no party should have a majority in the Lords, and most proposals for reform (see Chapter 10) have been based on a principle of party proportionality.

Routes into the Lords

As already indicated, there are three broad categories of members in the House of Lords: the life peers, the remaining hereditary peers and the bishops. The life peers predominate, so their method of appointment will receive the greatest attention here. But we begin with a brief account of the means by which the other two groups gain their seats in the chamber.

Bishops

The bishops are in practice appointed to their dioceses by the church, although such appointments are nominally made by the monarch on the advice of the prime minister. Five of the 26 seats in the Lords are reserved on an *ex officio* basis for the archbishops of Canterbury and York, and the bishops of London, Durham and Winchester. The remaining 21 are not associated with a particular diocese but instead are allocated on the basis of length of service in the church. Hence, the dioceses with representation in the chamber change regularly, as each senior bishop retires. Occasionally a bishop who already holds a seat in the Lords is promoted within the church, and thereby changes his title. As of May 2013, the church allowed only men to be appointed as bishops. No other religious group has formal representation, though appointments to other benches in the chamber are sometimes used to increase religious diversity.

Hereditary peers

The House of Lords Act 1999 provided for the retention of 92 hereditary peers as members. This provision was not originally in the government's bill, but was added by the 'Weatherill amendment' (see Chapter 2), which the government accepted. At the time, it was seen as a compromise solution, and also as a measure that would hasten the promised 'stage two' of reform, because it made clear that the chamber remained in what was termed a 'transitional' (i.e. semi-reformed) state.

The Act specified that two royal officeholders (the Earl Marshal and Lord Great Chamberlain), plus 90 additional hereditary peers, would retain their seats. The chamber's standing orders then set out the detail. The initial group of 90 were chosen in elections within the chamber in 1999.[4] At first, when deaths occurred vacancies were filled by 'best losers' from these elections, but by-election provisions were written in (by a government amendment, under pressure from the Conservative frontbench, not by Weatherill—see Crewe 2005: 56–7) to begin in the 2001 parliament. At the time, many imagined that these would never be used, because a second stage of Lords reform would follow. But the lack of progress on reform meant that by May 2013, 17 hereditary peer by-elections had been held.

When a hereditary peer dies the eligible voters in the majority of cases are the remaining hereditaries in the deceased peer's party (or Crossbench) group. Bizarrely, the only eligible candidates are 'excluded' hereditary peers, who by now include some descendants of members who sat in the chamber in 1999. In addition, the number of voters can be very small. For example, when Liberal Democrat hereditary Conrad Russell died in 2004, the electorate numbered only four. Elections for Conservative and Crossbench vacancies at least involve more voters, but are nonetheless difficult to defend. There have been various attempts to end the hereditary by-elections as part of large or small packages of Lords reform, as discussed in Chapter 10.

Life peers

The creation of all life peers continues to lie officially in the hands of the monarch, who acts on the advice of the prime minister. Although there has been limited formal change to the system, the pattern of these appointments has altered significantly since 1999. Nonetheless, the extent of prime ministerial patronage is still substantial. Unlike hereditary peers (who can still retain titles such as viscount or earl), all life peers are either barons or baronesses—barons are generally referred to simply as 'Lord'.

Before 1999 announcements of new peerages were often included within the queen's birthday and new year honours lists. These announcements were particularly used for 'grandees', many of them appointed to the Crossbenches, with separate more political lists of 'working peers' released periodically. The former pattern of honorific appointments has now largely ended, although no official announcement to this effect was ever made. Today, there is far more of an expectation that virtually all members appointed will be 'working peers'.

A key change in this period was the establishment of the House of Lords Appointments Commission in 2000. The Commission has two primary duties. First, it took over responsibility from the previous Political Honours Scrutiny Committee for vetting all appointments to the chamber for propriety.[5] Second, it was given primary responsibility for appointing members to the Crossbenches. These latter appointments mark a real break from the past, as the Commission openly advertises, then shortlists and interviews against a set of criteria in a transparent process tantamount to appointment for a job.[6] Although the number of 'vacancies' available to the Appointments Commission is not fixed, there is now an understanding that this will be about three or four appointments per year. Such nominations, when passed by the Commission to the prime minister, are forwarded automatically to the monarch, with no political input. But a semi-formal agreement between the Commission and the prime minister leaves the latter with the right to appoint 'up to 10 distinguished public servants, on their retirement, for non-party-political peerages' during each parliament (House of Lords Appointments Commission 2011: 6). These positions have been used, for example, to reward retiring heads of the civil service and the armed services.

The arrangements for appointment of peers to sit on the political party benches remain significantly less regulated, and far more controversial. Aside from the greater emphasis on 'working peers', and the change of vetting arrangements, the only recent development here was Tony Blair's confirmation in 1998 that he would not interfere with individual appointments by other parties. Instead, opposition party leaders are now invited to put names forward which—provided they pass the propriety test—are passed directly to the monarch. But the prime minister retains control over how many party peers are appointed and when, what the balance is between them, and who is chosen on the government side. This ultimately results in control of both the share of seats between the parties in the chamber and its overall size.

The number of appointments per year to the Lords by party 1999–2012, alongside the chamber's overall size and party balance, is shown in Table 4.2. This demonstrates that Blair, Brown and Cameron all made appointments from across the political spectrum, but tended to favour their own party (for a longer perspective on party appointments, see Table 2.3 in Chapter 2). From 1997 onwards Tony Blair began making large numbers of Labour appointments to counterbalance the Conservatives' previous advantage in the chamber.[7] In 2006 Labour eventually became narrowly the largest party. On taking office in 2010, David Cameron sought to rebalance again by making new Conservative and Liberal Democrat appointments. Indeed, the coalition agreement explicitly proposed that 'Lords appointments will be made with the objective of creating a second chamber that is reflective of the share of the vote secured by the political parties in the last general election' (HM Government 2010: 27). The sharp rise in numbers post-2010 can be seen in part as an attempt to reach this objective. But if such a rule was applied rigidly by incoming governments, the regular changes in the party in power combined with lack of retirement provision would lead to an exponential growth in the size of the chamber (for an analysis, see Russell et al 2011). Labour's 1997 general election manifesto had included a more modest

Table 4.2. Number of members and number of appointments by party, 1999–2013

	Total members (January)*					Appointments (Jan–Dec)†				
Year	Con	Lab	Lib Dem	Other	Total	Con	Lab	Lib Dem	Other	Total
1999						11	24	7	18	60
2000	232	181	54	195	662	4	20	9	3	36
2001	231	199	62	196	688	6	13	5	18	42
2002	221	200	65	214	700	0	0	0	3	3
2003	215	188	65	211	679	0	0	0	2	2
2004	210	181	64	209	664	6	25	8	13	52
2005	202	201	68	220	691	5	17	5	11	38
2006	205	208	74	230	717	7	7	5	17	36
2007	206	211	78	241	736	2	5	2	9	18
2008	202	216	78	242	738	1	3	0	6	10
2009	198	216	72	246	732	1	3	0	6	10
2010	189	211	72	234	706	47	39	24	11	121
2011	204	233	83	233	753	0	0	0	3	3
2012	218	239	91	239	787	1	0	0	2	3
2013	212	224	90	234	760					

Sources: Total members based on figures provided by House of Lords Information Office. Appointments drawn from Brocklehurst and Kelly (2012), updated to end of 2012.

* Excluding disqualified peers and peers on leave of absence.

† Excludes bishops and hereditary peer by-elections (which are both one-in-one-out). All appointments are listed in the year that they were announced (in some cases peers took their seats in the subsequent year).

aim that 'over time party appointees as life peers more accurately reflect the proportion of votes cast at the previous general election': i.e. implying that proportionality should apply to new appointments, rather than the chamber as a whole. But Blair's peerage creations nonetheless pushed the size of the chamber upwards.

An added problem is that while some pre-1999 conventions regarding appointment have been abandoned, others have not. In particular, there has long been a convention of a 'dissolution honours' list at the end of each parliament (used to appoint retiring MPs), and a 'resignation honours' list left by a prime minister departing office. Tony Blair did not leave a resignation list, but in 2010 Gordon Brown left a list of 32 names, which David Cameron felt obliged to appoint.[8] Thus, Cameron ironically created 29 additional Labour peers within a month of taking office.

As well as determining the number and party balance of appointments, the prime minister personally selects members of the governing party to be made peers. This patronage power, and the equivalent power of opposition party leaders to select their own members, can also be seen as problematic. The

Liberal Democrats did experiment briefly with internal party elections for these positions, which never became entrenched, and there have been no similar moves in Labour or the Conservative parties. Smaller parties, including the Greens and Plaid Cymru, have run internal ballots to choose nominees for the chamber, but the Greens have never yet been given a seat.[9] There are regular complaints that dissolution honours are used by party leaders to persuade MPs to retire, sometimes freeing up seats for their favoured Commons candidates.[10] In addition, there has long been an assumed link (see Chapter 2) between political donations and the award of peerages, with some peers having been major party donors. In 2006 the so-called 'loans for peerages' scandal blew up, when it emerged that the House of Lords Appointments Commission had rejected some of Tony Blair's Labour nominees on propriety grounds connected to their political donations.[11] This scandal damaged Blair's reputation, and the reputation of the Lords; but it at least demonstrated that the vetting system was effective, and hence boosted the reputation of the Appointments Commission.

What kind of people sit in the Lords?

The House of Lords' membership is often caricatured. On the positive side, the chamber is frequently praised for being more 'expert', and less 'political' than the House of Commons. More negatively, it is sometimes ridiculed for containing numerous elderly members, and is generally seen as being predominantly white, male and middle-class. There is some truth in all of these claims, though in each case the picture is not straightforward. In terms of gender and ethnicity, in particular, there have been important advances since 1999.

Two features of the chamber's membership providing a clear contrast to the House of Commons are that many members sit on the Crossbenches rather than for political parties, and that most are appointed quite late in their careers, often after distinguished achievements outside politics. These help to account for the chamber's 'less political' reputation, and its reputation as both 'expert' and elderly. But many also enter the chamber having been MPs, or having held other elected office, and some are appointed at a relatively young age. The composition of the chamber is in fact quite diverse, and increasingly so.

Table 4.3 summarizes the main professional backgrounds of members of the House of Lords in October 2009. Classifying members in this way is a far from exact science, because many have had complex and varied careers. But the figures give at least some indications of which groupings are best

Table 4.3. Primary professional backgrounds of House of Lords members, October 2009

Area	Number	% of House
Agriculture and horticulture	20	3%
Architecture, engineering, construction and transport	10	1%
Manual and skilled trades	1	0%
Banking and finance	59	8%
Business, commerce and other private sector	84	12%
Culture, arts and sport	14	2%
Journalism, media and publishing	25	4%
Education and training	64	9%
Medical and healthcare	15	2%
Legal professions	54	8%
Representative politics	151	22%
Political staff and activists	15	2%
International affairs and diplomacy	18	3%
UK civil service, and local authority administration	18	3%
Armed forces and police	20	3%
Other public sector	14	2%
Trade unions	21	3%
Voluntary sector, NGOs and think tanks	25	4%
Clergy or religious	29	4%
Unclassified	42	6%
Total	699	100%

Source: Adapted from Russell and Benton (2010), Table 10. 'Primary' background was defined as one in which a peer had worked for at least eight years, by default their most recent working area, but a prior area if this had applied for more than twice as long.

represented. What is immediately visible is that the biggest single category comprises members whose main background is 'representative politics', most of whom are former MPs.[12] The table also shows that private sector professions are well represented, as are the legal professions and education (mostly by current or former university academics). All of these groups have had strong representation for some time. One major change since the chamber's reform in 1999 is the decline in members with agricultural interests. An analysis in the 1980s found that the largest group in the chamber was the 44% of peers who could be classified as a 'landowner/farmer' (Shell 1992: 46). Now, fewer than 5% of peers have a primary background in this area.[13]

Two kinds of criticism may be levelled at the celebrated 'expertise' in the House of Lords. First, that some groups are over- and other groups under-represented. Notably, for example, only one member in 2009 was judged to have a primary background in manual trades (although this same criticism could be levelled at the modern House of Commons). The Appointments

Commission tries to some extent to balance backgrounds and interests, but this is clearly difficult, not least because it only selects around 20% of members (the remainder being chosen by the parties). The chamber undoubtedly includes various eminent scientists, academics, lawyers and others, but not all fields will be equally represented.[14] For example, one study recently suggested that the Lords lacks expertise in the welfare field (Bochel and Defty 2010); but this raises an important point. The primary objective should perhaps be for the Lords to complement the expertise in the House of Commons, where many MPs are familiar with the public's day-to-day concerns through their constituency work.[15] Peers do not have constituents, so may be less in touch in this way, but nonetheless may have a better grasp of policy detail in other areas. Another criticism levelled at peers' expertise is that much of it is in fact out of date, since many members are wholly or semi-retired from their original fields. Liberal Democrat peer Paul Tyler has therefore characterized the chamber more as one of 'ex-experts'.[16] This is true in part, but many other members do remain active in their professions outside the House.

This point about experts is clearly connected to more basic demographic questions about the chamber's membership. In May 2013 the average age of its members was 69 compared to 53 in the House of Commons. Among those not on leave of absence, there were 136 peers aged over 80, while only 26 were under 50. Membership is thus clearly skewed to the older age groups. It is also geographically skewed, although this is much harder to measure with certainty. The analysis of the chamber's members in October 2009 found that 70% had either a first or second home in London, which is unsurprising, given their need to attend the House. The proportion of peers with a home in the South East, South West or Scotland was slightly higher than that in the population, while disproportionately few peers had a home in some regions, including the North East and North West (Russell and Benton 2010).[17] In contrast, obviously, members of the House of Commons have a geographical base which is far more closely linked to that of the population.

Nonetheless, in some senses members of the Lords are as representative or slightly more so than MPs. Women were excluded from the chamber until 1958, and most hereditary peerages passed down the male line. The 1999 reform therefore greatly improved the gender balance in the chamber. In May 2013 the proportion of women in the Commons and the Lords was almost identical, at 22.5%. Undoubtedly, women remain under-represented, but they have held many senior positions in the Lords since 1999, most notably making up four of the seven Leaders of the House, and both of its first two Lord Speakers. Recent years have also seen many more ethnic minority peers appointed, particularly by the Appointments Commission. Figures on this question are less clear, as they depend on self-definition, but a study in January 2012 suggested that there were 28 minority ethnic MPs (i.e. 4%), and 42 minority ethnic peers (5%) (Cracknell 2012).

A key difference between the two chambers is that while MPs today treat membership of the Commons as a full-time job, most peers do not do the same. According to the 2007 peer survey, just 27% treated membership as full-time, compared to 41% who treated it as part-time alongside other paid work.[18] Additionally, many peers are obviously elderly, and some in poor health. All of this means that attendance falls well short of total membership; but it is nonetheless far higher than it was in the pre-reform House. In 1968, for example, the chamber had 789 eligible members (similar to now), of whom only 291 (37%) attended more than a third of sittings (Walters 2003). In contrast, in 2010–12, 597 members (71%) attended this regularly. Immediately before Labour came to power, in 1996–97, the chamber had 1067 eligible members, and an average daily attendance of only 381 (36%) (Vollmer 2012); but by 2010–12 the average daily attendance was 475 (60%). Hence the increase in the chamber's *active* membership has been far greater than the overall membership figures would suggest.

Key functions of the Lords

As the second chamber of the British parliament, the House of Lords carries out broadly similar functions to the House of Commons, though both its organization and its ethos—as further discussed later—differ in important ways. The three core functions of the chamber are scrutinizing legislation (which in practice largely means government bills), holding the executive to account for its broader policy-making and administration, and acting as a national forum for deliberation and debate. One key difference is that members of the Lords fulfil less of a 'linkage' function into local communities than MPs, as they are not elected and do not perform constituency duties.

With the obvious exception of the presence of non-party groups, and also the limited powers of the Lord Speaker (discussed later), the structure of responsibilities in the chamber is quite similar to that in the House of Commons. There are government and opposition frontbenches, both populated by members who cover particular policy portfolios. The Leader of the House of Lords is a member of the cabinet, but is often now the only such senior minister in the chamber. Until 2005 the Lord Chancellor was also drawn from the Lords and sat in cabinet, but following reform of this office (see Chapter 2) it can now be held by an MP. The prime minister is free to appoint other cabinet ministers from the Lords, as Tony Blair did when

Valerie Amos served briefly as Secretary of State for International Development in 2003, and Gordon Brown did when he appointed Peter Mandelson as Business Secretary in 2008 and Andrew Adonis as Secretary of State for Transport in 2009. But most Lords ministers hold more junior positions. Occasionally, members may be appointed to the Lords by the prime minister specifically to take up ministerial office straightaway, because by convention all ministers must be members of one or the other chamber of parliament.

It is normal for most government departments to have one minister in the Lords, who is responsible for guiding through departmental bills and answering questions (as ministers from one chamber cannot speak in the other). In May 2013 there were 82 ministers in the Commons (excluding junior whips) and just 16 in the Lords, meaning that each of the latter had to cover a far wider policy brief. Unlike in the Commons, whips also support departments (particularly those without Lords ministers) by answering questions and helping to pilot bills.

Table 4.4 summarizes how time was spent on the floor of the chamber in the long 2010–12 parliamentary session, and in the more 'normal' one-year session of 2008–09. The Lords normally sits for four days per week, and around seven hours per day. In 2008–09 there were 134 sitting days, and in 2010–12 there were 293—in both cases a very similar figure to the House of Commons.[19] So while some members of the Lords may be part-time the chamber itself is not. As seen in the table, the largest single item of business in both sessions was discussion of government bills, accounting for more than half of total hours. Smaller amounts of time were also spent on private members' bills and delegated legislation. Legislative business is discussed in detail in Chapters 6 and 7.

Table 4.4. Time in the chamber on different types of business, 2008–09 and 2010–12 sessions

	2008–09		2010–12	
Category of business	Hours spent	% of total	Hours spent	% of total
Government bills	479	53	1,131	54
Private members' bills	31	3	48	2
Delegated legislation	40	5	63	3
Ministerial statements	52	6	104	5
Oral questions	63	7	141	7
Debates	202	22	516	25
Procedural matters	5	1	17	1
Miscellaneous other business	35	3	86	3
Total	907	100	2,106	100

Source: House of Lords (2012).

In addition to scrutinizing government legislation, the chamber uses various other means to hold the executive to account: including oral questions and responding to ministerial statements. Statements are often made concurrently in both the Commons and Lords on major policy matters, and are followed by questions from peers. Oral questions to ministers are held in the chamber on most sitting days, and members can also ask written questions of government, which receive a published reply in *Hansard*. The various forms of debate in the chamber likewise act as accountability mechanisms, including on the annual queen's speech (which sets out the government's legislative programme), and policy matters chosen by members on which they wish to hear a government response. But debates also fulfil a wider function of enabling members to deliberate on policy matters and put their views on the record.

With the exception of written questions, all of these mechanisms relate to time spent in the chamber itself. But the Lords also conducts a lot of business through committees 'off the floor'. Unlike the Commons, it does not establish public bill committees (though temporary select committees are occasionally created to look at bills). But it does have a well-established set of 'select committees' specializing in particular policy fields. In contrast to the equivalent Commons committees, these are not structured by government department but are 'crosscutting' and may span several (or all) Whitehall departments. They conduct detailed inquiries and provide a further important accountability mechanism for government. The non-legislative work of the chamber—through questions, debates and committees—is further discussed in Chapter 8.

The powers of the Lords

A key question, though not one with a wholly straightforward answer, is what powers the House of Lords has over the government and its bills. The first place to look for a definition of the chamber's power is in the Parliament Acts 1911 and 1949. However, these statutory provisions are fairly narrow. In practice, the House of Lords' powers are also constrained to a great extent by established conventions, which are not set down in any binding document and therefore remain flexible and subject to change. Two important developments have put pressure on these existing conventions in recent years: the reform of the chamber in 1999 and, more recently, the formation of a Conservative/Liberal Democrat coalition government in 2010.

As described in Chapter 2, the 1911 Parliament Act ended the House of Lords' absolute veto over legislation, and replaced it with a power of delay over bills originating in the House of Commons. The delay period was then shortened by the 1949 Parliament Act. The Acts now provide that if the Lords rejects a Commons bill in two successive parliamentary sessions (or makes amendments to which the Commons does not agree), the bill may be passed by the Commons alone, providing that a year has elapsed between its initial Commons second reading and its final approval. In practice, this somewhat complex arrangement is often summarized as the Lords having a delay power of 'around a year' on most legislation. In fact, the period of delay depends on a number of factors, including the timing of the bill's initial introduction and the way that the Lords itself chooses to proceed. At one extreme, a bill introduced at the beginning of the long session 2010–12, had it been rejected by the Lords, would not have been eligible for reintroduction for two years. At the other extreme, when the House of Lords rejected the European Parliamentary Elections Bill in 1998 (over the government's proposal to introduce 'closed' rather than 'open' electoral lists), it 'cooperated' in the second session by rejecting the bill entirely at its second reading. This allowed it to be put onto the statute book straight away, just two months after the initial defeat. Had the Lords subjected the bill to a full committee stage, and subsequent stages, the delay could have been far longer.

It is important to point out, however, that any such case is unusual, as resort to the Parliament Acts is rarely needed. Instead, a compromise of some sort is usually agreed at an earlier stage between the two chambers (for further discussion see Chapter 6). Since the passage of the 1949 Parliament Act, only four bills have reached the statute book under its provisions.[20] In addition, it should be noted that the Parliament Acts only apply to Commons bills, and not to bills which begin their parliamentary passage in the Lords. Around one-third of government bills start in this way, which is necessary in order to ensure a smooth flow of legislation. Although the Lords retains an absolute veto over such bills, this has rarely proved to be a problem for governments.

The other important provision in the Parliament Acts relates to 'money bills'. These are defined quite narrowly, and must deal entirely with financial matters: including national taxation, public money and loans.[21] If the Speaker of the House of Commons certifies a bill as meeting these criteria, the Lords has only one month in which to pass it. Should the chamber fail to do so, the bill could be put on the statute book with the support of the Commons alone. Because of the narrow definition of money bills, many Treasury bills (sometimes including the annual Finance Bill implementing the budget) do not meet the criteria, but further conventions govern the Lords' treatment of financial matters, as discussed at the end of this section. To date, it has never been necessary to use the Parliament Acts to pass a money bill without the consent of the Lords.

This is the extent of the statutory limitations on the House of Lords' power, but the limitations flowing from established convention are far wider. One crucial example relates to the making and breaking of governments. By convention (though not by statute) a government must maintain the confidence of the House of Commons; yet no similar convention applies to the House of Lords. There is no expectation that peers can remove a government from office, and 'confidence votes' are never held.

The best known conventions relate to the House of Lords' treatment of government legislation: in particular, the 'Salisbury-Addison convention' (or simply 'Salisbury convention'), agreed by the two party leaders in the chamber after the 1945 general election. This recognized that the Lords should not block measures which had appeared in the governing party's election manifesto. In practice, it is interpreted as meaning that the chamber should not vote down bills implementing such measures at second or third reading, or pass 'wrecking' amendments to them. But in fact the chamber's restraint has gone far further than this, and it is rare for any government bill to be rejected in its entirety.[22]

Since 1999, the Salisbury convention has come under significant strain. When it was first agreed, Labour had just won a landslide victory in the Commons, but had only a handful of peers. The chamber consisted largely of hereditary peers, and was dominated by the Conservatives; had it not shown restraint, the new government's programme could therefore easily have been destroyed. But by the end of the century most hereditaries had departed the Lords, and the number of seats held by the two main parties was far more evenly balanced. Particularly after the 2005 general election (which Labour won on 35% of the national vote), Liberal Democrat politicians spoke out against the continued use of the convention. Then party leader Charles Kennedy claimed that it was 'absolutely ridiculous . . . [to] fall back on a 60-year-old convention relating to absolutely different political circumstances', while the party's Leader in the Lords, Tom McNally, referred to the convention as 'the last refuge of legislative scoundrels'.[23] Such pressures led to the establishment of a joint committee of both chambers to review the conventions governing relations between them, which reported in 2006. The committee concluded that the Salisbury convention could still be considered to apply, and further suggested that, in general, 'to reject Bills at Second Reading on a regular basis would be inconsistent with the Lords' role as the revising chamber' (Joint Committee on Conventions 2006a: 32).

Post-2010 a new difficulty arose. The Liberal Democrats and Conservatives had campaigned on separate manifestos, which differed in some important ways. The formation of the government therefore required the drafting of a coalition agreement, which became the key document setting out its legislative priorities. Despite this not having been put to the voters for approval, Conservative Leader of the House of Lords Tom Strathclyde claimed shortly after the election that the convention would 'of course' still apply.[24] A more realistic position was later suggested by the (Conservative) Cabinet Office Minister Mark Harper, when he told the Commons that the advent of coalition government meant 'the Salisbury-Addison convention does not operate in the same way, if at all'.[25]

There are two further areas where convention plays an important part in restraining the powers of the House of Lords. The first is with respect to 'secondary' or 'delegated' legislation, in the form of 'statutory instruments'. These set out the detail of policy, as allowed by normal 'primary' legislation, and require formal parliamentary approval which falls short of a full legislative process. The use of such measures was not considered when the Parliament Acts were drafted, but increased hugely during the course of the 20th century. Consequently, the Lords retains a formal veto over them, which is only very rarely used. The Joint Committee on Conventions (2006a: 62) concluded that the chamber 'should not regularly reject' secondary legislation, but 'in exceptional circumstances it may be appropriate for it to do so'. How this works in practice is further discussed in Chapter 6.

Finally, the chamber's restraint with respect to financial matters goes far beyond the Parliament Act provisions relating to money bills. As indicated in Chapter 2, the Commons' 'financial privilege' is an ancient convention, which was codified through parliamentary motions in the 17th century. These are not legally binding on the Lords, and are somewhat open to interpretation, but are generally respected. Today, for example, Finance Bills implementing the annual budget (even when they are not certified as 'money bills') are in practice considered non-amendable by the Lords. Both money bills and Finance Bills tend to be debated only at second reading in the chamber, with the remainder of their stages taken formally and without debate. On other bills, if the Lords passes an amendment with financial implications, this will be flagged by the clerks in the Commons as falling under financial privilege, and the Commons may choose to reject it on this basis alone (though MPs can also choose to 'waive' Commons privilege, and often do). When the Commons rejects a Lords amendment on grounds of privilege the Lords normally backs down, though it is under no statutory obligation to do so.

The Lords' ethos and organization

Aside from differences in powers, there are also important distinctions between the two chambers' organization and ethos. Some key organizational differences have already been referred to. For example, that Lords select committees are crosscutting rather than shadowing government departments, and that while the committee stages of most bills in the Commons are taken in small public bill committees off the floor, there is no equivalent arrangement in the Lords. Instead, many bills have their committee stage on the floor of the chamber, while the others are taken in a 'grand committee' which is open to all members to attend. As in the Commons, much of the day-to-day business is coordinated by the so-called 'usual channels' (the euphemistic name given to discussions between party leaders and whips). But the government's lack of a majority, coupled with fewer rigid rules, result in ministers having much less control of the chamber's agenda than in the Commons. While procedures such as the 'guillotine' motion (to limit debate) were introduced in the Commons more than a century ago, the same did not occur in the Lords (Wheeler-Booth 2001).

Another key difference between the operation of the two chambers is the lack of power of the Lord Speaker relative to the Speaker of the House of Commons. The Lords is officially 'self-regulating', which according to the chamber's *Companion to Standing Orders* means that 'the Lord Speaker has no power to rule on matters of order', and instead 'the preservation of order and the maintenance of the rules of debate are the responsibility of the House itself, that is, of all the members who are present' (House of Lords 2010: 60). In the Commons, the Speaker can call the House to order, call individual members to speak in debate, and select which amendments should be debated from amongst those which have been tabled. In the Lords, none of these apply. In advance of planned debates, peers will instead let the Chief Whip's office know of their wish to speak, and a list of all names is collated and circulated. In more spontaneous debates, including on legislation and particularly at question times, there may be competition to speak. But contributors must be selected based on the mood in the House itself, guided where necessary by the Leader of the House or frontbenchers in individual party groups, rather than the Lord Speaker. This arrangement relies on considerable courtesy and good judgement by peers wishing to be called, and the same applies with respect to the tabling and moving of amendments to legislation. If all peers asserted their rights in an unrestrained way, the result would be chaos. Most of the time these arrangements work, but they are fragile. They certainly create a much less certain environment for the government than exists in the Commons.

The tradition of self-regulation and the difficulty of maintaining it has been much discussed in recent years. These arguments came to the fore when the Constitutional Reform Act 2005 ended the centuries-old tradition whereby the Lord Chancellor acted as the chamber's presiding officer. This required new arrangements to be put in place, and resulted in the creation of the post of Lord Speaker. How the Lord Speaker should be chosen, and the appropriate functions for the holder of this new role, were considered by two specially-convened select committees. The first question proved relatively straightforward: the Lord Speaker is now elected in a secret ballot of members, using the preferential Alternative Vote system. But the question of functions was more difficult. The second committee concluded that 'any change in the role currently performed by the Lord Chancellor would be a "slippery slope" ending in a loss of self-regulation', and 'could ultimately lead to a Commons type speakership which nobody wants' (Select Committee on the Speakership of the House 2005: 7–8). Although some proposed that the new Lord Speaker should have more control of the chamber, particularly at question times, this was firmly rejected by members.

After the 2010 election demands re-emerged to strengthen the post, as a result of tensions around establishment of coalition government (particularly the speaking rights of Liberal Democrat peers), and the large increase in the size of the chamber, with many new members not yet socialized in its restrained mode of debate. A review group of peers was established to look at the chamber's working practices, chaired by the former Conservative minister Alastair Goodlad. It suggested that there was 'an increasingly fractious and at times aggressive atmosphere' at question times, and that the chamber should experiment with giving the Lord Speaker a more active presiding role (Leader's Group on Working Practices 2011: 13). But the chamber rejected these proposals in November 2011, with Leader of the House Tom Strathclyde describing them as potentially 'the start of the end of self-regulation'.[26]

Various other proposals for procedural change have been made in recent years.[27] The main source of these has been successive 'Leader's Groups' such as that chaired by Lord Goodlad (the Lords Procedure Committee playing a rather different role to that in the Commons). However, as should already be clear, not all proposals for procedural change find favour among members. One recommendation that has been made repeatedly is for greater use of grand committees (off the floor) for the committee stage of government legislation. For example, the Goodlad Group suggested that most bills should follow this mechanism, aside from major constitutional bills, emergency legislation and 'other exceptionally controversial bills' (Leader's Group on Working Practices 2011: 33). But peers rejected this change, partly because it would make life easier for government (since greater use of grand committees would free up time on the floor for yet more government bills, while votes on amendments in grand committee are not permitted). Conversely, proposals that would make government's life more difficult—such as the Goodlad Group's suggestion that clauses not previously fully debated in the Commons should be flagged for extra attention when bills reached the Lords—fail to find favour with government whips. Thus, major procedural change of any kind is relatively rare.

Administration and support for members

Continuing the theme of differences between the two chambers, there is a wide gulf between the pay, allowances and other resources made available to members of the Commons and the Lords. In May 2013 MPs received an annual salary of £65,738, costs for a second home in London and for travel to and from their constituency, sufficient allowances to employ three full-time members of staff, and office space in which to house them. By comparison, resources in the Lords were far more limited.

Rather than receiving a salary each peer can claim a daily allowance, which is paid only for days that the House sits and on which they actually attend. This system was first introduced in 1957, and the sums payable have gradually risen over time, reaching £300 per day in 2010 (Vollmer 2011). On this basis, a peer attending every single sitting day would be able to claim approximately £44,000 per year, and these payments are tax free.[28] However, few peers attend daily and, as indicated previously, many indeed attend far more rarely (for any who completely cease to attend, no pension is available). In addition to the daily allowance, members living outside London can claim for the cost of train travel to and from their homes. But there is no longer any allowance payable to such members for the cost of overnight accommodation in London. This did exist prior to 2010, but was ended following media allegations against some peers who were said to be abusing the system.[29]

Most notably, perhaps, there is no separate allowance for peers to employ staff. Until 2010 a modest staffing allowance of £75 per sitting day attended was available, but this officially ended when the system was reformed. Those wishing to employ a secretary or researcher must now pay for this out of their daily allowances or other funds. Some peers do employ staff, mostly on a part-time basis. Others who themselves are employed outside the House can sometimes make use of staffing support elsewhere (e.g. in a business, voluntary organization or university). The rest depend solely on the House authorities, and on the numerous briefings that they receive from outside lobby groups such as industry organizations, trade unions, and charities, with whom many have strong links.[30] Funding for party groups is much more limited than in the Commons: the so-called 'Short money' payable to opposition parties in the first chamber totalled over £6.5 million in 2010–12, while the equivalent 'Cranborne money' in the Lords was less than £600,000.

Like staffing, office space in the Lords is also at a premium, despite having increased significantly in recent years. Unlike MPs, few peers have an office to themselves, and most instead share offices or do not even have a desk.[31] As the Clerk of the Parliaments reported recently, the office space provided in the Lords amounts to only five square metres per member (which is roughly double the size of a desk). MPs in contrast are granted 12.5 square metres for themselves, plus considerable additional space for their staff (Joint Committee on the Draft House of Lords Reform Bill 2012b: 379–80).

The Clerk of the Parliaments is the senior official in the House of Lords, and serves both as chief clerk and as the head of the administration. A similarly ancient office is that of Gentleman Usher of the Black Rod (generally referred to simply as 'Black Rod'), the official with responsibility for security in the Lords, and having special duties at the state opening of parliament. In total, the Lords had 493 staff in July 2012, of whom 111 worked in catering and retail services (i.e. the canteens, restaurants and souvenir shop) and over 100 in either back-office functions such as finance and human resources, or in security.[32] Those of most direct importance to peers' political work are the clerks and other specialists, numbering around 100, who advise on procedure and support both the chamber and its committees. Given peers' lack of personal staff, the research support from the roughly 40 staff in the House of Lords Library, who can provide policy briefings for members as well as access to outside publications, is also important.

Overall therefore, the total cost of running the Lords is significantly lower than that for the Commons, as peers often proudly point out. For example, in the 2008–09 session, the costs of the two chambers were £107 million and £392 million respectively. The largest difference between their budgets came in terms of members' salaries, allowances and personal staff, which cost £157 million in the Commons, and only £19 million in the Lords.[33]

The Lords' image, outreach and communications

As Chapter 3 noted, second chambers are often relatively low profile institutions, due to their distance from the democratic process and lesser powers when compared to first chambers. This is certainly true of the Lords, which (as demonstrated by polling figures in Chapter 9) is little understood by the public. Most political 'big beasts' sit in the Commons, and since members of the Lords are unelected, few citizens come into contact with them. This is in some ways beneficial to the chamber, as peers are not distracted by the constituency work that is so time-consuming for MPs, and can engage in political negotiation out of the media spotlight. But it also means that the chamber can be seen as out of touch, and that it is easily caricatured, or even dismissed.

If most people were asked today to conjure up an image of the House of Lords, it would doubtless be of people—predominantly elderly white men—wearing red ermine-trimmed robes. This is the image that accompanies almost every story about the chamber in the newspapers and on television. But in fact these outfits are worn by peers only once a year, when gathered for the queen's speech. On every other day they look much like MPs, or members of any other modern parliament or professional workplace. True, many are older, but there are also numerous members below retirement age, and they are more diverse in gender and ethnic terms than many would assume. If the standard ermine-clad image was ever accurate, it is certainly now well out of date.

In recent years many peers have become frustrated that while the chamber's membership has been at least partly modernized, its image has not kept up. Increasing energies have therefore gone into 'outreach', including public information about the chamber and its work. In particular, the Lord Speaker has been able to develop a role as ambassador for the chamber outside parliament in a way that the former Lord Chancellor did not have time to do. One such initiative has been a programme of 'peers in schools' where a team of volunteer members tour the country to meet schoolchildren; by November 2012 over 1,000 such visits had been made. Technology also clearly makes communication much easier, and the parliamentary website has greatly opened up access to information about both chambers. Since 2008 a team of peers has collaborated with the Hansard Society to produce 'Lords of the blog', which provides short lively updates on the chamber and its work.[34] In 2011 the House of Lords opened a twitter account, and many individual peers also communicate in this way.[35] These initiatives present a very different image, of a relatively responsive 21st-century institution.

Conclusion: A chamber of paradoxes

This chapter has sketched out some of the key features of the contemporary House of Lords, and begun to demonstrate the complexities and contradictions in this famous parliamentary institution. These may be addressed by returning to three of the questions set out in the opening chapter of the book, each of which is further addressed in the chapters that follow.

In terms of change, and the extent to which the chamber remains 'unreformed', the Lords underwent significant change in 1999 that was in many ways transformative. It is no longer Conservative-dominated, and the fact that it is now controlled by no single political party gives it a potentially important role in holding the government to account. It is unelected, yet now more representative of how people vote in party political terms than is the House of Commons. But many anomalies remain. Leaving aside the question of election (which is discussed at length in Chapters 9 and 10), few would consider it appropriate for the prime minister to be able to determine the size and party balance of one chamber of parliament. The only constraints on his patronage are political (in terms of the fear of a public or media backlash), rather than legal. Since 1999, when the majority of hereditary peers departed, appointments by Tony Blair and David Cameron have caused the chamber's size to increase substantially. This is connected to another anomalous feature: that members are appointed for life, and therefore cannot permanently depart the chamber until they die. The Lords' reputation as an outdated institution is hence not wholly deserved, but is not wholly inaccurate either.

In terms of differences to the Commons, the Lords' relatively proportional party balance is now an important feature. Particularly under Labour 1999–2010, this was a stark contrast to the government's single party dominance in the first chamber. In addition, the Lords includes many independent members, which seems fitting in an age when only a minority of citizens express strong support for any political party.[36] In both of these respects its membership is surprisingly modern, and in gender and ethnic terms the Lords is also becoming more diverse. It has a positive reputation as a chamber of 'experts', and as 'less political' than the Commons, which helps to counterbalance concerns about its unelected nature. But untangling this reputation is complex, and it is linked to more problematic elements (most notably the chamber's relatively elderly membership). Like the Commons, the Lords is a full-time professional parliamentary institution, but many of its members are nonetheless part-time, and do not receive a salary or resources to pay for staff. The chamber retains a tradition of 'self-regulation', but this relies on self-control and cooperation by its nearly 800 members, which could potentially be fractured at any point.[37]

The Lords is therefore in many ways a chamber of paradoxes. The same can be said with respect to the third question—regarding its impact on the policy process. The Lords is officially the junior partner in the legislative process, much constrained by conventions resting on its unelected nature. The Commons enjoys primacy, as the chamber of democratic territorial representation and the main seat of government. Yet the fact that the government has no majority in the Lords, and that it contains many high-profile and 'expert' members, gives it potentially great leverage to hold government to account. The extent to which this is exercised, and how it works in practice, is explored in the chapters that follow.

Notes

1. For further general introductory reading on the House of Lords, the various high-quality materials now available on the chamber's own website are recommended. The House of Lords Information Office produces various factsheets and annual summaries, and the House of Lords Library produces more detailed research papers. All of these are freely available to the public. Some specific examples are cited throughout the book.
2. It is perhaps a little known fact that the Green Party's first member of the UK parliament was a member of the House of Lords: Tim Beaumont, who was originally appointed as a Liberal in 1967, but later defected to the Greens. He died in 2008.
3. Since 1999, 58 life peers have been appointed before their 50th birthday. These include, for example, Crossbencher Victor Adebowale, appointed in 2001 aged 39, Conservative Nat Wei, appointed in 2010 aged 33 and Labour's Oona King, also appointed in 2010 aged 43.
4. Standing orders state that 15 of the 90 are chosen to act as office holders in the House (e.g. Deputy Speakers) and the remaining 75 are divided between the parties on the basis of their strengths. All members of the House (hereditary and non-hereditary) could vote for the 15 officeholders, and the other 75 were elected only by hereditary peers, within their party groups. Similar arrangements now apply to by-elections.
5. The Commission defines propriety as meaning that 'the individual should be in good standing in the community in general and with particular regard to the public regulatory authorities', and 'the individual should be a credible nominee . . . [and] would enhance rather than diminish the workings and the reputation of the House of Lords itself and the appointments system generally' (House of Lords Appointments Commission 2011: 12).
6. See <http://lordsappointments.independent.gov.uk/>. Such appointees were for a while dubbed 'people's peers': a name never used by the Commission, but instead said to have been coined by Tony Blair's former press secretary, Alastair Campbell.
7. This volume of appointments was subject to much criticism. After less than three years in office, Blair had made more appointments to the Lords (214) than Margaret Thatcher did in 11 years (203).
8. This compared to just 10 names left by James Callaghan in 1979, and seven names left by Margaret Thatcher in 1990 (Shell 1992: 37).
9. But see note 2.
10. For an account of one such transaction, see Mullin (2011: 270). For criticism of this process, see Public Administration Select Committee (2006: 14).

11. For discussion, see Public Administration Select Committee (2006, 2007).
12. Note that not all former MPs in this study were classified as having a primary background in representative politics—for example, if they had served in the Commons fairly briefly and had a longer career elsewhere.
13. Though it must be noted that the 2009 analysis allocates each peer to a single unique 'primary' profession, whereas the earlier study allowed members to be classified in more than one professional group. The two sets of figures are therefore not directly comparable.
14. Note that the presence of scientists is not captured in the table, as most of these are classed under either higher education or 'medical and healthcare'. The more detailed analysis of peers' specialisms conducted by Russell and Benton (2010) showed that these included astronomy, epidemiology, geology, meteorology, nanotechnology, neurology, psychiatry, statistics, zoology and various others.
15. This view may in any case be rather out of date: the Lords took a strong interest in the coalition government's Welfare Reform Bill, as discussed in Chapters 6 and 7. Contributors included many peers with voluntary sector backgrounds who had been chosen by the Appointments Commission in the immediately preceding years.
16. See, for example, <http://lordsoftheblog.net/2008/03/11/trust-the-experts/> (accessed 11 May 2012).
17. This part of the analysis was based on survey responses from 65% of peers.
18. n = 377. Other alternatives were 'a part-time job' that 'I pursue alongside voluntary work only' or while being 'otherwise wholly retired' (27% combined), or 'I do not attend often enough even to consider it a part-time job' (5%).
19. Equivalent figures for the Commons were 139 and 296, respectively.
20. The War Crimes Act 1991, European Parliamentary Elections Act 1999, Sexual Offences (Amendment) Act 2000 and Hunting Act 2004.
21. The exact words in the 1911 Act state that a money bill must contain 'only provisions dealing with . . . the imposition, repeal, remission, alteration, or regulation of taxation; the imposition for the payment of debt or other financial purposes of charges on the Consolidated Fund, the National Loans Fund or on money provided by Parliament, or the variation or repeal of any such charges; supply; the appropriation, receipt, custody, issue or audit of accounts of public money; the raising or guarantee of any loan or the repayment thereof; or subordinate matters incidental to those subjects or any of them'.
22. Since 1999, there have been only three defeats during second reading of government bills, and only one attempt to reject a bill at a third reading (see Chapter 6).
23. *House of Commons Hansard*, 17 May 2005, column 51; *House of Lords Hansard*, 6 June 2005, column 760.
24. *House of Lords Hansard*, 25 May 2010, column 22.
25. *House of Commons Hansard*, 27 June 2011, column 724.
26. *House of Lords Hansard*, 8 November 2011, column 145.
27. For a summary, see Newson (2010).

28. Based on an average number of sitting days of 146 per calendar year. The number of sitting days was 147 in 2006, 148 in 2007 and 2008, and 141 in 2009 (House of Lords Information Office 2010).
29. Two peers—Lord Taylor of Warwick and Lord Hanningfield—were convicted of criminal offences in relation to these claims in 2011. Prior to the 2010 changes, all members were entitled to a daily allowance of £86.50 and a daily secretarial allowance of £75 for days attended, while members whose main residence was outside London could claim an additional overnight allowance of £174. See Vollmer (2011).
30. Although these relationships can be seen as beneficial in the development of policy (see Chapter 7), it is also sometimes suggested that peers are too dependent on outside groups (e.g. Bingle 2012).
31. In 1988–89 only around 175 peers had a desk on the parliamentary estate (Rush and Jones 1993). In July 2012 the comparable figure was 617; but only 51 did not share with another peer (figures from the House of Lords Information Office).
32. Figures provided by the House of Lords Information Office.
33. *House of Lords Hansard*, 5 October 2009, Column WA416.
34. <http://lordsoftheblog.net/>.
35. See @UKHouseofLords. Examples of individual peers' accounts include @LordPhilofBrum, @LolaHornsey, @bryworthington, @oakeshottm, @LordNortonLouth.
36. The British Election Study 2010 (pre-campaign in person survey, n = 1935, available at <http://www.bes2009-10.org/>) found that 11% claimed to be a 'very strong' supporter of one of the parties (including minor parties), and a further 35% a 'fairly strong' supporter.
37. Indeed, this system did almost break down over the Parliamentary Voting and Constituencies Bill in 2010–11 (as discussed in Chapter 7).

5

Political Actors in the Lords

The previous chapter provided a brief introduction to the composition of the contemporary House of Lords. This one goes considerably further, describing the make-up, organization and behaviour of each of the chamber's component groups in detail. This allows us to further explore several of the key questions set out at the start of the book. An analysis of the chamber's groups gives important insights into how the Lords has changed since its reform in 1999, and how its culture differs from that in the Commons. Examination of group behaviour can also start to address questions about the policy influence of the Lords, in particular in terms of which groups of members have greatest potential to decide legislative outcomes.

As the chapter demonstrates, these questions are closely linked. We already know that the reform in 1999 had a fundamental effect on the chamber's party balance. A body that had been dominated by the Conservatives, essentially for 200 years, ceased to be so. In this new environment the culture and organization of all of the component groups in the Lords altered in important ways. The chamber's 'no overall control' status meant that various sets of peers could potentially affect the outcome of votes, which put increasing pressure on members' attendance and voting records. When Labour was in power it was the Liberal Democrats in particular who attained a pivotal position in the chamber. Post-2010, when this party entered coalition government alongside the Conservatives, the independent Crossbenchers instead became the chamber's main 'pivotal voters'.

The chapter opens with a description of each of the main groups in the Lords. The focus is on what kinds of individuals make up each group, how they reached the chamber, and (in most cases) how they organize themselves when they get there. The second half of the chapter then goes on to analyse the different groups' behaviour, principally in terms of attendance and voting. It investigates the role of whips and party voting cohesion, and also explores voting patterns in the non-party groups. This sheds light on the extent to which the Lords is 'less political' than the Commons. An analysis is then conducted of all divisions in the chamber 1999–2012, to establish which groups influenced voting outcomes. This provides essential context for subsequent chapters, which look at the chamber's policy interventions. The chapter's conclusion sums up what has been learnt about the chamber's culture, policy influence and change since 1999.

The main groups in the Lords

As indicated in the previous chapter, there are six principal groups in the House of Lords: the three main parties (which mirror those in the House of Commons), the independent Crossbenchers, the bishops and other peers who fit into none of these categories. This section looks at each of the six in turn, starting with the parties, and also includes a short analysis of the remaining 92 hereditary peers as a group.

Labour

As of May 2013, Labour was marginally the largest group in the House of Lords. This was a hangover from the party's 13 years in government (1997–2010), and represented a radical departure from the pre-1999 period, when the chamber was dominated by the Conservative Party (see Table 2.2).

Table 5.1. Summary information on the main groups in the Lords, October 2012

	Lab	Con	Lib Dem	Cross-bench	Bishop	Other	All
Number of members	225	212	90	178	26	33	764
Average (mean) age	69	70	67	71	63	70	69
Proportion aged over 80	14%	20%	10%	21%	0%	21%	17%
Proportion new since 1999	54%	37%	60%	54%	96%	52%	51%
Proportion of former MPs	30%	32%	32%	5%	0%	33%	24%
Proportion of women members	29%	18%	29%	21%	0%	15%	23%
Number of former cabinet ministers	24	33	2	2	0	1	62
Number of members at end of 1996–97 session	116	477	57	322	26	69	1067
Change in size of group since May 1997	+94%	−56%	+58%	−45%	0%	−52%	−28%

Source: Author's database for October 2012 (based on data provided by House of Lords Information Office), Purvis (2012) for 1996–97. Dod's for cabinet ministers. All figures exclude peers on leave of absence.

As discussed in Chapter 4, Tony Blair created a large number of new peers, many of whom joined the Labour benches. This gradually brought his party level with the Conservatives and eventually Labour became the largest group in 2006. Appointments by David Cameron since 2010 have not yet eliminated Labour's advantage. However, the coalition government obviously relies on votes from Liberal Democrats as well as Conservatives, so comfortably outnumbers the main opposition party. It is therefore in a far stronger position than Labour was even post-2006.

Before Labour entered government in 1997 it was not only numerically under-represented, but its benches in the Lords were in greater need of renewal than those of the Conservatives. Margaret Thatcher and John Major created 173 new Conservative life peers during the party's 18 years in office (1979–97), compared to 96 peers for Labour. Immediately before entering government, Labour had just 116 peers (15 of them hereditary), against the Conservatives' 477 (including 328 hereditaries). Labour peers included some who had held senior cabinet positions in the 1970s, such as James Callaghan, Barbara Castle and Denis Healey, whose appointments were partly honorific. But many others had been appointed on recommendation of consecutive Labour leaders specifically to be 'working peers', and particularly to maintain an active frontbench presence. A high level of commitment was thus expected of most Labour appointees, given their lesser numbers. For example, in the 1988–89 session 58% of Labour peers had attended more than two-thirds of sittings; but only 22% of Conservatives did the same (Baldwin 1993).

After 1997, several large waves of Labour peers were added. Around a third of appointees were—as in the pre-1997 period—former MPs, including a few who had served in senior roles (e.g. former party leader Neil Kinnock). But many others came from the more junior ranks in the Commons, or were brought in from outside, with the clear intent that they would serve as active peers. These included numerous former party staff, trade union officials, and local councillors. Tony Blair also ennobled a number of prominent Labour-supporting figures from outside politics, particularly in his early years. Examples included the architect Richard Rogers, novelist Ruth Rendell, fertility expert Professor Robert Winston and broadcaster Melvyn Bragg. A few members, such as the barrister Charlie Falconer, were appointed to the chamber to serve immediately as ministers. Under Gordon Brown, post-2007, various other non-politicians were brought in as Lords ministers to serve in his so-called 'Government of all the Talents'. These members (dubbed 'goats') included the surgeon Ara Darzi, diplomat Mark Malloch Brown and businessman Digby Jones (Yong and Hazell 2011). Taking all of these appointments together (and following losses due to deaths) Labour's

Lords group increased by 82% during the party's time in government, from 116 to 211. Then, following the 2010 general election defeat, a further 39 Labour appointments were made by David Cameron, 29 of them resulting from Gordon Brown's resignation and dissolution honours lists.

In terms of organization, the Parliamentary Labour Party (PLP) Labour Peers Group meets weekly, and elects its own chair and officers. Members can also attend the equivalent meeting of the overall PLP—comprising MPs and peers together—but only in a non-voting capacity. The Labour peers' meeting hears a report from the group's leader (i.e. the Leader of the House of Lords when in government, Shadow Leader in opposition) and Chief Whip about the business for the week, and there is usually an invited speaker (often a Commons frontbencher). The chair of the Labour peers attends the weekly 'Parliamentary Committee' which meets with the Labour leader, and there are also two places for peers on the party's National Policy Forum. In addition, a weekly meeting is held of all Labour frontbenchers, which is possible in the Lords given the relatively small number of such members. This helps create a more collegiate sense than in the Commons. In government, the group's leader and Chief Whip are appointed by the prime minister, but in opposition these positions are elected by Labour peers.

Labour's loss of power in 2010 was clearly a major blow, and required its peers to adjust to opposition. But members point out that this was easier in the Lords than in the Commons, since (given their age and backgrounds) many Labour peers had served in parliament pre-1997. While the two governing parties had to adjust to working together, and also to a severe loss of funds (as discussed in the following sections), Labour faced neither of these challenges. Indeed, the Liberal Democrats' entry into government meant that Labour gained almost the entire allocation of 'Cranborne money' paid to opposition parties. This allowance was £522,102 in 2011–12 (Kelly 2011), enabling the group to employ nine staff.

Conservatives

Labour's relative gain in Lords strength post-1999 largely came at the cost of the Conservatives. As already indicated, the party had 477 peers immediately before Labour won power in 1997. Since the majority were hereditary, most departed in 1999. At the end of the 1999–2000 session the group numbered 232, comprising 52 hereditaries retained under the Weatherill amendment, plus 180 life peers (Purvis 2012). Like Labour, around a third of the party's life peers were former MPs, but their profile was rather different. The Conservatives' long period in government had left them with many 'grandees' who had held high ministerial office. As convention used to demand that senior cabinet ministers should be awarded a peerage after departing the Commons, many of these were ennobled. In late 2012 the Conservative benches in the Lords still included numerous members who served in Thatcher and Major's cabinets, such as Leon Brittan, Michael Heseltine, Nigel Lawson, Norman Tebbit and Margaret Thatcher herself. Since Blair created only 62 Conservative life peers (against 163 for Labour) these grandees accounted for a significant proportion of the party's seats, and many did not become active in the chamber. As for life peers drawn from outside politics, the largest professional block on the Conservative benches (accounting for 35% of the group in 2009) comprised those from banking, finance, business, commerce and the private sector (Russell and Benton 2010). Conservative peers included relatively fewer with backgrounds in higher education and the voluntary sector, compared to the other parties and Crossbenchers.

As in 1997 for Labour, the Conservative group in 2010 was in need of replenishment. Numbers had gradually declined to 185, of whom 79% predated the 1999 reform (compared to only 58% of Labour and 49% of Liberal Democrat peers). Consequently, Conservative members were on average considerably older than their counterparts in the other parties. David Cameron then created an unprecedentedly large number of new life peers in his first year, 49 of whom were Conservatives. These included a few former MPs, but the great majority came from outside politics. Like Blair and Brown, he brought some people in to serve immediately as ministers, such as banker Stephen Green and former Number 10 adviser Jonathan Hill (who became Leader of the House in 2013). In opposition Cameron had already used some of his small number of appointments—among them Sayeeda Warsi and David Freud—to bring new blood onto the shadow frontbench. When his 'big society' adviser Nat Wei was appointed in 2010 he became the chamber's youngest member, aged 33. Such creations helped Cameron to boost his party's image as younger, more ethnically diverse and female-friendly. Nonetheless, as shown in Table 5.1, Conservative peers in 2012 remained on average older, longer-serving and more male than those from the other parties.

The Conservative group's organization in the Lords is quite similar to Labour's. The Association of Conservative Peers (ACP) is an explicitly backbench body, which meets weekly and elects its own chair and officers. Peers can also attend the party's 1922 Committee in the House of Commons, though few aside from the ACP chair do so. This position tends to go to a senior parliamentarian, and recent holders include the former cabinet ministers Peter Brooke, Gillian Shephard and John MacGregor. The ACP's meetings hear reports from a representative of the 1922 Committee, from the party's Chief Whip in the Lords about the week's business, and from another frontbench or outside speaker.

After 2010 there were two important changes for the Conservatives to deal with—transition from opposition to government, and entry into coalition with the Liberal Democrats. Both were easier for the party's peers than its MPs. Relationships between all parties in the Lords are relatively informal, with the offices of the three sets of Leaders and Chief Whips in close proximity on a single corridor. Senior figures in the Conservatives and Liberal Democrats already spoke very regularly when Labour was in power, given that the two parties (as discussed later) could combine to defeat the government. One Conservative peer suggested in an interview in 2010 that the 'last 13 years have been spent in coalition with the Libs in this House'. But some things did change, such as the ACP occasionally being addressed by Liberal Democrat as well as Conservative frontbenchers (although the two parties' groups continued to meet separately). A set of 15 new ACP 'liaison groups' were also established to shadow government departments.

Liberal Democrats

The Liberal Democrat group in the Lords has also undergone very significant change since 1999, and more since 2010. The Lib Dems remain, as in the Commons, by far the smallest of the three main parties; but they have grown significantly in strength, both numerically and in other ways.

Immediately before Labour came to power in 1997 there were 57 Liberal Democrat peers, of whom 24 were hereditary. The party was therefore potentially very vulnerable to the effects of the 1999 reform. But Tony Blair was generous in appointing Lib Dem peers. In 1997 alone he created 11, and by the time he left office ten years later he had added a total 53 new peers to the party's benches. By the 2010 general election the group's size (following appointments, removal of the hereditaries and deaths) had risen to 72. David Cameron then made a further 24 Liberal Democrat appointments. Overall, over 1997–2012 the group increased in size by 58%. As Table 5.1 shows, the Lib Dem group contains a higher proportion of relatively new members than either of the other parties, and is on average younger.

Liberal Democrat peers, like those of other parties, include some political 'grandees' who previously sat in the Commons. Among them are Shirley Williams and Bill Rodgers, who served in Labour cabinets in the 1970s and then formed part of the 'gang of four' who left Labour in 1981 to establish the Social Democratic Party (SDP).[1] Both have been group leaders in the House of Lords (see Table 5.2). But the party's smaller number of MPs, and exclusion from government until 2010, left it with far fewer obligations to reward senior figures with peerages (notable exceptions being former party leaders David Steel and Paddy Ashdown). Instead, Lib Dem appointees have tended to include a higher proportion of members from the party's activist and councillor base. The group therefore includes a distinct mix of generations, some of whom are relatively young and others who have a background in politics older than the party itself. Tom McNally, the current leader of the group (and Deputy Leader of the House of Lords), is one of the latter, having been a Number 10 adviser to Labour's Callaghan government 1976–79. In terms of professional backgrounds, Liberal Democrat peers include a higher proportion drawn from the public and voluntary sectors, education and the legal professions than the other parties (Russell and Benton 2010).

Due in part to its size, but also its role in opposition, the Liberal Democrat group has historically been organized slightly differently to the two larger parties. Until 2010 it had no separate backbench leadership, and its weekly meeting (which is otherwise similar to the other two parties) was instead chaired by its leader. In opposition, there was thus a culture of collective decision-making, including all-group discussion of the line to take on government bills. Occasionally, given the party's pivotal position in 1999–2010 (discussed later), Labour ministers even addressed the group to try and win its support. Liberal Democrat MPs met separately, but departmental 'portfolio teams' met on a bicameral basis, again with something of a blurring between frontbench and backbench roles.

The party's move into government brought some important changes, including a more explicit, if somewhat awkward, separation of front and backbench. The Lords group now elects a backbench 'convenor' who chairs its weekly meeting. A new set of bicameral policy committees were also created, each co-chaired by a peer and an MP who have a kind of quasi-frontbench but non-governmental role as party 'spokespeople' (Yong 2012). The party's key challenge was to maintain its separate identity inside the coalition, and it notably kept its own whips' office and separate briefings, despite being subject to the government whip. But it faces major resource problems. In opposition, the Lib Dems were entitled to a share of the 'Cranborne money', amounting to £237,136 in 2009–10 (alongside the far larger 'Short money' in the Commons: an annual £1.75 million). On entering government these funds ceased, which was a far larger blow to the Liberal Democrats than the relatively better-funded Conservatives. Consequently, support to the party's group in the Lords was severely cut, and is now maintained at a reduced level in part through a levy on individual peers.

Crossbenchers

The fourth key group in the chamber, significantly larger than the Liberal Democrats, comprises the non-party-aligned Crossbenchers. As indicated in Chapter 2, although the presence of non-partisan experts may now be seen as quintessential to the Lords, the Crossbench group only formed after the 1958 Life Peerages Act. But it is now extremely well established, and its organization and level of influence has developed significantly since 1999. Immediately prior to reform there were 355 Crossbenchers, of whom 226 were hereditary, so the group therefore lost more than half its members as a result. But other changes have brought significant renewal, and far greater activism.

A study of the group up to 2007 suggested that there were six distinct routes by which members had reached the Crossbenches, three of which are now effectively closed (Russell and Sciara 2009). Of these defunct routes the most substantial was ennoblement in the annual queen's birthday and New Year honours lists of leading non-party figures drawn from industry, the arts, professions and academia. Such appointments effectively ended with the creation of the House of Lords Appointments Commission in 2000. A second route closed in 2009 with the establishment of the Supreme Court, before which 'Law Lords' conventionally sat as Crossbenchers. A third defunct route is dealt with later in this section.

Three means therefore remain to reach the Crossbenches. The first, as for the party groups, is election as a hereditary peer: 31 of the 92 remaining hereditaries are Crossbenchers. The primary route, however, is now through appointment by the House of Lords Appointments Commission. While the Commission has no direct role in selecting members of the political parties (merely vetting them for 'propriety'), it actually chooses Crossbench peers. By May 2013, 63 such appointments had been made. The Commission's criteria for selection have subtly changed over time, but currently require that applicants demonstrate 'a record of significant achievement' and 'are and intend to remain independent of any political party'.[2] When first created, the Commission advertised widely and received over 3,000 applications, appointing its first batch of 15 members in 2001. Since then applications have reduced to around 100 per year, of whom around 15 are invited for interview.[3] Of these, no more than three or four are likely to be appointed. In terms of who gets chosen, part of the Commission's remit is 'to consider nominees who would broaden the expertise and experience of the House and reflect the diversity of the people of the United Kingdom' (House of Lords Appointments Commission 2011: 9). Of its first 59 appointments, 21 (36%) were women and 13 (22%) were black and minority ethnic candidates (House of Lords Appointments Commission 2011: 9), while several people with disabilities have also been selected. Although the Commission chooses only around one-fifth of total appointees, this helps explain why the post-1999 chamber has become more demographically representative. In reflecting diversity, the Commission also explicitly seeks to fill gaps in expertise in the chamber. It has made far fewer 'celebrity' appointments than were chosen via the old honours lists, with many members drawn from the voluntary sector, as well as public sector bodies, science and industry. The Commission also makes some attempt to achieve religious diversity in the chamber, for example, appointing Chief Rabbi Jonathan Sacks in 2009, and Indarjit Singh, Director of the UK's Network of Sikh Organisations, in 2011.[4]

The third and final means of appointment to the Crossbenches is as a direct nominee of the prime minister, who retains (by agreement with the Commission) the right to select up to 10 'distinguished public servants' per parliament. These places have conventionally been used to reward retiring holders of certain very senior public offices, most notably Cabinet Secretary (i.e. head of the civil service), Chief of the Defence Staff (head of the armed services) and more recently Commissioner of the Metropolitan Police (the UK's most senior police officer). Such appointments are still seen as 'quasi-automatic'. The 2009 audit of expertise showed that the Crossbenches included relatively more peers than the parties whose main background was in higher education and the legal professions, as well as including the majority of members whose main background was in the civil service, police, defence and voluntary sector (Russell and Benton 2010). These groups collectively accounted for more than half of Crossbenchers. In contrast to party peers (as seen in Table 5.1), very few Crossbenchers are former MPs. Exceptions include former Commons Speakers, who give up party allegiance when in post, and have conventionally been appointed to the Lords on their retirement.

Even more than the parties, today's Crossbench group includes a wide mix of members who have entered via different routes, and at different times, with varying expectations on their performance. The appointment of 'quasi-automatics', and celebrity figures prior to 2000 was always partly honorific, with members not necessarily expected to contribute much to the chamber's work. This may still be true to some extent for the Prime Minister's direct nominees, but those chosen by the Appointments Commission now face different expectations, as discussed later in the chapter.

Not just Crossbench membership, but also organization, has changed significantly since 1999. In some ways the group organizes on similar lines to the political parties, but with obvious and important differences. For example, it does not have a 'leader', but does have a 'convenor'. The first such figure, Lord Strang, emerged in the 1960s. Since then the position has become more formalized, and is now elected by the group for a term of up to four years.[5] Unlike the opposition parties, until 1999 the Crossbenchers received no public funding at all and employed only a part-time secretary, funded by voluntary donations from members. Their weekly meeting was therefore vital for the exchange of information. But organization is now far more sophisticated and extensive. In 1999 the then convenor, Bernard Weatherill (a former Commons Speaker), negotiated a small annual allowance of £10,000 from the 'Cranborne money'. This increased gradually, reaching £67,063 in 2011–12 (Kelly 2011). The group now employs one full-time and one part-time member of staff, whose tasks include producing briefings on bills and regular updates for peers. Nonetheless, the contrast in funding to the parties is stark: as already indicated, the Labour peers (with roughly equal numbers to the Crossbenchers) receive approximately eight times the funding, while even the Liberal Democrats in opposition (despite having only around one-third the number of peers) received four times as much.

Perhaps understandably, there is significant suspicion on the party benches about the genuine neutrality of Crossbenchers. As Crossbench peer and constitutional historian Peter Hennessy (2011: 166) suggests, many members 'reckon that it is a bit of an act on our part . . . that we must really be closet Conservatives, Liberal Democrats or Labour people. They can't really quite grasp, some of them, that people can come into the Lords primarily because they know things, without partisan beliefs to fire them up every day'. Prior to 2010 such suspicions were greatest on the Labour and Liberal Democrat benches. In the 2005 survey only 45% of Labour peers and 51% of Liberal Democrats agreed that 'the Crossbenchers fulfil a genuinely independent role'; in stark contrast, 93% of Conservative peers believed this to be true.[6] The difference between the two main parties is explained both by historic Labour suspicions about the Crossbenchers and natural concern among those on the government side about peers who vote against its legislation. Public opinion is, however, much more positive about the inclusion of non-party-aligned peers. As discussed in Chapter 9, some polls have indicated far greater support for inclusion of 'independent experts' than party representatives in the second chamber.

The Crossbench group (particularly as represented by its convenor) has become increasingly sensitive about allegations of non-independence, and the group's rules have been tightened up to clarify its distance from the parties. The final defunct route onto the Crossbenches was as a member of a minor party, or temporary refugee from one of the major parties. A decade ago it was common for party members who fell out with their group, or who took a position (e.g. public appointment) that required political neutrality, to join the Crossbenches. But such members are no longer admitted. More anomalously, members of the Northern Ireland parties (UUP and DUP) historically sat as Crossbenchers, but were ejected in 2009. Hence, the group now pretty unambiguously includes only independents.

It is clear that while the Crossbench group has some 'party-like' features, it has no unified point of view. There are no clear 'left' or 'right' factions, and curiously neither are Crossbench vocational or interest groupings very strong. For example, the former Cabinet Secretaries and Chiefs of the Defence Staff rarely work as coordinated groups.[7] Indeed, Crossbenchers may not feel part of a cohesive entity at all: in the 2007 survey only 43% agreed that 'there is a strong feeling of unity in my group', compared to around 90% of party peers who said the same.[8] Historically, some Crossbenchers have even denied that they are part of a 'group', describing the collectivity instead as 'an amalgam' and as 'unbelievably heterogeneous'. This clearly creates challenges for members. One Crossbench interviewee described feeling 'very exposed and vulnerable', suggesting that in contrast party members are 'part of a club'. This has both its positive and negative sides. Another member suggested that 'it's terribly easy being whipped', whereas the Crossbenchers 'actually have to think'. A third conceded that a party would provide 'a more companionable environment', and more resources, but felt that subordination to a whip was too high a price to pay. As another put it, 'the best and the worst thing is that nobody tells us how to vote'. But while Crossbenchers may not act collectively, or even network a great deal together, they do tend to join or form networks which operate on a cross-party basis. They therefore play an important role in connecting people with shared policy interests across the chamber as a whole. In this and other ways, as discussed later, they greatly enhance the 'expert' and 'less partisan' ethos of the Lords.

Table 5.2. Leaders and convenors of the four main groups since 1999

Conservative	Labour	Liberal Democrat	Crossbench
Tom Strathclyde (1998–2013)	Margaret Jay (1998–2001)	Bill Rodgers (1997–2001)	Bernard Weatherill (1995–99)
Jonathan Hill (2013–)	Gareth Williams (2001–03)	Shirley Williams (2001–04)	David Craig (1999–2004)
	Valerie Amos (2003–07)	Tom McNally (2004–)	David Williamson (2004–07)
	Cathy Ashton (2007–08)		Frances D'Souza (2007–11)
	Jan Royall (2008–)		Herbert Laming (2011–)

Bishops

The other main non-party group in the chamber comprises the Church of England bishops. As described in Chapter 2, they sit in the Lords as of ancient right, but their numbers are limited to 26 by an Act of 1847. Despite being a much smaller group than the Crossbenchers, the bishops' presence in the chamber proves far more controversial.

As indicated in Chapter 4, five seats for bishops are *ex officio*, while the remaining 21 go to the longest-established holders of episcopal sees. A newly-appointed bishop may therefore wait several years before gaining a seat in the House of Lords, but will then retain it until retirement from the church. Bishops are the only members who can permanently retire from the chamber, but a few are subsequently granted life peerages. Former Archbishops of Canterbury are conventionally among those appointed directly by the prime minister. In May 2013 the chamber included two such members (George Carey and Rowan Williams), and one other former Lord spiritual (Richard Harries, formerly Bishop of Oxford). All three sat as Crossbenchers.

Various aspects of the bishops' presence prove controversial. Some question whether organized religion should be represented in the chamber at all, and others whether this should be restricted—particularly in a multi-faith Britain—to the Church of England, which is the only 'established' church. The merits of widening religious representation—or alternatively abolishing it completely—have therefore been much debated in the context of Lords reform (see Chapter 10). Polls suggest that there is fairly limited public support for the bishops' presence: in January 2012 a *Sunday Times* YouGov survey found that 58% believed 'bishops should not sit and vote in the House of Lords', while only 24% thought that they should.[9] Other polls have found more ambivalent attitudes, but not much support (Cruse 2012). Within the chamber itself, 71% of members in the 2007 survey agreed that 'I respect the role of the bishops in the House'. But support was significantly greater among Conservatives and Crossbenchers than Labour and Liberal Democrat peers.[10]

The bishops, in fact, project themselves as 'a voice for all people of faith, not just Christians', and have various formalized mechanisms for inter-faith dialogue.[11] They also point out that they are the only members of the chamber with any kind of formal geographic constituency, and occasionally intervene on issues relating to their locality. One recently suggested that the church allows bishops to 'bring to their contribution a network of connections into local communities which no other institution can begin to match', noting that the one million weekly attendees at Church of England services significantly exceeded membership of any political party.[12]

The bishops very rarely attend the chamber in large numbers, as further discussed later in this chapter. The daily proceedings of both chambers open with prayers, and in the Lords these are read by a bishop. For this purpose the group has a rota, and there is always a bishop 'on duty'. The rota excludes the five most senior (i.e. *ex officio*) bishops, which in practice requires the other 21 to be on duty for roughly two weeks each per year, during which time they will also participate in other debates. Additional bishops attend when there is business of interest, or when sittings coincide with other meetings in London. For example, when the General Synod meets (in Church House, nearby in Westminster) attendance can be markedly higher.

Organizationally, the bishops, like the Crossbenchers, nominate a 'convenor' who acts as the main point of contact for the group, including with the 'usual channels' (i.e. discussions between party whips). Although the group does not take a collective line, there is a degree of coordination on policy matters. Thus the bishops do discuss and agree who will be present to contribute to particular debates and bills; but each remains free to express his own view. For example, the former Bishop of Portsmouth (Kenneth Stevenson, who sat 1999–2009) was chair of the Church of England's Board of Education and thus regularly contributed to debates in the House on education matters; the current Bishop of Liverpool (James Jones) takes a particular interest in prisons. In pursuing these interests, each bishop will take some care to consult with colleagues, and also other faith groups. The group does not receive Cranborne money, but benefits from research and policy support by staff at Church House.

Other peers

The remaining members of the chamber comprise a collection of peers who fit into none of these categories. The stricter criteria now set down for Crossbench membership have contributed to a significant increase in their number over recent years: at the end of the 1999–2000 session there were only six such members, but by October 2012 this had risen to 33. These peers are not an organized group, and have no collective meetings or convenor. They comprise principally of two types of members. The first are peers allied to other smaller parties. As described in Chapter 4, these include representatives of the Ulster Unionist Party (UUP), Democratic Unionist Party (DUP) and Plaid Cymru, each of which gained representation through being granted appointees by the prime minister. Since all three also have members of the House of Commons, peers can share some research support with them. The UK Independence Party (UKIP) members, in contrast, all previously sat as

Conservative peers. They enjoy no public funding in parliament, as Cranborne money extends only to the main opposition parties and to the Crossbenchers, and the party has no MPs.

The remaining other members are non-aligned peers who for one reason or another do not sit on the Crossbenches. Some have been expelled from their parties, including the former Conservative peer Jeffrey Archer and former Labour peer Mike Watson, both following criminal convictions. The fact that those convicted of serious criminal offences cannot be permanently expelled from the chamber, as applies in the Commons, remains a bone of contention (see Chapter 10). Other members take a brief respite from political party affiliation for more benign reasons. For example, former Labour cabinet minister Chris Smith moved to these benches in 2008, having become chair of the Environment Agency and hence required to be independent of party. Such members often resume their seats on the party benches once their spell in such a role is over.

The remaining 92 hereditary peers

Finally, although they do not operate as a group, the 92 remaining hereditary peers are of sufficient curiosity value to merit a short description of their own. As already discussed in Chapter 4, these peers continue to sit in the chamber under the terms of the 1999 Act, and standing orders set out the detail. These specify that 42 hereditary peers are elected as Conservatives, 28 as Crossbenchers, three as Liberal Democrats and two as Labour. In addition, 15 are elected by the whole House as officeholders and two are royal officeholders. These 17 are also divided between the chamber's main groups.[13]

Accounts of the initial contest for the 92 hereditary seats are available elsewhere (e.g. Crewe 2005; Shell 2000). But suffice to say that seats were hotly contested, and one of the principal considerations was whether those elected would attend regularly and contribute to the work of the House. The hereditary peers in today's chamber are therefore far more assiduous attenders than was the norm prior to 1999. Baldwin (1993) found that in the 1988–89 session 44% of hereditary peers failed to attend at all, and only 13% attended more than two-thirds of sittings. In the 2010–12 session well over half of hereditary peers attended this regularly.

The profile of these peers is perhaps not quite what most people would assume. The tradition of hereditary membership dates back many centuries, and allowed seats to be passed down for generations; however, as Chapter 2 demonstrates, the hereditary peerage was always extremely porous. New peerages were regularly created in order to maintain the membership of the

House, strengthen party numbers, or reward favourites. Until the 1958 Life Peerages Act the only means of appointing somebody to the chamber was by creating a new hereditary peer. In the early 20th century many of these positions went—like life peerages subsequently—to industrialists, civil servants, military personnel and former MPs.

The background of the remaining 92 reflects this complex history. Of those with a right to sit in May 2013, by far the largest number of peerages—52—dated only to the 20th century, and a further 18 to the 19th century. Consequently, 14 were only the second holder of their titles (most having inherited from their fathers), a further 26 were third holders, and 10 were fourth holders.[14] Some were descendants of well-known 20th-century figures: for example, the grandson of post-war Labour Prime Minister Clement Attlee (Earl Attlee, who sits as a Conservative), the grandson of Liberal Prime Minister David Lloyd George (Viscount Tenby, Crossbencher) and the sons of wartime military commanders Field Marshal Montgomery and Field Marshal Slim (Viscount Montgomery of Alamein and Viscount Slim, both Crossbench). Many others were sons, grandsons or other relatives of lesser-known 20th-century politicians. Of course, some titles were significantly older. Seven dated to the 18th century, seven to the 17th century, seven to the 15th and 16th centuries and one to the 12th century. This most ancient title belonged to the Countess of Mar, who was its 31st holder, and also distinguished by being one of the only two women hereditaries in the chamber.

Attendance, voting and voting cohesion

Membership of the House of Lords is very different to that in the Commons, and indeed to most other elected legislatures. Unsurprisingly, therefore, the chamber's culture and its members' voting behaviour are very different as well. In particular, the Lords is often referred to as being 'less partisan' than the Commons. This is true, most obviously due to the presence of the bishops and Crossbenchers, but also because the parties operate in subtly different ways. However, it is important not to overstate these differences too much: key aspects of the parties' behaviour in the Lords also reflect those in other partisan assemblies.

A notable feature of the Lords, as indicated in Chapter 4, is that members' attendance is very variable. Many peers do not treat membership as a full-time job. In the past this was explicable partly by the presence of those who arrived in the chamber by accident of birth, rather than through choosing a political career. Reform in 1999 brought this to an end. Additionally, appointment to the Lords used often to be seen as an honour more than a job. This has gradually changed, but many members remain who were appointed under the old honorific system. These factors may be fading, but others nonetheless remain. One is that peerages (both life and hereditary) are essentially permanent, and cannot be renounced.[15] If a member's circumstances change—for example, in terms of place of residence or ill-health—they cannot resign their seat, only take voluntary 'leave of absence'. Few in practice do so, in part because there is no guarantee that they will be replaced by another from their party. Consequently, many members are elderly and find it difficult to attend. Another contributing factor is the tradition—indeed often the explicit objective—that 'expert' members should continue to pursue their professional interests outside parliament. Indeed, the fact that

Table 5.3. Peers' attendance and voting, by group

	Lab	Con	Lib Dem	Cross-bench	Bishop
2010–12 (Coalition government)					
Mean daily attendance (per peer)*	68%	61%	76%	45%	19%
Proportion attending 2/3 of sittings*	67%	50%	75%	35%	0%
Mean turnout in government whipped divisions (per division)**	57%	59%	66%	24%	5%
Maximum voting turnout in a single division	82%	89%	90%	52%	23%
Mean cohesiveness (Rice index) in whipped votes†	99%	97%	94%	46%	77%
1999–2010 (Labour government)					
Mean daily attendance (per peer)*	66%	55%	71%	35%	16%
Proportion attending 2/3 of sittings*	60%	46%	68%	20%	0%
Mean turnout in government whipped divisions (per division)**	53%	30%	48%	11%	3%
Maximum voting turnout in a single division	84%	89%	95%	48%	42%
Mean cohesiveness (Rice index) in whipped votes†	98%	98%	99%	45%	80%

Source: Author's database (based on *House of Lords Hansard*, and attendance figures provided by House of Lords Information Office).

* Mean attendance is calculated for each peer and then averaged across the group. Both of these figures are approximate, as they exclude all members who switched group during the period, but otherwise include all eligible members not disqualified or on leave of absence. Calculations are based only on those sittings that a peer was eligible to attend if not a member for the whole period.

** Voting turnout is calculated for each group in each division, and then averaged over the period.

† Calculated for Lab, Con, Lib Dem and Crossbench only on votes where more than 10 such members participated; for Bishops where more than two participated.

there is no salary associated with membership of the Lords means that many members consider work outside the chamber a financial necessity.

Table 5.3 shows a number of key indicators by group with respect to attendance and voting, while variations in voting turnout over time are illustrated in Figure 5.1. These demonstrate that there are significant differences between groups, and also over time. One notable feature is that attendance and voting in all groups falls well short of 100%. When Labour was in government the average turnout of its peers in divisions (i.e. votes) was barely over half the group, while Conservative turnout was far lower. When asked in the 2007 survey whether they treated membership of the chamber as a full-time job, only 38% of Labour peers claimed to do so, as did just 23% of Conservatives. The most assiduous in this regard were Liberal Democrat peers, of whom 46% claimed to attend full-time; this group also consistently has the highest actual attendance. In contrast only 16% of Crossbenchers (and understandably, no bishops) considered themselves to be full-time members.[16]

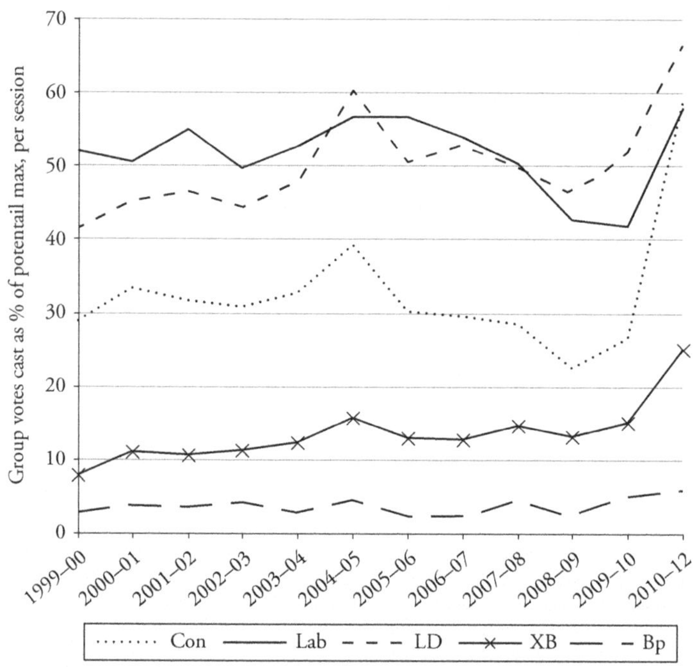

Figure 5.1. Turnout in divisions by group, 1999–2012

Source: Constructed from figures in Purvis (2012). Data includes all divisions (including unwhipped), and takes no account of strength of the whip. For highest turnouts by group see Table 5.3.

The culture of whipping in the Lords

Levels of attendance in the chamber, and of course voting, are closely related to the work of the party whips. The two primary roles of the whip are to encourage members to attend and, when they do so, to encourage them to vote the party line. As indicated previously, concern about these matters can begin even before members are appointed.

Prior to 1999, when the party still dominated the chamber, the job of Conservative whips was as much to discourage members from voting as to encourage it. Except on occasions when a Conservative government feared losing a key division, it was undesirable to display too flagrantly how Conservative peers' votes could swamp those from the other parties. As the party's former Chief Whip Bertie Denham put it, '[b]ecause we had this preponderance of Tories it would be embarrassing if too many people came too often' (quoted in Mitchell 1999: 52). Consequently, there was little need to vet incoming Conservative peers for their commitment to making an active contribution. These peers included many political grandees rewarded after years of active service in the Commons, while others with senior jobs in industry struggled to attend. One Conservative peer appointed in the 1990s after more than a decade in cabinet reported being told to 'turn up, but you know, don't make a thing of it'.

This was in marked contrast to the culture of the other parties, who were greatly outnumbered until 1999. Even before Labour entered government in 1997 most of its prospective peers were interviewed by the Lords Chief Whip, who emphasized that their presence was expected for three days per week. Only after this meeting would the party leader confirm their appointment. In Blair's early years as prime minister this practice slipped somewhat, but was quickly reinstated when attendance of some of his initial 'celebrity' peers turned out to be poor. The arrangements in the Liberal Democrat group were similar. The establishment of a coalition government in 2010 then put new pressures on both attendance and voting, particularly for the Conservatives. Figure 5.1 illustrates how voting turnout in all groups increased post-2010, with the increase among Conservatives sharpest of all.

The absolute exception to this kind of regime used to be on the Crossbenches, where non-partisan figures had received largely honorific peerages, and of course had no whip to encourage them to attend. But this culture has gradually changed since creation of the House of Lords Appointments Commission. Initially, there was no expectation by the Commission that Crossbenchers should be 'working peers'; but its first group of appointees in 2001 was subjected to fierce media criticism for poor attendance and voting, raising concerns that both the Commission and the Crossbenchers could fall into disrepute.[17] Applicants interviewed by the Commission are hence now pressed on their availability to contribute to the chamber. They are expected, in the words of the its chair, to 'spend, say, two days a week or thereabouts in the House of Lords'.[18] In addition, the Crossbench convenor has put increasing emphasis on both attendance and voting. One former convenor suggested that if Crossbenchers vote more often they are more likely to be seen as 'a force', and also as 'an asset' (as some fear for the group's existence should the Lords be replaced by a wholly elected chamber). Nonetheless, despite increased attendance and voting, the group's turnout remains significantly below that of the parties. Crossbenchers clearly confront greater challenges regarding how to cast their vote than party peers, who if in doubt can simply follow the directions of their whip. Hence, some would like abstentions to be officially recorded, in order to make clearer when they were present in the chamber and simply choose not to vote for either side. However such a change would be highly undesirable to party managers, as it would show up divisions within their own ranks.

As Table 5.3 and Figure 5.1 make clear, by far the lowest attendance and voting turnout is that of the bishops. In the whole period 1999–2012 there were just four occasions when as many as 10 bishops participated in a division. The highest turnout was 14, on the Assisted Dying for the Terminally Ill Bill in 2006 (discussed in Chapter 7).[19] Likewise, there were just four times when as many as 100 Crossbenchers voted (all on unwhipped votes on House of Lords reform in 2006). Crossbench turnout reached 50 members in only just over 10% of divisions; but such occasions are gradually becoming more common.

The three parties organize their whipping in quite similar ways, which bear close superficial resemblance to organization in the Commons. A weekly communication is sent to every member indicating the 'strength' of the whip on each sitting day, meaning how important it is that they should attend. More regular briefings are then sent throughout the week, by e-mail or text message, indicating the likely timing of votes. It is generally on the floor of the chamber itself that the whips indicate how they want members to vote, as it can be unpredictable exactly what (e.g. which amendment) will be voted upon.

In general, whipping is more genteel and low-key than in the Commons. The Conservatives and Liberal Democrats have traditionally both avoided the use of 'three-line' whips as far as possible, restricting these to a handful of times per year. Labour, in contrast, uses three-line whips (which literally comprise of an instruction to members underlined three times, in this case stating 'your presence is required') much more regularly. However, differences between the parties are to some extent semantic. Liberal Democrats and Conservatives distinguish between 'light' and 'heavy' two-line whips, with the latter broadly comparable to a Commons three-line whip. Nonetheless those responsible for whipping in all parties emphasize how relatively powerless they are to compel members to attend. One who had been a whip in both chambers characterized Lords whipping as needing to be 'more persuasive'. Whips have fewer sanctions than in the Commons: most notably, they cannot threaten to withhold promotion (as few peers aspire to be ministers) or deselection (as peers cannot be removed). Philip Norton—himself a Conservative peer, as well as an academic expert on parliament—has thus described the Lords as a 'discipline-free' environment (2003: 58). This is a slight overstatement, as the whips do, for example, control places on committees, and speaking time to some extent. But whips interviewed insisted that they had 'absolutely no powers with the members', and that there are 'absolutely no sanctions whatsoever'. A senior Conservative whip claimed instead to depend on members' 'devotion to duty'; a senior Labour whip spoke of the need to 'appeal to [members'] better nature' and a senior Liberal Democrat whip suggested that 'if in the end people don't feel able to go along with you, I think you've got to be reasonably relaxed about it and smile'.

Despite this comment, Liberal Democrats have conventionally taken whipping most seriously, and this is reflected in their attendance and voting turnout as shown in Table 5.3. In the 2005 survey, 89% of Liberal Democrat peers agreed that they had a duty to vote the party line, compared to just 58% of Conservatives.[20] A Lib Dem who defies the whip, or is absent for a 'three-liner', is likely to be called in by the Chief Whip. In contrast, Labour peers voting against the party line—even when the party was in government—rarely received more than a letter expressing the whips' displeasure. Such pressure was traditionally least heavy for Conservative peers. But post-2010 the number of Conservative three-line whips has increased, as has the number of 'telephone operations' by whips to cajole members to attend (with some peers even occasionally receiving such calls from the Prime Minister). This was in part an inevitable consequence of entering government, where the party needs sufficient votes to get its legislation through. But it was made more difficult by the nature of coalition, with peers being asked to support policies that were not in their party's original programme. Even the Liberal Democrats' previously high voting cohesion began to weaken, as discussed later.

Voting cohesion and party dissent

Given the relative weakness of the whips it is perhaps surprising that rebellious votes in the Lords are not more common. The standard measure of parliamentary party cohesion is the Rice Index, whose value is 100% when a party is wholly united, and 0% when its members are equally split.[21]

Table 5.3 gives the average Rice Index for all of the main groups 1999–2010 and 2010–12. This shows that voting is almost entirely united in all three parties, though it declined somewhat in the two coalition parties post-2010. Indeed, Norton (2003) has pointed out that the level of party voting unity in the Lords is similar to that in the Commons. This is clearly not explained simply by uniformity of political views, as many peers report ideological differences between themselves and their party leaders (see Russell and Sciara 2007). Instead, cohesive voting must be explained by the kind of 'devotion to duty' cited earlier, and by other psychological factors (for a longer discussion, see Russell 2012b). In the 2007 survey, just 4% of party peers expressed concern that if they voted against the party line 'the whips would take action against me'. In contrast, 44% said they would be concerned that this behaviour would 'upset other members of the group', and 73% that it would 'damage' the group.[22]

Voting outcomes in the Lords are therefore largely decided by parties voting as cohesive blocks. But one reason why recorded dissent is so low is that peers often simply absent themselves from divisions when they feel unable to support the party line. Unrecorded abstention in parliaments is important, but notoriously difficult to measure (Loewenberg 2008), and in the Lords there are clearly many reasons why a member may be absent from a vote. In the 2007 survey, 94% of respondents from the three main parties agreed that it was justified for party peers to abstain when disagreeing with the frontbench line, and 22% admitted to doing this 'very' or 'fairly' often.[23] It is clear that the party leaderships encourage their members to be absent rather than to vote actively against the line, and that abstention is not really punishable in any way. Indeed, even some frontbenchers admit to abstaining occasionally.

Nonetheless, rebellious votes do sometimes occur, and became considerably more common after 2010. These are both more likely on the government benches (because governments more than oppositions must take tough decisions), and also easier to trace (because the government almost invariably whips strongly on its own legislation, while other parties do not always do so). Table 5.4 therefore shows the number of divisions in which dissenting votes were cast by peers in the governing parties 1999–2010 (Labour) and 2010–12 (Conservative and Liberal Democrat).

This demonstrates that under Labour dissenting votes on the government benches occurred in only 29% of whipped divisions, and that 85% of the time there was no more than a single rebellious peer. Large rebellions were extremely rare—on only eight occasions in 11 years were there more than 20 Labour rebel peers. In contrast, in the Commons, both rebellions and large rebellions were far more common during Labour's time in power. In the

Table 5.4. Divisions including dissenting votes by government party peers, 1999–2012

	1999–2010		**2010–12**					
	Labour		Liberal Democrat		Conservative		Coalition total	
Number of rebels	n	%	n	%	n	%	n	%
0	949	71.2%	132	57.4%	164	71.3%	101	43.9%
1	179	13.4%	42	18.3%	26	11.3%	45	19.6%
2–5	144	10.8%	31	13.5%	27	11.7%	48	20.9%
6–10	30	2.3%	17	7.4%	8	3.5%	19	8.3%
11–20	22	1.7%	7	3.0%	0	0.0%	10	4.3%
21–30	6	0.5%	1	0.4%	4	1.7%	5	2.2%
31–40	1	0.1%	0	0.0%	1	0.4%	0	0.0%
41–50	1	0.1%	0	0.0%	0	0.0%	2	0.9%
Total	1,332	100.0%	230	100.0%	230	100.0%	230	100.0%

Source: Author's database of divisions (based on *House of Lords Hansard*). Includes government-whipped divisions only.

2001–05 parliament alone, there were 259 Commons divisions in which rebellious Labour votes were cast (Cowley 2005), and 18 of these involved more than 40 MPs (roughly equivalent proportionally to 20 peers, given the size of the PLP). Cowley reports that more than half of Labour MPs voted against the whip at least once during this parliament, and 32 MPs defied the whip more than 30 times. In the Lords there were far fewer rebellious Labour peers—over the entire period 1999–2010 only seven defied the whip more than 30 times. The two most rebellious were Helena Kennedy, who cast 93 votes against the whip, and Bill Wedderburn, who cast 59. In terms of proportion of dissenting votes these two peers, however, far surpassed their Commons colleagues, as both had a relatively low turnout in divisions overall.[24] Much of the difference between the chambers can thus be explained by peers' frequent absences from divisions. It is far more difficult for MPs to absent themselves on a regular basis given the expectations of their constituents and local parties, and they will often prefer to put their dissent on the record.

In 2010–12 the proportion of dissenting votes in the Lords increased sharply, with the coalition government suffering rebellions in a majority of divisions; though these were often confined to one coalition party only. The proportion of larger rebellions also increased. The Conservatives maintained a similar level of cohesion to Labour's record in government, but Liberal Democrat peers rebelled rather more. A similar pattern occurred in the

House of Commons (Cowley and Stuart 2012a). On one occasion early in the 2012–13 session (on so-called 'secret courts' in the Justice and Security Bill) almost the entire Liberal Democrat backbench in the Lords voted against the government.[25] That more dissent should occur is unsurprising, given the difficulty of one coalition party being asked to support policy primarily favoured by the other. Yong (2012: 109) quotes one peer as saying that 'we have a joke in the Conservative Party that we need three hands because we need to go through the voting lobby sometimes holding our nose and covering our ears'. As well as casting dissenting votes, it was widely noted that post-2010 more peers (again particularly Liberal Democrats) began to express dissent through explicit abstention, by sitting in the chamber during divisions.

Who has political impact?

A key question is which group or groups in the Lords have most impact on policy outcomes. The shift from Conservative dominance to a 'no overall control' chamber in 1999 gave several groups the potential to act as 'pivotal voters' (Krehbiel 1998) or 'veto players' (Tsebelis 2002). That is to say, it created the ability for these groups' votes to make the difference between government victory and defeat. The non-government actors likely to prove influential then changed under coalition post-2010.

Which group(s) prove influential will depend on three factors: first, obviously the size of the group, second, its members' turnout in divisions, and third, the extent to which it votes for or against the government. The first two factors were explored earlier, and the third is illustrated in Figure 5.2 for the period 1999–2012. This shows the proportion of each group's votes cast against the government, by counting up all individual group members' votes in each session. Unsurprisingly, we see a stark switch in positions between Labour and the Conservatives in 2010. Other groups divided their votes more between pro- and anti-government positions, though the Liberal Democrats also clearly switched to almost entirely pro-government in 2010.

Pivotal voters under Labour 1999–2010

A superficial glance at the membership figures (see Table 5.1) might suggest that the Crossbenchers would be the most influential group in determining the outcome of divisions. They hold a roughly equal number of seats to

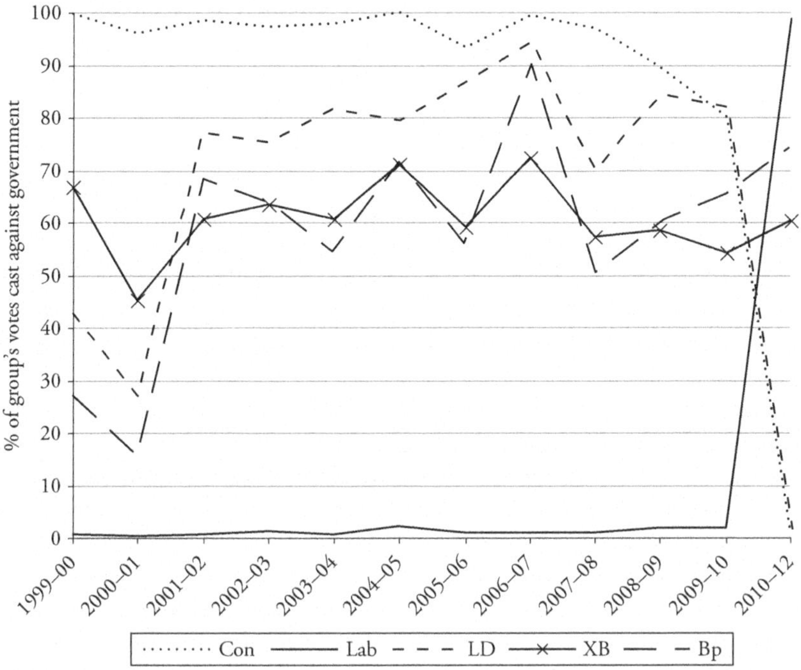

Figure 5.2. Proportion of individual peers' votes cast against the government, by group, 1999–2012

Source: Constructed from figures in Purvis (2012). Government-whipped divisions only.

Labour and the Conservatives, and many more than the Liberal Democrats. From 1999 onwards, therefore, it might seem likely that they held the balance of power. But because the group does not take a collective line, and Crossbench turnout is relatively low, the picture is considerably more complicated than that. Table 5.3 shows that Crossbench 'cohesion' in divisions is low: the Rice Index for the group during 1999–2010 was on average just 45%, while Figure 5.2 demonstrates that the group has no consistent pro- or anti-government line. From 1999–2012, 62% of individual Crossbench votes in government-whipped divisions (i.e. 23,891 of a total 38,768) were cast against the government; but in most individual divisions these votes were split. Crossbench involvement in a division can therefore involve a relatively small number of members voting, of whom some support the proposition while others vote against. Consequently, the group's votes can be marginal, and on occasion simply cancel each other out.

The peers who were more often pivotal when Labour was in power were the far less numerous Liberal Democrats. During 1999–2010 this group had a high voting turnout and was also the most cohesive in the chamber. Unlike the Crossbenchers, the Liberal Democrat votes shown in Figure 5.2 were thus invariably cast as a bloc. During Labour's early years in government the group was fairly supportive: for example, its official line in government-whipped divisions in 1999–2000 was in Labour's favour 52% of the time. But after 2001, when the Blair government focused increasingly on criminal justice, and anti-terrorism policies in the wake of the '9/11' attacks in the US, the smaller party's libertarian instincts led it more often to make common cause with the Conservatives. Thus, by the 2006–07 session the Liberal Democrats opposed the government in 83% of whipped divisions, and (as Figure 5.2 shows) over 90% of its individual members' votes were cast against the government.[26]

The extent to which different groups were pivotal during 1999–2010 is explored in Table 5.5, which summarizes each group's impact on the outcome of government-whipped divisions under both Labour and the coalition. For each division the outcome was recalculated to demonstrate the effect of a theoretical absence of members of the group (i.e. effectively assuming an abstention, but in the case of rebels, assuming that they voted loyally instead).[27] The table shows this both for total divisions, and also separately for government defeats, as it is mostly on the latter that the question matters. For example, if the Labour government won a division despite Conservative opposition, the absence of Conservative peers from that division would have made no difference to the outcome. But this party's absence from a defeat would almost always have allowed the government to win: the table shows that this was true in 98% of cases. Hence, had Conservatives always abstained there would have been only 11 defeats during 1999–2010. This is unsurprising, given the size of the Conservative group.[28] What is more striking is that an abstention by the far smaller Liberal Democrat group would have averted 62% of defeats. Indeed, if the counterfactual is changed to envisage the Liberal Democrats voting for the government, as they did more often in Blair's early years (not shown in the table), 91% of defeats would have been averted. This would have left only 39 defeats over the whole period of 1999–2010, rather than the 458 suffered by the Labour governments.[29]

These facts go a long way to explaining the types of informal relationships which developed between different groups in the post-1999 chamber, and particularly between different party leaders and whips. The government Chief Whip needed to keep in regular touch with both his Liberal Democrat and Conservative counterparts to listen to their concerns and work out whether trouble was brewing. Likewise, the opposition whips were in regular contact with each other, given their combined ability to defeat the government. This was a distinct change from the pre-reform House, where the

Table 5.5. Number of government-whipped divisions where different non-government groups' votes affected the outcome, 1999–2012

	1999–2010				2010–12			
	All divisions		Defeats		All divisions		Defeats	
	n	%	n	%	n	%	n	%
Conservatives (under Labour)	448	34%	447	98%	–	–	–	–
Liberal Democrats (under Labour)	309	23%	284	62%	–	–	–	–
Labour (under coalition)	–	–	–	–	47	20%	47	98%
Crossbenchers	91	7%	88	19%	39	17%	39	81%
Bishops	8	1%	6	1%	2	1%	2	4%
Government backbench rebels	15	1%	15	3%	15	7%	15	31%
Total whipped divisions/ defeats	1,332	100%	458	100%	230	100%	48	100%

Source: Author's database of divisions (based on *House of Lords Hansard*). Figures show notional outcome of divisions if each group had abstained (or in the case of backbench rebels, if these members had voted loyally).

Conservatives could always beat Labour on their own, allowing such contacts to be relatively rare. Indeed, post-1999 there was even some consultation between the opposition parties on whipping itself, since there was little point in one party applying a three-line whip if the other's members were to be absent. The close relationship that built up between the two opposition parties in the Lords, and the increasing accord that they found over policy (see Figure 5.2), was an important precursor to their eventual entry into coalition in 2010. For Labour, again in the words of a former whip, 'the whole job was trying to . . . reach an agreement with the Lib Dems on specific issues, or an agreement with the Tories on specific issues, or persuading one or other of them to go home'. A former Leader of the House summed up the situation in an interview in 2005 by saying that the Lib Dems 'hold the key to the way the place runs'.

Crossbench influence, pre- and post-2010

When Labour was in government the Crossbenchers were far less often important to the outcome of divisions than were the Liberal Democrats. Their absence from divisions during 1999–2010 would have averted only 19% of defeats, generally when the margin between victory and defeat was narrow. Crossbenchers were also far more difficult to negotiate with, given their lack of a coordinated policy line. The group's convenor, as one former Labour chief whip put it, 'could promise to deliver only one vote: his own'—

and was initially largely shut out of 'usual channels' discussions. However, this changed gradually, as the government lost Liberal Democrat support, allowing Crossbenchers to gain better access to key information such as when divisions were likely to be held. Such intelligence, coupled with the group's growing resources, allowed them to be far better briefed than previously, and in turn helped boost their participation. Over time, Labour ministers even began to attend and address the Crossbench group, particularly on controversial bills.

All parties had long worked to court support from individual Crossbenchers, and boasted a number of Crossbench 'friends'. Under Labour the Liberal Democrats worked particularly hard in this regard, even sending copies of their whip to some.[30] A few Crossbenchers do have voting records that are clearly tilted to one party or another: in October 2012 there were 17 who had historically cast 80% or more of their votes with Labour, and 14 who had done the same with the Conservatives.[31] Some were fairly obvious—for example Michael Martin, a former Speaker of the House of Commons, and before that a Labour MP, who voted with Labour 90% of the time. But most Crossbenchers split their votes far more evenly, and some assiduously so. As convenor of the group during 2007–10, Frances D'Souza (now Lord Speaker) cast 55% of her votes for, and 45% against, the government.[32] Her immediate predecessors did likewise.

After 2010, with the Liberal Democrats in coalition, the votes of Crossbenchers became far more critical to voting outcomes. Labour lacked adequate members to beat the government on its own, so aside from government backbench rebellions, or interventions by the Bishops, these were the only pivotal voters left. Given the Liberal Democrats' previous importance, it appeared at first that the new government might suffer few defeats in the Lords. But instead the Crossbenchers seem to have recognized their new responsibility, and changed their behaviour accordingly. Their turnout in divisions increased and, as Table 5.5 shows, their votes came to matter almost as much to inflicting government defeat as the votes of Labour peers. Although such defeats reduced somewhat in number they continued to occur with regularity.

The new importance of the Crossbenchers post-2010 is further illustrated in Table 5.6, which shows the lead sponsor of all amendments resulting in government defeat during 1999–2012.[33] When Labour was in power the majority of defeats resulted from amendments moved by Conservative peers (mostly frontbenchers), and 87% of all defeats were on opposition party amendments. In stark contrast, during 2010–12, opposition amendments accounted for just 23% of defeats. The gap was filled primarily by Crossbench amendments, which accounted for almost half the total. For the

Table 5.6. Defeats 1999–2010 and 2010–12 by party/group of mover

Party of mover	1999–2010		2010–12		Total
	n	%	n	%	
Conservative	300	66%	6	12%	306
Liberal Democrat	100	22%	4	8%	104
Labour	14	3%	11	23%	25
Crossbench	43	9%	23	48%	66
Bishop	1	0%	1	2%	2
Other	0	0%	3	6%	3
Total	458	100%	48	100%	506

Source: Author's database of divisions (based on *House of Lords Hansard*).

opposition, there are potential benefits in allowing/encouraging Crossbenchers to 'front' challenges to the government, as this may help maximize support across the chamber. Government backbenchers may be more likely to rebel (or at least abstain) if objections are raised by a non-partisan expert.

In February 2012 Labour's Leader in the House of Lords admitted that 'winning the support of Crossbenchers is a key part of our strategy.... But doing so is far from easy... Because the Crossbenches are not collective, every Crossbench vote won to a cause has to be individually secured' (Royall 2012). The convenor was far more warmly embraced by the 'usual channels', and on some crucial bills was even invited into discussions with party leaders. But the group continued to hold assiduously to its neutral stance. Even when a Crossbencher tables a high-profile amendment, the only appeal that they can make to their fellow group members at weekly group meetings is to 'listen to the arguments and consider voting for it'.[34]

Nonetheless, we have already seen that the Crossbenchers' political behaviour is controversial among party peers. When Labour was in power there was a common refrain that Crossbenchers were 'Tories in disguise', and fundamentally hostile to a left-leaning government.[35] But Crossbench votes are fairly evenly split, and showed no pro- or anti-government turn in 2010 (see Figure 5.2). Survey data from Crossbenchers also suggest that the group is biased neither to the left nor to the right (Russell and Sciara 2009). Reviewing the evidence under Labour, and looking ahead to a possible Conservative government, Russell and Sciara (2009: 43) noted that 'in future years Conservative peers might even complain of independent Crossbenchers being "Labourites in disguise"'. Sure enough, some coalition peers now complain that the Crossbenchers have become an organized anti-government bloc. One Conservative peer interviewed suggested that they were 'beginning to behave like a caucus', which is 'pretty dangerous' and another that they were 'in danger of creating the Crossbench party'. But the fact that such complaints are made is itself almost demonstration that Crossbenchers behave even-handedly. As a former convenor commented of both Labour and Conservatives, 'they desperately don't want us to be a group, but they [both] want us to vote for them!'.

Other pivotal groups

Returning to Table 5.5, it is of course important to note that others sometimes affect the outcome of divisions, particularly when numbers are finely balanced. The votes of bishops are occasionally decisive, but due to the small numbers attending and voting (and the fact that they, like the Crossbenchers, often split their votes), this is rare. There were just 10 government-whipped divisions during 1999–2012 when the bishops' votes made a difference between victory and defeat, in seven of which the government had won or lost the division by only one vote.[36] Nonetheless, the influence of bishops attracts far more criticism than that of the Crossbenchers. One notable example was on the Equality Bill in January 2010, when the votes of eight bishops were decisive on an amendment to widen the exemption for religious groups from requirements for equal treatment in employment. This was an unusually high bishop turnout, and an even more unusual example of influence in the division lobbies, yet it quickly attracted negative attention.[37] However, insofar as the bishops have a measurable impact, this shows no clear 'progressive' or 'conservative' bias. On only one occasion over this period did the bishops' votes make a difference in a division on a bishop-led amendment (indeed, there were only eight bishop-sponsored amendments in total). This was in 2002, on an amendment by the Bishop of Portsmouth (to the Nationality, Immigration and Asylum Bill) to require that asylum seekers' children had access to school education rather than being taught in detention centres. Three bishops voted for the amendment, and the government was defeated by one vote.

A mechanistic approach to determining parliamentary influence would suggest that the votes of government backbenchers were rarely important during 1999–2010, though they clearly became more so under the coalition. With relatively few rebellious votes cast, these made the difference between government victory and defeat only 15 times. But of course it would be quite wrong to conclude that government backbench peers' votes do not matter: they are in fact essential to the government. As Anthony King (1976) classically pointed out, in the Commons government backbenchers are usually the 'pivotal voters', on whom the government depends and to whom it must thus remain responsive. Backbenchers are equally (or indeed even more) important in the Lords, given the government's lack of a majority, and the whips' greater reliance on goodwill. Party leaders must work to maintain their peers' support, as members could easily stay away. Rebellions in the Lords can thus be troubling for ministers in their own right, but these can also signal further trouble ahead, from government MPs in the Commons and more widely in the party. The impact of this on the dynamics of government defeat is discussed further in Chapter 6.

Post-2010, Table 5.5 shows that the votes of rebels took on a new importance, helping to bring about almost a third of defeats—compared to just 3% under Labour. We know that government backbench rebellions became more common under the coalition (Table 5.4), and that a substantially higher proportion of defeats also occurred on rebel amendments (Table 5.6). All of this reflects greater backbench unease in a coalition situation. But the importance of rebel votes under the coalition is also simply a product of tighter voting outcomes, with Labour unable to defeat the two coalition parties on its own. Because there are now more narrow defeats, these votes start to matter more often.

As with government backbenchers, it is important not to view the influence of other groups in the Lords purely mechanistically. There are many more subtle ways of affecting outcomes than through votes in the division lobbies, or moving of amendments. These include questions, debates and committee work (as discussed in Chapter 8), and contributions to debate and behind-the-scenes networking on legislation (as discussed in Chapter 7). Peers agree that speeches in the chamber by non-partisan figures in particular can be important. In the 2007 survey only 25% of peers believed that 'the bishops' votes are influential in divisions' (a surprisingly high number, given the facts); yet 64% believed that 'speeches by bishops are influential in debate'.[38] The opinions, and votes, of other members may be swung by a powerful speech from a bishop. Similarly, Crossbench speeches can be important in determining the mood in the chamber, especially when made by a recognized expert on the topic at hand. One former Cabinet Secretary claimed that 'if you have been what I was, and if you speak fairly rarely in the House, when you do stand up and speak people listen'. Such effects apply not only to other Crossbenchers, but also party peers. Thus in the 2007 survey 91% of members believed that 'Crossbench speeches are influential in debate'.[39]

There is, however, one last, entirely immeasurable but extremely important influence from these groups of non-party-aligned members regarding the culture of the House of Lords. Their presence discourages use of partisan arguments by party peers, and by frontbenchers in particular. Such rhetoric may play well in the House of Commons, where the main objectives are to harden support amongst your party's backbenchers and to send signals to the public via the media. In the Lords, even party members are probably less susceptible to such appeals, and media reporting of debates is very limited. These factors alone encourage a different tone of debate to in the Commons. But more importantly the Crossbenchers and other non-party peers essentially sit in judgement of the arguments for and against propositions being discussed, being described by some members as 'acting like a jury' in policy debates. Party peers know that cheap point-scoring will be ineffective in influencing Crossbenchers, and indeed will probably be counter-productive. In the pre-1999 chamber Crossbenchers were described by members as 'guardians of the ethos of the House' who 'change the way the rest of us speak'.[40] More recently, former Leader of the House Jan Royall (2012) has emphasized that the chamber 'responds well to reasoned argument, to well-argued persuasiveness, to evidence-based cases, to rational thought and rational behaviour'. One central reason that this remains the case is the presence of non-party peers.

Conclusion: New dynamics in a 'no overall control' chamber

This chapter has outlined the nature of the different organized groups in the House of Lords, and their behaviour. It has provided a good deal of material to help answer three of the key questions at the start of the book. First, to what extent was the Lords changed by its reform in 1999? Second, to what extent, and how, does its ethos differ from the House of Commons? Third, what impact does the chamber now have on British politics?

Starting with the first question, it is clear that the membership of the Lords was significantly changed in 1999, but also that this one-off shock was followed by more gradual and subtle changes of two kinds: to the type of members appointed, and to members' expectations and behaviour. The reform was therefore not just an important event, it was also the beginning of a process.

The pre-1999 chamber was Conservative-dominated, and the majority of its members had received their seats as a result of accident of birth. Many others had been awarded a life peerage primarily as an honour. The removal of the hereditaries ended Conservative domination, and subsequent changes to the pattern of appointments (through both the parties and the new House of Lords Appointments Commission) mean that most members now enter the chamber as 'working peers'. This, combined with the pressure of a 'no overall control' chamber, has resulted in peers becoming far more active than they used to be. Unlike the Commons, where there is one big membership change every four or five years following an election, the Lords' membership constantly evolves. Every year a number of peers die, and in most years some new appointments are made. This results in constant gradual adjustments in culture. Over time, as one peer put it in interview, the chamber is 'more and more post-1999'. By 2012, only a minority of peers had served in the pre-reform chamber.

Turning to the second question, these changes have made the Lords in some ways more similar to the Commons. Members of the two chambers are increasingly alike in terms of class, gender and other demographic factors (though peers are on average significantly older), and attendance and voting are becoming more similar as well. But the Lords and the Commons nonetheless remain very distinct. One crucial difference is the presence of non-party peers, who have the capacity to affect voting outcomes, but perhaps more importantly greatly influence the tone of Lords debates. Additionally, party peers have a quite different relationship to the whip than do their Commons colleagues. This results from their age and experience, the fact that they are appointed for life, are not accountable to local parties or constituents, and often remain active in professions outside parliament. While few actively defy the whip by casting dissenting votes, it is largely just their sense of duty that keeps them from staying away. As one peer commented, most members have 'grown up—been there, done that', and are less susceptible to party pressure. Few have ambitions to high office, and, it is anyway now unusual for senior ministers to be appointed from the chamber. Whips therefore have relatively few sanctions against peers.

The Lords has a reputation for being both 'more expert' and 'less party political' than the Commons, and there are notable experts on all of the chamber's benches. They include many specialists from outside the world of politics, alongside others who are steeped in its traditions. Peter Hennessy suggests that the Lords is 'a rolling permanent reunion... [of] Britain's political class, its ministers, its officials, sometimes its industrialists, sometimes its military... a kind of human version of sedimentary rock' (2011: 165). This has certainly been the tradition since the early 20th century, though today's chamber also contains many members who are not part of the old-style establishment. Meanwhile, the need for peers to be more active means that the inclusion of retired political 'grandees' is now less automatic than it was, and more party activists are instead being appointed at a relatively young age. This has led to some claims that the Lords is becoming more 'party political'. But only 52% of peers in the 2007 survey accepted this premise, while in contrast, 64% believed that the chamber post-1999 had become 'more professional'.[41] Anyway, changes on the party benches have perhaps been balanced by those among Crossbenchers, who are now required to have very clear distance from the parties. In the words of one former Leader of the House reflecting on changes since 1999, 'the party links have got deeper, while the Crossbenchers have got more independent'.

A crucial element of the Lords' culture post-1999 is its relatively party-proportional membership. Before reform, Conservative peers had no need to build cross-party alliances in order to defeat Labour in government, while Labour had few serious opportunities to defeat Conservative governments. Now that numbers are more balanced, negotiation between parties (and indeed Crossbenchers) has become more common. This necessity for cross-party working means that relationships are better developed and more cordial than in the Commons. Partisan banter in the chamber is also limited by the fear of alienating Crossbenchers.

This leads to the third key question, of the Lords' impact on British politics. The chapter focused in particular on which groups can have impact on legislative outcomes in the chamber. An analysis of divisions during 1999–2012 demonstrated that various groups of peers now have the potential to be 'pivotal voters' in the Lords. When Labour was in power it was the Liberal Democrats who generally played this role. This position of influence for the third party was relatively little noted outside the chamber at the time. But the relationship that they established with the Conservatives in the Lords during Labour's period in government helped to lay the ground for the post-2010 coalition. Once the Lib Dems had entered government, the number of defeats in the chamber might have been expected to fall, given that the two coalition parties greatly outnumbered Labour. But defeats continued, with the votes of independent Crossbenchers instead taking on a new importance. This group, which had only rarely affected voting outcomes when Labour was in power, stepped into the new vacuum that had been created. The extent to which non-party politicians can now affect the outcome of policy decisions at Westminster is another development as yet barely noticed outside the Lords.

Whether these new political dynamics are important of course depends on whether policy decisions in the Lords are listened to by government. This crucial question is addressed in the next three chapters.

Notes

1. A third member of the 'gang of four', David Owen, also sits in the House of Lords but as a Crossbencher (having never joined the party—initially the Social and Liberal Democrats and later the Liberal Democrats—that resulted from the merger of the Liberals and the SDP). The fourth member, Roy Jenkins, was a Liberal Democrat peer until his death in 2003 (and led the group in the Lords from 1997 to 1998).
2. House of Lords Appointments Commission website, 'Criteria Guiding the Assessment of Nominations for Non-Party Political Life Peers' (<http://

www.lordsappointments.independent.gov.uk/selection-criteria.aspx>), accessed 9 January 2013.

3. Evidence by the chair of the Commission, Michael Jay (Lord Jay of Ewelme), to the House of Lords Constitution Committee, 25 January 2012, question 4.
4. Religious leaders were sometimes appointed under the old system: for example, the previous Chief Rabbi, Immanuel Jakobovits, was made a peer in 1988. But unlike the bishops, such seats are not guaranteed. Some religious leaders have also served on the party benches; for example, Rabbi Julia Neuberger is a Liberal Democrat peer.
5. For details of the seven Crossbench convenors to date, and other information about the group, see <http://www.crossbenchpeers.org.uk/index.html> (accessed 15 December 2012).
6. Labour n = 105, Liberal Democrat n = 47, Conservative n = 116.
7. There are occasional exceptions. For example, the former Cabinet Secretaries worked together to rescue the clauses of the Constitutional Reform and Governance ('CRAG') Bill in 2010 which put the values of the civil service on a statutory footing, when these risked being lost in the 'wash-up' at the end of the parliament. The former Chiefs of the Defence Staff do sometimes speak en masse in debates on defence.
8. Proportion selecting 'strongly agree' or 'agree' on a five-point scale, n = 100. Figures in the parties were Conservative 89% (n = 109), Labour 93% (n = 100), Liberal Democrat 98% (n = 44). No more than 2% in the parties selected a 'disagree' option, compared to 22% of Crossbenchers.
9. The question was 'Currently 26 senior Church of England bishops are entitled to sit in the House of Lords and vote on laws. Do you think bishops should or should not be entitled to seats in the House of Lords?', don't knows were 18%. Fieldwork conducted 26–27 January 2012 (n = 1,716).
10. n = 264. Those agreeing and strongly agreeing combined were 50% for Labour (n = 99), 51% for Liberal Democrat (n = 45), 80% for Crossbench (n = 107), 86% for Conservative (n = 111). Only 12% of Labour strongly agreed, contrasted with 41% of Conservatives.
11. Church of England website, 'Bishops in the House of Lords', at <www.churchofengland.org/our-views/the-church-in-parliament/bishops-in-the-house-of-lords.aspx> (accessed 9 January 2013).
12. Speech by the Bishop of Leicester, convenor of the Lords spiritual, British Humanist Association, 27 January 2010.
13. In May 2013, nine Conservative, three Crossbench, two Labour, one Liberal Democrat and two on leave of absence.
14. At the time of the 1999 reform all remaining hereditary peers of first creation were offered life peerages.
15. The 1999 Act amended the 1963 Peerages Act to end the right of the chamber's remaining hereditaries to renounce their titles.
16. For question wording see note 18 in Chapter 4. n = 89 Labour, 101 Conservative, 43 Liberal Democrat, 95 Crossbench, 8 bishops.

17. E.g. 'People's peers who rarely take part in votes', *Times*, 10 November 2003; 'What's the point? In one year they hardly turned up to the Lords, hardly voted and hardly made any difference', *Mirror*, 25 April 2002.
18. Evidence by Michael Jay to the House of Lords Constitution Committee, 25 January 2012, question 16.
19. On this occasion, all 14 bishops cast their votes against the bill (which was defeated by 48 votes). More often, including in 'free' (i.e. conscience) votes such as this one, bishop votes are split. This occurred, for example, on the Sexual Offences (Amendment) Bill in 2000.
20. The precise question was: 'Do you agree or disagree... [that] when party peers vote they have a duty to support the party line all or most of the time'. Responses were on a five-point Likert scale. n = 104 Conservative, 45 Liberal Democrat (and 102 Labour, of whom 83% agreed).
21. For any one division the Rice Index (Rice 1925) is the absolute value of the proportion of members in the group voting one way minus the proportion voting the other (e.g. if 95% vote yes and 5% vote no its value is 90%). The overall Rice Index for each group is simply calculated by averaging over all divisions, but here we exclude divisions where 10 or fewer members of the group voted, to avoid these skewing the results.
22. n = 247–8. The precise question was: 'To what extent would you be concerned about the following factors if you voted against your party group?'. There were only small differences between the parties.
23. The first question asked for levels of agreement to the statement 'It is justified for party peers to choose to abstain if they disagree with frontbench policy', and the figures quoted are for those responding 'agree' or 'agree strongly' on a five point Likert scale. n = 256. The second question was: 'In terms of voting in the Lords, how often would you say each of these occur?', and responses are to 'you personally choosing to abstain because you disagree with your party line'. Responses were recorded on a four point scale: other options were 'not very often' and 'not at all'. n = 249.
24. Baroness Kennedy voted loyally only 188 times during 1999–2010, so had a dissent rate of 33%; Lord Wedderburn (who sat on the Crossbenches for part of this period) cast 351 loyal Labour votes, giving a dissent rate of 14%. In contrast, Cowley reports that the most rebellious MP during 2001–05, Jeremy Corbyn, cast dissenting votes in only 12% of divisions.
25. This was on 21 November 2012, and only 12 Liberal Democrats (most of them frontbenchers) voted for the government, while 57 voted against. In a sign of how little attention the media pays the Lords, this was hardly reported.
26. The discrepancy between the two figures (both here and in 1999–2000) is explained largely by variations in turnout between divisions where the party supported and opposed the government.
27. Of course, this assumes that a change of behaviour by one group would not affect other groups, which is slightly unrealistic. For example, had Liberal Democrats abstained more Conservatives might have voted.

28. Indeed some may be surprised that there were any such exceptions at all. The 11 defeats included two where the Conservatives did in fact abstain, and the government was beaten by only a handful of votes. In the remaining nine cases the majority against the government was so large (including significant numbers of Labour rebels and large numbers of Crossbenchers) that Conservative votes were not needed.
29. In 17 of these, all or most Liberal Democrats did in fact support the government; in 13 very small numbers of Liberal Democrats (mostly in single figures) participated in the division; and in the remaining nine the size of the defeat was so large that a switch of Liberal Democrat position would have made no difference.
30. It must be emphasized (as explained previously) that the whip does not tell peers how to vote, but simply when important votes are likely to take place. The only place from where Crossbenchers could reliably acquire such information was the parties.
31. These figures include all government-whipped divisions since 1999 for which Crossbenchers serving in the chamber in October 2012 were eligible to vote, but excludes members who cast no more than 10 votes.
32. All of these figures count government-whipped divisions only. D'Souza figures are for the three full sessions that she was convenor. Martin figures are from his arrival to the end of the 2010–12 session.
33. An amendment in the Lords may be normally signed by up to four peers. The peer who is first signatory is seen as the primary sponsor, and generally speaks to the amendment.
34. For a discussion of the culture of Crossbench meetings (albeit now slightly out of date) see Crewe (2005: 150–1).
35. This impression was coloured by the documented behaviour of the group when the Conservatives were previously in power: in the 1988–89 session 61% of Crossbench votes were cast in favour of the government (Miers and Brock 1993). But this figure is clearly not comparable to today, as it refers to a chamber where the great majority of Crossbenchers were hereditary peers.
36. Likewise, among the 87 unwhipped divisions during this period, there was only one occasion (on a procedural division on the Mersey Tunnels Bill in 2004) that their votes affected the outcome. Again, there was only a difference of one vote, and one bishop voted.
37. See McLean (2010a). For a response to criticism from the Bishop of Winchester, see Michael Scott-Joynt, 'The churches stand for pluralism', *Guardian*, 3 February 2010.
38. n = 370–72 for these two questions. The figures quoted combine those responding 'strongly agree' and 'agree' on a five-point Likert scale.
39. n = 373.
40. Viscount Cranborne (former Conservative Leader of the House) and Earl Russell (Liberal Democrat), quoted in Mitchell (1999: 108, 73).
41. Those responding 'agree' or 'agree strongly' on a five-point scale. n = 346–7.

6

The Lords as a Barrier to Government: Legislative Defeats

In the previous chapter we saw how the profound change brought about by the removal of most hereditary peers in 1999 set in train various gradual and more subtle developments within all of the party groups in the Lords, and on the Crossbenches. Probably the most important effect of the 1999 reform was the chamber's transformation into one of 'no overall control', where different combinations of actors could potentially form a majority against the government. Under Labour, this gave the Liberal Democrats a pivotal position in determining the outcomes of divisions. Since 2010, in contrast, the Crossbenchers have gained an increasingly important role, as the Labour opposition needs sufficient of their votes if it is to defeat the coalition government.

Description of these membership changes and voting dynamics has laid the ground for exploring the chamber's policy contribution, which is the focus of the next three chapters. For several reasons the obvious place to start such an analysis is with the nature and policy impact of government defeats. First, defeats are where the Lords' political impact is most visible and high profile. When the chamber reaches the news, and therefore public consciousness, this is normally for two things only: its confrontations with the government, or controversies about its reform (the latter being the subject of Chapter 10). Second, defeats provide the clearest and most measurable indicator of those policy matters on which the government faces difficulty in the chamber. Defeats in themselves can potentially have a lasting effect on policy; but they also create the political backdrop for more negotiated outcomes, as discussed in Chapter 7. The fact that the Lords can readily defeat the government, and that certain groups in particular contribute to this, makes government more responsive to the demands of the chamber and to these policy actors in particular.

The chapter begins by outlining the basic legislative process in the Lords, and the process of agreeing legislation with the Commons. It then includes a detailed analysis of the more than 500 defeats suffered by governments during the period 1999–2012. This starts with a summary of how the defeats were distributed across time and legislative stage, and broadly what kinds of policy issues they related to. After a brief discussion of delegated legislation, the chapter goes on to explore whether defeats really matter in policy terms. Under the Parliament Acts the Commons can override the Lords on House of Commons bills, so it might be expected that defeats are largely symbolic, with little lasting effect. However, this analysis, based on detailed tracking of every defeat that took place during 1999–2012, shows that the truth is very different; many policy confrontations between the chambers are actually resolved in the House of Lords' favour. A new question therefore arises, of why the government gives in so frequently to peers' policy demands, and in what circumstances it does so. This is explored through a statistical analysis. The general trends are then illustrated by some example cases of defeats suffered by both Labour and coalition governments. The chapter's conclusion sums up what defeats tell us about one of the central questions in the book: the effect of the post-1999 Lords on British politics and the policy process.

The legislative process in the Lords

As a bicameral parliament, all bills at Westminster must be considered by both the House of Commons and House of Lords. The majority start their passage in the Commons, where they receive scrutiny both in the chamber and in committee before proceeding to the Lords. However, around a third of government bills instead begin their passage in the Lords and pass to the Commons afterwards. In the 2008–09 session, for example, there were 19 government bills introduced into the Commons, and eight into the Lords; in 2010–12 the figures were 36 and 11 respectively. Bills beginning their passage in the Lords tend to be those which are less controversial. This is first simply because the Commons is the 'primary' chamber, where most senior ministers sit. Introduction of a major bill there provides an opportunity for a high-profile debate, where government and opposition can set out their positions, and MPs contribute their views, in the full glare of the media. Debate in the Lords tends to be more low-key, and most bills must be guided through by junior ministers. An additional reason to start bills in the Commons is to ensure that the Parliament Acts can be used if needed, as these do not apply to bills starting in the Lords. In the event of conflict on such bills the Commons therefore cannot impose its will. Nonetheless, the smooth management of government legislation requires that a certain number of bills begin in the House of Lords in order that both chambers are occupied throughout the parliamentary session.

The stages of the legislative process in the Lords are fundamentally the same as those in the Commons. Bills have a first reading, second reading, committee stage, report stage and third reading. However, the detailed procedures that apply at each stage differ in some important ways between the chambers. In both cases the first reading is simply a formal introduction without debate, and the second reading is a plenary debate on the main principles of the bill. The committee stage in each chamber is then the opportunity for members to debate the bill in detail clause by clause, but here procedures differ. Most bills have their Commons committee stage in a small 'public bill committee', while the committee stage in the Lords is taken either in plenary or in a 'grand committee' open to all peers. Because there is no fixed membership of grand committees, and they can run in parallel with the chamber itself, the number of members attending is unpredictable and no votes are permitted. In contrast, bills taken in a Commons public bill committee, or on the floor in either chamber, can be voted on at committee stage. The report stage in both chambers is then a plenary debate, where members can reflect on the committee stage and resolve any outstanding issues. Finally, third reading is a last opportunity to debate the principles of the bill. Amendments can be made at this stage in the Lords, whereas in the Commons they cannot. In order to allow peers to reflect on the content of the bill, and any amendments made to it, the *Companion to Standing Orders* sets out minimum recommended intervals between each legislative stage.[1] This same degree of regulation does not exist in the Commons, where the stages of bills can be more rushed.

In general, peers pride themselves on their careful consideration of legislation. As Chapter 4 indicated, the chamber is 'self-regulating', and the powers of the Lord Speaker are much more limited than those of the Speaker of the House of Commons. The most notable difference in this respect is that there is no concept of the 'guillotine' to curtail debate in the Lords. In contrast, most bills in the Commons are now 'programmed', meaning that a fixed timetable is set for each stage of the bill. If a Commons committee runs out of time, certain clauses may therefore not be scrutinized fully, and the chamber may likewise run out of time at report stage. Such problems cannot occur in the Lords. Because of this, and because the government lacks a majority in the chamber, it must listen more attentively to the views of non-government representatives during 'usual channels' discussions than is necessary in the Commons. Self-regulation also means that individual members have far more control over the timing of debates, as the Lord Speaker cannot limit contributions or move the chamber on to next business, and crucially has no power to select amendments. Any peer can thus table an unlimited number of amendments and demand that they be debated, provided that they are relevant to the bill. Ensuring that debates do not continue interminably depends on self-restraint and good sense by members, coupled occasionally with polite collective pressure by those present if a certain peer is 'trying the patience of the House'.

Lords defeats may potentially occur at any stage of the legislative process at which a bill is actually debated (excepting grand committee) but usually apply to amendments rather than whole bills, so are concentrated at committee, report and third reading. (Some defeats also occur on other matters, particularly delegated legislation, as discussed further later.) Divisions are normally not held at second reading, because by convention it is judged that a bill should be able to progress to the committee stage and receive detailed consideration. In particular, the Salisbury-Addison convention demands that government manifesto bills should be granted a second reading, and should not be blocked at third reading or subjected to 'wrecking' amendments. In practice, the Lords treats very few bills—manifesto or not—in this way. In the 2007 survey, two-thirds of peers agreed that 'the House of Lords should not block government bills at second reading', though this statement was more strongly supported by Labour peers (i.e. those from the then governing party) than other groups.[2]

Whenever the Lords amends a bill, either as a result of defeat or more consensual amendments (including those moved by ministers), it must pass to the Commons for those amendments to be agreed. Except where the Parliament Acts are used, bills must be approved by both chambers in identical form. Hence, any amendments made in the chamber that is second to see the bill must return to the initiating chamber for approval. If the chamber where the bill began agrees the other's amendments, this completes the process and the bill proceeds to royal assent. Otherwise, if it disagrees with the amendments, the bill must return again to the other chamber. This process of back and forth—colloquially known as 'ping-pong'—continues until the two chambers reach agreement. At each stage one chamber may propose alternatives to the other's amendments, until a compromise is reached, or alternatively may choose to reject them outright and hope that the other chamber backs down.[3]

In practice, the government's position is crucial to how this process unfolds on its bills. Lords amendments that were supported by the government will normally be accepted by the Commons unquestioningly; extended ping-pong therefore tends to apply only in the case of Lords defeats. When the Lords has amended a bill against the government's wishes, ministers must decide how to respond when it returns to the

Commons. Sometimes they will decide to give in to the Lords' demands, and recommend that the Commons approves the amendment. At other times they will recommend outright rejection, or else propose a compromise amendment, which the Commons will usually approve. If the Commons rejects the Lords' position and the bill returns to the Lords, ministers there will invariably urge peers to accept the Commons' position. Peers supporting the original amendment must then decide whether to give up, try to reinsert their change into the bill, or propose a compromise. Such compromises (in either chamber) are known as 'amendments in lieu', and the stages in the respective chambers are simply known as 'Commons consideration of Lords amendments' (CCLA) and 'Lords consideration of Commons amendments' (LCCA).

Only when this process fails completely might government resort to the Parliament Acts, and attempt to pass a bill without the Lords' approval. This, however, can result in significant delay. In practice, agreement is almost always reached without this being necessary, either through the government backing down, the Lords backing down, or a combination of the two. As Chapter 4 indicated, only four bills since 1949 have been passed under the Parliament Acts against the Lords' wishes. Two of these occasions were after 1999: on the Sexual Offences (Amendment) Act 2000 and the Hunting Act 2004. But neither strictly speaking followed government defeat, since the disagreements between the chambers occurred on matters subject to 'free' (i.e. unwhipped) votes.[4]

The quantity and timing of Lords defeats

The number of divisions and defeats in the House of Lords in the period 1999–2012 is shown in Table 6.1. The first key point is the regularity with which government defeats occur. There were 506 such defeats in total over these twelve and a half years: 458 under Labour, and 48 during the coalition's first (two-year) parliamentary session. These figures stand in stark contrast to those for the House of Commons, where there were just seven defeats over the same period.[5] The reason for the difference is straightforward: that governments enjoyed a comfortable partisan majority in the Commons, but no majority in the House of Lords.

The table also demonstrates how defeats were distributed between the different legislative stages of bills, and over time. In terms of the latter we see that the number of defeats rose under Labour, reaching a high point in the period 2002–06. The start of this period coincided with the change in Liberal Democrat voting behaviour, as discussed in Chapter 5. Later, the number of

Table 6.1. Divisions and defeats in the House of Lords, 1999–2012

	Defeats by legislative stage (or n/a)							All divisions by legislative stage (or n/a)**							
Session*	2nd	Cttee	Rpt	3rd	LCCA	n/a	Total	2nd	Cttee	Rpt	3rd	LCCA	n/a	Total	%defeats
1999–00	1	4	15	11	2	3	36	2	65	71	36	11	7	192	19%
2000–01	0	0	2	0	0	0	2	0	10	15	7	0	8	40	5%
2001–02	0	4	26	18	8	0	56	0	36	65	39	16	16	172	33%
2002–03	0	19	35	17	12	5	88	1	59	87	36	23	20	226	39%
2003–04	1	2	37	13	10	1	64	2	10	75	47	32	10	176	36%
2004–05	0	7	9	6	14	1	37	0	12	21	10	19	5	67	55%
2005–06	0	8	30	8	15	1	62	1	29	83	40	24	10	187	33%
2006–07	1	9	20	3	10	2	45	1	18	45	9	15	15	103	44%
2007–08	0	6	19	2	2	0	29	0	22	70	15	9	5	121	24%
2008–09	0	4	16	1	1	3	25	1	18	53	2	7	7	88	28%
2009–10	0	4	5	1	0	4	14	1	17	12	1	1	11	43	33%
2010–12	0	6	27	6	7	2	48	3	34	128	26	26	17	234	21%
Total	3	73	241	86	81	22	506	12	330	725	268	183	131	1,649	31%

Source: Author's database of divisions (based on *House of Lords Hansard*).

* It should be noted that the lengths of sessions vary. A 'normal' session is 12 months, but over this period each general election has been preceded by a short session of only around four months (i.e. 2000–01, 2004–05 and 2009–10), and followed by a long session of around 18 months (2001–02, 2005–06) or two years in the case of the coalition (2010–12).

** Figures for total divisions include those which were unwhipped on the government side. These amount to 87 in total (i.e. 5% of all divisions). The largest number was in 2002–03 when there were 22 (10%). Seven of these were on House of Lords reform (see Chapter 10), and seven on the Hunting Bill. Divisions in the 'n/a' column mostly relate to delegated legislation (see later).

defeats fell slightly again, reflecting in part the changing policy agenda, and in part the government's more careful handling of the Lords. The pattern of defeats over a longer time period is illustrated in Figure 6.1.

In terms of the point in the legislative process, the largest number of defeats occurred at the report stage, with significant numbers also occurring at committee stage, third reading and during LCCA. Notably, there were only three instances of defeat at the second reading stage of government bills, none of which explicitly rejected the bill outright. In September 2000 a motion was agreed at second reading that the Criminal Justice (Mode of Trial) (No. 2) Bill should not be considered for a further six months. In March 2007 a similar motion was agreed with respect to the Fraud (Trials Without a Jury) Bill. These both formed part of the long-running battle between the Blair government and the Lords over trial by jury (summarized later, in the case study section of this chapter). In 2004 a motion was agreed that the Constitutional Reform Bill, which sought to abolish the office of Lord Chancellor, be referred for evidence-taking by a select committee rather than proceeding directly to its committee stage. By using procedural tactics of delay such as these, peers can argue that they are respecting the convention of not blocking government bills altogether—although in the first two cases their actions had the same effect. Of the nine remaining second reading votes (none resulting in defeat), seven used similar procedural tactics, but two did explicitly concern whether a bill should be given a second reading at all. One was essentially procedural, pressed by the Conservatives to test the quorum during debate in 2000 on the Disqualifications Bill late at night. As the quorum failed, this simply resulted in second reading being delayed by less than 24 hours. The other such vote, in 2011, sought to deny a second reading to the coalition's controversial Health and Social Care Bill. The *Companion to Standing Orders* had been amended in 2007, to advise peers that the six-month delay tactic was 'obsolete' (House of Lords 2010: 129), so the vote instead took place on a 'reasoned amendment' proposed by Labour backbencher Nicolas Rea. This quoted the coalition agreement, which had promised to 'stop the top-down reorganisations of the NHS that have got in the way of patient care', as an argument to reject the bill. Lord Rea emphasized that the reform was not in the governing parties' manifestos, and the Salisbury convention could not therefore be seen to apply. The Labour frontbench whipped in favour of his motion, but it was defeated. There was also an unsuccessful attempt to reject the bill at third reading (the first such division since at least 1970: most third reading divisions being on amendments). This further indicated conventions under strain.

After second reading, defeats become more likely. Although committee stage provides an opportunity to discuss the clauses of the bill in detail, fewer divisions are held at this point than at report stage for several reasons. First, obviously bills taken in grand committee cannot be subjected to divisions. Second, the parties tend not to whip the committee stage heavily, and some peers even claim that there is a convention of not calling divisions at this stage (though given the figures, this claim is clearly not sustainable). Relatedly, the committee stage is often used by peers to propose changes and invite ministers to go away and reflect on them. As there are two further stages when amendments can be passed, this gives the government an opportunity to come back with its own amendments in response to peers' demands (a process further discussed in Chapter 7). Nonetheless, there were 73 defeats at committee stage: or an average of around six per year.

Once the report stage is reached whipping tends to be heavier, and if government has not come forward with an adequate concession in response to peers' earlier concerns, matters are more likely to be pressed to a vote. There were 241 defeats at this stage. Sometimes, however, concerned peers will likewise withdraw their amendments at report stage and await the government's final word at third reading, when a final opportunity remains to press their amendments. In total, there were 86 defeats at this stage. The remaining legislative defeats were at LCCA as a result of peers insisting on their amendments for a second or subsequent time, as discussed later.

At this point, it is worth remarking that the proportion of divisions which result in defeat (shown for each session on the right-hand side of the table) should be interpreted with care. There are various reasons why divisions may be won or lost. The most obvious is the positions of the main parties and other individual peers, but this alone cannot explain the proportion of defeats. One factor is the strength of whipping in the opposition parties, which, as already indicated, is likely to be lighter at committee stage, and generally on legislation which the party is more ambivalent about. Another more mundane factor is the timing of votes, and its effect on turnout. Unlike the Commons, the Lords adjourns on most days between around 7:30 and 8:30 pm for a 'dinner break' (during which time unwhipped business such as questions for short debate may be taken). Attendance drops after this point, and it becomes more difficult for the opposition to win votes. A third factor is less intuitively obvious: that the opposition does not always hope, or even want, to win every vote. Sometimes an opposition party, or other group of peers, will push something to a division in the full knowledge that they do not have adequate support to beat the government. This may be in order simply to put their views on the record, or to force government peers to vote for something thought to be unpopular. In addition, Conservative peers in opposition used to be concerned not to look like they could beat the government too readily. In what was partly a hangover from the pre-1999 chamber, they therefore called some divisions that they knew they could not win.

Does the post-1999 chamber defeat the government more often?

One of the book's central questions is whether and how the post-1999 House of Lords differs from its predecessor. A key area of change seems to be the chamber's assertiveness. As shown later in the book (see Table 9.2), peers' survey responses clearly indicate that they consider the post-reform chamber to be more legitimate, and that this has increased their confidence to challenge government policy. As more and more members have joined the chamber post-1999, and a diminishing number remember the way things were previously, peers have become increasingly socialized in an environment where challenging the government on dubious policies is considered appropriate. We might expect this to be visible through more government defeats.

The question is, however, more complex than it might initially appear. To provide some longer perspective, Figure 6.1 shows the number of government defeats by session since 1975. We see that the post-1997 figures are relatively high compared to the immediately preceding period, but that the number during 1975–79 was greater still. This pattern is easily explained, because during 1979–97 the Conservatives were in power, and dominated the Lords as well as the Commons. In contrast, when Labour was in power in the 1970s, the Lords looks to have been as assertive as it is today.

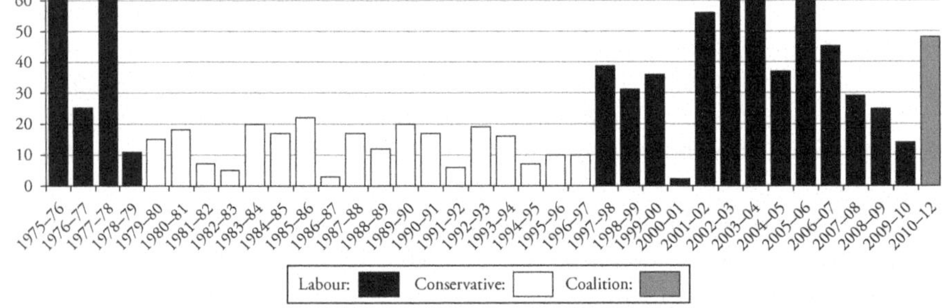

Figure 6.1. Government defeats in the House of Lords 1975–2012, by parliamentary session and party of government

Source: Constructed from figures provided by House of Lords Information Office. See note to Table 6.1 regarding session lengths.

Table 6.2. Number of bills per parliament on which the House of Lords has insisted on its amendments, 1974–2013

	Number of insistences				
Parliament	1	2	3	4	Total
1974–79	2	1	1	0	4
1979–83	0	0	0	0	0
1983–87	1	0	0	0	1
1987–92	0	1	0	0	1
1992–97	1	0	0	0	1
1997–2001	3	1	0	1	5
2001–05	12	3	0	2	17
2005–10	13	0	0	2	15
2010–13*	6	0	0	0	6
Total	38	6	1	5	50

Source: 1974–2005 drawn from the Clerk of the Parliament's evidence to the Joint Committee on Conventions (2006b), supplemented by information from author's database of divisions.

* Three years only.

Nonetheless, the straightforward total of defeats over this period does not tell the whole story. In the 1970s the Lords defeated Labour frequently, but almost invariably backed down if the Commons rejected its amendments (Baldwin 1995). This is illustrated in Table 6.2. During the 1974–79 parliament there were only four bills on which the Lords attempted to insist on its amendments following rejection by the Commons. On two of these it insisted once (i.e. sending the bill back to the Commons for a second time), on one it insisted twice and on another it insisted three times.[6] During the Conservative years there were of course relatively few insistences, because there were relatively few defeats. In the 1997 parliament the number of insistences was a little higher, and the Lords sent one bill (the European Parliamentary Elections Bill, in 1997–98) back to the Commons four times (this eventually passed only under the Parliament Acts, in the following session). But in subsequent years the number of insistences went up substantially, and further bills were subjected to extended 'ping-pong' of this kind (hence the 81 defeats shown in Table 6.1 at the LCCA stage).[7] This does seem to demonstrate clear evidence of the Lords' growing assertiveness over policy, although the total number of cases of extended ping-pong is small.

The 2010–13 figures cover only three years, so are not comparable with other sessions. But we see that as yet there has not been a sustained battle between the coalition and the Lords. It remains difficult to say whether the chamber underwent a transformation post-2010 that has made it less assertive than under Labour, but this may well be the case. While the opposition parties during 1999–2010 were often determined to push issues to repeated rounds of ping-pong, defeats now rely to a large extent on Crossbenchers. As well as being less organized and cohesive, these peers may also be more cautious about forcing government to rethink, given that the group has no electoral mandate at all (because it has no MPs). When Labour was in government the assertiveness of the two opposition parties did differ, with the Conservatives being less aggressive than the Liberal Democrats. A former Conservative Chief Whip pointed out that 'the potential party of government respects the right of the House of Commons to get its way'; something another Conservative peer described as a philosophy of 'do as you would be done by'. In contrast, the Liberal Democrats, with their belief that the voting system for the House of Commons was unfair, and their lesser expectation of being in government in future, showed less caution. Now that this group sits on the government benches its fiercer opposition has been neutered, at least temporarily.

The Lords and delegated legislation

Most government defeats in the Lords are on 'primary' legislation, and these are the focus of the remainder of the chapter. But a small number of defeats also take place on 'secondary' or 'delegated' legislation (in the form of 'statutory instruments').[8] Table 6.1 shows that over 1999–2012 there were 22 defeats on whipped business other than passage of government bills; 17 of these were on delegated legislation. In addition, there were 53 votes on such legislation which did not end in defeat.

Like votes at second reading, the conventions regarding delegated legislation have been controversial since 1999. As Chapter 4 indicated, the Parliament Acts do not apply, and the Lords consequently retains a veto. Statutory instruments cannot be amended, but only agreed or disagreed in their entirety, and there is no 'ping-pong' in the case of defeat, since the Lords' veto is absolute. However, prior to 1999 only one such measure (the Southern Rhodesia [United Nations Sanctions] Order 1968) had ever been blocked by the chamber. Lords restraint in these matters had therefore come to be considered a convention prior to the 1999 reform. But immediately afterwards the Conservative Leader in the House of Lords, Tom Strathclyde (1999), made a speech stating that 'I declare this convention dead', and the same day the chamber vetoed two orders on arrangements for the London Mayoral elections of 2000. The 2007 survey of peers found only 23% of members agreeing that 'the House of Lords should not block delegated legislation', most of whom were government party peers.[9] In interview one peer described the convention as 'hanging by a thread'.

Nonetheless, actual blocking of secondary legislation remains rare. Generally, when presented with a controversial measure of this kind, peers express their displeasure through a 'non-fatal' motion simply commenting upon it, rather than an actual veto. Such motions typically express 'regret' at the government's actions and ask it to reconsider. These account for the majority of delegated legislation votes: over the period 1999–2012 there were 27 'fatal' and 42 'non-fatal' motions voted upon (Newson and Purvis 2012). In the case of fatal motions while Labour was in power the number of Conservatives voting was generally fairly small, and easily outnumbered by government party peers.[10]

Only one further fatal motion in the period covered by Table 6.1 resulted in defeat. This was on the Gambling (Geographical Distribution of Casino Premises Licences) Order in 2007, which would have allowed a 'supercasino' to be opened in Manchester. But even here the circumstances were somewhat special. The original Gambling Act 2005, which delegated this power, had been passed by the Blair government. Gordon Brown, who was about to take over the premiership at the time of the vote, was in contrast rumoured to be sceptical about the policy. The division was lost by just three votes, and the official Conservative position had been to abstain (though 30 Conservative peers voted against the order, and six in favour). The defeat resulted from a whipped vote by the Liberal Democrats (50–0 against) and the balance of Crossbench votes (27–9), alongside 12 Labour rebels and three bishops. The latter were painted as responsible, since their votes were enough to secure defeat (and also because the Archbishop of Canterbury was present and made a speech against the policy, thought to be influential on other peers), but clearly the votes of Labour rebels and other groups were more numerous. This example further demonstrates how, despite Lord Strathclyde's earlier claim, the official opposition remained cautious, in another example of 'do as you would be done by'. But post-2010 Labour in opposition in the Lords has taken a more aggressive stance, whipping in favour of occasional 'fatal' motions. In early December 2012 there was another such defeat (which went largely unreported), in which 162 Labour peers voted against the government. This does suggest that the convention may be crumbling.

Although such occasions have so far been rare, the possibility of defeat over delegated legislation remains real and ever-present. This induces caution on the government side as well, and statutory instruments are occasionally withdrawn (either before or after debate) when peers are known to be unhappy. As discussed in Chapter 8, concerns are often signalled at an early stage by the Lords Secondary Legislation Scrutiny Committee.

The nature of Lords defeats

The preceding discussion has already given some indication of the kinds of policy matters on which the government gets defeated in the Lords. The issues most likely to spark defeat obviously depend to a large extent on the chamber's political make up, and the different constellations that may potentially form a majority against the government.

As we have already seen, when Labour was in power, most defeats depended on the two opposition parties uniting against the government. Hence this largely determined the kinds of policies where difficulties would occur. There was little opportunity for Labour to be defeated from the 'left': for example, through pressures to increase public spending. Though the Liberal Democrats, and Labour backbench peers, may have sometimes wanted to push the government in this direction, Conservative support for such amendments would not be forthcoming. Likewise, there was little real Lords pressure on the government in an authoritarian direction. Even if some Conservatives might have wanted policies such as tougher policing or longer jail sentences, amendments of this kind would alienate the more libertarian Liberal Democrats.[11] Instead, defeats tended to have moderating effects, taking place on issues where the two opposition parties could find common cause, or at least not oppose each other. There were two broad areas where this was particularly likely to occur. One was 'civil liberties', where the Blair governments (particularly post-2001) were seen as being illiberal through bills on issues such as immigration, counter-terrorism and access to justice. Such legislation frequently ran into problems in the Lords. The second, partly related, area on which the two opposition parties could easily unite was 'constitutional propriety', where they pressed the government to tighten up transparency, good governance and oversight. This applied quite broadly, both in the purely constitutional realm and more generally in terms of management of public services.

Of course, as outlined in Chapter 5, the Conservatives and Liberal Democrats were not the only influential actors—or 'pivotal voters'—in the Lords 1999–2010. The government also had to heed the concerns of its own backbenchers, and the Crossbenchers. The large Crossbench group did not often make the difference to voting outcomes, but could always potentially do so. While Crossbench votes generally split in a relatively evenhanded way, they could sometimes be heavily tilted against the government. For example, in 2006 on the bill introducing identity cards (discussed later), 46 out of 53 Crossbenchers voted in favour of an amendment to delay the scheme's introduction until an investigation into costs and benefits had been completed. On the Police and Justice Bill that same year, 24 out of 25 Crossbenchers voting supported an amendment to limit the Secretary of State's power to direct failing police forces. In the first case, the group's votes did not determine the outcome, as the overall majority against the government was 81. But in the other, party votes were more evenly balanced and the government lost by just 19. As these two examples illustrate, the Crossbenchers often reinforced opposition party pressure on civil liberties and constitutional propriety matters, which appealed to the group's many well-respected lawyers and former civil servants. Their speeches and amendments, in turn, could attract widespread support across the House.

Some examples of key defeats in the Labour era relating to civil liberties, broader constitutional proprieties, and other matters are given in Box 6.1. What happened following these defeats is discussed in the next section of the chapter.

Post-2010 the government was in a potentially stronger position, as the previous pivotal group (the Liberal Democrats) had entered coalition. Where there were differences between the two governing parties these could be expected to be largely settled behind the scenes. The constellation needed to defeat the government in the Lords was now completely different, comprising the Labour opposition plus sufficient Crossbenchers, and sometimes Liberal Democrat or Conservative rebels (or at least abstentions). In addition, the government's policy agenda, and the broader political context, was very different to that in the Blair and Brown years. One of the coalition's primary objectives was to reduce the fiscal deficit after the financial crash of the immediately preceding period, largely through reducing public spending. In contrast, the kind of law and order measures so frequent during Tony Blair's premiership did not feature on its early agenda. Instead, the primary focus of legislation was public service reform. The coalition agreement also included several key constitutional changes, including to parliamentary boundaries and public bodies (commonly known as 'quangos'), and through introduction of fixed term parliaments and elected police commissioners. All of these were legislated for in 2010–12.

Box 6.2 lists some of the key defeats during the first three years of the coalition. We see that the Lords continued to intervene on questions of constitutionality. Some of the biggest defeats also sought to limit the impact of the public spending cuts—for example, on legal aid and welfare benefits. These issues clearly reflected the concerns of the Labour opposition, but were ones on which it could manage to attract sufficient support from Crossbenchers and/or rebels on the government side.

This gives some indication of the topics on which governments have suffered defeat in the Lords. An additional question is the extent to which

Box 6.1. Examples of Labour government defeats in the House of Lords 1999–2010

Civil liberties

2001 Anti-terrorism, Crime and Security Bill: to prevent the Secretary of State from detaining suspected foreign terrorists indefinitely without judicial review, and to remove an offence of incitement to religious hatred.

2003 Criminal Justice Bill: to restrict the definition of 'bad character' as admissible evidence in court, and remove limitations on trial by jury.

2005 Prevention of Terrorism Bill: to place various restrictions on the use of 'control orders' for terrorist suspects, and to insert a 'sunset clause' so that the bill expires on a fixed date.

2006 Identity Cards Bill: to limit compulsion in the scheme, and to introduce significantly greater parliamentary oversight over the Secretary of State's ability to alter it in future.

2008 Criminal Justice and Immigration Bill: to remove the power of magistrates to give suspended sentences, and insert a freedom of expression clause.

2008 Counter-Terrorism Bill: to prevent the extension of pre-charge detention from 28 to 42 days.

Wider constitutional propriety

2000 Local Government Bill: to not compel local councils to adopt cabinet/mayoral structures.

2000 Criminal Justice and Court Services Bill: to prevent the merger of the Chief Inspector of Probation and Chief Inspector of Prisons.

2006 Police and Justice Bill: to prevent the merging of the five criminal justice inspectorates, and to limit the Secretary of State's powers to merge police forces and direct the police.

2007 Legal Services Bill: to require that the chairman of the Legal Services Board is appointed with agreement of the Lord Chief Justice, not just by the Secretary of State.

2009 Health Bill: to give parliament a role in determining the principles of the NHS Constitution.

Other matters

2002 Export Control Bill: to write protection of academic freedom into the bill.

2004 Energy Bill: to include a strategy for microgeneration, require the Secretary of State to have regard to sustainable development, and to strengthen future parliamentary oversight.

2004 Higher Education Bill: to ensure that new tuition fees should not apply to students awarded a deferred place the previous year.

2007 Mental Health Bill: to require that renewal of detention involves a fully qualified medical practitioner, and that young people are assessed by a clinician with specialist training.

2010 Equality Bill: to limit the application of equality legislation in the case of religious groups.

Box 6.2. Examples of coalition government defeats in the House of Lords 2010–13

2010–11 Public Bodies Bill: to limit ministerial power to abolish public bodies by delegated legislation, and remove several bodies from scope of the bill.

2011 Parliamentary Voting System and Constituencies Bill: to change the formula for calculating electoral boundaries, and exempt the Isle of Wight.

2011 Police Reform and Social Responsibility Bill: to remove the provision establishing elected police commissioners.

2012 Welfare Reform Bill: to exclude child benefit from the proposed welfare cap, exempt cancer patients from limits on benefits, and block the 'under occupancy penalty' on social housing tenants with one spare room.

2012 Legal Aid, Sentencing and Punishment of Offenders Bill: to guarantee legal aid to children, victims of domestic violence and claimants challenging benefit cuts.

2013 Growth and Infrastructure Bill: to remove a clause allowing company employees to trade in their employment rights in return for shares, and limit proposed deregulation of planning regarding home extensions.

2013 Enterprise and Regulatory Reform Bill: to outlaw caste discrimination.

these defeats demand a reversal of government policy. A defeat could be anything between the (extremely rare) complete rejection of a government bill, or central clause in a bill, to a minor tinkering with the technical detail. The examples given show that many defeats are on important policy matters. But to build a fuller picture (particularly when considering the extent to which defeats are overturned, as the chapter goes on to do) requires some overall assessment of the policy significance of such interventions.

To judge the policy significance of a defeat requires careful reading of both the bill and the proposed amendment. But such judgements risk being subjective. To increase reliability requires use of a carefully constructed coding scheme, and ideally two independent coders.[12] Exactly this kind of analysis was conducted for all 'unique' legislative defeats in the Lords during 1999–2012. The dataset here includes only defeats on government bills, excluding those on delegated legislation or non-legislative matters. It also excludes defeats that took place at the 'ping-pong' stage insisting on an earlier amendment, because including these would effectively mean that some policy disagreements were counted more than once. The exclusion of these two categories of division leaves 406 unique legislative defeats.[13] Each

Table 6.3. Policy significance of Lords legislative defeats, 1999–2012

Value	Policy significance	Number of defeats	% of defeats
2	Minor alteration to minor policy (1 + 1)	3	1%
3	Medium alteration to minor policy (2 + 1), or minor alteration to medium policy (1 + 2)	46	11%
4	Major alteration to minor policy (3 + 1), medium alteration to medium policy (2 + 2), or minor alteration to major policy (1 + 3)	145	36%
5	Major alteration to medium policy (3 + 2), or medium alteration to major policy (2 + 3)	129	32%
6	Major alteration to major policy (3 + 3)	83	20%
	Total	406	100%

of these was then coded for policy importance, as 'minor', 'medium' or 'major' on two dimensions, the first to capture the centrality of the policy to the bill in question, and the other the extent of policy change demanded by the amendment.[14] Finally, these two codes for each defeat were added together, to create a five-point scale of policy significance.

The meaning of each of the five points, and the breakdown of unique defeats between them, is given in Table 6.3. It shows that defeats falling into the two categories of lowest policy importance are relatively rare. This makes sense, as both government and opposition parties are unlikely to waste their energy battling over relatively trivial policy matters: ministers in the Lords will instead usually concede a minor policy change if necessary, to avoid a defeat (as discussed in Chapter 7). When defeats happen the nature of the policy change, or the centrality of the policy, are usually of at least 'medium' importance. As the table shows, in one in five cases a defeat was coded 'major' on both dimensions.

To what extent are Lords defeats overturned in the Commons?

One response to the large number of government defeats in the House of Lords could simply be 'so what?'. The Lords has limited powers over most bills, and can ultimately be overruled under the Parliament Acts on those that start in the Commons. It retains an absolute veto over bills starting in the

Lords, but these often cover less controversial matters. Furthermore, the elected Commons may be able to use its authority to get the Lords to back down. Defeats—however ambitious in policy terms—could therefore be little more than symbolic, with no real lasting effect.

We already know that disputes between the chambers are generally resolved through negotiation. Recourse to the Parliament Acts is slow and cumbersome, and is in practice rarely used. But negotiations could result in the Lords usually backing down, or the government usually backing down, or some combination of the two. To establish who 'wins' in such conflicts requires further study into what happened after the defeat at the later ping-pong stages in both chambers. This again requires careful reading (this time of *Hansard*, as well as the bill and relevant amendment/s), and coding of outcomes in as objective a way as possible.[15]

Such analysis was conducted for all 'unique' defeats of government legislation during 1999–2012, coding each on a five-point scale in terms of the extent to which it was overturned, or ultimately accepted by the Commons. Decisions at the two extremes are relatively straightforward: a defeat was coded '1' if it was totally overturned and the government's original words reinstated; or '5' if it was wholly accepted and the amendment wording remained in the bill (three cases where the entire bill was dropped because of the defeat were also included in this group). Between these two poles the boundaries are more blurred. Defeats that were largely overturned but with some minor concessions to the Lords were coded '2'; those where the government and House of Commons largely accepted the defeat were coded '4'; and those where a roughly halfway compromise was reached were coded '3'.

Table 6.4 shows the ultimate outcome of Lords defeats during 1999–2012 according to this classification, and demonstrates that many go on to be accepted, in whole or in part. Although the largest single category comprises defeats that the government managed to completely overturn, these account for only a minority of the total. The Lords also won a large number of conflicts outright, while in many more there was some form of compromise. If the outcomes are simplified to two categories, where the Lords is either wholly or largely overruled, or where it is met at least halfway in policy terms, these are relatively balanced. The Lords' position prevailed, and went on to make a lasting difference to the legislation, just under half of the time. For examples of defeats that succeeded, look back to the examples from under Labour in Box 6.1: all of these challenges were ultimately accepted by the government. (The outcome of coalition defeats in Box 6.2 was more mixed.) Some of these examples are discussed in greater detail later in the chapter.

Table 6.4. Extent to which Lords legislative defeats were overturned, 1999–2012

		Final policy outcome (see text for codes)					Lords 'win' or 'draw' (i.e. 3, 4 or 5)	
Session	Unique legislative defeats	1	2	3	4	5	Total	%
1999–00	31	10	4	2	3	12	17	55%
2000–01	2	1	0	0	0	1	1	50%
2001–02	47	13	15	5	9	5	19	40%
2002–03	75	37	11	8	6	13	27	36%
2003–04	52	25	6	4	9	8	21	40%
2004–05	22	9	3	1	7	2	10	45%
2005–06	46	21	5	5	8	7	20	43%
2006–07	34	11	3	11	6	3	20	59%
2007–08	27	13	2	4	2	6	12	44%
2008–09	21	5	2	2	6	6	14	67%
2009–10	10	4	0	0	1	5	6	60%
2010–12	39	18	8	4	2	7	13	33%
Total	406	167	59	46	59	75	180	44%
% of total		41%	15%	11%	15%	18%		

In terms of the extent to which Lords defeats are reversed, some comparisons with earlier periods can be made. Donald Shell (1992) analysed 148 such defeats during 1979–90 and concluded that 63 were accepted, 55 rejected, and 30 resulted in a compromise. This suggests a similar or rather higher success rate for the Lords than during 1999–2012, though it is not clear how exactly his categories were defined. Additionally, of course, the same party dominated both chambers over the period 1979–90, meaning that defeats signalled intra-party disagreements—on which the government may be more likely to concede (for reasons discussed in the next section). Nonetheless, this indicates that government has responded to Lords defeat with complete intransigence in only a minority of cases since at least the 1980s.

Factors associated with successful Lords defeats

The fact that many Lords defeats are overturned but numerous others are not raises a new question of why some succeed but others fail. There are many factors that could potentially be associated with the 'success' of defeats. Not all of these can be easily captured in a quantitative analysis: for example, the government may be more inclined to accept a defeat that is based on compelling evidence, chimes with ministerial doubts expressed behind the scenes, or is proposed by a widely-respected peer. But some other possible factors can be more easily measured, and the large number of defeats during 1999–2012 allows us to test whether any of these matter statistically. The success of the 406 unique legislative defeats is thus examined here in a multivariate regression analysis with respect to the following possible causal factors:

- *Policy significance.* One of the most obvious things that might be expected to be associated with a defeat's success is the extent of policy change that it demands. As we have seen, defeats vary in policy significance, and government might resist hardest those defeats which overturn the most important policies. A first look at the relationship between policy significance and the ultimate outcome of defeats does not suggest this kind of relationship, however. The examples in Box 6.1 demonstrate that defeats on many important policy matters succeeded. Looking at all 406 cases, we know that 49 defeats fell into the two most minor categories, and it turns out that only 19 (39%) of these resulted in a 'win' or 'draw' for the Lords, while a very similar proportion (90 out of 212, 42%) of the defeats in the two most major categories succeeded. So policy significance does not on its own immediately appear important, though it might matter when combined with other factors.
- *Chamber of introduction.* Another obvious factor could be whether the bill in question began its passage in the Commons or in the Lords. Because the Parliament Acts apply only to Commons bills, the government might feel a greater need to compromise with peers on Lords bills. Of the 406 unique legislative defeats in this period, 282 were on Commons bills, of which 115 (41%) resulted in a 'win' or 'draw' for the Lords. The equivalent figures for Lords bills were 124 and 64 (52%), suggesting that this factor may have an influence. But the figures also demonstrate that many Lords 'wins' occur on Commons bills, so this cannot be an overriding factor.
- *Size of the defeat.* A third obvious feature which might affect government thinking is the size of the defeat. Sometimes a division in the Lords is lost by just a handful of votes, and at other times the government is defeated convincingly. Large majorities may be difficult to overturn, as they indicate that a wide spectrum of peers are ranged against the government. The biggest defeat of all over this period was by 191 votes (309 to 118) in 2008, over peers' opposition to the proposal that maximum pre-charge detention of terrorist suspects be extended from 28 to 42 days. The second largest was by 187 votes in 2005, on the Prevention of Terrorism Bill. These defeats (both of which are further

described later) succeeded, as did nine of the total 14 where the government lost by more than 100 votes. In contrast, there were 84 times when the government was defeated by fewer than 10 votes, of which 34 (40%) succeeded. This suggests that a defeat's size might affect its success. But there could be relationships with other factors—for example, if large defeats occur disproportionately on more important policies. This illustrates why a multivariate analysis, which allows the effect of each factor to be tested independently of the others, is useful.

- *Government rebels.* Another possible factor is whether those opposing the government's policy include some of its own backbenchers. There are various reasons to think that this may be important, as already touched on in Chapter 5. First, the government depends on the support of its own backbenchers in the Lords, who are not paid a salary or answerable to an electorate, and party whips rely to a large extent on goodwill. For this reason alone it may be risky for ministers to alienate peers on their own side. Government may therefore prefer to back down when such dissent is expressed. But more importantly, backbench resistance signals problems in the party, which could extend to the backbenches in the Commons should the government seek to overturn a defeat. The presence of rebels effectively changes the nature of a dispute from one purely between Lords and Commons, or government and opposition, to a less partisan one between parliament and government. Earlier scholars (Miers and Brock 1993; Shell 1992) have thus claimed that defeats involving rebels are less likely to be overturned, and peers today also suggest that this is the case. Of the 16 cases of unique defeat during 1999–2010 where there were more than 10 Labour rebels, 14 resulted in a Lords' win or draw, suggesting that this factor is indeed important.
- *Government rebel amendments.* As well as backbenchers casting rebel votes, an even clearer sign of dissent can be when a government backbencher tables a hostile amendment on which a defeat takes place. As was seen in Chapter 5, this is relatively rare, but has become more common under the coalition. For similar reasons to those applying to rebel votes, this may make ministers more inclined to give in to a defeat.
- *Crossbench amendments.* Like government rebel amendments, Crossbench amendments help to demonstrate that there is widespread opposition across the chamber, beyond that on the opposition benches. Defeats on such amendments have become more common under the coalition. During Labour's time in office they were sometimes

associated with larger defeats, when a Crossbench figurehead was used to signal the breadth of opposition to the government. So we might expect such defeats to be more difficult to overturn, but a multivariate analysis is necessary to tease competing factors apart. In fact, of the 46 unique defeats on Crossbench amendments during 1999–2012 only 13 (28%) resulted in a Lords win or draw, suggesting that Crossbench opposition may not be as effective as it seems.

- *Coalition government.* Finally, we might expect behaviour to be different between the periods of Labour and coalition government. Table 6.4 showed that the proportion of defeats succeeding in 2010–12 was rather lower than the average since 1999. This could be a chance factor, or might indicate something more substantive. For example, as a new government, the coalition may have been more reluctant to give concessions on its flagship policies (Tony Blair's initial years in office were before 1999, so are not included in this analysis). Also, as the coalition is made up of two parties, policy changes are potentially more difficult to negotiate within government, perhaps making ministers more resistant to pressure from parliament. In addition, the cuts agenda meant that more defeats in 2010–12 probably had financial implications, and could fall prey to claims of Commons' financial privilege. But the coalition period is also closely related to other factors on this list such as size of majority (as the coalition is stronger numerically in the Lords than Labour was). A multivariate analysis can help us disentangle such effects and understand the data better.

The results of three regression analyses on the 406 unique defeats are therefore shown in Table 6.5. Each used ordinary least squares (OLS) regression, with ultimate outcome of the defeat (on a five-point scale) as the dependent variable. The independent variables are as just listed (with majority against the government and number of government rebel peers as continuous variables, policy significance as a five-point scale, and the remainder as dichotomous 'dummy' variables). Model 1 used data only from the period of Labour government, and models 2 and 3 include coalition defeats as well.

Looking at the results, the most notable feature of all three models is that the independent variables are very poor at predicting the outcome of government defeats. Altogether (as indicated by the R^2 figure at the base of the table) they explain no more than 5.6% of the variance in the dependent variable. Under Labour, just two independent variables proved to have a statistically significant effect: presence of government backbench rebel peers (which is highly significant), and the amendment being moved by a Crossbencher. In the latter case the relationship is negative, meaning that Crossbench amendments actually had a poorer success rate than those moved by others. In practice, this indicates that opposition-sponsored amendments had a marginally higher chance of success, since backbench rebel-sponsored amendments are the only real alternative, and the model shows that these had no particular effect. Number of rebel peers, however, shows a positive relationship with the success of defeats. That is, as predicted, a higher number of rebel supporters increases a defeat's likelihood of success.[16] The coefficient indicates that the presence of around 15 rebels results in a shift of one point on the 1–5 scale in terms of success. But backbench rebellions under Labour were relatively rare, which means that this factor clearly cannot account for much of the overall variance.

When the coalition data is included, in model 2, the same two independent variables remain statistically significant, with Crossbench mover appearing to grow in importance. But we already know that the number of Crossbench-sponsored defeats rose sharply in 2010–12, so this could be masking an effect of coalition itself. Model 3 therefore removes this variable. Here, the negative effect (B coefficient) of coalition increases, and this comes closer to being statistically significant, but still falls well short. Hence, there is no clear evidence that (once other factors are held constant) defeats were more often overturned by the coalition than Labour. But this could be due to the small amount of data for the later period.

Other variables included in the models did not prove statistically significant. Notably, there is no clear relationship between the policy significance of a defeat and whether or not it is overturned. There is also no evidence that defeats are more likely to succeed on House of Lords bills, despite the fact that the chamber has an absolute veto. The government appears equally likely to compromise on House of Commons bills. Likewise, the size of the majority against the government is not statistically significant.

The main conclusion from this analysis, therefore, has to be that the main factors associated with the success of government defeats in the Lords are more complex than those captured in this analysis. When rebel peers are present this does appear to matter, almost certainly in part because they indicate (or predict) discontent on the government benches in the Commons.[17] The other factors that matter are probably less measurable ones, such as those mentioned earlier. For example, whether a proposed amendment is broadly 'sensible' and whether the peer(s) promoting it are well respected. Other external factors, such as the state of public or media opinion, or the views of key interest groups, may also be important. But these would be extremely difficult to capture in quantitative terms.

Table 6.5. Multivariate analysis of factors influencing the success of Lords defeats

	Model 1: 1999–2010 only			Model 2:1999–2012			Model 3:1999–2012		
	B	Std. Error	Sig.	B	Std. Error	Sig.	B	Std. Error	Sig.
(Constant)	2.228	.395	.000	2.312	.381	.000	2.336	.383	.000
Policy significance	.031	.086	.718	.003	.082	.966	−.006	.082	.939
Lords Bill (= 1)	.202	.174	.246	.272	.170	.110	.286	.171	.095
Majority against the government	.002	.003	.422	.005	.003	.115	.003	.003	.233
No of government rebel peers	.076	.022	.001***	.042	.017	.014*	.041	.017	.017*
Government rebel mover (= 1)	−.842	.589	.154	−.683	.443	.124	−.430	.435	.324
Crossbench mover (= 1)	−.648	.316	.041*	−.696	.274	.012*	–	–	–
Coalition government (= 1)	–	–	–	−.053	.316	.867	−.390	.288	.178
	R^2.056			R^2.050			R^2.033		

Significance:
* at the 0.05 level;
** at the 0.01 level;
*** at the 0.001 level

Case studies of defeats

The preceding analysis using all defeats during 1999–2012 indicates some general trends, though mostly by clarifying where relationships do not exist (e.g. between policy significance and success of a defeat). But it lacks the finer-grained detail that may help us to really understand the political dynamics of such events. This section therefore discusses a few examples in greater depth. Given the multitude of defeats, a handful of cases cannot capture all of the relevant factors, so here we consider examples of four kinds. First, big civil liberties and constitutional showdowns between the Lords and the Labour governments, which demonstrate the kind of impact that the Lords often had during 1999–2010. Second, other cases under Labour where the role of rebel backbenchers was particularly important; and third, examples from this period where Crossbenchers played a central role. Finally, we discuss some examples of defeats under the coalition.

Key defeats on constitutional and civil liberties issues under Labour

Access to jury trial

As mentioned previously, one of the longest-running disputes between Labour and the House of Lords was over government attempts to restrict criminal defendants' access to trial by jury. The first confrontation occurred on the Criminal Justice (Mode of Trial) Bill, introduced into the House of Lords at the beginning of the 1999–2000 session. The bill was given a second reading, but subsequently became subject to the post-1999 chamber's first government defeat. This reversed the central provision to remove the right to opt for a jury trial in 'either way' cases (i.e. those that can be heard either by a magistrate or a jury). The amendment was sponsored jointly by the Conservative and Liberal Democrat frontbench, Crossbench former Law Lord Desmond Ackner and Labour human rights lawyer Helena Kennedy. Having lost by 95 votes the government simply abandoned the bill. But soon afterwards it introduced the Criminal Justice (Mode of Trial) (No. 2) Bill into the Commons, to allow the possibility of using the Parliament Acts. When this arrived in the Lords it was defeated by 96 votes at second reading. Ultimately it too was abandoned.

The government's next attempt was in the Criminal Justice Bill 2002–03. At Lords committee stage the clause allowing a defendant to opt out of a jury trial was defeated by 74 votes. During ping-pong the government trimmed its ambitions, proposing that restrictions on jury trials should only apply in complex fraud cases. But this compromise was also heavily defeated by peers. In the end a more shaky compromise was reached, giving ministers the power to introduce the latter change via delegated legislation subject to the affirmative procedure. In 2005 a statutory instrument was laid to this effect, but there were clear indications behind the scenes that this might be defeated, and it was withdrawn. A final attempt to legislate for this more limited measure, through the Fraud (Trials without a Jury) Bill 2006–07, was again rejected at Lords second reading by 73 votes.[18] The government argued that it had merely sought to streamline the criminal justice system and make it more efficient, but the Lords' hardline position was widely welcomed by civil liberties groups.

Prevention of Terrorism Bill 2004–05

The single biggest confrontation between the Labour government and the Lords was over the Prevention of Terrorism Bill, shortly before the 2005 general election. This bill was introduced quickly, following a court ruling that provisions in the earlier Anti-terrorism, Crime and Security Act 2001 (which followed the 9/11 attacks on the US) were contrary to the Human Rights Act. The original provisions allowed foreign terrorist suspects to be held potentially indefinitely without charge, and the new bill replaced this with a system of 'control orders', which could instead impose other restrictions such as house arrest. Altogether, the bill was subject to 18 Lords defeats and four rounds of ping-pong, lasting a record-breaking 32 continuous hours. The confrontation was unusually intense because the bill was an emergency measure, which needed to reach the statute book before the suspects were released from prison.

The main points of contention concerned the degree of discretion that judges (rather than ministers) should have over control orders, and peers' desire that the legislation be time-limited. During the initial Commons stages, 62 Labour MPs had rebelled on the first of these points. Appearing on BBC *Newsnight* that evening, Labour's Robin Cook, a former Leader of the House of Commons and Foreign Secretary, claimed that MPs had 'sent the House of Lords a message' about how to deal with the bill. When it arrived in the Lords, the government immediately moved some concessions, but peers judged that these did not go far enough. There were five defeats by over 100 votes, one of which (at 187 votes) was the second largest of Labour's time in government. This inserted a 'sunset clause' of 30 November 2005, and had support from 24 Labour rebels and 61 Crossbenchers. An amendment to restrict the Home Secretary's powers likewise attracted 20 rebels and

49 Crossbenchers. During ping-pong, various compromises were reached. A revised sunset clause of 31 March 2006 was proposed by Labour backbencher Helene Hayman (who later became Lord Speaker), and defeat on this was ultimately accepted by the government, alongside various restrictions on ministerial power.

There were several other major conflicts between the Lords and the government over anti-terrorism measures. Another example was rejection of the Brown government's proposal to extend maximum detention without trial from 28 to 42 days. This had been approved by the Commons by only nine votes—requiring the support of the Northern Ireland DUP, because 36 Labour MPs rebelled.[19] When the bill reached the Lords, an amendment to remove this provision was proposed by Crossbencher Geoffrey Dear, a widely-regarded former senior police officer. Peers speaking against the policy included former Director General of MI5 Eliza Manningham-Buller (Crossbench), and former Lord Chancellors Charlie Falconer (Labour) and James Mackay (Conservative). Following a defeat (including 24 Labour rebel peers), Gordon Brown chose not to risk another Commons vote, and dropped the policy.

Incitement to religious hatred

Another recurring issue was Labour's attempt to introduce a new criminal offence of incitement to religious hatred. Such a proposal was first included in the Antiterrorism, Crime and Security Bill 2001–02, but was rejected at Lords report stage by 99 votes. Opponents of the measure included eight Labour rebels and 45 Crossbenchers (with just 11 Crossbenchers supporting the government). They were backed by civil liberties campaigners outside parliament, who expressed concerns about the implications for free speech. The defeat was initially overturned in the Commons (despite 27 Labour rebel votes), but peers subsequently insisted on their position by an increased majority of 113, and the government retreated rather than risking the entire bill being lost.[20]

In the 2005–06 session a freestanding Racial and Religious Hatred Bill was introduced, which again ran into trouble in the Lords. At committee stage, the government was defeated by 149 votes on a joint Conservative/Liberal Democrat amendment, also signed by former Archbishop of Canterbury George Carey and Labour backbencher Professor Raymond Plant. This effectively gutted the bill, with opponents again arguing the case on free speech grounds (now supported by a high-profile external campaign). On the bill's return to the Commons, ministers sought to reverse the change, but were humiliated when MPs instead chose to back the Lords' position, resulting in a Commons defeat. This was extremely unusual, and Commons specialists Cowley and Stuart (2008) blame the result primarily on poor whipping, connected to the fact that many Labour MPs were absent campaigning in a by-election. But this was a hard reminder to ministers of the danger of asking MPs to overturn Lords defeats on issues where they lacked solid backbench support.

Exploiting Labour rebellions, successfully and unsuccessfully

Communications Bill 2002–03

As already discussed, large rebellions in the Lords under Labour were relatively rare. One of the largest occurred on the Communications Bill 2002–03, which revised the powers of the communications regulator Ofcom and arrangements for media ownership. There were five defeats in the Lords in total, including one led by Labour backbencher and film producer David Puttnam, to insert into the bill a principal duty on Ofcom to 'further the interests of citizens' as well as consumers. Puttnam had previously chaired a joint committee of both chambers which had scrutinized the bill in draft form and recommended such a change. His amendment attracted the votes of 33 Labour peers, while only 73 voted for the government (suggesting that there may have been government abstentions). In addition, 29 Crossbenchers supported the rebel amendment while only one voted for the government. The result was a defeat by 105 votes, which was largely accepted by the government in the Commons. As the previous example demonstrated, seeking to overturn an amendment which had such clear Labour support could have been risky for ministers.

Health and Social Care Bill 2002–03

On occasion, opposition parties in the Lords seek to exploit divisions in the governing party's ranks, but this does not always succeed. One example under Labour concerned the establishment of 'foundation hospitals' in the Health and Social Care (Community Health and Standards) Bill 2002–03. During the bill's initial passage through the Commons this measure had been hugely controversial, with 62 government backbenchers rebelling at report stage on an amendment to remove the foundation hospital clause from the bill. A leading rebel MP, former Health Secretary Frank Dobson, then took the unusual step of writing to peers to urge them to defeat the provision in the Lords. They obliged, inflicting a defeat by 50 votes on an amendment from the Conservative frontbench. But only four Labour peers rebelled, while 95 voted for the government, so this was essentially a defeat achieved by opposition votes. On the bill's initial return to the Commons the government sought to overturn the defeat, but did so by only 17 votes (the smallest majority since 2001), as 62 Labour MPs again rebelled. This encouraged the Lords to insist, but when the bill returned to the Commons for a second time, the number of rebels dropped to 35. Conservative frontbenchers in the Lords concluded that Labour opinion had swung behind the government, so they did not insist on the amendment again. The Commons having finally decisively spoken, the provision was instead allowed to pass into law.[21]

Crossbench leadership and brokering under Labour

Identity Cards Bill 2005–06

Another highly contentious bill, on which there were 12 Lords defeats and four rounds of ping-pong, was that introducing Labour's identity cards scheme. The confrontation again had a classic civil liberties and constitutional propriety focus. Many campaigners outside parliament opposed the whole notion of identity cards, and the associated 'national identity register', while peers raised additional concerns about the details of the scheme, and in particular the extensive powers for ministers to make future adjustments using delegated legislation. One major defeat removed a clause allowing the Secretary of State to make the cards (formally introduced on a voluntary basis) compulsory via this route. The proposal was highly contentious, not least because Labour's manifesto had promised a voluntary scheme; peers therefore claimed that they were merely holding the government to its own election promises. Perhaps fearing a Commons backbench backlash, ministers did not seek to overturn this defeat. Another defeat required that the bill could not come into effect until a report had been produced on the scheme's costs and benefits, and here the government accepted a compromise amendment in the Commons moved by a Labour backbencher to require regular reports on costs to be laid before parliament. Hence, both of these issues were resolved on the first round of ping-pong.

The more protracted argument was over peers' resistance to the proposal that those applying for a passport should be automatically entered onto the identity register and obtain an ID card. This again clearly affected the extent of voluntarism in the scheme. Originally, there was a Labour rebel amendment at Commons report stage, which was taken up in the Lords in a joint initiative by the Conservative and Liberal Democrat frontbench. Ministers successfully convinced the Commons to overturn this three times, but peers repeatedly reinserted it. The impasse was finally broken when Crossbencher Robert Armstrong, a former Cabinet Secretary, moved a compromise amendment specifying that entry onto the register would remain voluntary until 2010. Ministers initially resisted, so this too was pressed to a defeat, which there was no attempt to overturn in the Commons. As one peer involved in the dispute claimed, 'everybody saw that accepting an amendment from a Crossbencher was a way of not climbing down: a way out for the government and the opposition'. Another described it as 'accepting arbitration, if you like'. At the time, the deal looked like a climbdown by opposition peers (it is coded in the analysis as a 'draw'), but it was carefully designed to delay any compulsion until after the forthcoming general election. As the Conservatives and Liberal Democrats both opposed ID cards, this allowed the post-2010 coalition to abolish them easily before many had been taken up.

Corporate Manslaughter and Corporate Homicide Bill 2006–07

This kind of 'brokering' role by Crossbenchers is relatively common. What occurred less often under Labour was a Crossbencher leading Lords opposition to a bill. One rare case was on the government's legislation to introduce a new offence of corporate manslaughter. Debates on the bill in the Commons had focused largely on employment issues, with trade unions keen to maximize safety, and employers to contain costs and liabilities. However, at report stage there were two amendments moved by Labour backbenchers—the chair of the Home Affairs Select Committee, and chair of the Joint Committee on Human Rights—to extend liability to include deaths in prison and police custody. Both of these failed. When the bill reached the Lords there was then a major conflict over the issue. The group of peers calling for change, which included both the Conservative and Liberal Democrat frontbench, was led by David Ramsbotham, a Crossbench peer and former Chief Inspector of Prisons.

The initial defeat occurred at report stage, when the government lost by 96 votes to a wide-ranging coalition that included 36 Crossbenchers (with only one supporting the government), and 11 Labour rebels. Ramsbotham obviously had expert status, and he was part of a penal reform group on the Crossbenches which included other specialists such as Vivien Stern, a former director of Nacro (the National Association for the Care and Resettlement of Offenders). But he also worked closely with opposition party frontbenchers, as well as concerned Labour members and outside groups. From the parties' point of view it was beneficial to have Ramsbotham in the lead, both to maximize cross-party support and to limit the blame laid at their own door for challenging the Commons. The government initially strongly resisted his amendment, under pressure from the Association of Chief Police Officers and the Prison Officers Association, and persuaded the Commons to overturn it four times. But eventually ministers moved their own amendments effectively giving in to his demands.

The dynamics of Lords defeats under the Conservative/Liberal Democrat coalition

While the record of Lords defeats under Labour extends to 13 years, experiences under the 2010 coalition government are far more limited. There are dangers in drawing too many conclusions from the period 2010–12, when all members in the Lords were adjusting to the new political circumstances, and the government could enjoy at least something of a 'honeymoon' period. But it is clear that the arithmetic of defeat in the Lords became very different in 2010, and that the Crossbenchers began to play a more pivotal role. Two examples can help to illustrate.

Welfare Reform Bill 2010–12

This government's bill to reform the welfare system (discussed further in Chapter 7) suffered eight defeats and went to one round of ping-pong. In a manner fairly typical of the 2010–12 session, and very different from Labour's time in office, six of these were sponsored by Crossbenchers. Richard Best, a housing expert (supported by both a Labour and a Liberal Democrat backbencher with respected reputations on welfare policy) proposed changes to the government's plans to penalize social housing tenants for underoccupancy (the so-called 'bedroom tax'). Narendra Patel, a senior medical doctor, led on amendments to exempt those unable to work during cancer treatment from new restrictions on employment benefits. Two other defeats on benefits for disabled children were sponsored by Crossbenchers with established expertise in welfare, children's policy and disability, among them the former paralympic athlete Tanni Grey-Thompson. These proposals all won support from the overwhelming majority of Crossbenchers who voted, as well as the unanimous support of Labour peers; the margin of defeat ranged from 16 to 68. A further defeat sponsored by the Bishop of Ripon and Leeds, to exclude child benefit from calculations of the new 'benefit cap', proved more controversial.[22] Crossbenchers divided only 41:38 in favour, but 26 Liberal Democrat peers rebelled, while only 39 voted with the government. Some Lib Dems claimed privately to have received signals from Commons colleagues that pressure from the Lords on this point would help party leader Nick Clegg to win concessions from the Conservatives. A final defeat headed by former Conservative Lord Chancellor

James Mackay was won by an impressive 142 votes, including 34 Conservative and 16 Liberal Democrat rebels. This sought to block introduction of fees for parents pursuing claims for child maintenance from their ex-partners.

Despite the wide spectrum of peers ranged against the government, on the bill's return to the Commons all the defeats were judged to infringe that chamber's 'financial privilege', and the government convinced MPs to overturn them. Only some very minor concessions were given. This infuriated peers, including some on the government's own side, who claimed that the second chamber was effectively being sidelined. Lord Mackay suggested that it was 'a waste of time' and 'a waste of taxpayers' money' for the Lords to debate amendments which the government and House of Commons just dismissed out of hand.[23] Likewise, Labour's Patricia Hollis (co-sponsor of the housing amendment) claimed that if government behaved in this way peers 'might as well go home'.[24] Former Conservative Chancellor of the Exchequer Nigel Lawson suggested that financial privilege was being 'invoked promiscuously', in a way 'completely contrary to the conventions of the constitution'.[25] The episode raised new questions about the ability of the Lords to challenge a government from the 'left' by protecting public spending in a time of austerity, and demonstrated that there were further conventions that could come under pressure (but also that these were little understood).[26] The argument died down, with the criticisms from such senior figures no doubt encouraging the government to adopt a more conciliatory approach.

Public Bodies Bill 2010–12

As shown in Table 6.4, not all Lords defeats in the coalition's first session ended in failure. Peers had significantly greater success with respect to the Public Bodies Bill, introduced early in the session via the House of Lords, which allowed the government to abolish and merge 'quangos'. Of the numerous amendments made in the chamber many were achieved without defeat, as described in Chapter 7. But defeats also played a part. One example was a wide-ranging amendment by Liberal Democrat backbencher Anthony Lester at committee stage (regarding protection for bodies with judicial and human rights functions), which was ultimately accepted intact by ministers. Government amendments were moved at later Lords stages to flesh out his proposal. Three further defeats dealt with the status of particular bodies. An amendment sponsored by three Crossbenchers (headed by Ilora Finlay, a former president of the Royal Society of Medicine), alongside the Labour frontbench, removed the Chief Coroner from the list for abolition. The government was defeated by 112 votes, and a compromise was reached to protect the office but merge it with another body. A similar defeat on a

Labour frontbench amendment to remove the Youth Justice Commission from the list of bodies for abolition was initially overturned in the Commons, but when the bill returned to the Lords David Ramsbotham sought to reinsert this change into the bill. The government then chose to reverse its position and back his proposal, rather than continuing the conflict. A final defeat, sponsored by former Conservative cabinet minister Tony Newton, concerned the status of the Administrative Justice and Tribunals Council. Despite the high regard with which Newton was held, this was completely overturned in the Commons, perhaps in part because the government had lost the initial division by only six votes.

Conclusion: Defeats and the policy power of the Lords

This chapter has reviewed the Lords' role in inflicting legislative defeats on government during 1999–2013. In doing so it has told us a good deal about the chamber's policy influence in contemporary British politics. An analysis of defeats also provides important background for the chapters that follow, regarding the chamber's broader policy influence. In addition, this in-depth look at the British case suggests some general lessons about bicameralism.

The first conclusion from the analysis is that defeats matter, and that the House of Lords therefore has a real impact on the policy process. Lords defeats are frequent, and numerous: since 1999, occurring on average once every three to four sitting days. This is a sharp contrast to the House of Commons, where such incidents are extremely rare (occurring on average closer to once every two years during 1999–2012). Lords defeats are mostly on non-trivial policy matters, and indeed many are on large policies that are central to government bills—though outright rejection of bills remains unusual. Careful tracking of what happened after each defeat in the period 1999–2012 shows that just under half went on to be accepted by the House of Commons. That is, as Table 6.4 showed, 181 unique Lords defeats were largely or wholly accepted into government bills. We must therefore conclude that the chamber has a significant impact on policy outcomes in contemporary Britain.

An additional question is whether this situation represents a change from the past. We conclude that it does, as the pre-1999 Lords was seen as a weak policy actor. Earlier in the chapter we saw that Labour governments pre-1999 certainly suffered many Lords defeats, but these were almost invariably overturned when bills returned to the Commons (Baldwin 1995; Morgan 1975; Shell 1992). Now, the Commons gives in to Lords defeats far more often, at least in part because the chamber is much more prone to insist on its amendments when they are blocked. This new assertiveness by peers indicates a greater sense of confidence and 'legitimacy', as explored later in Chapter 9. Notably, the chamber's party balance now means that—in sharp contrast to the past—Conservative and Labour governments are equally likely to suffer defeat. Even the 2010 coalition, which can largely rely on the support of previously 'pivotal' Liberal Democrat peers, has faced substantial difficulties in the Lords. A single party Conservative government—while perhaps being stronger than the coalition in the Commons—would have been defeated in the Lords much more.

The reasons that governments now concede to the Lords—despite the chamber lacking both an absolute veto and a democratic mandate—are mostly quite familiar from standard accounts of bicameralism. Parliamentary time is precious, and governments face opportunity costs if they enter protracted conflicts with peers, including on other legislation. Ministers will often prefer to compromise than face lengthy delay resulting from ping-pong or recourse to the Parliament Acts. They will also not wish to aggravate peers unnecessarily, because government intransigence on one bill may reduce peers' cooperation on future bills.

But the multivariate analysis of 13 years of Lords defeats—while ultimately explaining little statistically about why some fail and others succeed—shed important light on the dynamics of these intercameral conflicts. This was further illustrated by the case studies at the end of the chapter. Mostly we see that the determinants of a defeat's success are difficult to measure. One important factor is probably the chamber's renowned 'expertise', in terms of the status of particular peers pressing for change. Faced with criticisms from some members, government can sometimes find it hard to say no. In the quantitative analysis, the only factor found to be relevant in encouraging government to back down was the presence of backbench rebel peers. This is an important insight, reinforced by the case studies, which demonstrated how dissenting votes by government MPs can also play a part in defeats that succeed. The government can only overturn a Lords defeat with the Commons' consent, and asking for this can be risky on policies that are controversial on its own side. To avoid conflict with their own Commons backbenchers, and possibly even a Commons defeat, ministers often prefer to concede to peers' demands.

The analysis in this chapter therefore demonstrates that bicameralism is not a zero-sum game, where strength exercised by one legislative chamber comes at the cost of the other. The new pivotal voters in the Lords can instead strengthen the negotiating power of the existing pivotal voters in the Commons, who are usually government backbench MPs. Despite the requirement for party loyalty in the Commons, rebellion in that chamber has markedly increased in recent decades (Cowley 2002, 2005; Cowley and Norton 1999).

Government may face limited problems on 'populist' policies such as criminal justice, and be able to dodge some difficulties through its significant control of the Commons and agenda; but a Lords defeat forces a policy dilemma to be put to MPs head-on (while at the same time often fuelling wider debate through the media). There is clear evidence that some government backbenchers have even encouraged the Lords (either privately or publicly) to challenge controversial policies. If the great majority of backbench MPs later choose to support the government (as occurred on Labour's Health and Social Care Bill and the coalition's Welfare Reform Bill), peers may back down. But otherwise, a policy change may be forced. This function of asking members of the first chamber to 'think again' is one of the classic purposes of bicameralism. But the mechanics, and indeed psychology, of how this works in practice have been relatively unexplored. In the UK, where MPs are increasingly prepared to act independently, but where the ultimate 'primacy' of the Commons is clear, it turns out that the revival of bicameralism post-1999 has acted to strengthen the Commons as well as the Lords.

So the direct impact of Lords defeats on government policy is substantial, and potentially strengthens both chambers. But the indirect effect of defeats may well be even greater. It is widely recognized by scholars (both in and outside the UK) that the primary influence of legislatures often comes through what Friedrich (1937) first dubbed the 'rule of anticipated reactions'. That is, that these bodies have a largely preventative effect (e.g. Arter 1985; Blondel 1970; McGann 2006; Mezey 1979; Norton 1993). There is a parallel dynamic commonly noted in international relations, in terms of so-called 'hard' and 'soft' power, whereby the threat of military action or tough sanctions can encourage compliance through more diplomatic routes (Nye 2004, 2008). In the parliamentary arena, if a government anticipates that its policy proposals will face parliamentary resistance it is likely to trim its ambitions accordingly. In extremis, it may choose to drop certain proposals altogether. But these kinds of preventative effects are virtually impossible to measure, because the government initiatives that were most likely to have caused difficulties never see the light of day. Nonetheless, there are some indications that such dynamics are important in the government's relationship with the Lords. Notably, the number of defeats increased during Labour's first few years in power (see Figure 6.1), but subsequently declined. This may in part reflect a changing policy agenda, but also more careful preparation by government for passage of its legislation through the Lords. The extent to which this happens, and how much subsequent negotiation takes place during the passage of bills, partly in order to avoid defeat, is the topic of the next chapter.

Notes

1. The minimum intervals are as follows: two weekends between first reading and second reading, 14 days between second reading and start of committee stage, 14 days between end of committee stage and start of report stage for 'bills of considerable length and complexity', and three sitting days between end of report stage and third reading (House of Lords 2010: 122).
2. Precise figures were overall approval (i.e. responding 'strongly agree' or 'agree' on a five-point scale) 66% (n = 370); Labour 89% (n = 100); Conservative 62% (n = 108); Liberal Democrat 58% (n = 45); Crossbench 56% (n = 106). Labour members were also far more likely to 'strongly agree': 64%, compared to 7% for Conservative peers.
3. This process could potentially go on indefinitely, but a bill can be lost either if both Houses twice insist on the same position on a particular amendment or if parliament is prorogued or dissolved. See House of Lords (2010: 159).
4. The first of these bills followed a ruling against the UK in the European Court of Human Rights over the equalization of the age of consent for gay and straight sex. In a free vote MPs strongly backed equalization, but peers disagreed (this dispute began before the 1999 reform, but continued afterwards). The use of the Parliament Acts on the Hunting Bill followed a free vote in the Commons where MPs had voted overwhelmingly for a foxhunting ban, but the Prime Minister himself had voted instead for a compromise option to allow hunting under licence. In both cases, the settlement could therefore be seen as imposing the will of the Commons, not the government.
5. Tony Blair suffered four defeats, two in 2005 on the Terrorism Bill over detention of terrorist suspects without charge, and two in 2006 over the Racial and Religious Hatred Bill (backing House of Lords amendments). Gordon Brown suffered three, all in 2009. One was on a trivial procedural matter regarding the venue for a regional committee meeting, while the others of greater substance related to UK residency rights for retired Gurkhas, and an amendment to the Parliamentary Standards Bill. David Cameron's government suffered an essentially procedural defeat, with no policy effect, on 7 December 2011. My thanks to Philip Cowley for this information.
6. Similarly, during the entire period 1964–70, there was only one Lords insistence (Morgan 1975), and in the 1940s 'though government defeats on bills were numerous... the Lords did not insist on their amendments if the Commons resisted them' (Jennings 1957: 429).
7. Bills sent back to the Commons four times were the European Parliamentary and Local Elections (Pilots) Bill (where the Lords sought to restrict the piloting of all-postal voting), the Prevention of Terrorism Bill, Identity Cards Bill and Corporate Manslaughter and Corporate Homicide Bill. These last three are discussed later in the chapter.
8. For a far more detailed discussion of this type of legislation see Page (2001).

9. The proportion responding 'strongly agree' or 'agree' on a five-point Likert scale (n = 357). Breakdown by the main groups was Labour 54% (n = 96); Conservative 12% (n = 104); Liberal Democrat 5% (n = 43); Crossbench 15% (n = 103).
10. Immediately after the 2000 defeat there were a handful of Conservative turnouts of around 70 peers, plus a similar case in 2006 and another in 2007; but in all of these the Liberal Democrats voted with the government, and it comfortably won. Later on, Conservative turnouts dropped to virtually zero in such divisions.
11. For a discussion of the British parties' ideologies, and definitions and data on the libertarian-authoritarian and socialist-capitalist scales applied to them, see Webb (2000). For data from the 2005 peer survey on members' beliefs on these dimensions (which clearly shows that it was on libertarian issues where the two opposition parties could unite) see Russell and Sciara (2009).
12. Due to the risk of bias and subjectivity, coding was conducted by two researchers independently, who met and discussed any cases of inconsistency. A third researcher adjudicated in cases of disagreement. Adjudication was needed on 51 defeats (on one or other of the dimensions described later). This work builds on an analysis originally published by Russell and Sciara (2008) for the period to 2006.
13. This is almost equal to the number of legislative defeats in Table 6.1, minus those at LCCA and second reading (all three second reading defeats being procedural ones which could not be overturned in the Commons). But there are six LCCA defeats that can be considered 'unique': two because they occurred on House of Lords bills and defeated new material inserted during passage through the Commons, two because they defeated new material inserted by the Commons at CCLA, and a final two because the initial Lords defeat occurred without a division (and was therefore not included in the figures for defeats at earlier stages of the bill).
14. Judgement about centrality to the bill was based on whether the policy addressed by the amendment featured heavily, only slightly, or not at all in the minister's initial second reading speech to peers. Judgement about the extent of policy change was based on reading the amendment against the bill itself, and whether it effectively reversed, significantly altered or only slightly changed the original policy provision. This scheme of classification is not perfect, and in particular takes no account of the bill's overall importance to the government's policy programme. But it is designed to minimize subjectivity and bias, as it is based as far as possible on pure textual analysis.
15. Coding was again conducted independently by two separate researchers, with a third researcher adjudicating in the (relatively rare) cases of disagreement. A third coder was needed only 26 times. This again updates an analysis first conducted for the period to 2006 (Russell and Sciara 2008). The updating uncovered some minor errors in this original analysis, so 1999-2006 figures in Table 6.4 are slightly different to those previously published.

16. This factor is closely correlated with size of the defeat, so models were also run which excluded one or other of these variables. Once number of rebels is excluded, size of the defeat appears significant; but the R^2 reduces far further than it does in a model that excludes defeat size and includes number of rebels—confirming that rebels are the more important factor.
17. Commons dissent is a possible important factor that was not included in the models, but doing so would be very difficult in practice because the Lords often votes on matters that have not been subject to a division in the Commons. This obviously applies in particular to defeats on House of Lords bills, which have not yet been to the Commons, but also in numerous other cases where the Lords has voted on an issue that was not selected for debate at House of Commons report stage.
18. As indicated earlier, in both cases the second reading defeat came through a procedural amendment to delay the bill by six months, which in practice had a fatal effect.
19. For an analysis of the vote in the Commons, see Cowley (forthcoming).
20. Data on Commons rebels taken from Cowley (2005). At the initial Commons stages 21 Labour rebels had supported an amendment to remove this clause.
21. For an analysis of the Commons dynamics on this issue, see Cowley (2005).
22. See T Kavanagh, 'Red revs out of touch with Britain today', *The Sun*, 30 January 2012.
23. *House of Lords Hansard*, 1 February 2012, column 1569.
24. *House of Lords Hansard*, 1 February 2012, column 1566.
25. *House of Lords Hansard*, 2 February 2012, column 1674.
26. Commons clerks make a technical judgement about whether an amendment engages privilege; MPs (acting on the advice of ministers) then decide whether to 'waive' privilege, or 'invoke' it and completely reject a Lords amendment. In the latter case, convention demands that the Lords does not insist on the amendment, though it may propose one in lieu (for a discussion, see Joint Committee on Conventions 2006a).

7

Negotiated Outcomes and the Wider Legislative Impact of the Lords

The previous chapter demonstrated that government defeats in the Lords are important, and that many have a lasting policy effect. Defeats are relatively frequent, and the government often makes at least some concessions to peers' demands. As a consequence of the ability to inflict defeat, there is also likely to be an impact in terms of 'anticipated reactions'. That is, through the government bearing in mind the Lords' possible reaction when drafting legislation, and subsequently making concessions to peers during its passage in order to avoid defeat.

These latter forms of influence are far more difficult to quantify, compared to the impact of defeats. When the government suffers a defeat it is clear that peers are trying to force ministers to change direction. In contrast, if a minister introduces an amendment in the Lords this may or may not be in response to other members' demands. Sometimes the government might simply have had a change of heart, or it may be responding to pressures from outside parliament, while at other times it may be conceding to parliamentary pressure. Peers do clearly consider negotiated outcomes to be important—in the 2005 survey, 85% of respondents agreed that 'the chamber's real influence is exerted as much through persuasion as through defeats'.[1] In the 2007 survey a slightly more detailed question was then posed to tease this out. When asked what mattered to the chamber's influence on the policy process, one-third (33%) of peers agreed that 'government defeats in the House of Lords' were very important. But more than half (54%) said the same about 'government bringing forward its own amendments under pressure from peers'.[2] It is clear that to understand the chamber's policy impact and its relationship with government more fully, some assessment of these less measurable effects is needed. This chapter therefore focuses on negotiated outcomes between the government and the Lords.

The next section gives some overall statistics about the number of amendments made in the Lords to government legislation. The rest of the chapter is then largely based on a detailed analysis of 12 government bills passing through the chamber during the 2005 and 2010 parliaments. Since many thousands of Lords amendments are proposed each year, this kind of case study approach is the only realistic means of exploring less visible forms of legislative impact. The first main section includes some basic information about the case study bills, and then a quantitative analysis of the extent to which they were amended in the Lords, by whom, and whether government amendments can be traced to pressure from non-government parliamentarians. The remainder of the chapter adopts a more qualitative approach. First, some general indications are given of how government prepares legislation for passage through the Lords and consults peers behind the scenes. Then six 'modes' of legislative debate in the Lords are identified, each illustrated with examples. A short section considers private members' bills in the Lords, to complement discussion of the chamber's treatment of government legislation. The chapter's conclusion then summarizes what has been learnt about the policy impact of the Lords, and the ways in which it complements the House of Commons.

Quantitative analysis of Lords amendments to government bills

Figures are readily available, and often quoted, regarding the number of amendments made by the House of Lords to government bills. These are published for each session in the chamber's *Public Bill Sessional Statistics*.[3] For example, in the one-year 2008–09 session there were 6,330 amendments proposed in the Lords to government bills, of which 1,806 were agreed and found their way into the legislation. In the two-year session of 2010–12 there were 9,431 amendments proposed and 2,405 agreed. On the face of it, these figures make the Lords appear very successful in persuading the government to change its policies. However, a high proportion of amendments agreed were proposed in the name of ministers, rather than backbench or opposition peers. According to figures provided by the chamber's Public Bill Office, 1,732 of those succeeding in 2008–09 (i.e. 96% of the total) were proposed by a minister. Likewise, in 2010–12, 2,268 of the amendments that passed (i.e. 94%) were government-sponsored. Once this is taken into account, the picture looks entirely different. We might conclude that government dominates the legislative process in the Lords, and that non-government peers make little impact.

If government brings forward its own amendments in response to points raised by peers (as the survey evidence suggests), the truth probably lies somewhere between these two extremes. But to verify this, and explore it further, it is necessary to look closely at the passage of individual bills, paying particular attention to whether amendments moved by ministers resemble those proposed by non-government peers at earlier stages, and to debates, where ministers and other peers often confirm that this is the case. For bills that begin their passage in the House of Commons (as the majority do) the picture can be even more complex, since ministers may also move amendments in the Lords to respond to points made earlier by MPs, and backbench and opposition peers may likewise pick up suggestions made by their Commons colleagues. So to fully understand the background behind all of the many amendments made in the Lords we need to look carefully at all stages of a bill in that chamber, and also how it was received in the House of Commons. Because this kind of work is very labour-intensive, only a few such studies have previously been conducted. The best known was by Griffith (1974), but is now several decades old. Griffith also paid far more attention to the Commons than the Lords, and his analysis of the links between the two chambers was fairly limited. Miers and Brock (1993) conducted a mixed quantitative and qualitative analysis of amendments to eight bills in the 1988–89 session, while Drewry and Brock (1993) presented overview data for all bills in that session. Other studies have taken a more qualitative approach, and focused largely on defeats (Baldwin 1995; Bromhead 1958; Shell 1992). In all such analyses there is some evidence of government amending its own legislation under pressure from peers, but this is largely unquantified, and the evidence is anyway now significantly out of date.

To gain a more contemporary picture, a detailed analysis was conducted of amendments to 12 bills in the 2005 and 2010 parliaments, as detailed in Box 7.1 (some of which were already discussed in Chapter 6, with respect to defeats). While these case studies made up only a small fraction of the roughly 200 government bills passed over the period 2005–12, they were selected as far as possible to be representative. Hence, some bills were large and others small, some were controversial and others not, and some began their passage in the Commons while others began in the Lords. They were also drawn from a variety of government departments. In two cases a bill from the coalition session 2010–12 overturned one of those studied in the 2005–10 parliament.

All amendments proposed to each of the case study bills in both chambers were logged in a database, alongside information about who tabled the amendment and whether it succeeded. Here, 'success' can be defined either narrowly or broadly. A narrow interpretation would only consider an amendment to be successful if it actually passed. A broader interpretation

Box 7.1. Summary details of the 12 case study bills

2005–10 parliament (Labour government)

- Identity Cards Bill 2005–06: introduced a national identity card scheme, underpinned by a national identity register database.
- Health Bill 2005–06: contained a wide variety of provisions, the most high-profile being a ban on smoking in public places in England and Wales.
- Corporate Manslaughter and Corporate Homicide Bill 2006–07: created a new offence allowing individuals to be convicted if a breach of an organization's duty of care resulted in a person's death.
- Further Education and Training Bill 2006–07: restructured the Learning and Skills Council, and created powers for further education institutions to award foundation degrees.
- Employment Bill 2007–08: contained a range of provisions on employment law, including enforcement of the national minimum wage and resolution of employment disputes.
- Saving Gateway Accounts Bill 2008–09: established the 'saving gateway', a scheme to encourage people on lower incomes to save.
- Energy Bill 2009–10: included measures to support carbon capture and storage, reduce energy bills for the most vulnerable and increase the powers of the industry regulator.

2010–12 session (Conservative/Liberal Democrat coalition government)

- Budget Responsibility and National Audit Bill 2010–11: established the new Office of Budget Responsibility.
- Identity Documents Bill 2010: abolished the identity cards scheme and national identity register.
- Savings Accounts and Health in Pregnancy Grant Bill 2010: abolished the saving gateway, and also the Labour government's child trust fund and health in pregnancy grant.
- Public Bodies Bill 2010–11: provided the framework to allow the government to abolish or merge numerous public bodies (commonly known as 'quangos').
- Welfare Reform Bill 2011–12: substantially restructured the benefits system.

would count all those amendments that ultimately made it into the bill, including through proposals from a different actor at a later stage (most likely a government minister). Both versions of success were recorded. This enabled us to see how many amendments proposed by non-government actors helped to bring about legislative change, and what proportion of government-sponsored changes were in fact provoked by opposition and backbench peers. Some summary data on these questions are included in Tables 7.1 and 7.2.

The tables give us some important indications of how the legislative process in the House of Lords works. An initial indication of where peers focus their attention is provided by the figures on time spent at each legislative stage. We see that the largest proportion of time is devoted to the committee stage, with some report stages also being quite lengthy. Second reading, and particularly third reading, generally take up less time.

Across all 12 bills there were 2,384 amendments proposed. The majority of these (1,496, or 63%) were at committee stage, and almost all of the remainder at report stage. This broadly mirrors how time was spent. However, a comfortable majority of the 498 amendments that were actually made (331, or 66%) occurred at the report stage, and far fewer at committee stage or third reading. Of those amendments made, 439 (88%) were proposed in the name of ministers—a similar but slightly lower figure than those cited for the 2008–9 and 2010–12 sessions.[4] In total there were 59 non-government amendments made, 50 of which resulted from defeat (once amendments 'consequential' to defeat are included: see next paragraph). Some of these were subsequently overturned during ping-pong. In only nine cases (two on the Health Bill, one on Corporate Manslaughter, one on Further Education and Training, and five on Public Bodies) were entirely non-government amendments accepted consensually, without a minister adding their name as co-sponsor.

So, consistent with the publicly available sessional statistics, the great majority of those amendments passed are promoted in the name of ministers. But a closer scrutiny of the content of amendments, and how those proposed by different peers relate to each other, allows us to understand better whether government really dominates. One key factor is that many government amendments do not have much legislative substance. Some are simply 'tidying up' measures, to correct errors in drafting, or are clarificatory, to ensure that the wording in the bill can be better understood. In addition, the amendments which have real policy substance will often be presented in a package with a number of 'consequential' amendments, also necessary for tidying up (e.g. if a definition is changed in one clause, this may require various other clauses referring to it to be reworded). Defining which amendments fall into each category can be somewhat subjective, but the distinction between substantive and non-substantive amendments is commonly made by scholars conducting such analyses (e.g. Kreppel 1999; Maurer 2003; Shephard and Cairney 2005).[5] Once drafting, clarificatory and consequential amendments are excluded, we are left with the number of government amendments that have actual policy substance. On the 12 bills there were only 130 such examples, representing 30% of all government amendments made. On some bills—for example, Health, and Further Education and Training—a large number of government 'tidying up' amendments were made to improve drafting. In others, such as Welfare Reform, non-substantive amendments were largely consequential.

The next important question is how frequently government amendments of substance responded to pressures from others in parliament, rather than being purely at government's own initiative. The tables show how many implemented a policy change very similar to that called for in amendments that had already been proposed by non-government peers (i.e. government backbenchers, opposition or non-party peers). In total, 72 substantive government amendments across the 12 bills (55% of the total) could be traced in this way.[6] Beyond this, a further three amendments on the bills that began in the House of Commons could similarly be traced to non-government amendments proposed there (and which had not been picked up in amendments by non-government peers). In addition, 12 substantive government amendments (as well as various less substantive ones) could be traced to recommendations from parliamentary committees (particularly the Delegated Powers and Regulatory Reform Committee (DPRRC), as discussed later).[7] This leaves only 43 government amendments of substance (33% of the total, and 10% of successful government amendments overall) which are not clearly traceable to parliamentary pressure. Even here there were often other factors besides government's own desire to change policy. For example, some amendments on the Public Bodies Bill were needed to accommodate changes resulting from the recent referendum in Wales on giving greater legislative power to the National Assembly, and others followed pressure from the devolved administrations. In fact, in only a small number of cases did government appear to simply change its own policy due to a change of heart.

If we take 2008–09 as a 'typical' one-year session and estimate that 30% of the agreed government amendments were substantive, this suggests that roughly 500 government amendments of substance are agreed to in the Lords in any one year. But if 55% of those (as in our sample) respond to amendments from other peers, these peers' amendments probably result in around 280 substantive changes each year. We would then expect another 12% (or around 58) to result from other pressures, from MPs or parliamentary

Table 7.1. Key data on eight bills starting in the Commons

	Identity Cards	Health	Corporate Manslaughter	Saving Gateway	Energy	Identity Documents	Savings Accounts	Welfare	Total (all eight bills)
Session(s)	2005–06	2005–06	2005–07	2008–09	2009–10	2010–12	2010–12	2010–12	n/a
Length (pages) at Commons introduction	47	92	20	17	31	16	6	175	n/a
Time (hours: minutes) spent in Lords at:									
- second reading	06:42	04:12	04:22	01:29	03:13	02:03	03:02	07:30	32:33
- committee	34:53	21:12	12:57	05:49	00:00	03:33	00:00	63:53	142:17
- report	17:02	07:30	05:07	01:30	00:00	01:56	00:00	35:10	68:15
- third reading	02:51	01:09	00:32	00:01	00:00	00:01	00:00	02:54	07:28
Total amendments proposed in Lords	513	205	154	68	9	26	0	632	1607
- proposed (and made) at committee stage	316 (1)	137 (10)	99 (3)	49 (3)	9 (9)	20 (0)	0 (0)	373 (45)	1003 (71)
- proposed (and made) at report stage	176 (58)	57 (39)	53 (32)	19 (5)	0 (0)	6 (1)	0 (0)	244 (59)	555 (194)
- proposed (and made) at third reading	21 (15)	11 (9)	2 (0)	0 (0)	0 (0)	0 (0)	0 (0)	15 (11)	49 (35)
Total amendments made in Lords	74	58	35	8	9	1	0	115	300
- Non-government amendments made	19	2	5	0	0	1	n/a	13	40
- Government amendments made	55	56	30	8	9	0	n/a	102	260
Government substantive amendments made	17	6	5	4	5	0	n/a	35	72
- traceable to other peers' amendments	12	4	3	3	0	0	n/a	16	38

- traceable to MPs' amendments (only)	0	1	0	1	0	n/a	n/a	1	3
- traceable to committees (only)	4	0	1	0	5	n/a	n/a	0	10
- none of the above	1	1	1	0	0	n/a	n/a	18	21
Total Lords amendments traceable to Commons	164	54	74	39	5	10	n/a	205	551
Divisions	15	4	2	0	0	1	0	14	36
Lords defeats	8	0	1	0	0	1	0	8	18
Number of insistences (i.e. rounds)	4	0	4	0	0	0	0	1	n/a

Source: Author's own research (based on *Hansard*, etc) for amendments, divisions and defeats; Journal Office for time spent.

Definitions:

- All figures exclude amendments and divisions during ping-pong (i.e. at LCCA). Hence, defeats are the same as 'unique defeats' in Chapter 6. Figures for 'amendments proposed' include those withdrawn prior to debate (so do not match Public Bill Office figures on all bills).
- Consistent with Public Bill Office data, government amendments are those including a government minister as a signatory, even if not first signatory. In four cases on the Welfare Reform Bill, one case on the Further Education and Training Bill and 14 cases on the Public Bodies Bill (Table 7.2) ministers added their names to amendments where the first signatory was a non-government peer, and which were agreed.
- Substantive amendments exclude those that are typographical, consequential and clarificatory.
- Traceable to amendments by others in the Lords means an amendment to achieve a similar policy aim was tabled by a non-government peer at the same or a previous legislative stage (including in those cases where a minister subsequently added their name). Traceable to MPs refers to non-government MPs only, and only where there is no relevant non-government amendment in the Lords. Traceable to committees is only where there were no prior non-government amendments in either chamber.
- Traceable to Commons means an amendment to achieve a very similar policy aim was tabled during the bill's Commons stages.
- Note that an individual defeat may include several amendments, particularly due to consequential amendments. Defeats are included in 'amendments made', but some were subsequently overturned.

Table 7.2. Key data on four bills starting in the Lords (and totals for all 12 bills)

	Further Education and Training	Employment	Budget Responsibility	Public Bodies	Total (all four bills)	Grand total (all 12 bills)
Session	2006–07	2007–08	2010–12	2010–12	n/a	n/a
Length (pages) at introduction	30	23	44	30	n/a	n/a
Time (hours: minutes) spent in Lords						
- second reading	04:55	03:38	02:41	08:37	19:51	52:24
- committee	06:48	13:07	08:46	45:25	74:06	216:23
- report	03:49	03:50	01:50	17:51	27:20	95:35
- third reading	00:38	01:16	00:04	03:17	05:15	12:43
Total amendments proposed in Lords	148	91	59	479	777	2,384
- proposed (and made) at committee stage	72 (3)	43 (3)	44 (0)	334 (39)	493 (45)	1,496 (116)
- proposed (and made) at report stage	66 (44)	38 (16)	15 (10)	135 (67)	254 (137)	809 (331)
- proposed (and made) at third reading	10 (8)	10 (4)	0 (0)	10 (4)	30 (16)	79 (51)
Total amendments made in Lords	55	23	10	110	198	498
- Non-government amendments made	3	0	0	16	19	59
- Government amendments made	52	23	10	94	179	439
Government substantive amendments made	8	5	6	39	58	130
- traceable to other peers' amendments	6	3	6	19	34	72
- traceable to MPs' amendments (only)	n/a	n/a	n/a	n/a	n/a	3
- traceable to committees (only)	2	0	0	0	2	12
- none of the above	0	2	0	20	22	43
Divisions	1	1	0	16	18	54
Lords defeats	1	0	0	4	5	23
Number of insistences (i.e. rounds)	1	n/a	n/a	0	n/a	n/a
Total Lords amendments continued in Commons	38	25	17	97	177	n/a

Source: see Table 7.1.
Definitions: see Table 7.1.

committees. In all, perhaps only 165 government amendments of substance are made per year that do not result from prior parliamentary pressure.

In terms of what actually changed, the tables give us some indication of how this differed by bill, and demonstrate significant variation. The Public Bodies Bill, Welfare Reform Bill and Identity Cards Bill were clearly the most controversial, as demonstrated by the amount of debating time that they took up. These bills were subject to many hundreds of attempted amendments, and several defeats. They also had the largest number of substantive government amendments made under pressure. Examples of these are given later, but it was the Public Bodies Bill where the negotiated outcomes were most important (and changed the bill quite fundamentally). There were a handful of negotiated amendments to most other bills. The Health Bill and Corporate Manslaughter Bill both saw many amendments proposed, but relatively few government amendments made that responded to peers. The Health Bill had been subject to significant changes in the Commons, as discussed later, while significant concessions occurred on the Corporate Manslaughter Bill following defeat (see Chapter 6). Some bills saw very few amendments. In two cases this was due to special circumstances: the Energy Bill arrived in the Lords shortly before the 2010 general election, and was rushed through under 'wash-up' procedures; the Savings Accounts and Health in Pregnancy Grant Bill was certified as a money bill, so had most of its stages taken formally in the Lords and was subject to no amendments. Both of these caused some frustrations among peers, some of whom had hoped to press changes.[8] Finally, Labour's Saving Gateway Accounts Bill and the coalition's Identity Documents Bill proved relatively uncontroversial.

A final key question is how much this situation differs from the past. Despite the earlier studies conducted, it is difficult to draw meaningful comparisons. Drewry and Brock (1993) indicate that in the 1988–89 session there were 2,359 amendments passed to government bills. These are not broken down by origin, but we can assume that most were government amendments. Among the eight bills analysed in greater detail by Miers and Brock (1993), there were 1,226 amendments made, of which just 65 (5%) were proposed by non-government peers. This is a significantly higher number of amendments (though lower proportion of non-government amendments agreed) than on our post-1999 bills. Miers and Brock did not attempt to quantify the number of government amendments that responded to earlier suggestions from non-government peers, but their discussion does make clear that this happened fairly frequently. However, they also demonstrate that the government amended its own legislation substantially as a result of incomplete drafting or changes in policy direction, as discussed in the conclusion to this chapter.

Government handling of bills in the Lords

The patterns found in the quantitative analysis can be illustrated by looking at some examples, as discussed later. But looking at government's prior preparation of legislation is also important to understanding this process. The fact that government can readily be defeated in the Lords requires ministers to prepare carefully for introducing legislation into the chamber, and then to negotiate it through with sensitivity and skill. This is a very different matter to navigating legislation through the House of Commons, where the government can rely far more on its partisan majority. In the Lords it has no such majority, and attendance at votes can be unpredictable. In addition, while many MPs focus largely on the big political picture, and are prepared to leave their frontbench to get the detail right, in the Lords there are many peers—often subject specialists—who pride themselves in focusing on the nitty-gritty of legislative drafting.

Government strategies for dealing with the Lords begin long before a bill is formally introduced. Before 1997 the Conservative Chief Whip simply attended the cabinet committee overseeing the legislative programme (which is chaired by the Leader of the House of Commons), and advised on any likely difficulties in the Lords as a bill was in preparation.[9] When Labour entered office, consideration of Lords 'handling' was made much more formal, and more demanding for government departments. Given the potential for difficulties in the still Conservative-dominated chamber, Labour Chief Whip Denis Carter introduced a requirement that the civil service bill team preparing the legislation should write a 'Lords handling strategy' and submit this for scrutiny to the cabinet committee. Over time, the process became increasingly elaborate. By 2012 the government's *Guide to Making Legislation* required a handling strategy for both chambers to be submitted, with indications of 'which areas are likely to be contentious, based on an awareness of the mood of the House', and of members 'likely to take a particular interest and what engagement with them is planned', plus details of 'possible concessions and fallback positions' (Cabinet Office 2012: 128–9). The Lords handling strategy was policed primarily by the Lords whips' office, which would advise and help with its preparation. In the 2005 parliament the whips' office created a 'handbook' for departments entitled *Getting Your Bill through the Lords*. The development of this system may help in part to explain why the number of defeats declined in the 2005 parliament (see Figure 6.1).

Once a bill is published, a regular part of the handling strategy, developed by Labour but continued under the coalition, is holding open consultation meetings with peers. Ministers often call a meeting before the bill's second reading, to which all peers are invited and at which they can raise any questions and concerns. These meetings are of particular use to Crossbenchers, as government and opposition parties will have private briefings about their group's line to take on the bill. Another practice introduced by Labour was for ministers to offer to attend the Crossbench weekly meeting and answer questions on their bill; this likewise continued under the coalition. Practice varies, depending on the bill's level of controversy and also on individual ministerial style. Some ministers, for example, hold open meetings before each committee day in the Lords, as well as before second reading. In some cases a Secretary of State from the Commons will address peers, while in others this will be left to Lords ministers. An analysis of the Crossbenchers' weekly mailing from February 2003 to May 2008 indicated that ministers held at least 89 open consultation meetings with peers on bills over these five years. No similar system of cross-party consultation exists in the Commons.

From the early stages of a bill in the Lords there will also be consultation with certain individual peers, who talk privately to ministers and often civil servants on the bill team as well. Again this kind of discussion would be unusual in the Commons, except within the confines of party groups. Some ministers will invite their opposition opposite numbers, in particular, to engage in such discussions. As one opposition frontbencher put it, a canny Lords minister will approach their shadow saying something like 'I'm so pleased to hear that you are leading on this bill—can we have a chat?'. If such a meeting takes place, often before second reading, the minister will ask 'which bits of the bill most concern you?'. This can help neutralize tensions, and allow ministers to start thinking through any compromises that may be necessary. No exact parallel exists in terms of consultation with Crossbenchers, given that they have no frontbenchers with particular policy portfolios. But in the second half of the 2005 parliament this group started to appoint 'liaison peers' on each bill, and also began routinely to circulate the contact details for the civil service bill team more widely among its members. Although the Crossbenchers' lack of a collective line means that liaison peers cannot set policy, they can at least act as a conduit: reporting back to colleagues and giving some indication to the government of where group members' concerns may lie. Some consultations even go on with opposition party backbenchers. One such peer, who entered the Lords after more than 20 years as an MP, recalled being 'gobsmacked' by the level of access that he had to ministers.

Despite the initial discussions, it is once a bill has actually begun its passage that the detail really begins to be discussed in earnest. As further outlined later, second reading allows peers to put on the record their response to the bill's principles, and to publicly outline any areas of concern. Then at committee stage amendments can be tabled, and these are used to structure debate. As one former opposition frontbencher put it 'negotiation starts as soon as you table the amendment at committee stage'. Such negotiation takes place in public, across the floor of the House, but also behind the scenes between peers, ministers and civil servants. The minister must respond formally to every amendment debated and will thus indicate to peers the government's view on the points raised. Sometimes ministerial assurances are all that is required to persuade the sponsor to withdraw their amendment. At other times they may consider the minister's explanation inadequate, and wish to press the point. In order to avoid a division (which will at a minimum waste time, and at worst result in a defeat), the minister will often offer to go away and think about the peer's amendment, after which further behind-the-scenes discussions may take place. Occasionally, the government even comes forward with its own amendment simultaneously at committee stage, to respond to the points made. But this kind of action more commonly occurs later—which explains why a far higher proportion of amendments are made at report stage.

The period between committee and report stages is therefore a key time for discussions between government and any peers who feel that their questions have not been adequately resolved. Ministers may then table amendments at report stage to respond to a peer's concerns, either with or without private discussion having taken place. Occasionally, non-government peers (including opposition frontbenchers) will actually be consulted on the wording of government amendments, to ensure that their concerns have been met. Even more occasionally—since all amendments may be signed by several peers—the agreed amendment will be tabled in the name of the non-government peer, with a minister as supplementary signatory to indicate the government's assent. Indeed, there are normally only four signatories allowed, but an exception exists in standing orders for when the fifth signatory is the minister sponsoring the bill.

If this process of negotiation is not resolved between committee and report stages, the same dynamic applies between report stage and third reading. Hence a non-government amendment may be proposed again at report stage, and the minister invited to go away and think about the issue. If the government appears hostile to the amendment, a vote (and possible defeat) is much more likely at this point. To avoid it, the minister may promise to reconsider, and perhaps even explicitly promise to bring forward an amendment at third reading. According to the *Companion to Standing Orders*, most outstanding matters should be resolved at report stage, but third reading amendments are specifically allowed 'to enable the government to fulfil undertakings given at earlier stages of the bill' (House of Lords 2010: 153).

Should peers not be satisfied with the government's response at this final point they can again try to inflict a defeat.

Before turning to some examples to illustrate this process further, some general points are worth noting. First, it is rare for the government (in either chamber) to actually accept a non-government amendment in its original form—as demonstrated by the tiny number of non-government amendments agreed consensually on the 12 bills. Ministers generally prefer to come back with an amendment of their own, even if this has an identical policy effect. This is in part because parliamentary counsel (the lawyers responsible for drafting government bills) want to ensure that the amendment is absolutely technically correct. It is also partly to allow the Lords minister to consult with other colleagues, including ministers in the Commons. The other important point to note is that, as the discussion about Lords handling strategies indicated, ministers may have been prepared from the start to concede some ground on the bill. They are far less likely to give concessions in the Commons, given that votes there can be more easily won, so it makes sense to save these up for the Lords (often much to the irritation of MPs). In this sense, the House of Lords' influence may look slightly exaggerated, and cannot be wholly separated from that exerted by the Commons.

Six modes of Lords legislative debate

The previous discussion has provided some generic indications of how government treats legislation in the Lords, and particularly the extent to which negotiation goes on behind the scenes. This section instead focuses principally on the public aspects of legislative decision-making, and the different types of debate that often take place on bills in the Lords. In doing so it suggests that there are six different 'modes' of legislative debate, each of which is illustrated with examples. They are, respectively, 'probing' mode, 'quasi academic' (expert) mode, 'interest group' mode, 'constitutional propriety' mode, 'second thought' mode and 'adversarial' mode.

As with any classification that tries to impose an artificial structure on complex real-world phenomena, this scheme is certainly not perfect. The six modes of debate are not mutually exclusive, and there is a distinct blurring between their boundaries, as we shall see. Others familiar with the Lords might suggest any number of different modes not included here.[10] But it is hoped that these six will help to illustrate some of the most important ways in which the chamber's legislative influence can work.

Probing mode

It makes sense to start with probing mode, because this applies particularly at the early stages of the legislative process, most notably in committee. This is the stage when, in the words of one peer, you can 'let a thousand flowers bloom', and move amendments to explore every aspect of the bill. Because the committee and report stage are structured around amendments, these provide the framework for debate on the detail of the bill. As seen in Tables 7.1 and 7.2, nearly two-thirds of amendments proposed to the 12 case study bills in the Lords were at committee stage, and this also takes up the largest share of time on those bills. However, only 8% of amendments in committee went on to be agreed, and these made up just 23% of agreed amendments overall.

There are various reasons for moving committee stage amendments. Some may be targeted directly at getting the government to change the bill, but others are simply 'probing': to explore the government's intent, and to get ministers to explain their policy on the record. Hence, an individual peer (and particularly opposition frontbenchers) will sometimes move amendments that are, as one peer suggested, 'wildly contradictory'. Voting on amendments is less common in committee than at report stage (for figures, see Table 6.1), and indeed when bills are taken in grand committee divisions are not permitted. The purpose of many amendments is therefore simply a kind of 'stress testing', to see whether the government's policy can stand up to scrutiny. Some probing amendments suggest the deletion of entire clauses or parts of the bill: these may look radical, but often, as one peer said, 'you simply move an amendment to get the minister to explain'. A typical probing amendment was Conservative frontbencher Sheila Noakes' proposed deletion of a subsection in the Saving Gateway Accounts Bill specifying that the scheme would be administered by Her Majesty's Revenue & Customs (HMRC). In debate, she sought to explore why responsibility had not been given to the Department for Work and Pensions instead. Having heard the minister's response, she withdrew her amendment and it was not pursued at later stages. Since it may not be the mover's intent that their amendment is inserted into the bill, figures demonstrating the number of non-government amendments that 'fail' can be misleading. Many of these were never really intended to pass.

The probing process occurs in the Commons as well, again largely in committee. Here, it is more often partisan, and the committee stage is strictly timetabled (with the result that often not all clauses will be discussed). Another difference is that any member may participate in the committee stage in the Lords, so various experts can materialize to question the minister on their areas of interest. As one Liberal Democrat peer who previously served for decades in the Commons put it, Lords consideration of legislation has 'a totally different mindset', where people are 'genuinely interested in what each other are saying'. Ministers can often appreciate this scrutiny by peers. As one suggested, 'you're bound to have areas where when fresh eyes look at it a bill can be improved'.

There are some particular reasons for getting government statements on the record, beyond straightforward explanation. One motive is partisan: to get ministers to spell out a policy that the opposition believes to be unpopular, or to later be able to say 'I told you so'. But another is strictly legal. Since the landmark *Pepper* v *Hart* decision of 1993, it has been possible for courts to use ministerial statements in *Hansard* to interpret legislation, as an indication of government intent (Bennion 2008). So again, a peer's objective may not be to get an amendment into the bill, but instead to get a ministerial statement about how the detail should be interpreted. The wording of such statements is sometimes negotiated privately in advance between ministers and non-government peers. This occurred, for example, on the Public Bodies Bill, over the rights of employees in bodies whose functions were to be merged. Attaining such on-the-record statements is an example of largely immeasurable legislative impact, as no amendments are made.

Quasi academic (expert) mode

This next mode is not entirely separate from probing, but occurs when many of those contributing to the debate (again particularly at committee, but also later stages) are respected experts in their fields. Sometimes, as peers are keen to point out, their collective expertise will exceed that of the civil servants who commissioned the legislation. Given the chamber's reputation, this could be seen as one of its classic operating modes. At times, though certainly not all of the time, its debates can be more akin to an academic seminar than to partisan debates held in other legislative chambers. This mode can occur particularly on bills first introduced in the House of Lords—in part because they have not yet been subject to partisan debate in the Commons, so are relatively unexplored, and in part because they are often less controversial.

The most obvious example among the case study bills occurred on the Budget Responsibility and National Audit Bill, fulfilling the coalition government's pledge to create a new Office of Budget Responsibility (OBR). This was to be an arm's-length body, charged with producing independent economic forecasts for the public finances. Its creation followed concerns that political control of Treasury forecasts had masked the looming budget deficit under Gordon Brown. The bill was relatively uncontroversial, as Labour did not fundamentally oppose the plans. Many peers commented on how, during debate on the bill, 'even by House of Lords standards, everyone was an expert'. The new minister, James Sassoon, had a background in financial services and at the Treasury, but was only ennobled in 2010. At all stages he faced a group of members described as 'quite formidable' and as having 'incredibly serious CVs'. John Eatwell, a professor of economics, led for the Labour frontbench. Active Labour backbenchers included Maurice Peston (also an economics professor), Joel Barnett (a former Chief Secretary to the Treasury) and Paul Myners (who was a Treasury minister during the financial crisis, having joined the government following decades in the financial sector). Others contributing included Crossbenchers Terry Burns and Andrew Turnbull (both former Permanent Secretaries at the Treasury), and Conservative Terence Higgins (a former chair of the House of Commons Treasury Committee).

Given that there was little disagreement over the principle of the bill, debate focused on the detail of the proposed arrangements, and issues such as how the new body's independence could be assured. There was much behind-the-scenes discussion, and all six of the substantive government amendments made responded to points from others. These largely came from Lord Eatwell, with similar issues having been raised by Lords Higgins and Peston. Although the bill didn't fundamentally change, the debates were widely seen as useful and constructive. One government insider commented that 'the fact that there was really serious scrutiny . . . by people of the highest economic and academic standing' meant that 'issues about . . . the independence of the OBR were given as thorough a testing as they possibly could have'. He concluded that 'as a consequence we got a better bill'.

Similar expert debates can be seen on some of the other case study bills. For example, contributors on the Further Education and Training Bill included numerous peers with university connections. Key amendments were moved by the respected Crossbencher Ron Dearing, who had chaired a government review into higher education in the 1990s, and Labour backbencher Diana Warwick, Chief Executive of Universities UK (the organization representing university vice chancellors). Six government amendments responded to these—for example, tightening up arrangements for the franchising of foundation degrees. The same happened to amendments by Labour backbenchers Bill Wedderburn and Muriel Turner on the Employment Bill, to ensure that those made subject to 'fast track' dispute resolution had given their consent. Wedderburn, an academic lawyer who helped draft Labour's employment legislation in the 1970s, was variously described by interviewees as 'formidable', 'very brilliant' and somebody who 'changed the world as far as labour law was concerned'. Yet some were less complimentary, suggesting that he had a mindset from 'the days of Michael Foot and a different sort of Labour'. This nicely illustrates how one person's expert can be another person's 'ex-expert', and the Lords' strength in this regard is disputed. But unarguably the chamber does include many employment specialists, including former senior trade union officials and industry figures.

Interest group mode

While there is clearly much expertise inside the Lords itself, the chamber also enjoys particularly close relationships with outside specialist groups. Many peers have paid or unpaid connections with such bodies, including companies, public sector organizations and charitable or 'third sector' groups. Other peers simply rely on such bodies for information and research, in the absence of funds to employ their own staff (see Chapter 4). One common means of contact with outside organizations is through specialist 'all-party parliamentary groups' (APPGs); these also include MPs among their membership, but peers are often more active given their lack of both research resources and constituency pressures. Many such groups have a specialist secretariat provided by an outside body—for example, the APPG on child protection is supported by the NSPCC and the APPG on food and drink manufacturing by the Food and Drink Federation (an industry group).[11] Wyn Grant (2000), an academic specialist on pressure groups, notes how the Lords became a target during the Thatcher years, due to the weakness of the Commons opposition, and greater openness of peers. This trend has almost certainly continued, as many outside groups realize that the lack of a government majority in the Lords, and the presence of Crossbench and relatively independent-minded party peers, create a better chance of influencing legislation than in the Commons.

When it comes to legislation, most outside groups will already have engaged with the government department sponsoring the bill—for example, through responding to earlier consultations. But parliament offers a last chance to influence policy, when ministers have to defend their decisions in a public setting. This can be seen as part of the 'stress testing' referred to earlier. A frontbencher suggested that 'part of your job in the Lords in opposition is to be a mouthpiece for legitimate outside organizations'. And the groups prioritized by peers can be slightly different to those chosen by MPs. One peer felt that 'the price of being in this unelected place is that I have a duty to stick up for the people who are really unpopular', such as 'travellers, asylum seekers, people with mental health problems'. Organizations such as Liberty (which campaigns on civil liberties) and Nacro (which supports ex-offenders) have many advocates in the chamber.

But peers interact with a wide multitude of groups. On the Welfare Reform Bill, for example, groups lobbying the Lords included Citizens Advice, the Children's Society, CarersUK, Disability Rights UK, Women's Aid and Macmillan Cancer Relief. On the Further Education and Training Bill, they included Universities UK and the Association of Colleges (which on the franchising of foundation degrees were pushing in opposite directions). On the Health Bill, interested groups included the British Medical Association (BMA), Royal College of Nursing, Royal Pharmaceutical Society, individual pharmaceutical companies, and both pro- and anti-smoking groups. Some organizations will draft amendments for peers, or help with preparing their speeches, but more often peers will do this themselves based on briefings from trusted groups. Groups (particularly those which are better resourced) will then lobby other peers to attend and support specific amendments.

The nature of external pressure on parliament is clearly changing, as illustrated by one high-profile issue on the Public Bodies Bill. The original bill contained provisions that would have allowed the government to sell off a large amount of public forestry land. This caused a public outcry and new bodies sprang up, such as 'Save Our Forests', which could quickly establish an internet presence and generate thousands of supporters via social media. The more general web-based lobby organization, '38 degrees' (which also campaigned on the coalition's Health and Social Care Bill), was likewise very active on the issue, which was extremely high-profile in the mainstream media as well. A large number of amendments were moved by the Labour frontbench, as well as key backbenchers, including Liberal Democrat Tony Greaves (co-chair of the party's parliamentary committee on environment, food and rural affairs) and Labour's David Clark (a former chair of the Forestry Commission). Under huge pressure, the government ultimately dropped the issue of forestry completely from the bill. Outside groups had encouraged their supporters to target peers, who were inundated with messages. This raises questions about how peers will cope in an environment where more and more outside lobby attention may come to focus on the Lords. Peers not only face resource issues, they also cannot easily limit their attention to residents of just one area of the country, as MPs routinely do. But this example also illustrates something else important about parliamentary influence: that this cannot easily be separated from influence by outside groups. Indeed, the outside pressure on government in this case was such that it might well have backed down even without peers' intervention.

Constitutional propriety mode

The Lords' particular interest in constitutional propriety was already seen in Chapter 6. The chamber has had this reputation since at least the 1980s, when it, for example, challenged Margaret Thatcher's legislation to abolish the Greater London Council (Shell 1992). The interest is based in part on many members' legal expertise, so could be seen as a special case of 'quasi academic' mode. But protection of due process and constitutionality is a responsibility felt widely amongst peers, and is not just confined to experts. As Chapter 6 demonstrated, challenging the government over constitutional propriety can often be adversarial; equally it may sometimes simply be probing. However, this is such an important and common mode for the Lords that it merits a category of its own. As one peer put it, the chamber 'can be influential and is disproportionately influential on issues around governance, conflicts of interest, liberties, Henry VIII clauses: i.e. unlimited powers, inadequate scrutiny, inadequate review, inadequate sunsetting'.

One of the commonest kinds of legislative change sought by peers is amendment to delegated powers. Many bills contain provisions allowing ministers to change policy in future without needing fresh primary legislation, by way of 'secondary' or 'delegated' legislation, which will be subject to limited parliamentary oversight. In practice, it is the Lords to a large extent that polices such delegation, and asks for changes when it believes that ministers are going too far. This scrutiny is greatly aided by the Lords DPRRC. More general constitutional oversight is also facilitated by the Joint Committee on Human Rights (JCHR) and the Lords Constitution Committee. All three of these committees (as described in Chapter 8) highlight constitutional shortcomings in legislation, and suggest changes. Their recommendations are often keenly taken up by peers.

Most of the case study bills saw some amendment to delegated powers. The Identity Cards Bill in its original form contained numerous such powers, and changes to these accounted for almost all of the amendments made in the Lords. The most far-reaching example was the clause (referred to in Chapter 6) allowing the government to turn the scheme from a voluntary to a compulsory one by delegated legislation. This was criticized by the Constitution Committee in particular, and removed after a defeat. Following pressure from the Conservative and Liberal Democrat frontbench the government made eight further such changes through its own amendments, while another three substantive government amendments (as well as numerous less substantive ones) responded directly to the DPRRC. Likewise, on the Welfare

Reform Bill, eight of the substantive government amendments made changes to delegated powers, following amendments from Liberal Democrat backbencher Mike German (co-chair of the party's parliamentary committee on work and pensions) and earlier DPRRC recommendations. Even the Energy Bill, whose consideration was greatly curtailed due to wash-up, was amended by the government at Lords committee stage following DPRRC recommendations. Changes included introducing requirements for parliamentary approval of future alterations to the definition of fuel poverty, and requiring the Secretary of State to table an explanatory memorandum to parliament if alterations were made.

Other changes to the bills followed recommendations from the Constitution Committee and the JCHR. An example of the latter can be found on the Employment Bill. One part of the bill sought to allow trade unions to exclude members belonging to extremist political parties. This followed a ruling in the European Court of Human Rights (*ASLEF* v *UK*), upholding a union's right to expel a BNP member—despite UK law until then having forbidden discrimination on grounds of party membership. In response, the government proposed simply to remove the previous legal exemption. At Lords committee stage Anthony Lester, a renowned human rights lawyer and member of the JCHR, tabled an amendment to replace this with a more limited right to expel. His proposal gained support in debate from both the Liberal Democrat and Conservative frontbench, but was withdrawn to allow ministers to reconsider. The JCHR subsequently suggested that the bill as it stood could breach an individual's right to freedom of association. At third reading, a government amendment essentially accepting Lord Lester's formulation was tabled and agreed.

Although there were pressures on nearly all of the case study bills on constitutional propriety grounds, the most far-reaching were on the Public Bodies Bill. Chapter 6 described the defeat, again sponsored by Lord Lester, which wrote protection of bodies with judicial and human rights functions into the bill. This was urged on peers by David Pannick, another highly regarded lawyer and a member of the Constitution Committee, and resulted in a package of government amendments to implement the proposal. But peers' constitutional objections went far further than this, and highly critical reports had been published by all three of the committees mentioned previously. Of particular concern were the various 'Henry VIII' clauses in the bill, which would allow the government to change primary legislation in future via secondary legislation. The most extreme example was a long list of bodies in schedule 7 of the bill which could be moved onto the list for abolition or merger by future ministerial order. Following widespread protest, and amendments from government backbenchers and Labour frontbenchers alike, the minister responsible for the bill added his name to an amendment led by Conservative backbencher Philip Norton (a former chair of the Constitution Committee) which deleted the schedule and thus removed this power altogether. The minister also added his support to a Labour frontbench amendment to insert a 'sunset clause', so that the eligibility of all bodies for abolition or merger would lapse after five years. Other government amendments (particularly following DPRRC complaints pursued in earlier amendments by various peers) significantly tightened up arrangements for orders abolishing or merging bodies, including requiring greater parliamentary oversight and public consultation. All of these major changes were achieved by negotiation, rather than defeat, although the threat of defeat was ever present.

Second thought mode

Obviously a classic function of second chambers is to provide a forum for 'second thought'. There are various ways in which this manifests itself in the Lords on bills that were first introduced in the Commons. Three of them are following up unfinished business from Commons debate, scrutinizing elements of the bill that were overlooked by MPs, and scrutinizing material introduced during Commons consideration of the bill. Each is here discussed in turn.

Dealing with unfinished business from the Commons is perhaps the most frequent form of second thought. As demonstrated in Table 7.1, policy concerns first raised by MPs often continue to be discussed in the Lords, and may well be resolved there. In total, at least 551 of the 1,607 amendments proposed in the Lords on Commons bills (i.e. 34%) followed very similar proposals made in amendments by MPs. Peers can sometimes extract concessions that were not previously forthcoming, as the combined forces of the opposition parties (or Labour plus Crossbenchers since 2010) can threaten defeat in a way not possible in the first chamber. Lords opposition frontbenchers frequently pursue points already raised in the Commons, and sometimes win. For example, on the Corporate Manslaughter Bill, there was pressure from the Conservative frontbench in the Commons to extend the provisions of the bill to unincorporated associations. These amendments were resisted, but government conceded the point to the Conservative frontbench in the Lords. Likewise, on the coalition's Welfare Reform Bill, the Labour frontbench in the Commons had pushed for a change to the eligibility requirements for recipients of the new 'personal independence payment' (which replaced disability living allowance). But only when similar proposals were made by Liberal Democrat backbencher Celia Thomas in the Lords did the government concede.

Generally, it takes further Lords pressure to extract government concessions on points previously raised in the Commons; but occasionally ministers table amendments voluntarily in order to honour commitments given to MPs. If proposals are made in the Commons that the government considers sensible, there may not be time to draft changes before the bill leaves that chamber. On these occasions, the Lords provides a second chance, as occurred on the Saving Gateway Accounts Bill, where government backbench MP Stephen Ladyman had proposed that recipients of Carer's Allowance should be made eligible for the scheme. In response, at Commons report, the minister stated that he was 'certainly minded to table an amendment for consideration' in the Lords.[12] At Lords committee stage, a government amendment was duly passed to extend the scheme as Ladyman had proposed.

It is also common for peers to pick up points that were overlooked during Commons consideration of a bill. Typical examples include the kind of technical changes to delegated powers outlined earlier. But peers also routinely complain that 'programming' in the Commons means that some clauses go unscrutinized in that chamber due to lack of time. There is some truth in this, though the Commons actually spends more hours debating most bills than does the Lords. The important difference is that time-wasting tactics are used much less in the second chamber, at least in part because non-government peers have a greater chance of getting their proposals accepted. The Commons also spends more time discussing the political 'big picture', often leaving the Lords to consider the detail.

A more unusual use of 'second thought' is for scrutiny of material introduced to a bill during its Commons passage. Among the case studies, there was a particularly clear example on the Health Bill. The biggest and most controversial issue in the bill was the introduction of a ban on smoking in public places. The government had originally proposed a partial ban, exempting pubs that did not serve food and private members' clubs. This was controversial in the Commons, and MPs pressed for a total ban, successfully inserting this into the bill through a free vote at report stage. When the bill arrived in the Lords, the clauses on a total ban had therefore not yet been fully scrutinized, and the Lords stages provided an opportunity. Many probing amendments were moved, to test the government's new position. Ministers had also conceded to backbench pressure in the Commons that the legal age for buying tobacco could be raised from 16. Following a Conservative frontbench amendment at Lords committee stage, a government amendment was agreed to specify that the age would not be increased beyond 18. Another small change, again responding to a point raised by Conservative frontbencher Freddie Howe, inserted an exemption for artistic performances, so that the ban would not, for example, prevent smoking in period dramas.

There are some clear limitations on second thought mode, however. The two chambers can often work together surprisingly well, with Commons frontbench teams handing over to their Lords counterparts and explaining any 'unfinished business'. At times, coordination is patchy, depending on individual frontbenchers' style, but it is clearly becoming more formalized as the parties adjust to the Lords being an important site of political compromise. Nonetheless, it would be a mistake to see the parties as monolithic blocks across the two chambers—frontbenchers must in each case be sensitive to the opinions of their backbenchers, and must also respond to what is going on in the wider environment. This can sometimes lead to intercameral tensions. For example, on the Welfare Reform Bill, the Labour frontbench in the Lords was faced with a decision over whether to support the amendment—proposed by a bishop—on raising the cap on welfare benefits. They chose to do so, and this led to a defeat (see Chapter 6). In the Commons, the Labour frontbench took a more populist line, as the cap was known to have widespread public support. Similar tensions faced the Conservatives and Liberal Democrats when opposing the Identity Cards Bill, with peers in both parties taking a more pro-civil liberties position than their Commons frontbench. On occasions like these it can be difficult to negotiate a united party line.

Coordination among backbenchers can be particularly challenging, as intercameral backbench networks are sometimes relatively weak, though party policy committees, and connections with outside groups (including through APPGs) can help to some extent. Former MPs who join the Lords tend to maintain good Commons networks at least for some years, but these can weaken over time; many senior peers are of course from a different political generation to their Commons colleagues.

Adversarial mode

This final mode of legislative debate is more unusual, but the threat of it is always present. There is definitely less adversarialism in the Lords than in the Commons, and, in particular, far less along pure party political lines. But clearly confrontations do occur between the government and the Lords, often ending in defeat—as described in detail in Chapter 6.

Second reading is the point at which the main principles of a bill are debated, and when the opposition may make a somewhat theatrical show of suggesting why the government's position is wrong. Even on the Budget Responsibility Bill, Labour's John Eatwell at second reading described the parts of the bill setting up the OBR as a 'failure', and proposed that they should be withdrawn.[13] Nonetheless, when a bill gets into committee, as occurred in this case, discussion tends to become much more measured and consensual. Partisan attacks at second reading may be seen as relatively harmless, given that votes are generally not held at this stage. But they are also necessarily muted, in order not to alienate Crossbenchers or wreck the chances for negotiation with ministers at subsequent stages.

When such negotiations succeed, and government gives ground, any sense of adversarialism is likely to dissipate. But where concessions are not forthcoming, and a large body of peers have real concerns about a bill, it may actually grow. At committee stage, amendments by opposition frontbenchers, backbenchers and Crossbenchers are moved in a largely uncoordinated way. But at report stage these different groups will often join forces, sometimes through co-sponsored amendments. Under Labour, discussions between Conservative and Liberal Democrat frontbenchers were often intense at this point. Since 2010, Labour has instead needed to network with particular Crossbenchers, and sometimes dissenters on the government side. Hence, even when adversarial showdowns do occur at report stage and third reading, it is always necessary to demonstrate that these are not purely partisan. An obvious example was David Ramsbotham's amendment on the Corporate Manslaughter and Corporate Homicide Bill, and the ultimate resolution of conflict on the Identity Cards Bill by fellow Crossbencher Robert Armstrong (both discussed in Chapter 6). In general, peers wanting to put real pressure on government try to signal the breadth of support for their amendments as clearly as possible, through cross-party signatories. As many peers pointed out, 'the real trick is to have four names: one Conservative, one Liberal Democrat, one Crossbench and one Labour'. Indeed, one opposition frontbencher claimed that 'it's partly a signal to the government that you're not serious if you do it [only] in your own name'. Thus discussions across party lines take place all the time, between both front and backbenchers, far more than in the Commons. As one Conservative frontbencher commented on the years of Labour government, Commons colleagues 'often looked at me with incredulity when I said that I was talking actively to my Liberal Democrat counterparts and seeking agreement with them'. But in the Lords such behaviour was the norm, and essential to the opposition's success.

In 2010–12 adversarialism worked rather differently, as Labour adjusted to opposition and parliament as a whole adjusted to coalition government. One episode described by peers as 'a very grim period' and 'deeply depressing' was the chamber's treatment of the Parliamentary Voting and Constituencies Bill 2010–11, which provided for a referendum on the voting system and for reorganization of Commons constituencies. Labour in the Lords opposed the bill hard, and there were many allegations of filibustering during its 17 days in committee (see Johnston and Pattie 2011). Ultimately, the government began to threaten that some kind of Commons-style guillotine arrangement would need to be introduced. The Crossbench convenor expressed concern that Labour's tactics were bringing the 'House into disrepute' and that it was reaching a 'dangerous crossroads'.[14] In interview, a senior government peer described the chamber at this point as having been 'hours away from the point of no return where it ceased to function'. All peers recognized that the introduction of guillotine arrangements would change the chamber fundamentally, and significantly weaken its effectiveness, so the blocking tactics ended. In any case, Labour frontbenchers concluded that 'if we carried on alienating the House... then we weren't going to get anywhere'. Instead they gradually realized that 'part of being in opposition was learning to be more subtle'. Hence, on the Welfare Reform Bill, for example, the opposition focused on the merits of the government's case, rather than procedural tactics, and relationships were carefully built with Crossbench experts, who sponsored many of the key amendments.

Private members' bills in the Lords

This and the previous chapter have focused so far only on the Lords' treatment of government legislation. But when considering the chamber's wider legislative impact, it is important also to give some consideration to private members' bills (PMBs).[15] Members of both Lords and Commons can introduce their own legislation, though it is much less likely to succeed than that of the government. Wherever a private member's bill originates, it must pass all its stages in both chambers if it is to become law; the Lords therefore considers PMBs promoted by both peers and MPs.

The total number of PMBs considered by the Lords in 2008–09 and 2010–12 is shown in Table 7.3. Overall, many fewer originate from the Lords than from the Commons. For example, in the typical one-year 2008–09 session MPs introduced 107 PMBs, while peers introduced just 17. But the majority of Commons PMBs do not make it through that chamber, and in 2008–09 only six arrived in the House of Lords (House of Commons 2010).

When peers receive PMBs from the Commons they face something of a dilemma. If they pass a bill unamended it then proceeds straight to the statute book, whereas any amendments will require it to return to the Commons for

Table 7.3. Private members' bills in the Lords, 2008–09 and 2010–12

	2008–09	2010–12
Lords private members' bills		
Bills introduced in the Lords	17	31
- Amendments tabled*	7	598
- Amendments made*	2	91
Bills falling in the Lords	12	21
Bills falling in the Commons	4	9
Bills receiving Royal Assent	1	1
Commons private members' bills		
Bills reaching the Lords	6	6
- Amendments tabled	0	2
- Amendments made	0	0
Bills falling in the Lords	2	0
Bills falling in the Commons	0	0
Bills receiving Royal Assent	4	6

Source: House of Lords *Public Bill Sessional Statistics* (see note 3).

* In 2010–12, 534 of the amendments tabled and 31 of those made were to a single bill: David Steel's House of Lords Amendment Bill.

CCLA, where it may die. Given the immense obstacles faced by MPs in getting their bills as far as the Lords, most are allowed through without amendment. Of the 12 Commons PMBs shown in the table, none were amended in the Lords, though two did fail due to lack of time.[16] In order to proceed, a Commons PMB must be picked up and sponsored by an individual peer, and likewise any Lords PMB reaching the Commons needs to be picked up by an MP.

Most private peers' bills, like their Commons counterparts, are on small and non-controversial areas of law. The two passed in 2008–09 and 2010–12 are fairly typical in this regard. In 2008–09 retired Crossbench judge Anthony Lloyd sponsored the Law Commission Bill, which comprised just two clauses requiring the Lord Chancellor to report annually to parliament on this body's work. The bill raised no objections and was subject to no amendments. In 2010–12 Liberal Democrat backbencher Tim Clement-Jones promoted the Live Music Bill, which amended the Licensing Act 2003 to make it easier for small venues to host live music events. At committee stage the bill was subject to 36 amendments; but all of these were proposed by Lord Clement-Jones himself following discussion with Whitehall officials, and most were purely technical. Bills like this are often promoted with the active support of a government department, which would otherwise have difficulty finding a suitable legislative vehicle for such small changes.

Not all private peers' bills are uncontroversial, however, and some are indeed the reverse. The clearest example in recent years was the succession of bills promoted during 2002–06 by Crossbencher Joel Joffe to allow terminally ill adults to request 'assisted dying'. The proposals were supported by the Voluntary Euthanasia Society (now Dignity in Dying), and had an important role in raising this sensitive issue up the political agenda. The second of Lord Joffe's bills was referred to a specially-convened Lords select committee for consideration, which created a forum for evidence-taking from interested groups and individuals (see Select Committee on the Assisted Dying for the Terminally Ill Bill 2005). Debates in the Lords included many carefully-considered contributions, but also became quite heated, and the bill was eventually denied a second reading in May 2006.[17] The bishops came under some criticism for their involvement, as 14 voted (the highest such turnout in any division since 1999), all of them against the bill. But the issue also showed how other religious networks (most notably Roman Catholics, informally organized at this time by Conservative peer Detta O'Cathain and Crossbencher David Alton) can be effective in the chamber despite having no formal representation. This was a classic 'conscience' issue of a kind that used regularly to be resolved through private members' bills, but which are now more often dealt with through 'free votes' within government legislation.

The fact that few private peers' bills reach the statute book directly does not necessarily imply that they are unimportant. As in this example, a bill can be a vehicle for drawing attention to an issue, and gathering support, as part of a longer campaign. Proposals in private peers' bills are also sometimes taken up later by government, or by other peers as amendments to government bills. Indeed, as discussed in Chapter 10, clauses for incremental House of Lords reform promoted in successive bills by former Liberal leader David Steel did find their way into a Labour government bill in 2009–10. But these were controversial in the chamber (as the note to Table 7.3 demonstrates), and have not yet made it into law.

Conclusion: A key site of legislative negotiation

This chapter has built on the preceding one, by looking at legislative change achieved in the Lords through negotiation, rather than defeat, and thus giving us a more complete picture of the chamber's legislative impact. While defeats can be high-profile, negotiated outcomes are rarely noticed outside the chamber, but are nonetheless important. The chapter included a quantitative analysis of amendments in the Lords to 12 case study bills, and suggested six common modes of legislative debate in the chamber. This material sheds particular light on two of the questions at the start of the book: the ways in which the Lords' ethos and culture differ from those in the Commons, and the extent to which the chamber influences policy. These questions are closely interrelated.

When discussing the Lords with those who have experienced its treatment of legislation (as either members, government officials or representatives of outside groups), two features are often emphasized. The first is that peers actually listen to each other during debates, and outcomes in the chamber can be determined by the strength of argument. A peer with significant prior experience in the Commons suggested that in the Lords 'you have to win the argument' and 'you have to make an intellectual case', while another claimed that in the Lords 'on the whole if you win the argument, you may well win the vote'. This image of rational non-partisan dialogue can of course be overstated; in the end, most votes are cast on the advice of party whips. But the chamber's party mix is crucial to the tone of its debates, as is the presence of non-party members. The parties must decide their positions in front of a very different audience to that in the Commons, which includes many who will not be swung by partisan arguments alone. The outcome for government is generally uncertain, so the strength of argument is important.

The second claim frequently made by observers of the Lords is how its influence resides with certain highly-regarded individuals—some of them non-partisan subject specialists, and others experienced party politicians. Presence of these members is undoubtedly important—as shown in some of the previous examples. But again there is far more to influence than expertise. A devastating speech from a respected figure may help to swing the mood of the House, but in the end most members' default setting will be to follow their whip. Hence, effective coalitions against the government normally require organization, often by other less well-known peers who act as foot soldiers in such campaigns. But some individuals in the chamber do manage to combine expertise, political judgement and networking skills. One example is Labour's Patricia Hollis, who won concessions on women's pension rights from the Conservative government in 1996 as a shadow minister, and later led a successful rebellion against the Blair government on pensions in 2007, having served eight years as a social security minister. This illustrates something else important about the chamber: that party frontbenchers can also often build a reputation as experts. Lacking the research backup available to their Commons colleagues, they tend to be reshuffled less often and stick closer to fields that they know well. A striking example is Conservative Freddie Howe (cited earlier on the Health Bill), who shadowed the Department of Health throughout Labour's entire time in office (1997–2010), and then became a minister in the department. This kind of frontbench longevity is unknown in today's House of Commons.

Turning to the extent of the chamber's influence on policy, the last two chapters have pointed to three distinct routes through which this can operate:

- First, and most visibly, government defeats.
- Second, negotiated changes—which are less immediately visible, but can be seen through careful tracing of amendments, as was carried out in this chapter. This demonstrates how ministers often concede points to peers, normally through government amendments, and suggests that such responses make up the majority of government amendments of substance, while others take up points made by parliamentary committees or MPs. Hence, figures on the origin of amendments cannot be taken at face value. This also applies to non-government amendments, many of which are simply 'probing' and not intended to make it onto the face of the bill.
- The third form of influence, through 'anticipated reactions', may actually be the most important, however. It operates through government taking peers' likely demands into account during the original planning and drafting of bills. Such influence is notoriously difficult to measure, but was detected during the period 1999–2012 through changes to Whitehall procedures and the development of 'handling strategies'. Evidence was also found through interviews with ministers and civil servants.

This chapter began by citing peers' views about the relative importance of defeat versus negotiation in terms of achieving policy change. An analysis of just 12 bills cannot enable us to reliably quantify this balance. But it is in any case a false divide, as these two forms of influence are inextricably linked. Ministers do listen carefully to debate in the House of Lords in part due to the expertise and persuasive powers of peers; but the clearest reason why the Lords is successful in achieving legislative change is the lack of a government majority. Putting this in terms of the six modes of debate discussed previously, it is ultimately the threat of adversarial mode that makes all of the others work. As one opposition frontbencher put it, 'on the whole, government ministers will bend over backwards to help you and have meetings, because the last thing they want is a vote'. If a vote occurs, the government may well lose. Consequently, behind-the-scenes discussions between ministers and non-government peers are far more frequent and intense than in the Commons. In the words of one minister, 'when it comes down to it, it's defeats that make this place work'.

The changes achieved to the 12 case study bills through negotiation were in most cases quite modest. With the exception of the Public Bodies Bill, none of them was substantially rewritten as a result of negotiation in the Lords. There were only 72 substantive amendments from non-government peers adopted via government amendments in total. But again, it would be simplistic to think that parliamentary influence can be entirely quantified in this way. The whole purpose of 'handling strategies' is to take peers' likely concerns into account before legislation is introduced. Indeed, if this system worked perfectly, no changes would be made at all, because bills would be introduced in a form wholly consistent with the desires of parliamentarians. Legislation now certainly has to be as robust as possible, and this requires careful planning in government. Returning to the studies of the 1988–89 session, Miers and Brock found that peers were frustrated by ministers' approach of 'legislate as you go' (1993: 134), whereby large numbers of government amendments were moved to change policy after bills were introduced. Two of their case study bills that started their passage in the Lords were subsequently 'largely rewritten' in the Commons (1993: 130). In both cases—having already been subjected to hundreds of amendments in the Lords—the bill returned containing over 100 pages of new material. Governments are far less likely to behave in that way today. The better planning that now goes into the legislative process cannot be wholly ascribed to the Lords' post-1999 revival, but this has certainly helped.

The extent to which the Lords now matters is clear from comments by Whitehall bill managers made in interviews on our case study bills. One responsible official claimed that from the department's perspective, influence on his bill was 'all about the Lords'. Another suggested that starting a bill in the Commons 'is nice, because you get a bit of a practice, a bit of a warm up'. Asked whether this implied that the Lords passage is more important than that through the Commons, the official added:

> If I had to say where I felt the most pressure, the most parliamentary scrutiny, where we were under the most pressure to come up with good intellectual arguments in response to points, where we felt the importance was really on winning the argument and explaining things then I would say largely the House of Lords more than the House of Commons.

This view may not be universal, but no official suggested to the contrary that the Commons was more important.

These conclusions might be interpreted as suggesting that the Lords is somehow superior to, or more powerful than, the Commons. But the reality is that the two chambers have different and complementary roles. The elected Commons is clearly the 'primary' chamber, in legal terms through the Parliament Acts, through numerous conventions, and because senior ministers are concentrated there. It is primarily MPs who debate the big political principles of bills, and this fulfils an important democratic purpose. Commons debates are high-profile, and members can be held to account publicly for their decisions, in particular by their constituents. The parties are likewise largely judged by their actions in that chamber. The Lords, in turn, requires ministers to justify their policy in an environment where they cannot rely on party loyalty alone. It is a key site of negotiation over legislative detail, which often includes pursuing points that were previously raised by MPs. Reflecting on relations between the two chambers, one peer suggested that 'although the senior spokespeople are at the Commons end this is the place where things get done, and they know it'. Consequently, another claimed that 'a strange feel comes up the corridor from the other place' in that they 'resent that we can do it but also are grateful for it'. But the two chambers' negotiating capacity cannot be separated; they operate as a partnership. This occurs within a framework where the Commons ultimately has primacy, and can if necessary have the last word. As another senior frontbencher put it, 'absolutely no doubt, the policy is made at the Commons end'.

Notes

1. n = 377. This was part of a set of questions which began 'Do you agree or disagree with the following statements about the role and functions of the House of Lords?', with responses on a five-point scale from 'strongly agree' to 'strongly disagree'. Only 6% disagreed with this statement.
2. n = 364–70. The exact question was 'How important do you think each of the following are in terms of how the House of Lords influences the policy process?', and there were four options: 'very important', 'important', 'not very important', and 'not at all important'. Just 7% selected either of the negative options with respect to defeats, and 1% with respect to government proposing amendments under pressure.
3. See <http://www.publications.parliament.uk/pa/ld/billstat.htm> (accessed 20 August 2012).
4. Note that—in line with Public Bill Office official figures—all amendments to which a minister was signatory (even if not first signatory) are included in this category. In a few cases ministers signed amendments that had initially been proposed by non-government peers (see notes to Table 7.1).
5. Due to the volume of amendments to be coded, the analysis in this section is based on work conducted by only one coder, using a clearly written coding scheme. In all cases, this work was checked by another researcher, but independent 'blind' coding (as was used in Chapter 6 for defeats) was beyond our capacity.
6. Note that this analysis takes no account of concessions that are made by government in non-legislative form, which also occur with some regularity—

for example, by indicating how ministers intend to interpret a clause, or what guidance they plan to issue their civil servants.

7. Amendments are only classed here as responding to a committee if there had been no prior non-government amendment calling for the same change. In various other cases, peers proposed amendments to implement recommendations of the DPRRC and Constitution Committee and these were incorporated via government amendments. These are classified as responding to non-government peers' concerns.
8. Certification of money bills only happens once the bill has completed its Commons stages, in case amendments are made in the Commons which would change its status. Peers and MPs therefore have no advance warning that Lords' consideration will be limited. In the case of the Savings Accounts Bill, there had been hopes that concessions on points raised in the Commons would be won in the Lords.
9. This cabinet committee has held various names over the years, including recently Legislative Programme Committee (referred to among civil servants and ministers as 'LP'), Legislation Committee (likewise 'LegCo') and Parliamentary Business and Legislation Committee ('PBL').
10. Other less sympathetic modes might, for example, include 'hobby horse' mode, where a small number of peers (usually fruitlessly) pursue a favourite topic, or 'self congratulatory' mode, when peers celebrate their own achievements or those of the House as a whole (for example, when debating Lords reform). But as these rarely result in legislative success, they are not considered here.
11. A register exists of all-party parliamentary groups, their officers and financial supporters: <http://www.publications.parliament.uk/pa/cm/cmallparty/memi01.htm> (accessed 22 August 2012).
12. Ian Pearson, *House of Commons Hansard*, 25 February 2009, column 296.
13. *House of Lords Hansard*, 8 November 2010, column 18.
14. Frances D'Souza, *House of Lords Hansard*, 24 January 2011, column 683.
15. It should be noted that private members' bills are a different thing from 'private bills', which are promoted by organizations external to both government and parliament. These bills used to be common but are now increasingly rare and are not discussed in this book. A recent example was the Mersey Tunnels Bill in 2003–04, which allowed the tunnel operators to increase tolls.
16. One of these arrived in June 2009 and had its second reading in July (following the summer recess, the session ended on 12 November); the other did not arrive until October and had no time even for a second reading.
17. As a private peer's bill, a vote against second reading could not be considered a breach of convention.

8

Non-legislative Policy Work

The previous two chapters focused on the House of Lords' treatment of legislation. This occupies a large proportion of the chamber's time, and represents its most obvious means of influencing policy. Numerous changes are made to government bills as a result of peers' intervention, both following defeats and less confrontational debates and negotiation. But parliament has important policy functions beyond legislation, in particular through holding the government to account (executive accountability), and debating issues of importance to the public (deliberation). These functions are shared between the Commons and the Lords, and exercised via mechanisms such as written and oral questions to ministers, general non-legislative policy debates, and inquiries by parliamentary committees. This chapter describes these various forms of work in the House of Lords.

In terms of the key questions presented at the start of the book, the chapter addresses how the processes of executive accountability and deliberation differ between the two chambers at Westminster. Many people are familiar with Commons question time (and in particular Prime Minister's questions), while that chamber's debates and select committees both regularly also make the news. The equivalent activities in the Lords are far more rarely reported. Procedurally, there are important differences between these activities in the two chambers. But less straightforwardly there are also significant cultural differences—resulting in part from the procedural dissimilarities and also from differences between their members. Another question addressed by the chapter is whether and how non-legislative activities in the Lords actually matter to policy. It is difficult (as we have seen) to assess policy impact with respect to the chamber's legislative role; going beyond this is harder still. Changes to bills can be measured fairly objectively, through tracing the outcome of defeats and other amendments. In contrast, how debates, questions or committee reports influence government is far less tangible, potentially more subtle, and therefore more open to dispute. As with legislation, the role of 'anticipated reactions' is important.

The chapter is structured in three main sections, covering questions, debates and committees respectively. As so much energy goes into the chamber's committee work, this is assigned the greatest amount of space. Here, the work of each of the chamber's main committees (some of which actually have a legislative as well as non-legislative role) is briefly reviewed in turn. The conclusion of the chapter returns to the opening questions, and reflects in particular on the challenges of assessing the impact of the Lords' non-legislative policy role.

Written and oral questions

As in the House of Commons, one of the key ways in which peers hold the government to account is through the tabling of questions for oral and written answer. But there are important procedural differences in this respect between the two chambers.

The most important of these relate to arrangements for oral questions. In the Commons, questions are directed at particular government departments. Ministers in each department answer oral questions roughly once a month, according to a rota, with large departments such as the Home Office and Department of Health having a one-hour question session, and others having shorter slots (for details, see Table 8.2). The prime minister also answers questions for half an hour once a week. In contrast, all questions in the House of Lords are directed at the government in general instead of a particular department. The topics for daily questions are therefore not fixed and can range across all departments.

Another important difference is that there are far fewer oral questions in the Lords: in the typical one-year session of 2008–09 there were just 484, compared to 1314 in the Commons.[1] A half-hour question period is held at the start of Lords business on Monday to Thursday, during which just four oral questions are taken. In contrast, a half-hour session in the Commons will include 10 questions or more. Consequently, the time devoted to each Lords question, and the number of members able to comment, is significantly greater. The minister is required to give a short reply (the *Companion* states that this should normally comprise no more than 75 words), after which the original questioner may ask a supplementary question. When the minister has answered this, there is time for up to six or seven other members to ask further supplementaries. In addition, members can ask 'private notice questions' (now known as 'urgent questions' in the Commons), which the Lord Speaker may decide to grant on the day itself. But these must meet strict criteria of urgency and importance, and few are granted (there were only 10 in the long 2010–12 session, compared to 73 in the Commons).

Written questions are more explicitly focused on extracting information than sparking a debate. These operate in a similar way to the Commons, but with some restrictions. The government is expected to provide an answer within 10 working days, which is published in *Hansard*. As shown in Table 8.1, the number of written questions has risen significantly in recent years. Between 1999 and 2012 the average number per sitting day more than doubled, to 58 (and had previously done the same since 1992–93, when there were only 13 per day). A recent analysis conducted for the House of Lords Procedure Committee of 2,390 written questions from October–December 2011 found that 10 members between them tabled over 1,000 questions (45% of the total), and the top three members tabled 653 (27%).[2] Consequently, in 2012 the House agreed to limit each peer to 12 written questions per week, in addition to a pre-existing limit of six questions per day. No such limits exist in the Commons, where question inflation has been even steeper, with around 400 written questions now asked daily.[3] Compared to this, the number of Lords questions appears quite modest. But the Procedure Committee (2012: 5) still estimated that the cost to the government of answering peers' written questions in 2010–12 was £9,500 per sitting day.

Table 8.1. Oral and written questions in the House of Lords, 1999–2012

Session	Sitting days	Oral questions	OPQs/ sitting day*	Written questions	WPQs/ sitting day
1999–00	177	630	3.6	4,511	25.5
2000–01	76	270	3.6	1,993	26.2
2001–02	200	713	3.6	5,798	29.0
2002–03	174	687	3.9	5,084	29.2
2003–04	157	634	4.0	4,524	28.8
2004–05	63	228	3.6	1,877	29.8
2005–06	206	743	3.6	7,374	35.8
2006–07	142	519	3.7	5,118	36.0
2007–08	164	595	3.6	5,814	35.5
2008–09	134	484	3.6	5,655	42.2
2009–10	68	248	3.6	2,906	42.7
2010–12**	293	1,080	3.7	16,980	58.0

Source: Vollmer (2012), supplemented by House of Lords (2012) for 2010–12 session.

* The average number of questions is fewer than four, due to occasional Friday sittings, when oral questions are not taken.

** Two-year session.

Table 8.2. Approximate distribution of oral questions by government department, 2010–12 (with House of Commons for comparison)

Department	Number of questions	% of total	% of Commons time*
Attorney General's Office	1	0%	2%
Cabinet Office	20	2%	3%
Department for Business, Innovation and Skills	76	7%	6%
Department for Communities and Local Government	34	3%	6%
Department for Culture, Media and Sport	55	5%	4%
Department for Education	53	5%	6%
Department for Environment, Food and Rural Affairs	48	4%	4%
Department for International Development	16	1%	3%
Department for Transport	53	5%	4%
Department for Work and Pensions	43	4%	6%
Department of Energy and Climate Change	23	2%	6%
Department of Health	108	10%	6%
Foreign and Commonwealth Office	166	15%	6%
Government Equalities Office	5	0%	1%
Home Office	98	9%	6%
Leader of the House of Lords/ Chairman of Committees	35	3%	1%
Ministry of Defence	24	2%	6%
Ministry of Justice	102	9%	6%
Northern Ireland Office	6	1%	3%
Scotland Office	6	1%	3%
Treasury	103	10%	6%
Wales Office	5	0%	3%
Total	1,080	100%	100%

Source: Constructed from data provided by House of Lords Journal Office. Questions were initially allocated based on the minister/whip answering and their departmental responsibilities, supplemented by reading of the question itself (and if necessary the answer) where this was not sufficient.

* House of Commons time is fixed by departmental rota for each five-week period, and figures reflect this: 15 minutes (1% of total), 20 minutes (2%), 30 minutes (3%), 45 minutes (4%) or 60 minutes (6%). Percentages exclude questions to the prime minister and deputy prime minister, as these do not apply in the Lords.

Because of the less regulated nature of question topics in the Lords, these give a good indication of peers' policy interests. Table 8.2 shows the approximate distribution of oral questions by government department in the Lords in the 2010–12 session, based on a coding of all 1,080 questions. The time allocations in the Commons are shown for comparison. The Lords figures can obviously only be approximate, as questions are not officially answered on a departmental basis (and sometimes cross departmental boundaries). But they show fairly clear concentrations of interest. The department attracting the greatest number of questions was the Foreign and Commonwealth Office, followed by the Department of Health, Treasury, Ministry of Justice and Home Office. All of these occupied a substantially larger share of questions than in the Commons. Other large departments, such as Education and Work and Pensions, attracted rather fewer questions in the Lords, and a smaller proportion than in the Commons (in part, probably reflecting peers' lack of constituency responsibilities). We have already established peers' interest in constitutional matters from previous chapters; the question distribution demonstrates their interest in foreign policy (which is subject to little legislation) and health matters as well.

Partly due to procedural differences, and partly due to the culture and nature of its members, the conduct of question time in the Lords feels quite different to that in the Commons. This has potential implications for any policy impact that Lords questions may have, which is difficult to measure. On the negative side, those answering questions in the Lords are generally more junior, since nearly all Secretaries of State sit in the Commons. (A special procedure for Secretary of State's questions was agreed in January 2010, when Peter Mandelson and Andrew Adonis were both serving in the cabinet from the Lords, but since the formation of the coalition government this has not been needed.) As some departments do not have a minister in the Lords, questions must often be answered by whips, who cover for several departments. This means that the minister answering the question does not usually have full departmental responsibility for the policy.

Nonetheless, there are various reasons to believe that Lords questions may be quite effective. Unlike Commons departmental questions, where the number of members present in the chamber may be limited to a few with a strong interest in the department's affairs, Lords question time is well attended every day—in part, precisely because the topics covered are so varied. The person answering must therefore do so in front of a full house. They also face lengthier questioning on each topic, with contributions potentially coming from former Secretaries of State, senior civil servants and subject specialists. This means questions are far more difficult to dodge than in the Commons. In addition, the culture in the Lords requires that—in the words of one former minister—'you can't get away with party political knockabout' and instead 'have to treat people seriously'.[4] All of this requires Lords ministers, and the civil servants who brief them, to put a great deal of time into preparation. Examples of ministers (or whips) being caught off-guard are relatively rare, but this should not be taken as an indication that questions have no real effect. Often, the impact is instead felt behind the scenes in Whitehall, as ministers prepare. Another former minister reported reading the briefing pack prepared by civil servants before he was due to answer a question and discovering that it contained inaccuracies. Recognizing that the government's position couldn't be defended, he referred the matter upwards to the Secretary of State, and the policy was changed. Such impacts are hidden, and it is impossible to know how often they occur.

Further, more subtle, benefits may also result from both written and oral questions. They raise awareness of issues around the chamber, as well as with ministers and civil servants; they also help members to communicate to each other who is interested in what issues, and therefore to form issue networks. In addition, questions are read by interest groups outside the chamber—in the public, private and voluntary sectors. Groups then often contact members who have shown interest in their topic, and build relationships in preparation for future legislation or debates.

General policy debates in the House of Lords

Beyond questions, there are various kinds of non-legislative debate in the Lords, as illustrated for the 2008–09 and 2010–12 sessions in Table 8.3.

Again the organization and culture of debates differ substantially from those in the first chamber. Unlike the Commons, the Lords has no provision for 'opposition days', the topics of which are chosen by the opposition frontbench. Instead, Thursdays during the first half of each session are set aside for general debates, most of which are allocated to the parties and other main groups. These are treated largely as backbench debates, with the number allocated to each group agreed (on a roughly proportional basis) through the usual channels, and the groups then choosing which backbenchers should be allowed to sponsor each debate. In the Conservative Party the allocation is made by the Association of Conservative Peers (ACP), while for Labour it is done by a backbench coordinating committee. In addition, one Thursday per month during this period is given over to short balloted debates, for which any backbench or non-party peer can enter, with two taken on each allocated day. Towards the end of the session, most Thursdays

Table 8.3. Number of debates by type, 2008–09 and 2010–12 sessions

	2008–09		2010–12*	
	Chamber	Grand committee	Chamber	Grand committee
General debates allocated by party/group	27	–	78	–
General debates allocated by ballot	12	–	21	–
Questions for short debate	38	18	92	30
General debates initiated by the government	2	–	15	–
Debates on select committee reports	14	7	28	18
Ministerial statements debated	66	–	145	–

Source: House of Lords (2012).

* Two-year session.

are instead dedicated to discussion of government bills. The other primary opportunity for backbenchers to sponsor debates is through the system of 'questions for short debate' (previously known as 'unstarred questions'), which are similar to House of Commons adjournment debates. In the chamber, these are taken at the end of business for up to 90 minutes, and during the dinner break for up to an hour, and they may also be taken in Grand Committee. They are extremely oversubscribed, and allocation of time ultimately lies with the Chief Whip's office (both factors which have caused some recent frustration). When a member manages to win time for a debate, they will often encourage others with a known interest in the topic to attend and contribute, and may publicize it to outside groups.

Another form of debate is that on reports from House of Lords select committees. Time for debating reports is not guaranteed in standing orders, as it is in the Commons, but agreed through the usual channels. Nonetheless, the far smaller number of committee reports in the Lords means that when a committee wants a report debated, it can usually be found time. In addition, the government occasionally sponsors debates on matters of widespread interest. In the case of all of these kinds of debate, the *Companion to Standing Orders* sets down strict limits on speaking time for the sponsoring member and respondent from the government, with the remaining time divided equally between all other members who have indicated in advance their desire to speak (meaning that all members are guaranteed a slot, however small). Most debates are held on a 'take note' basis, and do not end with a vote. In addition, short discussions on ministerial statements—for example, announcing the publication of a new white paper, or the government's response to an external event—take place about twice a week. These are not strictly 'debates', but an opportunity for extended questioning, lasting for 30–40 minutes.

As with oral questions, there is no regulation of the kind of topics debated, so the issues chosen can be useful indicator of the policy interests of members of the House of Lords. An analysis of debate topics in the 2008–09 session finds that (like oral questions, discussed earlier) there were more in policy areas covered by the Foreign and Commonwealth Office (FCO), and Department of Health, than other departments. FCO-related debate topics included, for example, Afghanistan, Africa, Iraq and Russia, while health debates included NHS doctors, contaminated blood products, stem cell therapy and dementia.

Some issues have historically been returned to in debates on a fairly regular basis, which can be seen as both a positive and a negative. Some peers have relentlessly pursued relatively obscure or unfashionable subjects, such as female genital mutilation or Gulf War syndrome, through lengthy campaigns using debates and questions. These can help to raise awareness and may eventually elicit a positive response from government (or sometimes outside bodies). As two former ministers suggested, such debates are 'a way of keeping an issue alive' and can 'help the government to make up its mind'. But the committee on working practices chaired by Alastair Goodlad complained about debates that '[t]here may be overlap or repetition, with similar subjects being tabled in close proximity', and that the combination of ballots and usual channels negotiation prevents 'intelligent selection' of topics (Leader's Group on Working Practices 2011: 45). The position in the Lords was unfavourably contrasted with that in the Commons, where in 2010 the usual channels gave up control over topics for many debates to a 'Backbench Business Committee' (Russell 2011). The Group's proposal that the Lords should adopt a similar system has not yet been acted upon, though there is pressure from members to do so.

Just as it is difficult to assess the usefulness or policy impact of questions in the House of Lords, the same applies to debates. One notable aspect is again, of course, that contributors can be very expert. For example, an emergency debate on Iraq in September 2002 attracted contributions from three former Foreign Secretaries, two former Secretaries of State for Defence, two former Home Secretaries, and various former military chiefs, ambassadors and civil servants. In November 2007, in a debate on defence spending sponsored by a Conservative peer, the Labour government found itself criticized by five former Chiefs of the Defence Staff. Yet, as Shell has suggested, the 'mere fact that peers taking part in a debate have an impressive list of qualifications is not in itself evidence for the political importance of those debates'

(1992: 209). The government is under no formal obligation to do as peers suggest. Most Lords debates are less high profile than those just mentioned, and the Goodlad group suggested that 'too many... take place in an empty Chamber, are ignored by the media and the public, and have no discernible impact upon Government' (Leader's Group on Working Practices 2011: 41). But this may be too harsh. As with questions, the primary impact of debates is inside Whitehall, when ministers and civil servants prepare themselves, and through 'anticipated reactions'. Crucially, a minister must respond to every debate and put the government's position on the public record.

Lords committees

The House of Lords' committee work is an important part of its contribution to the policy process. The suggestion that the chamber should establish a set of specialist investigative committees was first made in the 1960s (Torrance 2012). Since then, Lords committees have gradually grown in both number and importance.

Again, it may be useful to first point out the key differences between committees in the Lords and Commons. Just as the committee stage of legislation is significantly different in the two chambers, so too are their systems of select committees. In the Commons, the main select committees are structured to shadow government departments, whereas Lords committees are intentionally 'crosscutting', and far fewer in number.[5] The Goodlad group suggested—broadly in line with current practice—that Lords committees should meet three key criteria: making best use of members' knowledge and expertise, complementing (rather than duplicating) the work of Commons committees, and addressing cross-departmental issues (Leader's Group on Working Practices 2011). It also suggested some changes to committee organization, which were further elaborated in a report of the House of Lords Liaison Committee (2012)—the body that makes strategic decisions about committee work and resources—and have since been put into effect.

Summary details of the main committees in 2012–13, excluding new ad hoc and pre-legislative scrutiny committees, are shown in Table 8.4. There are two very well-established policy committees, on the European Union and Science and Technology, while the other policy committees are all relatively more recent additions. In addition, there are two important committees dealing with delegated powers and secondary legislation. Each of these is discussed in more detail in the following sections, together with a short

Table 8.4. Principal policy committees in the House of Lords, 2012–13

	Year estd.	Size	Chair 2012–13	Chair's party/ group	No. of reports 2010–12
European Union*	1974	19	Tim Boswell	Other**	34
Science and Technology	1980	14	John Krebs	Crossbench	5
Constitution	2001	12	Margaret Jay	Labour	25
Economic Affairs	2001	13	John MacGregor	Conservative	6
Communications	2007	13	Richard Inglewood	Conservative	3
Delegated Powers and Regulatory Reform	1992	10	Celia Thomas	Lib Dem	25
Secondary Legislation Scrutiny	2004	11	Alastair Goodlad	Conservative	60

* Includes members of the main committee only (see later for subcommittees).

** The chair of the European Union Committee also holds the position of Principal Deputy Chairman of Committees and consequently (like the Lord Speaker) drops any party affiliation. Until taking this role Tim Boswell was a Conservative peer.

section devoted to other committees. The latter include joint committees with the Commons, ad hoc committees, and more administrative committees.

The procedural differences between the chambers have become greater since recent reforms in the House of Commons. The organization of Lords committee work remains less formalized and places more trust in coordination by the whips. Since 2010, select committee members in the Commons have been elected within party groups, and their chairs elected by the whole House in a secret ballot (Russell 2011). In contrast, committee memberships in the Lords continue to be negotiated through the usual channels, as occurred in the Commons pre-2010. Hence, a peer wanting to serve on a committee must approach their whip or convenor. There has recently been some pressure from members for a more transparent mechanism of appointment to be introduced.[6] Appointments are made broadly in line with group strengths in the chamber, so that in the 2012–13 session a typical 13-member committee comprised four Conservative peers, four Labour peers, two Liberal Democrats and three Crossbenchers. A similar proportionality principle operates in the Commons, which normally gives the governing party (or parties) a majority on select committees. But, in practice, this makes relatively little difference to political dynamics, as work by investigative committees in both chambers is largely non-partisan.

Most committees meet weekly, and (like their Commons counterparts) can choose their own topics for investigation, take written and oral evidence, and publish reports. Staffing for committees in the Lords is more limited, however, with each having an average of 2.5 full-time members of staff. Part-time specialist advisers can also be appointed to support specific inquiries. In 2012 the Liaison Committee estimated that the cost of one 'unit' of committee activity (i.e. committee or subcommittee) was £225,000 per year. It recommended creation of two new ad hoc investigative committees, in part to accommodate the large growth in membership since 2010, and also more focus on pre- and post-legislative scrutiny (Liaison Committee 2012). These changes resulted in a net gain of one 'unit' (with some savings through the abolition of two pre-existing subcommittees).

The culture of Lords committees is, as for debates and questions, rather different to that in the Commons. Investigative committees tend to tackle more strategic, longer-term issues, and often more technical ones—partly due to their crosscutting nature, and partly the interests of their members. Inquiries are often longer and more in-depth, and reports therefore less numerous. The Commons committees are well respected but perhaps, as one peer put it, more 'hit-and-run'. Lords committees also tend to be less adversarial in their relationship with government and other groups that they scrutinize, and their inquiries and reports have a more academic, research feel. As in the Commons, the government is expected to reply to all committee reports within two months.

The European Union Committee

The longest-established committee in the Lords is the European Union Committee, which was created in 1974, shortly after Britain's entry into the then European Community.[7] As Shell (1992: 224) describes, the Lords was well placed to establish such a committee, as its members were more pro-European than MPs at that time, and it was also used to being 'a chamber of influence, rather than of power'. National parliaments have no direct role in approving most decisions of the European institutions, so the key role was to influence British ministers going into negotiations. Since the committee's early days, the European Parliament has developed its oversight of the Commission and Council of Ministers considerably, but the Lords committee (and its counterpart in the Commons) provide a link to British politics that remains important. Both benefit from the 'scrutiny reserve', which requires ministers not to agree policy proposals in the Council of Ministers that are still under consideration by the UK parliament.

The crucial difference between the Lords committee and the Commons' European Scrutiny Committee is that the latter puts its energy into filtering all EU policy proposals for their importance, in order to draw these to the attention of the House as necessary. The Lords committee also looks widely at EU policy, but selects a small number of topics for more in-depth scrutiny. It operates largely through an extensive set of subcommittees, each focusing on one policy field, and drawing in additional peers (see Table 8.5). The number of subcommittees was reduced in 2012 from seven to six, but the system still involves over 70 peers, supported by 24 specialist staff. The main committee conducts broad work, such as reviewing the EU budget and questioning the Minister for Europe, with input from the subcommittees (and its membership includes at least one representative of each). Its secretariat also filters the roughly 1,000 European documents each year received from ministers, which come with an explanatory memorandum setting out the government's view. The more important amongst these are forwarded to subcommittees for consideration. A subcommittee may then raise questions through correspondence with ministers, and occasional one-off evidence sessions. Aside from this highly reactive work, the committee and subcommittees also have a more proactive role conducting detailed inquiries into big policy issues, often trying to get 'upstream' of European decision-making. Each such inquiry results in a report, all of which are officially published by the main committee. In the (two-year) session 2010–12, there were 34 reports published, of which 20 were debated by the end of the session (and several others debated in 2012–13). It also heard evidence from over 300 witnesses, and sent 1,230 letters to ministers (European Union Committee 2012).

The committee is frequently praised. It describes itself as 'the most elaborate system of national parliamentary scrutiny of EU legislation in the EU' (European Union Committee 2010: 5), and is certainly far more

Table 8.5. Subcommittees of the European Union Committee, 2012–13

Subcommittee	Size	Chair	Chair's party/group
A. Economic and Financial Affairs	12	Lyndon Harrison	Labour
B. Internal Market, Infrastructure and Employment	12	Detta O'Cathain	Conservative
C. External Affairs	13	Robin Teverson	Liberal Democrat
D. Agriculture, Fisheries, Environment and Energy	12	Patrick Carter	Labour
E. Justice, Institutions and Consumer Protection	12	Peter Bowness	Conservative
F. Home Affairs, Health and Education	12	David Hannay	Crossbench

sophisticated than that in many other parliaments. Giving evidence to the committee in January 2012, former Italian Prime Minister Giulio Amato suggested that 'the best reports that we read throughout the Union, on whatever European documents, are coming from here'.[8] As with all Lords committees, the subcommittees include various experts. For example, a former head of the diplomatic service and ambassador to the EU, John Kerr, sits on subcommittee A, which is chaired by Lyndon Harrison, a former MEP. Kerr's predecessor as EU ambassador, David Hannay, chairs subcommittee F.

It is very difficult nonetheless to assess the extent of the committee's influence. Its work may be primarily targeted at the UK government, but it can potentially influence the EU institutions and other member state governments as well. Many remark on how the committee's reports are well used in other EU member parliaments, and in the European Parliament itself. The committee also has a basic role in informing the Lords on EU affairs, which can feed into wider debates. Although it clearly exists to hold the government to account, the two may even collude at times on European matters: for example, a critical committee report on EU fisheries or agriculture policy could strengthen UK ministers' case when negotiating in Brussels. On top of this, even where committee recommendations get taken up, there will always have been numerous other voices in the debate Europe-wide, and its focus on large, strategic issues means effects will tend to be diffuse, and longer-term. However, claims by Eurosceptic UKIP peers that the committee 'has virtually no influence' on EU affairs are almost certainly incorrect.[9]

The Science and Technology Committee

The next oldest committee in the Lords is the Science and Technology Committee, which was initially set up in 1980 after the House of Commons abolished its committee of the same name. The Commons committee was subsequently re-established, so the two now coexist. Like the EU committee, this one used to operate through two subcommittees, but was scaled back to a single unit in 2012. It is notable for its expert membership. In 2012 its chair was John Krebs, a professor of zoology and former chair of the Food Standards Agency. Other members included Narendra Patel, a former President of the Royal College of Obstetricians and Gynaecologists, Martin Rees, a former Astronomer Royal and President of the Royal Society, Alec Broers, a former President of the Royal Academy of Engineering and Robert Winston, a professor of fertility studies and well-known communicator of science. The latter two are former chairs of the committee.

The Science and Technology Committee describes itself as concentrating on three things: public policy areas which ought to be informed by scientific research, technological challenges and opportunities, and public policy towards science itself. It tends to conduct long and detailed inquiries, often at the interface of science and policy, and its reports are well respected. Those cited as particularly successful include a 1998 report on *Resistance to Antibiotics*, which led to changes in prescribing policy, and a report on *Science and Society* in 2000, which drew attention to the importance of public understanding of science and made influential recommendations about science communication. Reports such as these not only potentially influence government, but are also used within the academic and scientific communities, including overseas. In terms of operating style, the committee is known for its habit of returning some years on to follow up previous inquiries and check on progress. For example, its successful 1998 report on *Air Travel and Health*, which drew attention to deep vein thrombosis, was followed up in 2007, and in 2012 the committee revisited a report from 2006 on *Science and Heritage*. In the Commons, such follow-up work is fairly rare, but has been identified as helping lead to successful committee impact (Russell and Benton 2011).

In 2010–12 the committee was keeping a careful eye on the actions of the coalition government. It grilled the Liberal Democrat Secretary of State for Energy and Climate Change, Chris Huhne, a sceptic on nuclear power, for its inquiry on *Nuclear Research and Development Capabilities*. The committee's report, which concluded that there was a need for 'fundamental change in the Government's approach to nuclear R&D', was later said by the Conservative Minister for Universities and Science to have 'focused minds very much on that issue, which is leading to quite a big rethink across government'.[10] The committee's 2011 report on *Behaviour Change* expressed scepticism about the government's so-called 'nudge' agenda; and a report on *The Role and Functions of Departmental Chief Scientific Advisers* sought to protect these government experts and clarify their role.

The Constitution Committee

The Constitution Committee is one of a more recent set of additions to the House of Lords' committee system. Its establishment was recommended by the Royal Commission on Lords reform in 2000. The Commission suggested that an important role for the second chamber was 'to act as a "constitutional long-stop", ensuring that changes are not made to the constitution without full and open debate and an awareness of the consequences' (Royal Commission on the Reform of the House of Lords 2000: 48). It therefore suggested that a committee on the constitution should be established, 'to enhance the ability of Parliament as a whole to take full account of all the constitutional implications when considering proposed legislation and scrutinising the actions of the executive' (Royal Commission 2000: 53). The committee was subsequently created in 2001.

As indicated in this description of its putative role, the committee has a twofold function, rather like the EU committee. Its reactive work involves scrutinizing legislation for any constitutional implications, but it also conducts proactive inquiries. It seeks to issue its reports on bills before second reading in the Lords, to maximize their impact on debate. Deciding which bills have 'constitutional implications' in the British system is clearly not straightforward, as there is no distinct written constitution. The committee acts with the support of a legal adviser, and has interpreted its remit fairly broadly.

This is again a committee with an impressively expert membership. In 2012 its chair was Margaret Jay, a former Leader of the House of Lords; other members included former Attorney General Peter Goldsmith, former Lord Chancellor Derry Irvine, former Director of Public Prosecutions Ken Macdonald, senior barrister David Pannick and Professor of Government Philip Norton (a former chair of the committee). An analysis by Norton, presented at an event marking the committee's tenth anniversary, showed that it had published 126 reports, of which 71 commented on legislation, 20 reported on inquiries and a further 35 simply reported to the House (e.g. following evidence sessions with the Lord Chief Justice or chair of the House of Lords Appointments Commission).

The Constitution Committee's reports on legislation are taken seriously, and points are often pursued by peers through amendments if the government's response is not convincing. In recent years, the committee has begun to publish ready-made amendments in its reports. In 2010–12 it expressed particular concern about the Public Bodies Bill (discussed in Chapters 6 and 7), which it claimed affected 'the very heart of our constitutional system' and threatened a 'fundamental principle of the constitution that parliamentary scrutiny of legislation is allowed to be effective' (Constitution Committee 2010: 5, 3). Its scathing report had a significant impact, alongside reports from the Delegated Powers and Regulatory Reform Committee and Joint Committee on Human Rights. Lords Pannick and Norton were among those who proposed major amendments and won concessions from the government. Likewise, in 2010–12 an amendment from the committee to the coalition's Health and Social Care Bill regarding the constitutional relationship between the Secretary of State and the NHS led to government concessions being made.

The committee was so concerned about the coalition's hastily-prepared constitutional legislation (which also included the Fixed-term Parliaments Bill, Parliamentary Voting and Constituencies Bill and European Union Bill) that it conducted an inquiry and reported on *The Process of Constitutional Change* in 2011. Its central proposal was that bills should be accompanied by a ministerial statement indicating whether they provided for 'significant constitutional change', and that for those which did, the government should have to state what pre-legislative scrutiny and consultation had taken place. The committee has therefore not only carved out a role for itself as a constitutional guardian, but is also gradually helping shape notions of 'constitutionality' in the UK. Other notable inquiry reports include *Waging War: Parliament's Role and Responsibility* (2006), which helped secure an in-principle government commitment that parliament will be consulted on future military commitments, and *Surveillance, Citizens and the State* (2009), whose recommendations helped to inform the coalition government's Protection of Freedoms Bill.

The Economic Affairs Committee

Another relatively recent addition is the Economic Affairs Committee, dating to 2001. This grew from an ad hoc select committee established in 1998 to monitor the Bank of England's Monetary Policy Committee (MPC). Labour's post-1997 legislation to make the Bank independent contained provision for the MPC to be scrutinized by the Commons, but an amendment by Labour backbenchers Maurice Peston (a professor of economics) and Joel Barnett (a former Chief Secretary to the Treasury) proposed that scrutiny be extended to include the Lords. The government agreed to this, despite the Commons' formal primacy on financial matters, and the committee was created with Peston as chair. He maintained this position when it gained its new permanent status and broader remit. Controversy increased when the committee chose to establish a subcommittee to scrutinize the annual Finance Bill (which implements the government's budget). The then Chancellor Gordon Brown fiercely resisted the move, without success, and the government has since suggested that the subcommittee 'risks intruding on Commons financial privilege' (Joint Committee on Conventions 2006b: Ev 10). Nonetheless, since 2002 it has reported annually on the Finance Bill before report stage in the Commons. It officially sticks strictly to technical issues of administration, clarification and simplification, not policy, though this dividing line is not necessarily clear.

In 2012 the Economic Affairs Committee was chaired by John MacGregor, who had been (amongst other things) Chief Secretary to the Treasury under Margaret Thatcher. Other members included former Chancellor of the Exchequer Nigel Lawson, former deputy chair of the Monopolies and Mergers Commission Denise Kingsmill, several senior business people, and former chair of the Commons Treasury Committee John McFall. In contrast to the Commons committee, the Economic Affairs Committee focuses on longer inquiries and more strategic issues, and was described by one senior clerk as liking to 'query prevailing orthodoxies'. For example, its reports on *The Economic Impact of Immigration* and *The Economics of Renewable Energy* (both in 2007) argued that these were not as economically beneficial as the government at the time supposed. While the Commons Treasury Committee has had quite fierce exchanges both with ministers and industry figures (see Russell and Benton 2011), reports from the Lords committee tend to have a more academic tone. A good example was the 2002 report on *Globalisation*, which sought to define and understand this concept as well as its impact on the UK economy.

The Communications Committee

The Communications Committee also grew out of an ad hoc committee, this time on renewal of the BBC charter (2005–06). It was established in 2007 but, unlike the other committees, has not gained 'sessional' (i.e. effectively permanent) status, and instead simply been recreated each session. Its remit is 'to consider the media and the creative industries', which somewhat overlaps with that of the Commons Department of Culture, Media and Sport (DCMS) Select Committee. But it is both more industry-focused than the Commons committee and allows peers to consider interaction with several government departments.

The committee's first chair (until 2010) was Norman Fowler, who had held various cabinet positions when in the Commons under Margaret Thatcher and John Major. He is widely acknowledged as having been very effective in following up the committee's reports with ministers and industry figures. Again, the committee takes a less inquisitorial and more strategic approach than its Commons counterpart. While the DCMS committee ran high-profile and adversarial witness sessions with Rupert and James Murdoch and their colleagues following the *News of the World* phone hacking scandal of 2011–12, the Lords committee had held sessions with some of the same figures for its inquiry on *Media Ownership and the News* in 2007–08 which were far lower-key. Its report recommended that the public interest test for proposed media mergers should be strengthened. Other topics of inquiry have included *Public Service Broadcasting* (2009), *Regulation of Television Advertising* (2011) and *The Future of Investigative Journalism* (2012).

The committees on delegated powers

The two House of Lords committees on delegated powers are rather different to those discussed earlier, as they do not have an investigatory role. Their sole purpose is, in fact, legislative—so their work is closely related to that described in the previous two chapters. Both committees carry out quite technical scrutiny in connection with the powers that are delegated in primary legislation to ministers, and which thus allow future policy to be pursued through secondary legislation (i.e. 'statutory instruments', in the shape of orders or regulations). An order might, for example, allow ministers to alter the level or eligibility criteria for a social security benefit, or to change the selection criteria for membership of a public body. Such orders are subject to far more minimal scrutiny by parliament than is primary legislation. The Delegated Powers and Regulatory Reform Committee (DPRRC) was established in 1992 and looks at every government bill to consider the appropriateness of any new powers delegated within it to ministers.[11] The DPRRC reports to the House before the bill's committee stage. The Secondary Legislation Scrutiny Committee (SLSC) was created in 2004 (under its original name of Merits of Statutory Instruments Committee) to instead consider the importance of individual pieces of delegated legislation as they are laid before parliament. Its creation was recommended by the Royal Commission on Lords reform in 2000, to complement the work of the already-existing Joint Committee on Statutory Instruments (comprising of MPs and peers) which considers only the technical legality of such instruments, rather than their merits. The SLSC sifts the roughly 1,500 orders and instruments laid before parliament each year for policy importance, and draws any that might be deemed problematic to the attention of peers. Neither the DPRRC nor the SLSC has an equivalent in the Commons. In addition to carrying out their highly technical duties, both occasionally produce broader reports. For example, in 2006 the SLSC reported on *The Management of Secondary Legislation*, calling for better planning and greater clarity for those affected, and in 2012 the DPRRC reported on *Strengthened Statutory Procedures for the Scrutiny of Delegated Powers*, expressing concerns that the plethora of different kinds of parliamentary procedures for the approval of instruments was becoming too complex and might need rationalization.

The two committees share a secretariat, which includes a clerk and two full-time legal analysts. It is their responsibility to conduct the initial sift, prepare papers for committee members, and engage in correspondence with government departments. The SLSC, in considering the merits of new instruments published, frequently takes written and oral evidence from affected groups. The DPRRC tends not to do so.

The two commonest kinds of statutory instruments that allow parliamentary input are known as 'negative' and 'affirmative'. Negative instruments must be laid before parliament, but will come into effect automatically after a given time (usually 40 days) unless objections are raised. Affirmative instruments instead require the explicit approval of both chambers, but can only be voted upon, not amended. As the affirmative procedure is more onerous there are fewer such instruments, and they are reserved for more important or controversial policy matters. In the 2010–12 session 269 affirmative and 1178 negative instruments were laid. Fairly often, when the DPRRC considers a government bill, it may recommend that a power to amend policy by the negative procedure should be changed to the affirmative procedure. The SLSC, when considering instruments published, will also pay particular attention to negative instruments, as they might otherwise pass into law without any parliamentary consideration at all. Each instrument considered by this committee is placed in one of three categories: as being brought to the 'special attention' of the House (these will tend to be the most controversial), as having only an 'information paragraph' provided for interested peers, or as requiring no comment at all. In 2010–12 the committee brought 53 instruments (17 affirmative and 36 negative) to the attention of the House, and provided information paragraphs on an additional 362 (Merits of Statutory Instruments Committee 2012).

Despite the largely technical nature of these committees' work, they have a committed membership. In 2012 membership of the DPRRC included Alex Carlile, a senior barrister, and Robin Butler, a former Cabinet Secretary, plus other members with mixed political experience. The strength of the committee was described by one member as its ability to combine 'good legal advice and common sense'. The SLSC also combines members with different backgrounds: for example, former Secretary of State Estelle Morris brings a knowledge of education, London Assembly member Sally Hamwee a knowledge of local government, while Michael Bichard is a former Whitehall Permanent Secretary.

The committees are well respected, in particular because they approach legislation from a largely technical, rather than political, point of view. Both appear to have a high degree of success. Data collected by the DPRRC suggest that 80–85% of its recommendations for changes to bills are subsequently introduced through government amendments (for examples, see Chapter 7). The government's own *Guide to Making Legislation* devotes an entire chapter to how civil servants should handle the committee, and states that '[i]t is usual for the Government to accept most, if not all, of the DPRRC's recommendations' (Cabinet Office 2012: 116). Any proposals not immediately accepted are often pursued in amendments by non-government peers, so are ultimately likely to succeed. As Chapter 7 described, the Identity Cards Bill (2005–06) and Public Bodies Bill (2010–12) were both examples where the committee was particularly influential. These were considered 'skeleton' bills, largely providing for future changes through delegated powers, on which the committee was particularly concerned about 'Henry VIII powers' (allowing future instruments to amend primary legislation). In 2006 the committee also helped secure fundamental changes to the Legislative and Regulatory Reform Bill, nicknamed by some in its original form the 'Abolition of Parliament Bill' (Hansard Society 2008).

The SLSC also makes a visible difference, with two forms of impact possible after it identifies a statutory instrument as problematic. One is for the government to withdraw the instrument, perhaps re-laying it later in an amended form. For example, in 2008, when the committee expressed concerns about the complexity of arrangements for licensed premises in the new 'alcohol disorder zones', the government withdrew and re-laid the regulations twice. Sometimes the changes between versions can be major: as when the government's plans for 'home information packs' were withdrawn in 2006 and re-laid in a much watered-down form.[12] The other kind of action that may follow a critical report—particularly if the government has proved unresponsive—is a debate in the House, and sometimes a vote of censure. In the 2010–12 session such votes took place on eight separate occasions, five after the committee had brought the instrument in question to the chamber's 'special attention'. Usually (as discussed in Chapter 6) such votes take place on 'non-fatal' motions, that would not actually defeat the order but only express concern or 'regret' about it. However, they act as a warning. When the chamber did pass a 'fatal' motion against the Manchester supercasino order in 2007 this followed a lengthy report from the committee. The fact that such things can happen helps explain why the government proceeds with caution when faced with committee criticism.

Other Lords and joint committees

The committees discussed are some of the main ones contributed to by peers, but there are also others. These include temporary ad hoc investigative committees and select committees on legislation, permanent and temporary joint committees (with the House of Commons) and internally-focused administrative and 'domestic' committees.

As already mentioned, the chamber can set up ad hoc investigative committees on policy issues that it believes require concentrated attention—the BBC Charter Review Committee (2005–06) which preceded the Communications Committee being one such example. Other recent cases include committees on Intergovernmental Organizations (2007–08), the Barnett Formula (2008–09) and HIV and AIDS in the UK (2010–12). These committees have a flavour somewhat like an external expert commission, and can sometimes tackle issues that prove too sensitive for MPs. In 2012 the Liaison Committee proposed creation of two new ad hoc committees, on Public Services and Demographic Change, and on Small and Medium-Sized Enterprises. These were established in the 2012–13 session and expected to report within a year. The Liaison Committee later consulted with members and made recommendations for new ad hoc committees in the 2013–14 session, and this annual review process looks set to continue. Another innovation introduced in 2012–13 was establishment of a post-legislative scrutiny committee to review the law on adoption of children, chaired by the retired judge (and former President of the Family Division) Elizabeth Butler-Sloss. Again further such committees are likely in future sessions.

The chamber can also set up select committees to give closer scrutiny to legislation during its formal passage, but this is quite unusual. Such committees have the benefit of being able to take outside evidence from experts, which is otherwise excluded from the Lords legislative process (unlike the public bill committee process in the Commons).[13] But establishing a select committee can also be a deliberate delaying tactic. In 2004, for example, when the Lords voted at second reading to send the government's Constitutional Reform Bill (which established the Supreme Court) to a select committee, this was seen as a hostile gesture. But the committee helped to defuse tensions and acted as a forum for negotiation over the future of the Lord Chancellor, so the bill was ultimately agreed. Similar attempts were made in 2010–12 to refer the coalition's Public Bodies Bill and Health and Social Care Bill to select committees, but both of these failed to find adequate support among peers.

Joint committees, comprising equal numbers of peers and MPs, are used rather more often to consider bills, on occasions when these are published by government in draft form (i.e. before their formal introduction). This mechanism may be helpful for sensitive issues where government seeks to build consensus. A recent example was the joint committee in 2010–12 on the coalition's draft House of Lords Reform Bill. Others include joint committees on the Mental Health Bill (2003–04), Human Tissues and Embryos Bill (2006–07) and Bribery Bill (2008–09).

There are also important permanent joint committees. The Joint Committee on Statutory Instruments (JCSI) has already been mentioned, and carries out a very low-key and technical task (for a discussion, see Page 2001). Far more visible is the Joint Committee on Human Rights (JCHR), which was established in 2001 following Labour's introduction of the Human Rights Act. Although this committee comprises equal numbers of peers and MPs (six of each) its reports are used significantly more in the Lords than in the Commons. This builds on an interest in rights and liberties among peers that dates back at least to the 1980s. Peers on the committee in 2012 included the prominent human rights lawyers Anthony Lester (Liberal Democrat) and Helena Kennedy (Labour).

The JCHR has attracted significant attention from legal scholars interested in human rights. Assessments have been conducted by academics acting as legal advisers to the committee (Feldman 2002, 2004; Hunt, Hooper and Yowell 2012), other specialists brought in to review its working practices (Klug and Wildbore 2007), and committee members themselves (Lester 2002). Like the Constitution Committee, the JCHR has two principal modes: a reactive one assessing government legislation against human rights standards, and a proactive one conducting inquiries into related matters such as *Children's Rights* (2009) or *Facilitating Peaceful Protest* (2011). The committee also has a special responsibility to scrutinize 'remedial orders', which government can use to amend primary legislation when it has been found by a court to breach human rights requirements. But the committee's biggest, and potentially most influential, role is that of scrutinizing government legislation. Each bill must be accompanied by a statement on its compatibility with the Human Rights Act, and this is carefully studied by the committee and its legal adviser alongside the bill itself. Where there are rights considerations, the committee will report, as it did on 15 bills in the 2010–12 session. The study cited by Murray Hunt and his colleagues found that in the 2005–10 parliament there were over 1,000 substantive references to the work of the JCHR in debates, of which two-thirds were in the Lords rather than the Commons. Many related to issues of counter-terrorism and criminal justice policy, and over half to the importance of protecting minority rights. The committee has moved over time to proposing specific amendments to bills, and many of its recommendations find their way into law.

The final group of committees in the Lords are those playing a more administrative role. The Liaison Committee has already been mentioned, and oversees the work and resources of select committees. But it does not set them 'core tasks' as does the Commons Liaison Committee (Tordoff 2005). The Procedure Committee more broadly considers the chamber's rules and practices, and makes periodic recommendations for change. Unlike its counterpart in the Commons it does not tend to conduct investigations and invite outside evidence. Both of these committees—in contrast to their counterparts in the Commons—are dominated by whips and other frontbenchers, rather than backbenchers. The House Committee is chaired by the Lord Speaker and has a similarly senior membership, and a role overseeing the chamber's administration (similar to that of the House of Commons Commission). More narrowly-focused committees oversee specific areas of administration.[14]

Conclusion: Non-legislative activity and the influence of the House of Lords

This chapter has summarized the most important policy mechanisms in the Lords beyond the formal stages of the legislative process: through debates, questions and committee work. Like Chapters 6 and 7, it has provided important material to answer two of the key questions at the start of the book: how the culture in the Lords differs from that in the Commons, and what contribution the chamber makes to the policy process. Non-legislative policy work in the Lords proves to offer important insights into the chamber's culture. Regarding impact, this work is important in its own right, but also complements the chamber's legislative contributions.

Starting with culture, we see important differences of two kinds between Lords and Commons: first, in terms of how they organize non-legislative work, and second through the expertise and policy interests of their members. Procedurally, question topics in the Lords are unregulated and do not follow the kind of departmental rota used in the first chamber; select committees are likewise deliberately 'crosscutting' rather than shadowing individual government departments. In both cases, this leaves peers relatively free to focus on their own subject interests. Committee reports and questions are also both less 'quick fire' than in the Commons, which enables members to go into greater policy depth, and often to focus on more technical, long-term, and less party-political matters. Though it is always important not to underestimate partisanship in the Lords (or overestimate it in the Commons).

The second main point of cultural difference between the chambers comes through their members' policy interests and expertise. While MPs must be responsive to their constituents, peers often base their policy focus on the professional specialisms which led them to be appointed to the chamber.

The analysis of oral questions in this chapter showed that there is greater focus in the Lords on topics such as foreign affairs, health, the economy and constitutional matters. This is partly reflected in the chamber's committee structure. The Lords lacks a foreign affairs committee (though many members would like one), but its European Union committee is particularly well-established and involves more than 70 peers. Other committees play to peers' strengths in science and technology, economic affairs and constitutional matters, while the importance of temporary ad hoc committees is growing. Committees often include distinguished subject specialists that governments may find difficult to ignore.

This links to the much more difficult question of how the Lords' non-legislative work contributes to the policy-making process, and to Westminster's wider culture. Such influence is difficult to assess, and no systematic analysis was included in the chapter of the kind applied to legislation in Chapters 6 and 7. We are therefore dependent to an extent on the work of earlier scholars, which is fairly limited. Insofar as parliament's non-legislative impact has been examined, the main focus has been on committees in the Commons (e.g. Benton and Russell 2012; Drewry 1985; Hawes 1993; Hindmoor, Larkin and Kennon 2009; Russell and Benton 2011), though some attention was given to Lords committees pre-1999 (Grantham 1993; Shell 1993b). The general consensus is that there is no straightforward measure of committee influence. In particular, tracing committee recommendations, while having its uses, can overstate influence (e.g. if successful recommendations echo those proposed previously by key outside groups) or understate it (if committees have more important preventative effects). These latter effects operate like those of 'anticipated reactions' discussed in previous chapters. Because ministers and civil servants must attend committee hearings, and respond to committee reports, they brief themselves on policy issues that might otherwise have been overlooked. But also, awareness of possible future inquiries leads—as two former ministers suggested to Russell and Benton (2011: 89)—to 'risk management', whereby policy-makers ask themselves 'how would this look if there was an inquiry into it?'.

Similar patterns of influence apply to today's Lords committees, and to joint committees, which have received more recent attention. A number of studies of the JCHR have drawn attention to particular instances of committee influence (Feldman 2004; Lester 2002), and sought to quantify the success of recommendations (Hunt, Hooper and Yowell 2012; Klug and Wildbore 2007). But other studies suggest that the committee's greater contribution may come through creating a 'culture of rights' in Whitehall (Hiebert 2006), and through the government bearing JCHR scrutiny in mind when drafting legislation (Joint Committee on Human Rights 2006: 53–4). A study of delegated legislation likewise found that this was drafted by government lawyers 'as if the JCSI is looking over their shoulder' (Page 2001: 175).

The DPRRC and SLSC in the Lords almost certainly have a similar deterrent effect to this regarding delegated powers. The government statements cited earlier, and the fact that government lawyers routinely seek the committee advisers' advice at the drafting stage, provide clear evidence. Even so, both committees also often make recommendations for change once legislation is published, which frequently succeed. The Constitution Committee probably also has something of a preventative effect, while its inquiry reports—and those from the other 'pure' investigatory committees—have made various successful recommendations. The policy importance of debates and questions is more difficult to assess than that of committees—even internationally there is little literature on this question. But some similar dynamics almost certainly apply. In particular, the rules of both chambers require that debates as well as questions receive a ministerial response. The cumulative effect on the Whitehall policy agenda may well be significant, but is ultimately unquantifiable.

In general, the focus by peers in their non-legislative work on particular issues, many of which are less well covered by MPs, enhances government accountability in these policy fields. This applies in various areas where peers bring expertise, from international affairs to disability rights or medical ethics. It has long operated through bodies such as the European Union and Science and Technology committees. But it is probably now clearest in the field of constitutional affairs, where arrangements in the chamber have developed in parallel with changes in the constitution itself—from the growth in delegated legislation, through to Labour's post-1997 reform programme. The chamber has established a clear role for itself as a constitutional guardian, and one expert has gone so far as to describe the JCHR, DPRRC and Constitution Committee as 'three new pillars of the constitution' (Hazell 2004: 495). This focus by peers contributes something unique to Westminster, helping create a new sense of 'constitutionality' in the UK, and of the appropriate boundaries between executive and parliamentary power.

Returning finally again to the question of culture, we have seen that, just as with legislation, the Lords' tradition of 'self-regulation' means that the rules governing debates and committee work are less rigid than in the Commons. But self-regulation combined with the need for some coordination means that power largely rests in practice with the usual channels—that is, largely with party whips. Because of the government's lack of majority in the chamber, this does not mean (as it has historically done in the Commons) handing power to the governing party. Relations in the Lords are necessarily more inclusive than that. But nonetheless informal arrangements, which give whips significant control in the allocation of scarce resources such as debates and committee seats, have recently come under increasing strain. This partly results from a greater desire for professionalism and efficiency post-1999, but has grown further post-2010 under pressure of a bigger chamber, where two parties now operate as a government block. In coming years there may be more demands for internal reform along the lines seen in the Commons, to give backbenchers, rather than party whips, greater power to influence the chamber's running.

Notes

1. Note that until 2006 oral questions in the Lords were known as 'starred questions'.
2. This kind of concentration of questions amongst a small group of members is nothing new. Shell (1992) reports that in the 1984–85 session, seven peers were responsible for one-third of all written questions. In 2010–12 the three top questioners were John Laird (UUP), Roy Kennedy and Paul Myners (both Labour).
3. In the 2008–09 session there were 56,375 written questions asked in the Commons, and in the 2010–12 session there were 97,703 (Sandford 2012).
4. Though it should be noted that there have been increasing complaints about rowdiness at question time, particularly following the large influx of new members in 2010–11 (Leader's Group on Working Practices 2011: 77).
5. There are currently 19 departmental select committees in the House of Commons. It also has other permanent policy committees of a more crosscutting nature, including the Public Accounts Committee (PAC), Public Administration Committee (PASC), Science and Technology Committee and Environmental Audit Committee.
6. See, for example, the debate on working practices held in the chamber on 1 November 2012.
7. Originally named the European Communities Committee.
8. Oral evidence to the committee's inquiry on the euro area crisis, 23 January 2012, question 98.
9. Malcolm Pearson, *House of Lords Hansard*, 26 March 2012, column 1178.
10. David Willetts MP, oral evidence to the House of Lords Science and Technology Committee, 17 April 2012, question 412.
11. The committee's original name was the Delegated Powers Committee.
12. The government's initial intention had been that these should include both a 'home condition report' and an energy efficiency certificate. The original form of the order provided for both, but this was withdrawn and the requirement for a home condition report removed. The change cannot be ascribed to the committee alone, as there was also a great deal of external pressure.

13. The select committee to discuss Lord Joffe's private peer's bill on Assisted Dying was one example (see Chapter 7).
14. In 2012 these were the Administration and Works Committee, Audit Committee, Information Committee, Works of Art Committee and Refreshment Committee.

9

Is the House of Lords 'Legitimate'? Attitudes Towards the Chamber

The last three chapters have looked in detail at the work of the House of Lords, and concluded that this has a significant impact on public policy in Britain. However, the chamber, and in particular the nature of its membership, remains highly controversial. It is often claimed that, as an unelected institution, the Lords lacks the necessary 'legitimacy' to contribute to the policy process. This chapter thus moves on to one of the other big questions in the book, to explore claims and counterclaims about the chamber's legitimacy.

The chapter begins by considering how the concept of legitimacy has been applied in recent debates about the House of Lords, with respect to both the chamber's reform and its day-to-day policy role. Legitimacy is a much disputed concept in political science, so the chapter looks at the various meanings of this term. Having established these parameters, it then seeks to explore as objectively as possible whether the Lords can be considered 'legitimate'. This analysis follows the approach taken by many mainstream political scientists, who base such assessment on empirical study of attitudes. The chapter draws on public opinion poll evidence, evidence from surveys of MPs and peers, and an analysis of newspaper editorials, to assess the attitudes of both voters and political elites towards the Lords. This demonstrates that 'legitimacy' is best seen as multifaceted, and that it is also open to different interpretations. According to some definitions, the unelected chamber clearly cannot be considered legitimate, yet at the same time it has features that are widely valued. It lacks 'democratic legitimacy' as commonly understood, but may nonetheless be said to enjoy some 'procedural legitimacy', 'output legitimacy', and other forms of 'input legitimacy'. The ambiguity that exists about the House of Lords' legitimacy is important in restraining the extent to which the chamber in practice uses its substantial formal powers. It is thus central to the functioning of bicameralism at Westminster.

All of this is important when considering Lords reform, which is discussed at greater length in Chapter 10. Conflicting interpretations of legitimacy have contributed greatly to the difficulty in reaching agreement about reform. But such dilemmas are not restricted to Britain, as already touched on in Chapter 3. The legitimacy of second chambers can always be questioned, even where they are elected by the people. Disputes about legitimacy are therefore intrinsic to bicameralism. This is where the discussion in the chapter begins.

Legitimacy and bicameralism

Chapter 3 demonstrated that bicameralism is relatively common worldwide, and that modern bicameral institutions are extremely diverse. Some are elected, while others are appointed or contain a mixture of elected and appointed members. Some use direct elections, while others are 'indirectly' elected by MPs, councillors or other groups. Some are extremely powerful, and can be considered 'coequal' to their respective first chambers, while others have very limited powers to force policy change. But, despite these differences, one thing that unites many second chambers is the controversial nature of their role in the policy process. Hence Mughan and Patterson's characterization of these bodies as 'essentially contested institutions' (1999: 338).

There are two primary reasons why the legitimacy of second chambers may be questioned: one quite obvious in the British context, and the other rather less so (Russell 2013). The first reason concerns composition. Put simply, many second chambers do not enjoy a direct electoral mandate from the people. As shown in Table 3.1, only 21 of the world's 74 national second chambers in existence in October 2011 were wholly directly elected. The other 53 included either indirectly elected or appointed members, in whole or in part. The House of Lords is probably the most glaring example of this lack of democratic involvement, comprising mainly of members appointed by consecutive prime ministers, but still including some whose presence depends in part on accident of birth. Nonetheless, numerous other second chamber members have no direct connection to the electorate. In contrast, members of first chambers almost invariably have a direct electoral mandate. Hence, when conflicts arise between the two bodies, there are often vigorous claims (not least from MPs themselves) that the first chamber has the greater authority and should enjoy the last word.

The second reason why second chambers' legitimacy is frequently questioned relates instead to their core role in the policy process. This factor potentially affects all such bodies, whether directly elected or not. First chambers exist to reflect the will of the majority of the people (though the extent to which they genuinely do so depends on the electoral system), whereas second chambers exist explicitly to scrutinize and challenge their decisions, and can thus be seen as undermining majority rule. Whether this is perceived as a good or a bad thing may depend on both principled and pragmatic factors. That is, on how you believe political systems are best constructed, and also often on your own position within the system. Advocates of 'strong government' may argue that interference by a second chamber (or other veto players such as courts) is anti-democratic, because it undermines the executive's electoral mandate. More pragmatically, supporters of the executive—which often enjoys a majority in the first chamber—are at any one time particularly likely to see things this way. The alternative view is a more pluralist one, which values bicameralism as a useful part of building 'consensus democracy' (Lijphart 1999). This conception fears the 'tyranny of the majority', and hence can see second chambers as beneficial, even if they get in the majority's way. This too is a principled philosophical position, but may be particularly attractive to opposition politicians and their supporters, who are likely to appreciate the benefits of 'checks and balances'. In short, second chambers will tend to be unpopular with at least some of the people most of the time.

Concerns about second chambers' role and membership are connected, and frequently become confused. If a chamber's legitimacy to interfere in decisions taken by the first chamber is questioned, this may feed allegations about the 'illegitimacy' of its membership, even where it is elected. A good example is found in Australia, where the first chamber is elected by a majoritarian voting system (the Alternative Vote) and the Senate by a proportional system. As a consequence, the party balance in the two chambers differs significantly, with a single-party majority government of either left or right generally facing a Senate where small parties and independents hold the balance of power. Some can argue that the Senate is the more representative of the two chambers, as it more closely reflects the balance of party voting nationwide. Hence small parties and independents claim an electoral mandate to oppose the government's policies. But the equal distribution of Senate seats between the six states of Australia, despite their widely differing populations, allows ministers to claim that the first chamber instead has the stronger mandate. And these 'mandate wars' can get very heated indeed (Goot 1999; Uhr 1997: 75). Most famously, in 1992 Prime Minister Paul Keating referred to senators as 'unrepresentative swill'.[1] We therefore see that legitimacy concerns are not confined to the House of Lords, or indeed only to unelected second chambers, but are arguably inherent to bicameralism itself.

Legitimacy and debates about the Lords

In debates about the House of Lords the notion of legitimacy is rarely far from view. In recent years this has applied in particular to discussions of the chamber's reform, where concerns about legitimacy tend to be linked to the nature of the chamber's *composition.* But they also arise frequently as a result of the Lords' policy interventions, most notably when inflicting government defeats, where they fundamentally relate to its *role.* However, these two sets of concerns can rarely be fully teased apart. As in Australia, when the unelected Lords challenges decisions of the elected Commons, it is often the nature of its membership that is objected to, rather than its role per se. These are generally heard most loudly from politicians on the government side.

The concept of legitimacy has been present in Lords reform debates since well before 1999. Here, we just look briefly at the language used in reform proposals since Labour's white paper of that year, which set out the 'first stage' reform. This used the term 'legitimate' or 'legitimacy' 19 times in its 51 pages. It suggested that the predominantly hereditary House of Lords 'suffer[ed] from a lack of legitimacy because of its anachronistic and unrepresentative composition'; hence, a stated objective of the reform was to 'give the House a new legitimacy' (Cabinet Office 1999: 3, 51). As the reform was going through, the then Leader of the House of Lords, Margaret Jay, stated that 'I have no hesitation in asserting that the transitional Chamber will be more legitimate than that we have today':[2] a comment which came to be dubbed by some as the 'Jay doctrine'. The claim subsequently took on a greater importance than perhaps originally intended, as the 'transitional' chamber (i.e. the House of Lords post-1999 but awaiting further reform) became semi-permanent.

References to legitimacy continued to dominate debates about the second stage of reform. The report of the Royal Commission published in 2000 used the term 'legitimate' or 'legitimacy' only 15 times in 216 pages, but was much preoccupied with this topic (often referring to it instead as the chamber's 'authority'). The Commission agreed with the government that 'the old House of Lords . . . lacked the political legitimacy and confidence to do its job properly' (Royal Commission on the Reform of the House of Lords 2000: 7). But it also raised the prospect that a next stage of reform could make the second chamber *too* legitimate. Hence, the Commission stated that it 'would be strongly opposed to a situation in which the two Houses of Parliament had equivalent electoral legitimacy' (Royal Commission 2000: 105). It expressed concern that 'the greater the "democratic legitimacy" of the second chamber, the greater the risk of damaging constitutional conflicts arising between the two Houses of Parliament' (Royal Commission 2000: 97). Nonetheless, it concluded that the chamber's authority did need to be boosted, and that the system of prime ministerial appointment in particular was problematic, claiming that '[t]he abolition of such patronage is essential if the chamber is to have the legitimacy and confidence required' (Royal Commission 2000: 130). Its solution rested in large part on giving control of appointments to an independent appointments commission so that 'individuals will have been chosen through a specific process of selection and their legitimacy will rest on the established independence of this process' (Royal Commission 2000: 131), though the Commission also proposed inclusion of a small number of elected members. An appointments commission was of course established, but remains non-statutory, and has not been given responsibility (as the Royal Commission proposed) for selecting party peers.

After this point, legitimacy became something of a battleground in debates about reform. A report by the House of Commons Public Administration Committee used the term 'legitimate' or 'legitimacy' 37 times in just 48 pages. Its primary concern was that a minority elected second chamber (as both the Royal Commission and the government had proposed) would lack the required legitimacy to do its job. Later that same year, a joint committee of both houses of parliament suggested that there were five key qualities essential in a reformed second chamber: legitimacy, representativeness, no domination by any one party, independence and expertise (Joint Committee on House of Lords Reform 2002). But it concluded that these objectives conflicted at least to some extent: a fully appointed chamber might be representative, independent and expert whilst lacking legitimacy, but a fully elected one might have legitimacy while lacking these other features.

As reform debates wore on (see Chapter 10), proposals shifted towards a largely or fully elected chamber. A white paper published in 2007 used the terms 'legitimacy' and 'legitimate' 30 times in its 60 pages, suggesting that '[t]he issue of legitimacy goes to the heart of the question of reform' (Cabinet Office 2007: 26). It claimed that this remained a problem for the Lords, and that '[d]espite a recognition that the House is working, its unelected basis means that, in many people's eyes, it still lacks the necessary legitimacy to carry out its current role' (Cabinet Office 2007: 26). One of the key reasons for further change was therefore to enhance the chamber's legitimacy. But it was suggested that '[t]he "extent" of the reformed House's legitimacy needs to be balanced against the principles of primacy of the Commons and the complementarity of the second chamber' (Cabinet Office 2007: 26). The paper's proposed compromise was a chamber in which 50% of members were directly elected; but this suggestion was later rejected by the House of Commons. A subsequent white paper proposed an 80–100% elected chamber, and most recently similar plans were put forward by the coalition government in 2012. When appearing in front of the joint parliamentary committee scrutinizing the government's draft bill, evidence from Deputy Prime Minister Nick Clegg and Conservative Minister for Political and Constitutional Reform Mark Harper included no fewer than 42 references to legitimacy in just 25 pages. Clegg emphasized throughout that one of the key purposes of reform was to 'improve legitimacy' of the second chamber (Joint Committee on the Draft House of Lords Reform Bill 2012b: 437). Responding to concerns about Commons' primacy, Harper suggested that 'our 80 per cent option balances legitimacy with the concerns that people have about the relationship between the two Houses' (Joint Committee 2012b: 446). When challenged by a member of the committee that he wanted 'legitimacy, but not too much legitimacy', the Deputy Prime Minister suggested that '[a] bit of legitimacy and a bit of democracy—just a smidgen—might be better than none in a House which makes the laws' (Joint Committee 2012b: 446).

This last remark implies that the current House of Lords enjoys no legitimacy at all—which must surely be an overstatement, given that its involvement in the legislative process is tolerated. This is further explored later in the chapter. But the chamber's legitimacy when challenging decisions of the House of Commons is certainly regularly questioned, particularly in parliament itself. Ministers in both chambers frequently evoke the right of the Commons to get its way during disputes over legislation, and use the elected chamber's greater legitimacy as a justification. For example, when urging peers to back down in 2000 following a defeat on a government bill, Charlie Falconer suggested that 'the elected Chamber of this Parliament has now clearly indicated its wishes with regard to this Bill and I hope that your Lordships will recognise the legitimacy of that view'.[3] Other ministers have often made similar claims, sometimes couched explicitly in terms of legitimacy and sometimes not. For example John Hutton, as a Health minister asking the Commons to overturn Lords amendments to the Health and Social Care Bill in 2003, suggested that these represented a 'naked attempt to thwart the democratic decisions of elected Members of Parliament'.[4]

But equally, both peers and MPs find reasons to claim during intercameral disputes that it is justified for the unelected chamber to interfere with the decisions of the elected one. Here, they evoke arguments that might counteract the Commons' electoral legitimacy, thus seeming to suggest alternative legitimacy claims (though again not always using that term). One frequently cited justification is the alleged poor scrutiny of legislation in the first chamber. As Tom McNally suggested when leading the Liberal Democrat opposition in the Lords in 2004, 'it is not healthy that the democratically elected House does not consider Bills with the thoroughness required'.[5] Another argument often cited by Liberal Democrats in opposition was the relative imbalance of seats in the House of Commons. As Simon Hughes MP put it in 2006, 'the Government may have a majority of Members of [the House of Commons] but it has a lower share of the vote than any majority government since 1832. It has no justification for complaining that the House at the other end of the corridor should not do its job'.[6] Both the procedures and the policy positions of the Lords are also used as justifications for its interventions in policy. Hence in 2002, when ministers had just tabled an amendment to meet the Lords' concerns, Conservative frontbencher Lord Kingsland suggested that had the provisions 'not been scrutinised and amended in your Lordships' House then we would not have arrived at the position where the Government have recognised the anomalies in their original proposal'.[7] As another Conservative peer suggested during a similar dispute, '[t]he issue is not the legitimacy of the House of Lords but the legitimacy and wisdom of the Government's policy'.[8]

What does 'legitimacy' mean?

As legitimacy is so central to debates about the House of Lords, it is worthwhile to stop and examine in more detail exactly what this term means. As Kelso (2006: 563) has noted, recent debates in Britain have been plagued by significant 'conceptual confusion', particularly where legitimacy is concerned. Such confusion—and indeed disagreement—is not surprising, since the term is also a disputed one in political science. Indeed, while a status as 'essentially contested' is applied by Mughan and Patterson to second chambers as *institutions* (1999: 338), this phrase is borrowed from its classic application to *concepts*. 'Essentially contested concepts' are those 'the proper use of which inevitably involves endless disputes about their proper uses on the part of their users' (Gallie 1956: 169). That is, where there is disagreement not only about whether the concept applies (e.g. in this case to the House of Lords), but also fundamentally about what it means. It seems clear that legitimacy, which is much disputed by academics as well as political practitioners, falls into this category (Hurrelmann, Schneider and Steffek 2007).

One issue on which there is much scholarly disagreement is whether legitimacy effectively lies in the eye of the beholder. A key contributor here is David Beetham, who points out that different disciplines use the term to mean different things: lawyers equate it with legality, political philosophers with moral justifiability, and social scientists with support demonstrated through public opinion. Political scientists are therefore divided between the latter two camps. Some political theorists, in debating the legitimacy of either whole political regimes or individual institutions, suggest that this should be judged against relatively fixed standards. Beetham agrees, arguing that legitimacy requires power to be 'acquired and exercised according to justifiable rules' (1991: 3).

The alternative political science perspective is an empirical one, which draws on the legacy of Weber (1957) and Lipset (1959). As Beetham notes '[m]ost social scientists in the twentieth century have followed Max Weber in defining legitimacy as the *belief in legitimacy*', so that arrangements are 'legitimate where those involved in them, subordinate as well as dominant, believe them to be so' (1991: 6—italics in original). This approach has the benefit of rendering legitimacy measurable, through opinion polls. But the risk of confusing actual legitimacy with the belief in legitimacy is that morally illegitimate political systems could be perceived as legitimate, or vice versa. In order to avoid such traps, it is wiser to distinguish between two distinct concepts: 'perceived legitimacy' and 'moral legitimacy' (Saward 1992: 47). The latter depends on defined standards, which are always likely to be difficult to agree. Beetham's suggestion is that these require a political structure to 'be justified in terms of people's beliefs, ... their values or standards ... [and] the normative expectations they have of it' (1991: 11); but this seems to take us back to perceptions. Hence, even scholars who in principle recognize the importance of moral legitimacy sometimes suggest that 'the first place we would want to look if we want to know if a regime is legitimate or not is whether its citizenry is happy with it; or in other words the prevailing level of "perceived legitimacy"' (Saward 1992: 34).

This dichotomy is one key focus of academic debate. Another concerns the different factors that might cause people to perceive an institution as legitimate. This issue has been considered extensively with respect to unelected institutions, as well as elected ones—which is clearly of potential interest when discussing the House of Lords. Within this sizeable literature, three distinct justifications for perceived legitimacy are cited. These have been termed 'input', 'output' and 'throughput' legitimacy (Papadopoulos and Warin 2007, Schmidt 2013), or 'source', 'substantive' and 'procedural' legitimacy (Bodansky 1999), respectively.

The first of these, 'input' legitimacy, refers to how members are selected to serve in an institution, and the characteristics of the members who are chosen. As indicated from the earlier quotations, when discussing Lords reform 'legitimacy' is often used synonymously with 'democratic legitimacy': i.e. whether or not an institution's members are elected. This is clearly a key input factor. It feeds one of the best-known claims about legitimacy and bicameralism, by Arend Lijphart, who suggested that '[s]econd chambers that are not directly elected lack the democratic legitimacy, and hence the real political influence, that popular election confers' (1999: 206). Lijphart's theory appears to have been heavily influenced in this regard by the House of Lords immediately prior to the 1999 reform, and the institution's extreme caution in using its extensive formal powers.

An approach that equates legitimacy with democratic input legitimacy does not, however, fully account for the special role of second chambers, as *complementary* to first chambers. The legitimacy of unelected second chambers may undoubtedly be questioned, but—as we have seen with respect to Australia—so may be the legitimacy of elected ones. If there were just one ideal of legitimate composition, then all parliamentary institutions would need to be alike. Paul Keating's remark used the difference in the two chambers' electoral systems (and particularly the Senate's over-representation of less populous states) to question senators' legitimacy. But in Italy, where the first and second chambers have historically used very similar electoral systems and resultantly had almost indistinguishable memberships, this very similarity has led the Senate's utility to be disputed. A second chamber must thus in some sense have a 'competing' form of legitimacy to the first—such that both are considered sufficiently legitimate in their own right, but for different reasons. Achieving this is clearly very challenging indeed, and may require the second chamber to compensate in some way for perceived shortcomings of the first chamber.

Here, the wider literature on unelected institutions is useful. In particular, much recent attention has been given to the legitimacy (and perceived legitimacy) of courts, and of international bodies, including within the EU. All of these are designed in some sense to complement the work of elected national governments and parliaments, without being directly elected themselves. Hence, when forming a judgement about the legitimacy of such bodies, other 'standards' may be required (Majone 1998).

Remaining with input legitimacy, Rodney Barker suggests that a political institution may benefit from being 'like those whom it governs, in terms of its national, racial, religious or ideological identity' (1990: 51). This standard might apply to both elected and unelected bodies. For example, many would consider an elected parliament with only a tiny proportion of women members, or lacking representatives from key racial groups, to be less legitimate than one more closely reflecting the balance of the population. Some second chambers are explicitly designed to represent groups underrepresented in the first chamber, though this does not apply in any formal sense with respect to the Lords. But another form of 'representativeness' which does apply, and may be equally important, is proportionality of party representation. As the Liberal Democrats frequently argued when in opposition (see the quotation from Simon Hughes, and others in Chapter 4), the Lords' relatively proportional share of seats between the parties when compared to the Commons could give it some legitimacy in asking that chamber to at least think again.

Other potential sources of input legitimacy recognized in the literature include policy expertise, and independence from the party political process. These are important justifications for the recent growth in arm's-length bodies, such as regulators and 'watchdogs', which some suggest demonstrate a trend towards 'depoliticization' of policy-making (Hay 2007; Vibert 2007). While few would consider it valid to replace an elected first chamber with an appointed body of non-political experts, such forms of input legitimacy may be more appropriate for bodies which sit alongside elected parliaments. The Lords could be seen as falling into this category.

Another potential contributor to satisfaction with both elected and unelected institutions is 'output' legitimacy. This refers to support for the institution's policy decisions, and again clearly chimes with some quotations earlier about the Lords. As Mezey (1979: 29) suggests, when considering the question 'of why people support a legislature', one possible reason is 'policy satisfaction'. The concept of output legitimacy is widely applied with respect to both the courts (e.g. Gibson and Caldeira 1995, 2003; Gibson, Caldeira and Baird 1998; Mondak 1994) and international bodies (e.g. Beetham and Lord 1998; Bodansky 1999; Majone 1998; Menon and Weatherill 2008), where it may to some extent compensate for a lack of democratic input legitimacy. Here, it has been suggested that citizens maintain a 'running tally' of an institution's policy decisions to build up a longer-term view of its legitimacy, which can withstand the effects of occasional unpopular decisions (Gibson, Caldeira and Spence 2003a: 364; Grosskopf and Mondak 1998; Hoekstra 1995). Members of the House of Lords seem well aware of the ability of the chamber's policy decisions to influence public attitudes towards the institution. One very senior Conservative commented in interview that he 'set out to make the Jay doctrine true' when in opposition, by picking issues which were 'in the mainstream of public opinion, and where the government was being ridiculous'.

The final form of legitimacy recognized by the wider literature is 'procedural' or 'throughput' legitimacy. This refers to the means by which an institution reaches its decisions. With respect to international bodies, Steffek suggests that 'there might be other reasons than democratic participation and control for people feeling that they should accept rules and decisions of governance', among them, 'expert deliberation' (2003: 257). Likewise, it is widely noted that the courts may be perceived as legitimate precisely because their procedures are less partisan, and may be seen by many as more 'fair', than those of elected institutions (Baird 2001; Tyler and Rasinski 1991). Indeed, such bodies may even enjoy greater popular support than elected legislatures (Gibson, Caldeira and Spence 2003a; Hibbing and Theiss-Morse 1995).[9] The Lords has a reputation for conducting careful and relatively non-partisan legislative scrutiny, so could be perceived as having some procedural legitimacy—particularly if the Commons is felt not to be performing this function well.

The continued tolerance of the House of Lords suggests that the chamber is believed to have at least some redeeming features. The literature on legitimacy clearly echoes comments made by contributors to debates on the Lords, by suggesting that three forms of legitimacy—input, output and procedural—may be important. And it is worth noting that there are both complementarities and conflicts between these three forms. For example, if an institution is seen as procedurally legitimate this may confer legitimacy on its policy decisions; US researchers have found that voters view policies more positively when told that they result from decisions of the Supreme Court (Mondak 1994). But also, as Kelso points out, '[a]n institution that is deemed to have input legitimacy may not also be considered to have output legitimacy, and vice versa' (2006: 566). When it comes to the House of Lords, different desirable elements of input legitimacy (e.g. election versus presence of experts and independent members) may even conflict with each other, and may in turn conflict with aspirations for procedural or output legitimacy.

Evidence on key groups' views on Lords legitimacy

We have established that it is hard to identify whether an institution is 'morally' legitimate in an objective way. Some people equate moral legitimacy with democratic election, but it is clear from the heated debates on Lords reform (further discussed in Chapter 10) that others disagree. It also appears that the same standard of moral legitimacy cannot be applied to all institutions. There are few in the UK who suggest that judges should be elected, for example. The role of a second chamber of parliament in this respect is somewhat ambiguous.

Whether the Lords *is* legitimate is a normative question, over which there is evident disagreement. We are therefore reduced in practice to assessing the chamber's *perceived* legitimacy—despite the shortcomings of this approach identified by some theorists—because it can at least be assessed more objectively. The remainder of the chapter therefore gathers and presents evidence on this empirical question. This is not just to dodge the more difficult question of moral legitimacy, but because perceptions of legitimacy are in themselves extremely important. They help to determine whether an institution's formal *de jure* political power can be used in practice. Michael Mezey's well-known classification of legislatures recognized this, by basing assessment of each body's real-world policy influence on two dimensions: its formal power and its level of 'support', where support meant 'a set of attitudes that look to the legislature as a valued and popular political institution' (Mezey 1979: 27). This resulted in legislatures that lacked support being classified as 'marginal' (if they had modest policy-making powers) or 'vulnerable' (if they had strong formal powers). The strong formal powers of the House of Lords might put it in the 'vulnerable' category, which certainly seems consistent with the long debates about its reform or abolition.[10] The 1999 reform, however, had the potential to enhance perceptions of the chamber's legitimacy, as predicted by the Jay doctrine. Evidence in previous chapters suggests that this helped it to become a more active and influential contributor to the policy process.

Mezey (1979: 28) proposed that support should be gauged through 'the attitudes towards the legislature extant amongst mass and elite publics'. This suggestion guides the analysis in the remainder of the chapter. We consider attitudes towards the House of Lords among three groups: parliamentarians, the wider public, and the national newspapers. The attitudes of parliamentarians are clearly important; those of peers determine how the House of Lords acts, while those of MPs determine how its actions are interpreted by the House of Commons. Public opinion is then the fundamental test of support for the system. Media commentators also form an important political elite, whose views may well significantly shape the opinion of voters (and indeed parliamentarians). We therefore consider the evidence on each of these three groups in turn.

Parliamentarians' views

Some examples of parliamentarians' public statements with respect to Lords legitimacy have already been cited. Ministers are inclined to dismiss the legitimacy of the Lords when it subjects government legislation to defeat, usually referring to the chamber's unelected basis. Opposition spokespeople are more liable to defend the chamber's decisions, instead citing its procedural or output legitimacy. But to understand better the opinion of all MPs and peers, survey evidence is needed. These matters were explored in a survey of MPs in 2004, as well as in the peer surveys of 2005 and 2007.[11] These included questions explicitly about the chamber's 'legitimacy', and also about its appropriate role in the policy process.

Direct questions on legitimacy explored whether MPs and peers believed that the 1999 reform made the House of Lords 'more legitimate', as the Jay doctrine had suggested. The results from 2004 (MPs) and 2005 (peers) are shown in Table 9.1. At this time, four or five years after the reform, a majority of respondents from both chambers agreed that the Lords was more legitimate than its hereditary-dominated predecessor. In the Commons in particular there was a clear party split, whereby three-quarters of Labour MPs felt the chamber was more legitimate, but fewer than a third of Conservative MPs agreed. These responses are consistent with the 'party line', since the Conservatives had opposed the 1999 reform, while Labour members had supported it. Among peers, however, a comfortable majority from all parties believed that the reform had enhanced the chamber's legitimacy (though only a minority suggested that it had become 'far more legitimate').

A similar question was included in the 2007 peer survey, alongside others on the potential effects of the 1999 reform. Responses are shown in Table 9.2. As in 2005, three-quarters of peers believed that the reform had

Table 9.1. MPs' and peers' beliefs about impact of the 1999 reform on Lords legitimacy (2004/2005 survey)

	Far more legitimate	More legitimate	No change	Less legitimate	Far less legitimate	Total more legitimate
MPs						
Labour	18%	57%	23%	2%	0%	75%
Conservative	5%	23%	21%	32%	18%	29%
Liberal Democrat	4%	50%	46%	0%	0%	54%
All (including other parties)	12%	45%	28%	10%	5%	57%
Peers						
Labour	18%	69%	12%	0%	0%	88%
Conservative	3%	62%	22%	10%	3%	65%
Liberal Democrat	15%	69%	17%	0%	0%	63%
Crossbenchers	11%	66%	17%	5%	1%	77%
All (including other groups)	11%	67%	17%	4%	1%	78%

Source: 2004 MP survey (n = 195); 2005 peer survey (n = 374). Exact question was 'Do you believe that the reform of the House of Lords in 1999 to remove the majority of hereditary peers made it . . . '.

Table 9.2. Peers' beliefs about the impact of the 1999 reform (2007 survey)

	Increased a lot	Increased a little	Not changed	Decreased a little	Decreased a lot	Total increased
The 'legitimacy' of the House of Lords	22%	55%	19%	4%	1%	76%
Public support for the House of Lords	20%	53%	22%	5%	1%	72%
Peers' confidence to demand policy change	25%	61%	13%	1%	0%	86%
Attention government pays to the House of Lords	8%	60%	24%	5%	2%	69%

Source: 2007 peer survey (n = 327–354). The exact question was 'To what extent do you believe that the following have changed, if at all, since the reform in 1999?'.

increased the chamber's legitimacy, and a similar proportion believed that it had increased 'public support for the House of Lords' (with very little difference between party groups). Perhaps because of this sense of greater legitimacy and support, 86% of respondents felt that reform had increased peers' confidence to demand policy change. A smaller but nonetheless comfortable majority (69%) believed that the reform had also increased the attention paid to the chamber by the government. This last judgement certainly seems consistent with the facts, as discussed in Chapters 6 and 7.

Both MPs and peers were also asked in 2004–05 about the circumstances in which they would consider the Lords justified in voting against a government bill. Because of the Salisbury convention, this question distinguished between manifesto and non-manifesto policies. Summary responses are shown in Table 9.3. Predictably, MPs were significantly less likely than peers to think it justified for the Lords to act in this way in general, as were Labour members in both chambers. But actually a fairly high proportion of members in all groups, with the exception of Labour MPs on popular manifesto bills, believed it justified for the Lords to at least sometimes intervene.[12] Opposition members in both chambers, and Labour peers (i.e. supporters of the then government), were relatively supportive of the chamber's right to block legislation in most circumstances. Hence, most groups seemed to believe that the Lords had a legitimate role in the policy process, even when challenging decisions of the elected Commons.

The 2007 peer survey explored in more detail the factors that members believed to be associated with legitimacy of the House of Lords. Respondents were offered a menu of possible options—which might contribute to input,

Table 9.3. Proportion of MPs and peers believing it is justified for the House of Lords to vote against a government bill (2004/2005 survey)

	Labour		**Conservative**		**Lib Dem**		**All**	
Type of bill	MPs	Peers	MPs	Peers	MPs	Peers	MPs	Peers
Manifesto policy, strong public support	13%	50%	79%	81%	64%	81%	41%	72%
Manifesto policy, little public support	32%	81%	95%	97%	84%	98%	59%	93%
Manifesto policy, many Labour rebels	40%	88%	100%	97%	88%	100%	65%	96%
Non-manifesto policy, strong public support	44%	89%	98%	100%	92%	100%	68%	96%
Non-manifesto policy, little public support	56%	92%	98%	98%	92%	100%	74%	96%
Non-manifesto policy, many Labour rebels	60%	92%	100%	99%	98%	100%	77%	97%

Source: 2004 MP survey (n = 187–195); 2005 peer survey (n = 368–372). MPs were asked 'Do you believe the House of Lords is justified in blocking a government bill that implements . . . '; for peers wording was slightly softened to reflect real-world practice, with 'blocking' replaced by 'voting against elements in'. Wording of options has been slightly shortened. Respondents could select 'always', 'often', 'sometimes' or 'never'. Figures relate to those responding at least 'sometimes'. Also see note 12.

procedural or output legitimacy—as illustrated in Table 9.4. Peers' views on these various factors differed widely. Procedural legitimacy (expressed in terms of detailed legislative scrutiny) was very highly valued, and output legitimacy (in terms of acting in accordance with public opinion) much less so, although a majority of peers still considered this to be important.[13] Among the input legitimacy factors, 'trust in the appointments process' was considered most important. Fewer peers considered presence of experts, independent members, or party balance 'very important' to legitimacy, but large majorities nonetheless considered these important. Perhaps unsurprisingly, fewer than a quarter of peers thought addition of members elected by the public to be important to the chamber's legitimacy.

Public views

Peers' belief that the chamber's legitimacy has increased since 1999 is important, as it is liable to affect their behaviour, and thus the chamber's assertiveness in challenging government policy. But obviously it is public opinion that must ultimately be satisfied if the Lords is to be accepted as legitimate. A more assertive chamber depends on public support.

Table 9.4. Peers' views of factors important to determining Lords legitimacy (2007 survey)

	Type of legitimacy	Very important	Important	Not very important	Not at all important	Total important
Process of detailed legislative scrutiny	Procedural	65%	33%	1%	0%	98%
Trust in the appointments process	Input	70%	25%	4%	1%	95%
Presence of experts	Input	46%	48%	5%	2%	94%
A fair balance of seats between the parties	Input	30%	57%	11%	1%	87%
Presence of numerous Crossbenchers	Input	30%	49%	16%	5%	79%
Acting in accordance with public opinion	Output	11%	45%	38%	6%	55%
Addition of members elected by the public	Input	12%	11%	32%	45%	23%

Source: 2007 peer survey (n = 357–371). The exact question was 'How important do you consider each of the following in determining the legitimacy of the House of Lords?'.

In studying the legitimacy of unelected institutions, scholars of the courts have drawn on detailed public opinion surveys about these bodies' input, procedural and output legitimacy (e.g. Gibson and Caldeira 1995). But relatively little comparable evidence about public attitudes to the House of Lords (or indeed other second chambers) exists. Public opinion is regularly surveyed with respect to House of Lords *reform*, which is a slightly different matter (for a summary, see Cruse 2012). These surveys are often commissioned by either proponents or opponents of reform, who sometimes ask 'leading' questions, making results somewhat unreliable. Nonetheless, when asked a straight question, public opinion consistently leans towards a largely or wholly elected replacement for the Lords. For example, the large British Social Attitudes survey has asked regularly since 2000 about 'what should happen to the House of Lords' in future. In 2010 just 6% of respondents believed that 'all or most of its members should be appointed', while 31% believed that it should be 'all or most elected'. The remainder either believed that the chamber should be appointed and elected in equal shares (28%), abolished altogether (22%) or didn't know (12%).[14] These responses have been highly consistent over the past 10 years.

While public attitudes are generally supportive of election, they are rather less supportive of the likely consequences, including the involvement of political parties and possible reduction in numbers of non-party peers. These attitudes have been less often explored. But in the 2011 British Social Attitudes survey, 55% of respondents agreed that 'the House of Lords should consist of independent experts, not party politicians', while only 7% disagreed.[15] Again, this is consistent with earlier findings: a survey by YouGov in 2003 found only 10% believing that 'the reformed House of Lords should consist mostly of representatives of the main political parties', while 32% thought that it 'should consist mostly of non-party-political people', and 48% that it 'should consist of roughly equal numbers of representatives of the main political parties and non-party-political people' (10% didn't know).[16] This demonstrates some of the dilemmas and inconsistencies in public thinking. Likewise, in a Populus poll for *The Times* in 2006, 72% of respondents agreed that 'at least half of the members of the House of Lords should be elected so that the upper chamber of parliament has democratic legitimacy'; but 75% of these same respondents agreed that 'the House of Lords should remain a mainly appointed house because this gives it a degree of independence from electoral politics and allows people with a broad range of experience and expertise to be involved in the law-making process'.[17] These last two attitudes are clearly inconsistent, and demonstrate the difficulty of balancing different forms of (perceived) legitimacy, and of satisfying public opinion through reform.

Public surveys have far less often included questions about the operation of the Lords as it is, or the effects of the 1999 reform. Polls commissioned by the author from Ipsos MORI, in 2005 and 2007, made some attempt to bridge that gap.[18] These used similar questions to the ones cited previously from the surveys of peers and MPs.

When considering attitudes to the House of Lords, it is important to note that the chamber has relatively low salience with the public, and is not widely understood. This is something freely admitted to by survey respondents. For example, a YouGov survey for the Hansard Society in 2006 found that only 5% of respondents claimed to understand the House of Lords 'very well', and 33% 'fairly well' (the comparable figures for the House of Commons were somewhat higher, at 9% and 47%).[19] Likewise, the author's 2007 poll found that only 4% of respondents claimed to know 'a great deal' about the Westminster parliament, and 31% 'a fair amount'.[20] This suggests that public responses to questions about the Lords depend to some extent on instinct, rather than close consideration.

The 2005 survey explicitly canvassed opinion on what impact (if any) the 1999 reform had had on the Lords' legitimacy, and responses are shown in

Table 9.5. Public views on the impact on legitimacy of the 1999 reform (2005 survey)

	Far more legitimate	More legitimate	No change	Less legitimate	Far less legitimate	Total more legitimate
Labour voters	19%	32%	36%	10%	4%	51%
Conservative voters	9%	19%	26%	20%	26%	28%
Liberal Democrat voters	19%	30%	28%	11%	11%	49%
All (including other/no party)	16%	27%	31%	13%	13%	43%

Source: Author's 2005 Ipsos MORI poll. The exact question wording was: 'In 1999, the House of Lords was reformed to remove most of the hereditary peers. It is now made up mostly of appointed peers. What effect do you think this has had on the legitimacy of the House of Lords?'. Around 14% responded 'don't know'; these respondents are omitted from the analysis.

Table 9.5. This shows a similar party split to that found amongst MPs on the same question, with Labour voters more likely to feel that the reform had enhanced legitimacy, and Conservative voters less likely to agree. Overall, only a minority felt that reform had made the chamber more legitimate.

This line of questioning contained various weaknesses, however. First, it relied on *post hoc* self-reporting of how respondents' attitudes had changed over time; second, many respondents may not in fact have considered this question previously; and third, it tells us nothing about how legitimate respondents actually believed the chamber to be. The same survey therefore also replicated the questions asked to peers and MPs about the appropriateness of Lords challenges to government legislation, to gauge reactions to its actual behaviour. The responses are shown in Table 9.6. The first notable feature here is that—although the poll was conducted less than a month after the 2005 general election—the public attached little importance to whether or not a bill was in the governing party's manifesto. Instead, they were significantly more likely to support Lords' intervention where a bill lacked public support, or support amongst governing party MPs. As in the MP survey, there were some party differences; opposition party voters were more likely to support the Lords' right to intervene. These figures suggest that the public consider the Lords' participation in the policy process to be justified, at least to some extent. The chamber seems therefore to enjoy some output (and perhaps procedural) legitimacy even though it lacks democratic input legitimacy.

The subsequent public survey in 2007 reinforced this conclusion. Table 9.7 shows responses to questions (not asked of MPs and peers) regarding the composition and policy role of the two chambers of parliament.

Table 9.6. Proportion of public believing it is justified for the House of Lords to block a government bill (2005 survey)

Type of bill	Labour	Conservative	Lib Dem	All*
Manifesto bill, strong public support	41%	59%	52%	48%
Manifesto bill, little public support	59%	76%	68%	66%
Manifesto bill, many Labour rebels	60%	78%	77%	70%
Non-manifesto bill, strong public support	45%	64%	57%	54%
Non-manifesto bill, little public support	57%	68%	67%	64%
Non-manifesto bill, many Labour rebels	59%	76%	75%	68%

Source: Author's 2005 Ipsos MORI poll. Wording was similar to that for the MP survey reported in Table 9.3, but the public were asked to distinguish between a *bill* that had been in a government manifesto, while MPs were asked about a bill implementing a manifesto *policy*. Around 6% of the public responded 'don't know' to these questions. These respondents have been omitted from the analysis.

* Includes supporters of other parties and none.

Table 9.7. Public views of the House of Lords and House of Commons (2007 survey)

	Strongly agree	Tend to agree	Neither agree or disagree	Tend to disagree	Strongly disagree	Total agree	Total agree: knowledgeable only
The House of Commons generally carries out its policy role well	8%	45%	25%	17%	5%	53%	57%
The House of Lords generally carries out its policy role well	9%	48%	28%	11%	4%	57%	66%
The process for choosing members of the House of Commons is a good one	17%	46%	22%	12%	4%	62%	64%
The process for choosing members of the House of Lords is a good one	6%	30%	29%	23%	12%	36%	34%

Source: Author's 2007 Ipsos MORI poll. After some brief introductory words about the Lords and Commons, respondents were simply asked 'to what extent do you agree that . . . '. Figures exclude don't knows, which were for the House of Commons 12% (policy role) and 15% (composition) and for the House of Lords 15% (policy role) and 18% (composition) for the full sample.

Here a majority of respondents believed that the House of Lords 'carrie[d] out its policy role well', which was a similar figure to that for the House of Commons. Yet, simultaneously, only a minority believed that 'the process of choosing members of the House of Lords is a good one', compared to a comfortable majority who said the same about the Commons. Amongst respondents who claimed to know 'a great deal' or 'a fair amount' about the Westminster parliament, the latter divide was similar, but there was a clear split between respondents on 'policy role', with more rating the Lords than the Commons. Little other polling evidence exists on attitudes to the work of the House of Lords, but one rare exception also suggested that the public viewed this positively. A poll conducted by ICM for the Conservative think tank Politeia in 2005 asked 'overall, would you say that the House of Lords does a very good job, a fairly good job, a fairly bad job, or a very bad job?'. The combined respondents believing that the chamber did a good job were 72%, and those believing that it did a bad job were 23%.[21]

Finally, the 2007 public survey asked which factors were important to the legitimacy of the House of Lords, repeating questions asked to peers. Responses are shown in Table 9.8. This shows important similarities and differences between elite and public views. Like peers, public respondents attached strong importance to procedural legitimacy (considering legislation 'carefully and in detail'), and among the input legitimacy factors placed greatest importance on 'trust in the appointments process'.[22] These two factors attracted the greatest overall support in the surveys of both groups, and were considered 'very important' by far more members of the public than other factors. The presence of independent members and experts was also considered to be important, but clearly less so. A key difference between the two polls—perhaps unsurprisingly—was that the public expressed far higher support for the chamber acting 'in accordance with public opinion'. This suggests that output factors may be crucial to defining the public's overall view of the Lords. When asked to pick which two factors were most important, it was output legitimacy that ranked highest amongst the public (not shown in the table: total support was 40%, followed by 32% each for the two otherwise highest ranking factors). Notably, the inclusion of elected members was considered less important than procedural, output and some other input factors—but this result must be read with caution, as it of course referred to a notional future reform, while all other questions referred to factors present in the contemporary chamber.

Table 9.8. Public views of factors important to determining Lords legitimacy (2007 survey)

	Type of legitimacy	Very important	Fairly important	Not very important	Not at all important	Total important
That the House considers legislation carefully and in detail	Procedural	73%	23%	3%	1%	96%
Trust in the appointments process	Input	76%	19%	3%	2%	95%
That many members are experts in their field	Input	54%	36%	8%	2%	90%
A fair balance of seats between the parties	Input	46%	41%	9%	3%	88%
That the House acts in accordance with public opinion	Output	53%	32%	11%	4%	85%
That there are some members elected by the public	Input	50%	34%	12%	4%	84%
Presence of numerous independent members	Input	41%	42%	13%	4%	83%

Source: Author's 2007 Ipsos MORI poll. Exact question wording was 'for each statement I am going to read out about the House of Lords, some of which are true at the moment, and some of which are not, please tell me how important it is to you in determining how legitimate the House of Lords is as a chamber of parliament'. Figures in the table exclude don't knows, which were around 10% on each question.

The expressed views of the media

So we see that input, output and procedural factors may all be important to public perceptions of the legitimacy of the House of Lords. But many members of the public also readily admit that they do not understand the Westminster parliament, and the Lords in particular, very well. In these circumstances, public opinion is likely to be influenced not only by the wording of survey questions, but also more routinely by messages in the wider environment. In particular, perceptions are susceptible to influence from the mass media. The role of the media in shaping opinions about other political institutions that voters have little direct contact with, such as the courts, is accepted by academics (e.g. Gibson, Caldeira and Spence 2003b). In general, the media's ability to 'frame' issues, and for these frames to 'serve as bridges between elite discourse about a problem or issue and popular comprehension of that issue', is widely noted (Chong and Druckman 2007; Nelson, Oxley and Clawson 1997: 224).

It would be a huge task to conduct a full analysis of the media's coverage of the House of Lords, including broadcast and print media. Here, only a subset of that coverage is analysed, through focus on the editorial columns of the main national newspapers. Editorials are where the newspaper itself expresses a collective view on one of the issues of the day, without an author 'byline'. They therefore reflect the general position of the paper, as opposed to that of individual contributors, and so provide a good indicator of the overall media environment. This analysis uses all editorials including the term 'House of Lords' from the period 1 January 1999 to 30 April 2012 appearing in nine national daily newspapers (and their Sunday equivalents), drawn from the commercial database LexisNexis.[23] This resulted in a dataset of 610 articles, once those relating to the Lords acting in a purely judicial capacity had been excluded.

Clearly not all editorials mentioning the Lords make a claim about its legitimacy. In total, just 43 included the term 'legitimacy' or 'legitimate' (or illegitimacy/illegitimate) within their text. But a further 306 were judged to include some statement from which a judgement about the chamber's input, output or procedural legitimacy could be inferred. Each such article was then coded for whether it gave a positive, negative or mixed/unclear impression of Lords legitimacy, and which conception(s) of legitimacy it invoked, as well as basic attributes such as date and newspaper.[24] For example, on 23 February 2000 the *Daily Telegraph* evoked output legitimacy (positively) when it claimed that 'the House of Lords was abundantly justified' in voting down delegated legislation relating to the London mayoral election (the first such action by the chamber since 1968). The *Financial Times* on 1 February 2003 evoked input legitimacy (negatively) when it claimed that the chamber was 'a toothless body packed with political hacks'. The same paper evoked procedural legitimacy (positively) on 13 June 2009, when it suggested that '[t]he House of Lords has long been a better forum for debate on complex questions than the Commons'.

The overall pattern of positive and negative coverage (at the level of whole articles, rather than individual mentions) is shown in Figure 9.1. We see that the picture painted by editorials is mixed, with some interesting variation over time. In total, 154 editorials (44%) presented a negative impression of Lords legitimacy, 121 (35%) a positive impression, and the remaining 74

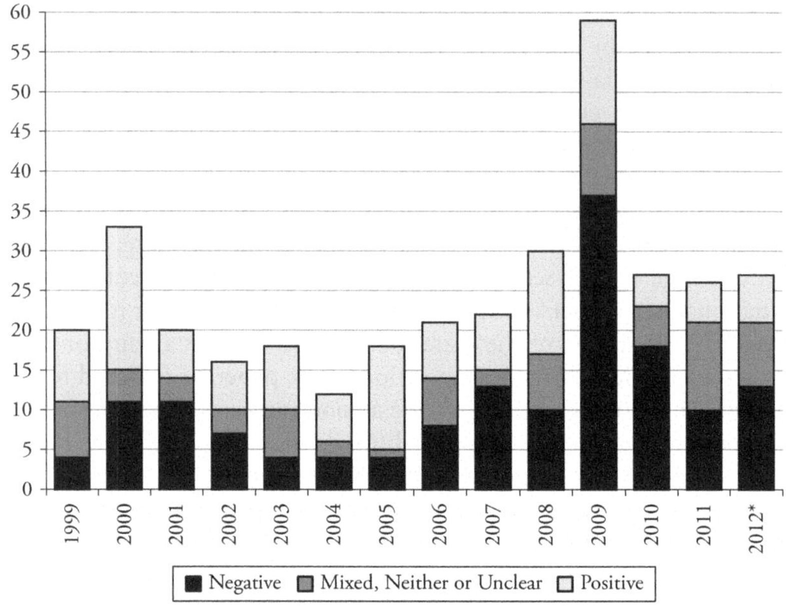

Figure 9.1. Number of editorials making positive, negative and mixed/unclear reference to the Lords legitimacy, 1999–2012

* Figure for 2012 is to 30 April only.

(21%) an impression that could be considered neither positive nor negative (often because they included a mix of positive and negative statements). Across the period, the picture is therefore quite evenly balanced. In several years (most notably 2000 and 2005) the number of positive stories outweighed negative ones, though at other times (particularly in 2009 and subsequently) the reverse was true.

The overall impression communicated by an article is closely related to the forms of legitimacy that it evokes. This is demonstrated by the data in Table 9.9. A large majority of negative articles made reference to the chamber's input legitimacy (i.e. commenting on its composition), while a majority of positive articles made reference to its output legitimacy (i.e. commenting on its policy positions). A relatively small number of articles evoked procedural legitimacy, but very few of these were negative. In other words, media coverage mirrors the attitudes of both politicians and public, by being on balance positive about what the Lords does, but negative about how it is composed. As with politicians, literal mentions of the Lords' 'legitimacy' tend to present this negatively, and to connect legitimacy to election. For example,

Table 9.9. Presentation in newspaper editorials of Lords legitimacy by type, 1999–2012

Presentation of legitimacy (articles)	Total	Conception(s) of legitimacy invoked						
		Input	% of total	Output	% of total	Procedural	% of total	Literal
Positive	121	30	25%	90	74%	17	14%	3
Mixed/neither/unclear	74	56	76%	22	30%	18	24%	19
Negative	154	129	84%	25	16%	4	3%	21
Total	349	215	62%	137	39%	39	11%	43

on 1 January 2001 the *Daily Mail* referred to the Lords' 'absence of electoral legitimacy' and on 22 December 2009 the *Daily Telegraph* referred to how it 'lacks the democratic legitimacy bestowed upon the Commons by its electoral mandate'. As shown in the table, literal mentions of legitimacy rarely appear in positive articles; but when going beyond these the wider picture is far more mixed.

The changing pattern of media coverage over time is of course related to the political agenda, and the reason why the chamber is in the news. Editorials about the Lords appear primarily when it is part of one of the biggest news stories of the day, which is when the chamber is most likely to enter wider public consciousness. This primarily occurred because of debates on Lords reform, or government defeats, though in 2009 there were other reasons.

In 2000, for example, the number of articles was relatively large, and on balance positive. Some commented on the effect of the 1999 reform, as when the *Daily Mail* (9 February) implied that input legitimacy had increased by noting that there was 'no longer an in-built Conservative majority' in the chamber. Other reform-related stories (e.g. surrounding publication of the Royal Commission's report) were more negative about input legitimacy. But many editorials also referred to the chamber's interventions in the policy process (output legitimacy), and these presented a mixed view, largely based on the newspapers' opinions on the policy concerned. Thus, the right-leaning *Daily Mail* (8 February) celebrated the chamber's blocking of the government's attempt to repeal Section 28 (which restricted discussion of homosexuality in schools) as 'a demonstration of democracy at its best'. But the left-leaning *Independent* (26 July) blamed such action on 'the unholy alliance of bishops and bigots presently assembled in the upper chamber'. Around this time, there were a number of such disagreements, including one on the

Sexual Offences (Amendment) Bill over the age of consent (which actually began before the 1999 reform). The *Observer* (3 December) summed up the period by suggesting that the chamber's 'debates on gays and lesbians during the last two years have offered one of the most repulsive spectacles in recent British politics'.

As the policy agenda changed, the newspapers became more united in their positive presentation of the Lords' output legitimacy, particularly on constitutional propriety and civil liberties matters. This was notable, for example, over the Prevention of Terrorism Bill in 2005 (a year when editorials about the Lords were on balance extremely positive). The chamber's challenge to the Blair government attracted approval from newspapers on both left and right. Thus, on 12 March the *Independent* suggested that 'it is appropriate that the House of Lords, unelected though it is, should have cast itself as the guardian of our rights and freedoms', and was united with the *Daily Mail*, which declared the outcome 'a victory for parliament and particularly a robust and courageous House of Lords'. Later, the right-leaning *Daily Telegraph* (12 June 2008) noted that the chamber in recent years had 'shown a surer grasp of our rights and liberties than the party cockpit of the Commons', while the left-leaning *Guardian* (14 October 2008) congratulated peers for having 'crushed the government's bankrupt scheme to lock up terrorist suspects for 42 days', which it described as a 'poisonous proposal'. The *Daily Telegraph* (15 July 2008) also celebrated this Lords' victory, commenting that the debate 'was sober, measured and immensely well-informed—not accusations you can often level at the House of Commons'.

Subsequently, with civil liberties battles and the overall number of defeats both in decline (see Figure 6.1) coverage became more negative. In 2009 there were a very large number of negative stories, mostly evoking input legitimacy. This resulted partly from fallout from the MPs' expenses crisis, which put parliamentary reform back on the agenda. The *Guardian*, for example, (26 May) claimed that the 'House of Lords is indefensible in principle and is increasingly emerging as a source of cronyism'. The chamber also suffered a scandal of its own, when four Labour peers were alleged by the *Sunday Times* to have accepted money in return for influencing legislation.[25] When this story broke on 26 January the *Sun* wrote of 'amazing corruption allegations' and the *Daily Mail* of the 'stench of sleaze', which the *Mirror* suggested 'turns the stomach'. The next day the *Times* reflected that it 'would be ideal if the Lords had a source of legitimacy other than its own conduct. But, for the moment, that is all it has. And that is now under threat'.

The conclusion from this analysis is that newspaper readers are given a complex and varied picture of the House of Lords' legitimacy. Discussion of its input legitimacy is largely (though not wholly) negative, while coverage of its output and procedural legitimacy is far more positive. When the Lords has challenged the government on some matters it has received plaudits from newspapers of both left and right. At other times, these same papers are more divided, depending on their views on the policy at hand, or on Lords reform. But recent editorials have communicated the complexity of the situation, and the potential contradictions between input, output and procedural legitimacy. As the pro-reform *Guardian* (8 February 2007) suggested, 'most people . . . agree that the House of Lords as it stands does its job well. Its greatest weakness lies in the way members are chosen'. The equally reform-minded *Independent* (28 January 2009) has argued that it is 'difficult for a democracy to tolerate an upper chamber that is, in many respects, a feudal relic' but that it is 'important to remember that many peers do much good work painstakingly picking through the legislation that is sent up by their professional colleagues in the Commons'. On this occasion, the paper concluded that it would be right to 'let the Government clean up and reform the Lords, but in the process we need to be careful not to wipe out what makes the chamber such a valuable check and balance on our democracy'.

Conclusion: A 'more legitimate' House?

One of the key questions at the start of the book was whether the unelected House of Lords, which we have seen plays an important part in contemporary British politics, can be considered 'legitimate'. The concept of legitimacy is frequently cited in debates about the Lords and its reform. But the meaning of this term is far from straightforward, and is much contested in political science. Some interpret legitimacy as meaning that a regime or institution has moral authority according to agreed rules, while others equate it with public and elite support. The question of the House of Lords' moral authority is hotly disputed: many claim that unelected legislators have no place in a modern democracy, but others oppose proposals to move to an elected replacement for the Lords. Furthermore, even those who support an elected second chamber in principle tend to defend the existing chamber's policy interventions when these accord with their own point of view. That is, one may dispute the chamber's lack of democratic input legitimacy, while nonetheless believing that its policy outputs, and perhaps also its procedures, are legitimate. This is in line with the academic literature, which notes that an institution may enjoy input, output or procedural legitimacy, and that there are complementarities and conflicts between the three. This chapter has purposefully avoided the long-running argument about whether the House of Lords' composition is morally right, and instead focused principally on attitudes towards the chamber, and the extent to which it has public and elite support. This was assessed against the three aforementioned forms of legitimacy, and uncovers a complex picture.

With respect to 'input' legitimacy, there is widespread agreement that the 1999 reform had a positive effect. The presence of hundreds of legislators chosen by accident of birth, who disproportionately supported the Conservative Party, had plainly become anachronistic. The reform therefore resulted in the chamber being seen as more legitimate—by MPs and peers, and to an extent also the public and the media. Peers' perceptions, backed up in particular by Liberal Democrat claims of enhanced input legitimacy due to greater party proportionality, helped give the chamber an increased confidence to challenge government policy. Hence, both the removal of the hereditary peers in itself, and the change in party balance that resulted, added to the chamber's confidence and assertiveness. The effects of peers' increased confidence and the new party balance were in turn mutually reinforcing. They did not necessarily make the Lords legitimate per se, but did change perceptions in important ways.

Political elites frequently point out that the unelected Lords lacks democratic input legitimacy. Claims to this effect are key to the House of Commons' assertion of its primacy during policy disputes with the Lords, and ensure that the second chamber continues to show caution in using its significant formal powers. But some do challenge aspects of the Commons' legitimacy (in particular, its over-representation of the governing party), while the Lords is perceived as having input legitimacy of other kinds. It is thus important to note that 'legitimacy is not an all-or-nothing affair, but a matter of degree' (Beetham and Lord 1998: 9). Public opinion surveys show significant support in particular for the presence of non-party-aligned members and 'experts' in the chamber, and there is little desire to see these replaced by party representatives should reform proceed. Public understanding of the Lords in general is limited, but its image as independent and expert is propagated by the media. With an electorate increasingly sceptical of party politics (Hay 2007; Stoker 2006), this image has a clear appeal. The Lords notably shares some common features with the kind of arm's-length, expert bodies to which politicians have delegated some of their power in acts of 'depoliticization' (Flinders 2012; Vibert 2007).

Hence, democratic legitimacy is not the only form of input legitimacy, though it may be the most important. Similarly, input legitimacy is not the only kind that matters: procedural and output legitimacy matter as well. Among parliamentarians, the media, and to some extent the public, the House of Lords' role in careful scrutiny of government policy is recognized and appreciated. This forms an important part of the chamber's reputation, and is linked to its image as relatively independent, expert and non-partisan. If the Lords were to turn into an oppositionist chamber, dominated by party politicking, this reputation could soon be damaged.[26] But it is clear from interviews with peers that they are well aware of such risks, which helps ensure that their battles with the government are at least cloaked in politeness, and are rarely pushed too far.

The outcomes of these policy battles, when they do occur and are won by the Lords, tend to boost the chamber's reputation, and enhance perceptions of its output legitimacy. One of the Lords' notable successes after 1999 was to gradually win the support of the left-leaning as well as right-leaning media for its conflicts with Labour governments over civil liberties matters. Hence, while newspapers like the *Guardian* and the *Independent* supported reform of the chamber's composition, they also helped enhance its reputation for independent political judgement. This media spotlight again ensures that peers (particularly opposition frontbenchers) pay considerable heed to public opinion in picking battles with the government and the Commons. This may at first seem counterintuitive, given the chamber's unelected nature, but it is partly its precarious existence as an institution constantly under threat of reform that holds the Lords' assertiveness in check.

The legitimacy of the House of Lords continues to be disputed, and probably always will be. At root, it is not just the chamber's composition which is controversial, but also its core role as a revising chamber. This inherent tension in bicameralism is likely to exist whether a second chamber is elected or not. Even if the Lords were replaced by a directly elected chamber like the Australian Senate (as the coalition's failed bill would largely have achieved), its interventions would almost certainly still be disputed. It is to proposals for Lords reform, and their prospects, that the book turns next.

Notes

1. Parliamentary Debates, 5 November 1992. For a longer discussion, see Russell (2013).
2. *House of Lords Hansard*, 14 October 1998, column 925.
3. *House of Lords Hansard*, 30 November 2000, column 1473.
4. *House of Commons Hansard*, 19 November 2003, column 905.
5. *House of Lords Hansard*, 18 November 2004, column 1657.
6. *House of Commons Hansard*, 13 March 2006, column 1259.
7. *House of Lords Hansard*, 6 November, columns 852–53.

8. Lord Brabazon of Tara, *House of Lords Hansard*, 29 November 2000, column 1325. A third example, from the Commons, came in the same debate on the Health and Social Care Bill cited previously, when Douglas Hogg disagreed with the minister by suggesting that 'the noble Lords have expressed their view. It was largely a free view, unconstrained by the Whip . . . I am bound to say that that view has a greater legitimacy in my eyes than that of Labour Members, bound by the Whips, most of whom are looking for jobs. I prefer the views of those in the other place in this matter. They know what they are talking about and they have not been bought by ambition' (19 November 2003, column 888).
9. Most detailed research of this kind has been US-based. As a (crude) comparator, the 2009 Eurobarometer in the UK (1,322 participants, fieldwork October–November 2009) found that 48% of respondents said they 'tended to trust' 'justice/the UK legal system', while only 19% trusted the House of Commons, and 9% trusted political parties.
10. It should be noted that Mezey's classification applied to entire legislative institutions, not individual chambers. And indeed he considered election to be an essential prerequisite for a body to be considered a 'legislature' at all, so a certain degree of licence is used here.
11. The survey of MPs was circulated in February 2004, and received 197 replies (a response rate of 30%).
12. In some, but not all, groups the proportion responding 'always' or 'often' was much lower. For example, on a non-manifesto policy with little public support, only 11% of Labour MPs and 31% of Labour peers gave such a response, while among Conservative MPs and peers around 70% did so, as did 48% of Liberal Democrat MPs and 78% of Liberal Democrat peers. When the scenario was changed to an equivalent policy with strong public support, the proportion in both opposition parties was 24–40% lower.
13. An important piece of context is that the 'loans for peerages' affair had reached the headlines in March 2006, and a police investigation into Tony Blair's peerage creations was still ongoing at the time of the survey.
14. 28th British Social Attitudes survey: fieldwork conducted June–September 2010, n = 1,081.
15. 29th British Social Attitudes survey: fieldwork conducted June–September 2011, n = 1,909.
16. Fieldwork conducted 17–20 January 2003, 2,018 respondents.
17. Fieldwork conducted 31 March–2 April 2006, 752 respondents. There were some relatively small differences between supporters of the two main parties: 88% of Conservative voters supported a largely appointed chamber, and only 69% supported a largely elected chamber; 75% of Labour voters supported both.
18. First survey: fieldwork conducted 27–29 May 2005. 1,007 valid respondents. Second survey: fieldwork conducted 18–23 October 2007, 2,044 respondents.
19. Fieldwork conducted 17–18 October 2006, 1,980 respondents. The exact question was 'As you probably know, Parliament consists of the House of

Commons and the House of Lords. How well do you feel you know how they work?'.

20. Here, the exact question was 'How much, if anything, do you feel you know about the Westminster Parliament?'. Other available responses were 'not very much' (42%), 'nothing at all' (20%) and 'don't know' (2%).
21. There was some difference between supporters of the different parties, but a majority of supporters of all parties believed the chamber did a good job: 84% Conservative, 71% Labour, 67% Liberal Democrat. Fieldwork dates and respondent numbers for this survey are no longer available.
22. Regarding timing, see note 13.
23. The newspapers were *Financial Times*, *Times* (and *Sunday Times*), *Daily Telegraph* (and *Sunday Telegraph*), *Guardian* (and *Observer*), *Independent* (and *Independent on Sunday*), *Daily Express* (and *Sunday Express*), *Daily Mail* (and *Mail on Sunday*), *Daily Mirror* (and *Sunday Mirror*) and *Sun*. LexisNexis had no articles stored for the *Daily Express* for dates between 1 June 2006 and 6 January 2009 so data is missing for this period. It also has no consistent means of classifying editorials, so this had to be identified for each newspaper by trial and error (e.g. 'Sun Says' and 'Editorial' sections for the *Sun* and 'Leader' section for the *Guardian*, but trawling through all articles for the *Daily Mail* manually). Non-editorial pieces were manually excluded, as were those referring to the Lords solely in its judicial capacity. The remaining articles were imported into Nvivo software for coding and analysis. Once our searches were complete we checked them against paper files of press cuttings on the Lords from all national newspapers kept since 1999 and found a small number of editorial articles which had not emerged from our electronic search. These were added to our dataset.
24. Unlike the coding of Lords defeats in Chapter 6, not all of this was completed by two independent coders, due to time and technical constraints. So results should be treated as somewhat less robust, though coding was conducted against clear written definitions.
25. In an undercover investigation, reporters posing as businessmen claimed that the peers had agreed to take payment for promoting legislative amendments. This triggered further stories about peers' links with outside organizations. The matter was referred to the chamber's Privileges Committee, and consequently Lord Taylor of Blackburn and Lord Truscott were suspended in May 2009.
26. For example, during the arguments on the coalition's Parliamentary Voting and Constituencies Bill (discussed in Chapter 7), the *Telegraph* (19 January 2011) claimed that 'Labour is importing into the Upper House heavy-handed Commons methods in pursuit of its objectives. This threatens to damage the civilised and well-informed conventions with which the Lords has traditionally conducted its affairs'.

10

The Politics of Lords Reform

Most of this book has been concerned with the House of Lords as it is now: how it has changed since 1999, its internal dynamics, the contribution it makes to the policy process, and how it is viewed from outside. These questions are all relatively little-studied, and therefore important. But no book on the Lords can end without also discussing the prospects for the chamber's future reform. This has been an endlessly debated topic in the last 15 years, with numerous pamphlets, reports and articles produced on the options—to the point that there is little new to be said. Yet the very intractability of Lords reform, if nothing else, makes it fascinating. The constitutional historian Peter Hennessy, who became a member of the chamber in 2010, has described its reform as 'the Bermuda Triangle of British politics'.[1] That is, a zone that is perilous to enter, and from which many have never returned.

Since Labour's removal of the bulk of hereditary peers, Lords reform has remained constantly on the British political agenda—albeit usually low down. The House of Lords Act 1999 was originally billed as 'stage one' of a two-stage process; but despite many initiatives by government, and proposals from parliamentarians and outside groups, the promised 'stage two' has remained elusive. In fact, as Chapter 2 demonstrated, Labour's reform might more appropriately have been presented as the next incremental step in a gradual process, which began more than a century earlier. In retrospect, this is how it looks. The most recent ambitious proposals for reform, from the Conservative/Liberal Democrat coalition in 2012, failed fairly spectacularly. The coalition may yet manage to achieve some small-scale changes; however, at time of writing, it looked unlikely.

This chapter starts by briefly reviewing the key proposals for Lords reform since 1999.[2] Over the 13 years to 2012 there were five fully-formed sets of government proposals, in the shape of white papers and bills, plus a Royal Commission report, reports from several parliamentary committees, and three high-profile votes in the House of Commons (two of which were repeated in the Lords). A review of the period demonstrates how the reform debate, and consecutive sets of proposals, evolved. The chapter then turns to the obvious question: given all of this activity, why was further reform not achieved? As the analysis shows, various well-established stumbling blocks exist.

Given the successive failures of proposals for 'wholesale' Lords reform, the second half of the chapter discusses some incremental changes that might prove more achievable. Most of these have been floated repeatedly since 1999, and with particular energy since the failure of the coalition's proposals. The chapter concludes that further incremental change might look timid, but—as seen throughout the 20th century—it is probably the most that can be achieved. Plus, given what we now know about the effects of the 1999 reform, small changes could prove surprisingly effective in further boosting the effectiveness and power of the Lords.

What's wrong with the House of Lords?

Before turning to the proposals themselves, it is sensible to stop and reflect on exactly what Lords reform is trying to achieve. The earlier chapters looked in detail at the chamber and what it does, leaving us in a good position to consider this question. We have seen that the 1999 reform removed some of the most anachronistic elements of the 'old' House of Lords: in particular, the inheritance of large numbers of seats, and the chamber's dominance by the Conservative Party. Members post-1999 have all been chosen by some kind of merit principle, and the chamber's party balance is now relatively proportional to general election votes. As discussed throughout the book, and particularly in Chapter 9, these fundamental compositional changes gave the Lords a greater confidence to use its powers, and to demand policy changes from government.

Nonetheless, many problems were clearly left unresolved by Labour's 'first stage' reform. The primary route into the chamber remains prime ministerial patronage, with the head of government ultimately controlling the size of the chamber, the balance of parties (and independents) within it, and who any new representatives of his or her own party should be. As members serve for life, many are elderly, and some only rarely attend. Women are under-represented (though no more so than in the Commons), and the only formal religious representation is of the Church of England (despite occasional appointment of other faith leaders). When peers disagree with government policy they can thus sometimes face difficulty getting their points taken seriously, and risk being dismissed as outdated and undemocratic. Although, as Chapter 9 illustrated, the chamber is often praised by the media, it is also regularly subjected to caricature and ridicule.

Labour's 1997 manifesto promised that stage two of reform would involve the creation of a 'more democratic and representative' second chamber. This clearly implied the introduction of elections, which had been Labour policy since 1992.[3] For many, this is first and foremost a principled objective, based on the fundamental belief that in a democracy members of the legislature should be elected. In addition, election might result in the chamber being considered more legitimate, and therefore boost its ability to convince the first chamber and executive of its case. So, as well as being a matter of principle, in pragmatic terms election could be considered essential for a second chamber to enjoy real power.

It was certainly easy to see things this way before the effects of the 1999 reform had been felt. In considering the options for stage two, it seemed likely that 'a wholly appointed upper house, like the House of Lords to date, would have insufficient legitimacy to use its powers and would not command public respect' (Russell 2000: 337). This was implied by prior experience of the Lords' timidity, but also, for example, by the *de facto* weakness of the wholly appointed Canadian Senate. Contrary to the claims of the 'Jay doctrine', some even anticipated that the 1999 reform would weaken the Lords, as it would make the chamber more prey to executive patronage (see, for example, the quotation from the *Daily Telegraph* at the opening of Chapter 1). But how reform would change things in practice was unpredictable. At the time, it was suggested that '[t]he best way of predicting the long-term outcome from a wholly appointed house will be to watch the performance of the transitional House of Lords' post-1999 (Russell 2000: 326–7). It has now been possible to observe the chamber for 14 years, and we have learnt that it was not in fact weakened by removal of the hereditary peers, but strengthened. Yet if anxieties about the toothlessness of an unelected chamber were gradually dispelled, this meant that the pragmatic argument for election lost its force. Indeed, new anxieties about an overpowerful second chamber could develop. This did not, of course, change the principled case for election. But it did perhaps make this objective more difficult to achieve.

The long road to Lords reform since 1999

At the same time as publishing its bill to remove the hereditary peers, the 1997 Labour government announced the establishment of a Royal Commission to consider the future options for Lords reform. The Commission was chaired by (Lord) John Wakeham, a former Conservative Leader of both the Commons and the Lords. It started work in early 1999, took extensive evidence, and published a report nine months later (Royal Commission on the Reform of the House of Lords 2000). This was a serious analysis, starting from first principles of what the reformed House of Lords should do, and drawing conclusions about its appropriate composition. Several of the Commission's proposals for the chamber's functions have since been implemented (for example, the establishment of a Constitution Committee and a committee on the merits of statutory instruments); but its compositional proposals have not. Nonetheless, elements of these were very influential on subsequent proposals (as illustrated in Table 10.1).

The basic model set down by the Royal Commission was for a second chamber with a mixed membership, comprising both elected and appointed members plus a small number of faith representatives. The Commission proposed that, in line with bicameral arrangements in many overseas states (see Chapter 3), elected members should be drawn from large regional constituencies matching those used for European Parliament elections, serve long terms of office, and be renewed only in parts. Specifically, it suggested that one-third be chosen at each election, and that they should serve either three House of Commons terms (then around 12 years) or three European Parliament terms (15 years). These terms should be non-renewable, to encourage independence from party leaders and whips, and to discourage constituency work. The Commission agreed that the reformed chamber should include only a minority of elected members, but could not agree on the precise proportion. Three composition options were thus set out, for either 65, 87 or 195 such members (12–35%) in a chamber of 550. In each case, most of the remaining members would be appointed, by a new statutory appointments commission, also for 12–15 year terms, and 20% of the chamber's seats would be reserved for independents. The appointments commission would (unlike now) have responsibility for picking party as well as non-party representatives. The Royal Commission proposed that party appointments be strictly proportional, based on votes at the previous general election, and that elections to the second chamber should also use a proportional system.

The most controversial aspect of this package was the proposal that elected members should make up only a minority. The Labour Party's own submission to the Royal Commission had failed to recommend an elected chamber.[4] While many in the party still favoured election, it was rumoured that Tony Blair was against this. As indicated in Chapter 9, the Commission expressed concern that a largely or wholly elected body could enjoy a surplus of democratic legitimacy.[5] Its report was, however, received badly, being

Table 10.1. Key proposals for a reformed House of Lords, 1999–2012

Source, and whether government (G) or non-government (N)	Size	% Elected	Elected details	% Non-party	Bishops	Other faiths	Change to powers	Break peerage link?	Other key points (AC = Appointments Commission)
Royal Commission 2000 (N)	550	12–35%	Proportional in regions, in thirds, non-renewable terms of 12–15 years.	20%	16	15	Delegated legislation only	Yes	AC selects appointed party peers, proportionally to general election votes.
White Paper 2001 (G)	600	20%	Proportional in regions, renewable terms of 4–15 years.	20%	16	None	Delegated legislation only	Yes	Parties select own appointees. Appointments proportional to general election votes.
Public Administration Select Committee 2002 (N)	350	60%	Proportional in regions, in halves, non-renewable terms of 8–10 years.	20%	None	None	None	Yes	AC selects party peers, proportionally to general election votes.
White Paper 2003 (G)	600	None	n/a	20%	26	None	None	No	Remove remaining hereditaries, allow retirements, disqualify peers convicted of serious criminal offences.*
'Breaking the Deadlock' 2005 (N)	385	70%	Proportional in regions, in thirds, non-renewable terms of 12–15 years.	20%	16	None	None	Yes	AC and prime minister can appoint a small number of party members.
White Paper 2007 (G)	540	50%	Proportional in regions, in thirds, non-renewable terms of 15 years.	20%	~16	None	None	Yes	Parties propose nominees, AC chooses, proportionally to general election votes.
White Paper 2008 (G)†	250–450	80–100%	In thirds, non-renewable terms of 12–15 years.	[20%]	[~16]	None	None	Yes	Non-party appointments only (if 80% elected).
Constitutional Reform and Governance Bill 2009 (G)	n/a	None	n/a	n/a	26	None	None	No	End hereditary by-elections, allow retirements, disqualify peers convicted of serious criminal offences.*
House of Lords Reform Bill 2012 (G)‡	450	80%	Proportional in regions, in thirds, non-renewable terms of 15 years.	20%	12	None	None	Yes	Non-party appointments only.

* Removal of hereditaries and introduction of retirement also appeared in all other packages listed here; disqualification of serious criminals appeared in most of them.

† Non-party appointees and bishops only apply under 80% elected option. No agreement between the parties on electoral system or size of the chamber.

‡ The draft bill published in 2011 differed in proposing 300 members, and elections in smaller sub-regions.

described in the *Times* as 'shallow, minimalist and deeply conservative'.[6] Despite many Labour MPs sharing this disquiet, the government went on to publish a white paper the next year proposing a minority elected second chamber (Lord Chancellor's Department 2001). This was broadly based on the Royal Commission's proposals, but omitted some of its suggested safeguards over both appointments and election. The paper was so badly received when debated in the House of Commons that the government decided not to proceed with a bill.[7]

Discussions over Lords reform had thus moved from the Royal Commission's emphasis on the chamber's role and functions to an argument about its composition. This began a virtual bidding war over the proportion of members that should be elected. The House of Commons Public Administration Select Committee (2002) conducted a survey of MPs, and used this to support its proposal for a 60% elected chamber. To work out where the 'centre of gravity' of parliamentary opinion lay, the government then initiated a joint committee of both chambers to devise a range of options on which MPs and peers could vote. This committee's report suggested seven options, all based on a mixture of appointed and directly elected members, with proportions of each ranging from none to 100% (Joint Committee on House of Lords Reform 2002).[8] There followed a somewhat farcical set of officially unwhipped votes in both Lords and Commons on 4 February 2003, where the Commons rejected all of the options presented and the Lords supported only a 100% appointed chamber. The options which received most backing from MPs were an 80% elected chamber (defeated by just three votes), or a wholly elected one (defeated by 17 votes).[9] However, it soon became clear that various errors (in the absence of whips), and deliberate wrecking tactics, had played a part in the confused outcome (Dorey and Kelso 2011; McLean, Spirling and Russell 2003).

At this point, the government considered introducing a more modest 'tidying up' reform, which was presented in its third white paper on Lords reform since 1997 (Department for Constitutional Affairs 2003). These proposals would simply have removed the remaining hereditary peers, put the House of Lords Appointments Commission (established in 2000) on a statutory basis, and capped the size of the chamber at 600. But they too proved controversial, as it was claimed that they would cement a wholly appointed chamber—which the Commons had just strongly rejected. Reformers thus faced a difficult dilemma of whether to accept some change rather than none. For example, when the Liberal Democrats debated the proposals, they judged that support would—in the words of one interviewee—mean 'giving away the only weapon they had'. That is, that the absurdity of the remaining hereditary peers at least made clear the need for future reform.

The longest hiatus between Lords reform white papers in this period was the four years 2003–2007. At this point those favouring a largely elected chamber sought to maintain pressure for such an outcome. A key publication was the *Breaking the Deadlock* report, produced by a cross-party group of senior MPs, including the former Commons Leader Robin Cook. This set out detailed proposals for a 70% elected House, and included a draft bill to this effect as an appendix (Tyler et al. 2005).

Two years later, Leader of the House of Commons Jack Straw sought to regain momentum by publication of yet another white paper (Cabinet Office 2007). This was the first sign that the government was prepared to accede to demands from reformers wanting a larger elected element. The paper included many by-now familiar features—including members serving long terms, elected using a proportional system in large regional constituencies—in a chamber with half of its members elected and half appointed. Recognizing that there had been problems with the 2003 parliamentary votes, and anyway now in a new parliament, a repeat round of unwhipped votes on the options for reform was held. These took place in March 2007, with a somewhat more decisive outcome than previously. The 50:50 solution in the white paper proved unpopular, being defeated in the Commons by 418 votes to 155. MPs supported an 80% elected chamber by 305 votes to 267, and an all-elected chamber by 337 to 224, though there were again signs that not all had voted sincerely.[10] The House of Lords, as before, voted heavily against all of the elected options.

Clearly, the government again needed to reconsider its plans, and—in a move reminiscent of the many 20th-century attempts at reform described in Chapter 2—Jack Straw initiated cross-party talks to discuss the way forward. These included frontbenchers from the three main parties, the Crossbench convenor and a representative of the bishops. The result was Labour's fifth and final white paper on Lords reform (Ministry of Justice 2008). This did not make a fully-formed reform proposal, but indicated two principal options: for an 80% or 100% elected chamber. However, not all who participated in the talks had supported either of these, and on more detailed matters—particularly the proposed electoral system—no agreement was reached.[11] Gordon Brown's government had originally suggested that draft bill clauses would be published for consultation, and that a bill might even be proceeded with before the impending general election, but neither of these things occurred. Instead, the government tried to use an existing legislative vehicle to achieve more minor reforms. The Constitutional Reform and Governance (colloquially, 'CRAG') Bill, published in July 2009, largely comprised of other measures, such as clauses to put the civil service on a statutory footing. To this the government added a set of clauses on the Lords.

These would have ended the hereditary by-elections, disqualified members found guilty of serious criminal offences, required suspension or expulsion of miscreant peers, and allowed members to retire and renounce their life peerages. But there was now very little time left for Labour to legislate. The provisions were approved by the Commons, but the bill reached the Lords only in March 2010, just before parliament was prorogued for the election. It therefore became dependent on the end of session 'wash-up', when the political parties make final private deals on the remaining bills to be allowed through. The Conservatives were not prepared to accept the clauses without full debate in the Lords, so they were simply dropped.[12] That this was storing up problems for the Conservatives in government seemed clear at the time.[13] Hence, Labour left office without having implemented the promised 'stage two'. Had the party been united on the question, it could easily have used its Commons majority to force Lords reform through. But instead it was split, and there was little public pressure for reform. The baton for the next stage therefore passed to the Conservative/Liberal Democrat coalition.

All three main parties had fought the 2010 election with manifesto pledges committing in principle to a largely or wholly elected chamber. But Conservative leader David Cameron had previously indicated that he considered Lords reform a 'third term issue': that is, a very low political priority. In contrast, reform was a key demand of his Liberal Democrat coalition partners, who had a long-standing commitment to an elected chamber. The coalition agreement hence included a commitment to 'establish a committee to bring forward proposals for a wholly or mainly elected upper chamber on the basis of proportional representation' (HM Government 2010: 27). Cross-party talks were restarted, chaired by the Deputy Prime Minister Nick Clegg, and a white paper and draft bill were published the following year (Cabinet Office 2011).

The coalition's package provided for an 80% elected chamber, using similar principles of election to numerous earlier proposals (see Table 10.1), and also left open the option of an all-elected chamber. The draft bill was sent to a new joint committee of both Houses for consideration. It held a large number of evidence sessions, collected written submissions, and published its report ten months later (Joint Committee on the Draft House of Lords Reform Bill 2012a). Fairly predictably, opinion on the committee was extremely split. While a majority endorsed the government's broad approach, 12 of the 26 members signed an 'alternative report' opposing elections to the second chamber. The coalition subsequently published a slightly altered bill for introduction into the Commons (but notably rejected one of the committee's key recommendations, that the proposals should be subject to a referendum before being put into effect). This bill comfortably passed its second reading on 10 July 2012, by 462 votes to 124, but with a total of 91 Conservative MPs voting against it.[14] Most Labour MPs were prepared to support the bill in principle, but Labour, and many Conservative rebels, indicated that they would vote against the 'programme motion' needed to get it considered by the Commons in good time. Facing almost certain defeat, the government withdrew the motion at the last minute, leaving little prospect of getting the bill through. Within a few weeks, Nick Clegg announced that the whole package had been abandoned.

With the coalition government's bill in trouble, alternative options began to be floated, including returning to the kind of more incremental measures that had been included in the CRAG Bill. One compromise that was initially suggested was reverting to a more minimalist package of election, perhaps including just one-third of the number of elected members proposed in the government's bill (i.e. 120 in a chamber of 450 members).[15] Ironically, this had moved the debate full circle, back to precisely the kind of package proposed by the Wakeham Royal Commission, which had been so derided by MPs in 2001.

Issues that confound 'wholesale' Lords reform

So, while the 15 year period 1997–2012 was littered with proposals for reform, including by successive governments, reaching agreement has proved impossible. In terms of composition, in particular, all of the options between a wholly elected and a wholly appointed chamber were proposed, and failed to find support. The obvious question, then, is why Lords reform is so difficult. A supplementary question is whether there is any package of reforms around which sufficient consensus might be found. The first of these questions is considered here, and the second in the subsequent section.

Those who have read Chapters 2 and 3 will have seen that second chamber reform is notoriously difficult, not only in the UK but in numerous other bicameral states. Second chambers are fundamentally controversial institutions, which exist to complement—and indeed to interfere with—the work of elected first chambers and executives. While citizens will often want to see them strengthened, governments may prefer them to be weakened or even abolished (Russell and Sandford 2002). Second chambers too similar to their respective first chambers are often criticized as superfluous, while those differing substantially can see their legitimacy questioned. All of these patterns have been visible in recent UK debates.

There are many interrelated factors which make Lords reform complex and difficult. This section discusses just four particularly well-rehearsed issues: the inclusion of elected members, the powers of the reformed chamber, the retention of its expertise and independence, and the retention of religious representation. The first two in particular have dominated recent debates.

Election

As we have seen, discussions about reform since 1999 have focused largely on the question of what proportion of the second chamber's members should be elected. The full range of options have been considered, but positions have primarily polarized between those who favour a largely or wholly elected chamber on the one hand, and those who oppose introduction of any elected members on the other. Some have tried to bridge this gap by suggesting a compromise solution; but the Royal Commission's model of a minority elected chamber found little support, and Jack Straw's model of a 50:50 chamber did no better.

This issue is one on which compromise is difficult, because for most involved in the debate it is a matter of principle. Those who favour election see it as a democratic necessity. As one such proponent put it during debate on the coalition's bill in 2012, the 'most fundamental principle of any democracy is that those who exercise political power over us must be elected by us'.[16] Both main political parties include some firm supporters of election, but both are split—as was clearly demonstrated during the parliamentary votes in 2003 and 2007.[17] This is therefore a polarized argument, but the main split is not along traditional party lines. Between 2000 and 2012 proponents of election seemed gradually to be gaining the upper hand, but when the government finally proposed a majority-elected chamber, support for this nonetheless collapsed. It transpired that, while a fragile majority on the principle might by that point have existed, there was a great deal of disagreement on the detail. Ironically, some of these details had been introduced in order to meet pragmatic concerns about introducing House of Commons-style election.

One example was over concerns that elected members would inevitably engage in constituency work, creating needless competition and duplication on MPs' home turf.[18] It was partly to avoid this that most reform packages including elected members (see Table 10.1) proposed single, long terms of office with no opportunity for re-election. Yet these elements—which were based in part on common practice overseas—added to, rather than diminished, the complaints of those opposing election. The objection became that such arrangements would make second chamber members unaccountable to their electorates. However, for some (notably including the Labour frontbench), these simply appeared to provide a convenient excuse to oppose the coalition's bill. In fact, as former Labour Home Secretary Alan Johnson pointed out during the debate in the Commons, 'everybody who has looked at this matter in any depth has come to the conclusion that there should be long, single terms with no further right to stand again'.[19] In other words, the coalition's bill closely resembled proposals previously championed by Labour.

Additionally, many opponents have expressed concern about the kind of electoral system proposed for the second chamber. As the principle that no party should have a majority in the chamber has been widely accepted, all serious proposals for reform have been based on election by proportional representation (PR). This clearly addresses a basic tenet of bicameralism: that the two chambers should have distinct but complementary memberships. However, some wishing to protect Commons' primacy fear that it could result in the reformed House of Lords being seen as more 'representative', and perhaps even more 'legitimate', then the House of Commons. Others object to the kind of mechanisms necessary to achieve proportionality, such as party lists in large regions, which could give party leaders significant control over the selection of candidates. Again in debate on the coalition's bill, senior Conservative Sir Malcolm Rifkind claimed that the government's proposals provided for 'a sham democratic Chamber, consisting overwhelmingly of Members who . . . will be elected under a party list system that is an insult to the electorate'.[20] His Conservative colleague Graham Brady suggested that '[i]nstead of a simple, transparent democratic process, the Bill proposes an absurdly complex hybrid assembly', which he summed up as 'a ridiculous fudge'.[21]

Debates about election for the Lords are thus riddled with paradoxes. The Commons has now accepted a largely elected second chamber in principle on two occasions (in 2007 and 2012), but seems unable to agree the detail. Those compromises designed to ensure that the reformed Lords does not simply duplicate the Commons, and retains its independent character, are seen as a 'fudge' that strays from democratic ideals. Yet complementarity between the memberships of two chambers is essential to the effectiveness of bicameralism. British MPs clearly do not want an elected second chamber that is a mere replica of the House of Commons. But—perhaps having only one fixed model of what they see as 'proper' election in their minds—neither do they seem prepared for it to be any different. Meanwhile, as seen from the polling evidence in Chapter 9, the public favours election but does not wish to see a chamber full of party politicians. Perhaps partly as a result, there has been limited public pressure for reform.

Power

One of the interesting features of the last 15 years of debate is how little attention has been paid to the appropriate powers of the reformed second chamber. As shown in Table 10.1, all proposals have essentially sought to leave the formal powers of the chamber as they are now. The only exceptions were some relatively minor proposals early on to limit the Lords' veto on delegated legislation. Instead, argument has focused almost exclusively on matters of composition.

However, one of the primary concerns of those opposed to election is the effect that this would have on the power relationship between the two chambers of parliament. Their principled position is that the House of Commons must remain the primary chamber, and many are keen to hold on to Britain's majoritarian traditions and reputation for 'strong' and stable government. Most people believe that a largely or wholly elected second chamber would be seen as more democratically legitimate than the present Lords, and hence that it would make greater use of its substantial powers. Although the Parliament Acts would ensure that the Commons usually retained the last word, the Lords could still become quite disruptive if it used its current powers to the full. From the Royal Commission onwards, there have therefore been suggestions that the reformed chamber could become 'too legitimate' and destabilize arrangements at Westminster. This has been used as a key argument for limiting the number of elected members, and for having at most a mixed elected/appointed House. It is also a further reason for proposing long terms of office and renewal of the chamber in parts, so that the Commons always has the fresher mandate.

Arguments about power have therefore always been present to some extent in the long debate about the reformed chamber's composition. But they were largely in the background. They came to the foreground only once the government had finally succumbed to arguments that the chamber should be largely elected. In other words, just when one debate seemed to be settled, another even bigger one began.

The relationship between composition, legitimacy and power was emphasized by the joint committee which met to consider the conventions governing the two chambers' relationship back in 2006. This committee was established because of fears that the existing conventions—including the Salisbury convention over treatment of manifesto bills—were breaking down. The committee concluded that established conventions could still be considered operative, but stressed that '[o]ur conclusions apply only to present circumstances. If the Lords acquired an electoral mandate, then in our view their role as the revising chamber, and their relationship with the

Commons, would inevitably be called into question' (Joint Committee on Conventions 2006a: 23).

Such concerns were elaborated substantially by the later joint committee that considered the coalition's draft bill in 2011–12. A particular focus of criticism by those giving evidence to the committee was clause 2 of the bill, which declared that relations between the chambers would be unaffected by a change in the second chamber's composition. The committee concluded that, in line with what it described as 'the overwhelming view expressed' by witnesses, 'Clause 2 of the draft Bill is not capable in itself of preserving the primacy of the House of Commons' (Joint Committee on the Draft House of Lords Reform Bill 2012a: 17). It further suggested that 'following election the increased assertiveness of a reformed second chamber will affect the balance of power between the two chambers in favour of the House of Lords' (Joint Committee 2012a: 20).

These concerns hence came to dominate debates on the 2012 bill. But as Chapter 2 demonstrated, they were far from new. For example, the 1945 Labour government feared, as cabinet minister Herbert Morrison (1964: 205) later put it, that 'the democratisation of the Second Chamber . . . would have added to its authority and would have strengthened its position as against that of the House of Commons'. Labour was always divided on the issue (see Dorey 2006), and similar divisions afflicted the Conservatives. The coalition's best defence in 2012 could perhaps have been to make a virtue out of the likely strengthening of the Lords: as Lord Strathclyde sought to do when suggesting that 'the only purpose in having the Bill on reform of the House of Lords . . . is that this House should be . . . more assertive, stronger and better able to hold the Government to account and if it can challenge the views of the House of Commons'.[22] However, these words clearly contradicted the claims in clause 2 of the bill. They also fuelled the objections of the bill's opponents that it would lead to gridlock and 'constitutional crisis'.[23]

It is well-established in the academic literature that the *de facto* powers of a political institution may be significantly less great, or indeed greater, than its formal constitutional powers imply (see, for example, Levitsky and Murillo 2009). This is clearly the case with respect to the Lords, which—as demonstrated in Chapter 3—enjoys substantial formal powers in comparison to many other second chambers, but uses them with caution. If the chamber's membership was elected, this would probably change. The impasse in 2012 suggests that MPs will only accept a bill to create a largely elected second chamber if it also includes a reduction in the chamber's formal powers (perhaps to something like a delay power of six months, as was proposed in 1968). Yet herein further paradoxes lie. The public and the political class are broadly happy with the Lords' existing powers, but see problems with the chamber's composition. Yet changing this would almost certainly also change its *de facto* power. A bill to reduce the powers of parliament would be highly controversial, as well as being complex to draft. Once the Pandora's box of powers has been opened, any resulting proposals might face even greater obstacles than those that previously sought to deal with composition alone.

Expertise and independence

Another concern, closely related to those surrounding election, is that any reform should maintain the 'expert' and 'independent' ethos of the present chamber. As was demonstrated in Chapter 9, these characteristics are valued by the public as well as political elites. We have seen throughout the book that both expertise and independence are relatively ill-defined, and at least to an extent disputed. Some claim that the Lords contains too many 'ex-experts', and point out that few votes are cast against the party whip. Yet the picture is more complicated than that: contributions to debates and committee work by members who are subject-specialists are widely appreciated, and may influence the votes of others. Party cohesion in the Lords remains looser than that in the Commons, particularly in terms of members' tendency to abstain.

Consequently, there is anxiety that something important could be lost if the chamber were elected. As the former Commons Speaker Baroness Boothroyd put it during debate on the coalition's bill, '[i]n what way would the nation benefit and parliamentary proceedings be enhanced by the abolition of this House of experts and experience, and its replacement by a senate of paid politicians?'.[24] Such concerns are shared by many in the charity and pressure group world, who have good connections to the chamber and are grateful for its members' willingness to take up causes, including those which are unpopular. Shami Chakrabati, Director of pro-human rights campaign group Liberty, has for example spoken publicly against an elected chamber, suggesting that peers 'have been great protectors of fundamental rights and freedoms'.[25] In a briefing responding to the coalition's plans, the Campaign for Science and Engineering likewise lamented that the 'proposed reforms to the House of Lords will almost certainly reduce the number of experts it currently has, across all disciplines' (CaSE 2012: 1).

Most accept that senior scientists, public servants and even retired political grandees would be unlikely to stand for election, while those without a party affiliation would face difficulty getting elected. Hence, almost all proposals have allowed for a 20% independent elected element (see Table 10.1). But this presents two difficulties. First, not all of the currently celebrated experts sit on the Crossbenches: many are party peers. Second, a mixed elected/appointed chamber raises new objections about a 'two-tier' membership, where controversy might arise over decisions on which the votes of appointed members determined the outcome. The proposal of a mixed membership (although, again, such arrangements are common in overseas second chambers) contributes to accusations that proposals are an uncomfortable 'fudge'. Other possible solutions, such as using some kind of 'vocational' system of representation, have been widely dismissed as impractical.[26]

Religious representation

Another complicating factor is the issue of religious representation. This has not been central to debates about reform, but must be faced in any wholesale package. In particular, an all-elected chamber would clearly require eviction of the bishops. But any reform that seeks to modernize the chamber's composition, and even simply to reduce its size, raises questions about reform of the bishops' benches.

This topic received careful consideration by the Royal Commission which (as shown in Table 10.1) has been the only body in recent years to suggest diversification of formal religious representation in the chamber. The Commission proposed that the number of Church of England representatives should be reduced, in order to make space for representation of other Christian denominations, and that there should also be 'at least five members of the second chamber specifically selected to be broadly representative of the different non-Christian faith communities' (Royal Commission on the Reform of the House of Lords 2000: 155). But—as with vocational representation—this approach opens up difficult new questions about which groups should be represented, and in what numbers.[27] Other proposals, recognizing these difficulties, have taken a more pragmatic approach of simply suggesting a reduction in the number of bishops.

But for many, the question of religious representation—and more broadly the relationship between religion and the state—is one of high principle (McLean 2010b; Morris 2009). Any wholesale package of Lords reform must take a position on the bishops' presence, either suggesting that they be removed, reduced in number, or left alone. But whichever option is chosen will be controversial in the House of Commons, and to an extent in the country at large. This could be an unexpected stumbling block for any bill. A more practical approach might be to deal with the bishops' presence as a standalone issue, for example in a private member's bill. That way, the Commons could express a view, which it has not yet been invited formally to do.

Options for more incremental changes

This final point leads neatly to the question of whether there are smaller changes that might successfully be agreed. As Chapter 2 summarized, the history of Lords reform has been largely one of inaction, punctuated by occasional incremental change. No 'wholesale' reform package seeking to put in place a new permanent settlement has ever been agreed. Instead, reforms that succeeded were always seen at the time as incomplete and temporary, to simply address the most urgent problems. The Parliament Acts of 1911 and 1949, the Life Peerages Act of 1958, the Peerage Act of 1963 and the House of Lords Act of 1999 all fall into this category. Possibly, then, it is more sensible to look at what are the most indefensible and problematic aspects of today's House of Lords—aside from its unelected basis—and seek to deal with these in a similar incremental manner.

As already discussed, there have been some recent attempts to proceed in this way, including the Labour government's CRAG Bill of 2009 and (in non-legislative form) its 2003 white paper. Incremental changes have also been proposed in a series of private peers' bills, most notably those introduced repeatedly by the Liberal Democrat peer David Steel in every parliamentary session since 2006–07 (see Rushbrook 2012). A menu of possible reforms was also presented to the Joint Committee on the Draft House of Lords Reform Bill (2012b: 355) by former Lord Speaker Helene Hayman. Since incrementalism is ultimately the most likely way forward, this section summarizes some of the smaller changes that might sensibly be implemented next.

Removing the remaining 92 hereditary peers

The most obviously anomalous element of today's House of Lords is the continuing presence of hereditary peers, and, in particular, the bizarre by-election system used to replace such members when they die. Labour's original intent in 1997 was to remove all hereditary peers, but a compromise was made to secure easier passage of the bill through the Lords. In retrospect, the government's acceptance of the so-called 'Weatherill amendment' was probably a mistake. Weatherill himself performed a classic Crossbench function by fronting the amendment, which was in truth a deal between the two main parties. But the by-elections were not included in his original plan. Indeed, he subsequently proposed a private peer's bill to end them, but this was strongly resisted by the Conservative frontbench.[28] The proposal later featured in slightly wider-ranging bills by David Steel, and also in the government's CRAG Bill.

This measure has considerable support among members of the chamber. In the 2007 peer survey, 71% agreed that 'there should no longer be automatic rights for hereditary peers to sit in the chamber'.[29] Nonetheless, this element of the Steel bill faced significant resistance in the 2010–12 session from a small group of peers, who tabled hundreds of amendments which threatened to wreck its passage. Consequently, Steel was forced to remove this provision from the bill. One difficulty is that then Lord Chancellor Derry Irvine had pledged during passage of the 1999 Act that the hereditary peers would 'go only when stage two has taken place. So it is a guarantee that it will take place'.[30] This has clearly not proved to be true, but a one-off measure to remove the hereditaries would still be seen by some as a breach of faith. Evicting the existing 92 completely (except in the context of a major reform) would be somewhat brutal, as many contribute usefully to the chamber. But there is widespread agreement that the by-elections damage the chamber's image, and should be ended (to clarify matters, the current 92 might at the same time be made into life peers). A government bill on these lines would be less prey to time wasting procedural tactics than was the Steel bill.

Allowing permanent departures from the chamber

The other main proposal in the Steel bill, which remained intact after its passage through the chamber in 2010–12 (and again in 2012–13) was to allow members of the Lords to permanently and irrevocably retire. Particularly given the chamber's spiralling size (see Chapter 4), this has been a growing preoccupation among both peers and external reformers. The government's CRAG Bill included provisions for voluntary retirement, to go beyond the existing leave of absence arrangements. These would have allowed peers to keep their titles, but nonetheless depart the chamber. Following the clauses' abandonment before the 2010 election, the new Leader of the Lords, Tom Strathclyde, established a committee chaired by Conservative peer David Hunt to look at the options for a retirement scheme. This recommended the current system whereby peers can indicate that they intend their leave of absence to be permanent (Leader's Group on Members Leaving the House 2011). But there are two obvious problems with these arrangements. First, there is nothing to prevent a peer from reversing such a decision, as they retain their sitting rights under the 1958 Life Peerages Act.[31] Second, as the Hunt committee pointed out, departing peers will weaken the numbers in their party/group, with no guarantee (at least until appointments become more regulated) that these will be replenished. Hence by May 2013 only three peers had chosen to 'retire' in this way. A statutory retirement provision (i.e. amending the 1958 Act) would deal with the first of these problems, but it would not deal with the second. Peers would probably remain reluctant to volunteer unless this were combined with other measures. One option could be for each of the chamber's groups to shed a certain proportion of members, by agreement, perhaps through internal elections (like those used for hereditary peers in 1999) or simply through seeking volunteers. Simultaneous action by all groups would almost certainly succeed better than an unregulated voluntary retirement scheme. But agreeing the appropriate balance between the groups could prove difficult.

Another option which has been much discussed is the possible introduction of compulsory retirement. The most straightforward means would be a statutory age limit. If this were set at 80 it would (as of May 2013) result in the departure of around 135 members, or if set at 75, of around 240.[32] This would clearly help with numbers, but be somewhat arbitrary in two senses. First, that many members aged 75+ make valuable contributions, and second, that its effect would be uneven between the parties (see Table 5.1). An alternative is a limit on length of service, discussed later in this chapter. Such changes would most securely be made via legislation, but in the short term conventions might also be established that members depart the chamber after a given age or term of office.

A slightly separate issue, which formed the third main proposal in the original Steel bill (and was also in CRAG), is disqualification for peers convicted of serious criminal offences. Such a restriction applies in the Commons, and it is almost universally agreed that the same should apply in the Lords. This is a tiny 'tidying up' measure, but would only be enforceable through legislation.

Regulating appointments and limiting the Prime Minister's patronage power

The measures already discussed both tackle anomalies in the Lords' existing membership, but changes are also needed to how new members reach the chamber, if past problems are not to recur. This requires far greater regulation of prime ministerial patronage powers.

The first problem is the age-old one of the chamber's size, and the fact that there is no limit on the number of new members that can be created. Controversy over new peerage creations long pre-dates Blair and Cameron; indeed the first bill to cap the size of the chamber was proposed in 1719 (see

Chapter 2). It has been pointed out repeatedly in recent years (e.g. Russell et al. 2011; Seyd 1998, 1999) that these unregulated appointments create an upward ratchet effect, as each new prime minister seeks to counterbalance their predecessors' appointments with new peers from their own party, while maintaining the appearance of decency by appointing a few from other parties as well. Tensions have been particularly high under the coalition, given Cameron's large number of appointments and desire to rebalance with Labour. In February 2013 the government was heavily defeated on a motion reiterating the Hunt committee's plea that 'restraint should be exercised by all concerned in the recommendation of new appointments to the House'—at 172 votes it was the third largest government defeat since 1999. The original motion (proposed by David Steel) had asked the chamber to temporarily block all new introductions of peers. Some members clearly considered such action too radical, and the words were toned down. But anger at the chamber's growing size could see such proposals returned to.

Ultimately, the only way to stop these kinds of problems is to cap the size of the House. Almost all recent proposals for reform (see Table 10.1) have assumed that a new chamber should have a fixed size, and this is normal in other parliaments around the world. To be enforceable, it would need to be set in statute, though a first step could be for the prime minister to voluntarily announce and respect a limit. Prior proposals for the chamber's size have ranged between 250 and 600 members, and if a part-time appointed membership is to be retained, the upper end of this range is probably necessary. But even this is well below the chamber's current size. To reach the cap more quickly, some shrinkage in the existing membership would thus be needed.

A cap on the chamber's size would need to be accompanied by an agreed proportionality formula for future appointments, as future prime ministerial restraint would become essential. Such a formula is anyway needed for transparency and fairness between the parties, since under the current arrangements a prime minister could still in theory appoint disproportionate numbers of government peers (for example, to overcome problems with Lords defeats). Ending this degree of executive control is long overdue. From the Royal Commission onwards, proposals for reform that have included continued presence of party appointees have consistently proposed that new appointments mirror party vote shares at the preceding general election, and this is the obvious formula to choose. (It is important to note that this is different to the formula suggested in the 2010 coalition agreement of bringing the chamber's whole membership into line with each general election result, which is far more problematic.[33]) Applying proportionality to each new group of appointees would result in a fairly stable balance between the parties, which would level out electoral fluctuations. New members might be appointed in groups of 10 or 20 (as has tended to occur in recent years), with the appropriate balance applied to each batch. But a standard proportionality formula (such as d'Hondt) could easily be used even if appointments were made one by one.[34] Any such formula would ideally be specified in statute, though a non-statutory agreement would be a possible improvement on the status quo. It would need to be regulated by some responsible body—most obviously the House of Lords Appointments Commission.

Reform could go further than this, and the Appointments Commission also be given some powers over the selection of party peers. The Royal Commission suggested that this power should extend to actually choosing party peers but, despite apparent public support, party leaders considered this proposal a step too far.[35] A more moderate suggestion, made by the House of Commons Public Administration Committee (2007), is that the Commission should gain a degree of discretion in picking from lists of names provided by the parties. This would better allow it to maintain balance in the chamber, for example, in terms of gender, professional expertise and geography. One of the chamber's strengths is its diversity of membership, but the Commission cannot guarantee this while only picking around 20% of members.

Finally, it has frequently been suggested (for example by the Public Administration Committee and in the Steel bill) that the existing Appointments Commission should be made statutory. It was originally set up on the Prime Minister's initiative, and acts under his guidance rather than having powers and responsibilities set out in law. If the Commission were given statutory responsibility for safeguarding proportionality and/or to select party members, it would make sense for the legislation to also set out a more general framework for its powers and membership. Provisions to this effect were included in the Labour government's CRAG Bill, and also the coalition's bill of 2011–12.

It is worth pointing out that, like so much else in debates on Lords reform, these proposals are far from new. More than 20 years ago Donald Shell (1992: 255) noted that constraints on prime ministerial patronage remained limited and informal, and '[a]ssuming that any reform would leave the Upper House still, in part, composed through appointment, a more formalised machinery for initiating suggestions [of new peers] should be composed'. He suggested that a body 'obliged to report on the balance of party membership in the range of expertise and experience represented in, and omitted from, the House of Lords' would be desirable, and that there was a need to 'define a formula which prime ministers would be required to observe in making nominations' (1992: 255). That two decades have passed since these proposals were made indicates the extent to which they are overdue.

Introducing term-limited appointments

Some further proposals could more radically shake up the system, though still falling short of introducing elections. One would be introduction of fixed-term appointments for members of the Lords. Recent proposals have largely been for 10–15 year terms for either elected or appointed members. Term limits for future appointees would be an alternative to a fixed retirement age, retaining flexibility to, for example, appoint a distinguished 67-year-old for 15 years. They would also help to keep the size of the chamber under control, while allowing a regular (and predictable) pattern of new appointments. This principle was proposed before the publication of the CRAG Bill by the Conservative MPs Andrew Tyrie and George Young (2009), who sponsored amendments to the bill to this effect on a cross-party basis, without success. Fixed terms were more recently on the list of proposals made by Helene Hayman.

This would be a fairly major change, and its detail would need careful thought. For example, many MPs (let alone peers) currently serve for more than 15 years, so it might be desirable for some members to be able to serve two terms. But if renewal lay in the hands of party leaders, this would give them far greater control than now over members' behaviour. Such problems might be resolved by leaving renewal at the discretion of the House of Lords Appointments Commission.

Breaking the link with the peerage

Another change which could have important effects of both a practical and symbolic nature would be to break the link between the peerage and membership of the chamber. This has already occurred with respect to the hereditary peerage, as the majority of such peers no longer have a right to sit. But life peerages remain inextricably connected to Lords membership. A change would seem necessary if fixed-term appointments were to be introduced, and was included in most post-1999 proposals (as Table 10.1 shows). Some members would feel more comfortable being appointed to the chamber if this did not require them to accept a peerage, while others might want to accept a peerage for purely honorific reasons. In the past this was possible, given the limited expectations on attendance for non-'working peers', but practice has changed since 1999. Breaking the link would clarify that appointment to the chamber is a job, not an honour. If honorific life peerages continued to exist, there would be nothing to stop a recipient being appointed to the chamber, or indeed elected to the House of Commons (as excluded hereditary peers can be now), but the two positions would become independent. This proposal was also recently made by Helene Hayman.

Enhancing the chamber's image: A 'Clause IV moment'?

All of the previous proposals involve substantive change to the chamber's membership. This last one is, in contrast, purely symbolic. Despite all of the changes in the last 13 years (and indeed since 1958), the visual image of the House of Lords remains largely unaltered. Invariably, the media use pictures of the chamber where massed peers are gathered wearing their red, ermine-trimmed robes. However, these are in fact worn only once a year, on the day of the queen's speech.[36] This image therefore essentially misrepresents the chamber: peers do not wear robes for their daily business. More normally they dress like any other 21st-century politicians.

Ironically, the single thing that might best communicate how much the Lords has changed is thus symbolic: for peers to simply abandon this dress code for the queen's speech. If these annual images did not exist, the media would be forced to show the chamber as it really is. This has previously been described as a potential 'Clause IV moment' for the House of Lords.[37] The phrase refers to the birth of so-called 'new Labour' in 1995, when the words on aims and values in the party's constitution were revised. It was widely recognized that the clause, which committed the party to the public ownership of industry, no longer reflected its actual policy positions. Yet, following Hugh Gaitskell's failed attempt to rewrite the clause in 1959 when he was party leader, most saw it as far too troublesome to change. When Tony Blair was elected leader in 1994 he recognized that its revision provided a symbolic opportunity. The new Clause IV was widely heralded as marking the birth of 'new Labour', despite the fact that much modernization had already been achieved by Blair's predecessors (Neil Kinnock and John Smith) and that much else in the party remained unchanged (Fielding 2003; Russell 2005). If the British public is ever to believe that it really has a 'new' House of Lords, a similarly bold symbolic change seems necessary.

Conclusion: Lords reform, large and small

This chapter has provided a brief account of attempts to reform the House of Lords since the passage of the 1999 Act. Over this period, debate has largely focused on the possible introduction of elected members, but this reform has so far proved elusive, and looks unlikely in the near future. The chapter has therefore also reflected on why Lords reform has proved so difficult, and considered whether there are smaller, more incremental reforms that might more successfully be pursued.

In terms of the questions at the start of the book, the chapter most obviously addresses just one of these, on the most likely future for the House of Lords. Based on events since 1999, and the longer history set out in Chapter 2, the prospects for 'wholesale' Lords reform do not look good. In asking why this is the case, however, other core questions in the book are important. In particular, the way that the chamber has changed since its last reform, and the impact that it now has on the policy process, have played a part in hindering further progress.

Many, particularly inside the Labour Party, have long been nervous about a reform that would significantly enhance the Lords' legitimacy, because this could threaten the pre-eminence of the Commons. There were good pragmatic reasons for Labour in 1997 to propose a two-stage reform, because the presence of hundreds of hereditary peers, many more of them Conservative than Labour or Liberal Democrat, was glaringly anachronistic. It was the chamber's obvious Achilles heel, and clearly the most urgent problem to deal with. But it was also the only progress on which Labour could easily agree, while any 'second stage' was far more likely to cause problems. Had the party sought to proceed with a single 'big bang' reform, it is quite possible that no change would have occurred.

Although many (particularly Labour's opponents) feared that the 1999 reform would weaken the Lords, it soon became clear that, if anything, the reverse was true. As documented throughout the earlier chapters of the book, the departure of the hereditaries resulted in peers becoming more confident, more active, and (particularly after the Liberal Democrats began to vote more often against Labour) extracting more policy concessions from government. The extent to which an unelected chamber, buoyed in particular by its newly proportional membership, was prepared to challenge the executive surprised many people. It thus became clear to ministers that a supposedly partial, temporary reform could have a substantial effect.

This is a key contextual factor in explaining why the second stage of reform proved so difficult. Had the Lords remained a timid institution post-1999, those campaigning for an elected chamber, which most believed would strengthen parliament against the executive, might well have had greater success. But while the principled argument for election remained unchanged, the pragmatic case for rejuvenating the second chamber got weaker. From the point of view of Blair and many of his key ministers, it had already been rejuvenated quite enough.

Nonetheless, by 2010, when the coalition government entered office, all three parties were officially committed to introducing a largely or wholly elected chamber. Response to the Royal Commission's report, and Labour's early 'stage two' proposals, resulted in a bidding upwards of the proposed elected element, in line with what polls suggested were the public's views. But only the Liberal Democrats were wholeheartedly in favour of such a reform. When an elected chamber was championed by Nick Clegg in government, opponents could even argue that he was motivated by self-interest, given that the proportional representation system would have cemented the position of his party as the pivotal group in the second chamber. The period 1999–2010 had already seen the Liberal Democrats use this position in the unelected chamber to achieve significant policy concessions from a single party majority government, while claiming the rights to do so on the basis of non-proportional share of seats in the Commons. Conservative MPs, resentful at the Lib Dems' influence inside the coalition, and naturally hostile towards PR, did not want to bolster the third party's influence. Thus, many voted against reform.

Given that both main parties are extremely split on the question of elections to the chamber, prospects for this reform now look poor. The likeliest scenario in which it might be pursued is a deal between Labour and the Liberal Democrats after a future general election, should Labour be the largest party. But such a deal might well collapse in a very similar way to that in 2012. After all, had Labour really wanted this reform, it could easily have been implemented between 1999 and 2010. Since then debate has moved on, as a result of the Clegg proposals, to what the correct powers should be for an elected second chamber. Any new package would have to address this, but it leads to a different quagmire—which so far remains relatively unexplored. Since Labour's 2010 manifesto promised that proposals for an elected chamber would be put to the people in a referendum, and this is the only sure means of avoiding Labour splits, the party would probably also make this a condition. But there is no guarantee that proposals would pass a referendum, given the public's complex views on the Lords (as set out in Chapter 9). Any reform seen as threatening the chamber's expertise, independence, or indeed powers, would find many opponents.

So, in terms of the future, the realistic choice seems to be between no reform at all, or some smaller-scale changes such as those set out in the second half of this chapter. Nick Clegg himself suggested, when presenting the coalition's plans, that 'the key thing is not to make the best the enemy of the good. That approach has stymied Lords reform for far too long'.[38] In this he was entirely correct.[39] The whole history of Lords reform tells us that it is seemingly small and incremental changes that succeed, while ambitious large-scale reform packages always fail. The 1999 Act was simply one in a long line of such incremental reforms, each of which had been viewed as a temporary stopgap at the time. But, despite not giving the chamber 'democratic legitimacy', it had an important revitalizing effect. The next small steps, if focused on the least defensible elements of the present settlement—such as the remaining 92 hereditary peers and the extent of prime ministerial patronage—might also incrementally strengthen the chamber.

Notes

1. Quoted in *Islington Tribune*, 19 July 2012 (available at <http://www.islingtontribune.com/reviews/books/2012/jul/house-call-why-debate-lords-reform-bermuda-triangle-british-politics>, accessed 25 October 2012.
2. Given the number of proposals, their descriptions here are necessarily brief. For more detail, see Clarke and Purvis (2010) and Dorey (2008).
3. Labour's 1992 manifesto had promised 'replacement of the House of Lords with a new elected second chamber'.
4. The Labour Party submission instead emphasized that the reformed second chamber must be 'distinctive', 'representative' and 'independent', warning of the danger of 'it being simply the mirror image of the House of Commons' (1999: 21). While the document did not explicitly rule out election, it also failed to repeat Labour's previous commitment to a wholly elected outcome. But it also suggested that the second chamber's 'members should have equal standing, and there should be no opportunity for some to assert that they have a greater legitimacy than others' (1999: 20). This also suggested hostility to a mixed elected/appointed chamber.
5. This could have been seen as breaching a clause in the Commission's terms of reference, set by the government, which required its proposals to 'maintain the position of the House of Commons as the pre-eminent chamber of Parliament'.
6. Editorial, 8 November 2001.
7. For an account, see Dorey and Kelso (2011: 191–7), Cook (2003).
8. The complete set of options were: fully appointed, 20% elected, 40% elected, 50% elected, 60% elected, 80% elected, fully elected. The House of Commons also voted on (and defeated) a motion on abolition of the second chamber.
9. The government's previous preferred option of 20% elected was unanimously defeated, without a division.
10. As in 2003, the other options were 20%, 40% or 60% elected (which were rejected in both chambers). The Commons also voted again against abolition of the House of Lords, by 163 votes to 416. Subsequently, several anti-election MPs admitted to having supported the largely elected options as a voting tactic, to wrong-foot the government. For example, 'I certainly voted for an 80% elected Upper Chamber . . . but Members who were present at the time know that they were no more than wrecking votes' (Stuart Bell, *House of Commons Hansard*, 27 June 2011, column 677); 'I eventually voted for a 100% elected

House . . . if I voted for that, the establishment of a directly elected House of Lords would somehow be prevented . . . we were told that at the time' (Paul Murphy, *House of Commons Hansard*, 27 June 2011, column 680).

11. The Conservatives indicated support for a majoritarian system, such as that used for the House of Commons; other parties favoured proportionality.
12. One small exception was the clause in the bill that required members of the Lords (and MPs) to be resident in the UK for tax purposes, and allowed peers not wishing to accept this condition to permanently depart the chamber. This clause did make it into the final Constitutional Reform and Governance Act, and consequently five peers resigned their seats in July 2010.
13. The Constitution Unit (2010: 2) suggested: 'David Cameron would be well advised to accept the Lords clauses . . . to make life easier for himself if he enters government. First, Lords reform will otherwise be irritating unfinished business and he may be forced to reintroduce some of these clauses himself. Second, he will want (and deserve) to appoint numerous Conservative peers to refresh his benches. The space created by allowing retirements, and over time freed up by the hereditaries, could prove very useful. Otherwise he will stand accused of creating a chamber that is much too large'.
14. This had the distinction of being the largest government rebellion on second reading of any bill in the post-war period (Cowley and Stuart 2012b). One difficulty was that, following the unwhipped votes in 2003 and 2007, MPs had grown accustomed to being able to make up their own minds on this issue, and indeed many Conservatives were already on the record as having voted against an elected chamber.
15. See, for example, 'Lords reform: Cameron plans to offer Clegg watered-down deal', *Guardian*, 11 July 2012.
16. Graham Allen MP (Labour), *House of Commons Hansard*, 9 July 2012, column 60.
17. For example, in the 2007 vote, 80 Conservative MPs voted in favour of an 80% elected chamber, and 98 against; 157 Labour MPs supported this outcome, and 162 voted against. In contrast, all 62 Liberal Democrat MPs voting were in favour.
18. These arguments were influenced by recent experience of 'turf wars' between Scottish and Welsh MPs and members of the devolved assemblies over constituency work. See Russell and Bradbury (2007).
19. *House of Commons Hansard*, 9 July 2012, column 58.
20. *House of Commons Hansard*, 9 July 2012, column 50.
21. *House of Commons Hansard*, 9 July 2012, column 64.
22. *House of Lords Hansard*, 14 February 2012, column 691.
23. For example, Nicholas Soames MP (Conservative), *House of Commons Hansard*, 9 July 2012, column 104.
24. *House of Lords Hansard*, 21 June 2011, column 1173.
25. Speaking at a public debate organized by Intelligence Squared on 23 November 2010, in favour of the motion 'an elected House of Lords will be bad for British

democracy'. Available at <http://www.news.bbc.co.uk/democracylive/hi/comment/newsid_9261000/9261535.stm> (accessed 19 November 2012).

26. For discussion see, for example, Royal Commission on the Reform of the House of Lords (2000) and Russell (2000).
27. For a discussion, see McLean (2010b: 235, 296–7), and for more detail, his evidence to the Royal Commission.
28. House of Lords (Amendment) Bill, session 2002–03.
29. n = 371. This combines those responding 'agree' and 'strongly agree' on a five-point Likert scale.
30. *House of Lords Hansard*, 30 March 1999, column 207.
31. Notably, the Liberal Democrat peer Andrew Phillips took leave of absence in 2006, announcing that he intended to retire permanently. But he later chose to return in 2009, and has remained active ever since.
32. The latter policy was adopted in Canada in 1965, before which appointments to the Senate were for life.
33. For words from the coalition agreement, see Chapter 4. In the short term this would have a disastrous upward effect on the size of the chamber, and also require appointment of peers from extremist parties (see Russell et al 2011); if applied consistently it might even encourage the Lords to claim a greater legitimacy than the Commons, and create perverse incentives for citizens to vote tactically.
34. Such methods are generally used for elections in multi-member seats, but also, for example, in some parliaments for distribution of committee seats between parties. The basic principle is that the group which is currently most under-represented compared to strict proportionality criteria is given the next seat.
35. A 2001 poll by ICM found that 83% of respondents believed that appointments to the Lords should be made by an Appointments Commission, and only 12% believed that this power should rest with the prime minister (see Cruse 2012).
36. They are also worn by individual newly-appointed peers and their sponsors during their introduction ceremony. This could usefully end as well.
37. See this author's evidence to the House of Lords Information Committee (2009: 160–3).
38. *House of Commons Hansard*, 17 May 2011, column 156.
39. He did, however, later appear to change his mind. During questioning on his statement that the bill had been abandoned, on 6 August 2012, he dismissed the Steel bill as a package that would 'dignify an illegitimate house'.

11

Conclusions: The House of Lords, British Politics and Legislative Bicameralism

In explaining the House of Lords as an important but little-understood contemporary institution in British politics, this book has covered a wide range of topics. It provided context in terms of the Lords' history, and legislative bicameralism around the world, and described the behaviour, culture and impact of today's chamber in detail. It also reflected on how the institution is perceived, and prospects for its reform. The role of this final chapter is to pull the main arguments together, and draw conclusions based on the breadth of the material in the book.

Chapter 1 identified six questions particularly pertinent to the contemporary House of Lords, which helped to structure the analysis. These are used to create the sections that follow, which address the original questions one by one:

- First, is it right to consider the House of Lords as 'unreformed'? How does the post-1999 chamber differ from its predecessors? Does Britain have, to some extent, a 'new' House of Lords?
- Second, how does the chamber's culture and behaviour differ from that in the House of Commons? For example, is it right to see the Lords as a 'more expert' or 'less political' chamber? In what senses are the two chambers complementary to one another?
- Third, and crucially, what impact does today's House of Lords have on culture and policy outcomes at Westminster? Has this also changed since 1999? If so, what effect has this had on the balance of power in British politics?
- Fourth, given that the Lords remains unelected, can it be considered 'legitimate'? What effect do questions about legitimacy have on how the chamber operates, and its impact?
- Fifth, as the oldest second chamber in the world, the Lords was important in developing comparative scholars' understanding of legislative

bicameralism. If it has now changed, does this have implications for such theories?

- Finally, as a perenially controversial institution, what is the likely future for the House of Lords?

The House of Lords: 'Unreformed' or 'reformed'?

Britain is commonly seen as having an 'unreformed' and outdated second chamber. Many people no doubt still primarily associate the House of Lords with red robes, ermine, the state opening of parliament and the aristocracy. This image—which continues to be propagated by the media—was in truth already somewhat outdated in the mid-20th century (as discussed in Chapter 2). But 1999 marked a key turning point, when hereditary peers ceased to outnumber life peers in the chamber, and were instead reduced to a small minority. This had an immediate transformative effect. It was then followed by further gradual changes, and the cumulative impact has been substantial. The results can be seen in four broad areas: the nature of the chamber's members, its party balance, attendance and voting patterns, and peers' confidence to challenge government and the House of Commons. In each case, it is instructive to compare the chamber as described in this book with the pre-1999 body, as described by Donald Shell in 1992. Two decades on, the chamber that he depicted is almost unrecognizable.

Starting with membership, in 1990 the House of Lords included 22 dukes, 27 marquesses, 156 earls and countesses and 102 viscounts (Shell 1992). The *Sunday Times* 'rich list' indicated that 44 of Britain's 200 wealthiest people were among its members. The largest professional grouping (comprising 463 members) were those who could be described as a 'landowner/farmer'. Women made up only 73 of a total 1,186 peers (6%). In contrast, the overwhelming majority of members in today's chamber are barons or baronesses, who were appointed in their own right. The link between wealth and membership has largely been broken; the equivalent 2012 rich list included only seven peers among its 200 entries.[1] Those appointed to the chamber are nonetheless drawn from the senior ranks of their professional fields, among which the largest today include business, banking and finance, the law, higher education, and politics itself. Many members also have backgrounds in the voluntary and public sectors, while a wide range of policy specialisms are present.

It would plainly be wrong to claim that the Lords is fully representative in a descriptive sense (Pitkin 1967); the chamber falls well short of being a 'microcosm of the nation'. It can perhaps even still be described as an 'elite' body, but no longer in a class sense—it instead largely comprises professional high achievers. The modern House of Commons is also largely middle-class. It is more demographically representative than the Lords in terms of age, but the proportion of women is now almost identical in both chambers (at around a quarter), while the Lords contains substantially more members from minority ethnic groups and with disabilities.

Looking beyond the one-off change in 1999, gradual further changes have made the Lords a 'new' chamber purely in terms of personnel. There has been a constant stream of new arrivals, and many departures (largely due to death), so that by late 2012 only a minority of the chamber's members had served pre-1999. And each new member appointed brought new expectations of what was required, which led to major changes in behaviour. The starkest illustration of this is in the case of the Crossbenchers. Shell describes how during the 1989–90 session a majority of this group did not attend the chamber at all, while only 65 of a possible 508 (13%) were present for as many as a third of its sittings. Aside from hereditary peers, Crossbenchers had mostly received peerages in the queen's birthday and New Year honours lists, and faced little pressure to attend. In contrast, today's Appointments Commission peers are expected to be active, and in 2010–12 69% of Crossbenchers attended at least a third of sittings. The parties have also revised their appointment practices to put increasing emphasis on active membership. Reflecting on peers in general, Shell (1992: 48) noted how 'some belong so loosely that they are scarcely members in any real sense'. Today, in all of the chamber's groups, membership is no longer viewed primarily as an honour, but as a job.

A key driver of these changes was the transformation in the chamber's party balance in 1999. From the age of Pitt to the late 20th century the Conservatives had dominated the House of Lords. Overnight, that domination ended, and there is now general acceptance that no party should have a majority in the chamber. In practice, the balance of voting power is held by the Liberal Democrats (the main pivotal voters when Labour was in government) and the Crossbenchers (who became particularly important post-2010). For contrast with the past we can look to Shell's description of how in 1988, faced with some backbench dissent and fierce opposition party resistance, ministers issued a three-line whip to Conservative peers to support introduction of the 'community charge' (more commonly known as 'poll tax'). This prompted an unusually high attendance, and peers approved the policy by a majority of 133. It went on to become a well-known policy disaster (Butler, Adonis and Travers 1994; Dunleavy 1995). This shows how Conservative governments, despite suffering occasional Lords defeats, could ultimately depend on peers to pass their legislation—irrespective of widespread protests, even extending to their own backbench MPs. The picture for Labour governments was very different; the Conservative preponderance in the chamber ensured high numbers of Lords defeats. But '[b]ecause a Labour Government [was] defeated as a matter of routine in the Lords' division lobbies, the Commons also, as a matter of routine, [was] asked to cancel Lords' amendments' (Shell 1992: 253). As Shell put it, this was a 'manifest consequence of the absurdity by which a parliamentary chamber contain[ed] a permanent built-in superiority for one party' (Shell 1992: 254).

With respect to the chamber's confidence, we can recall that Shell summed up the Lords as 'reasonably diligent and generally dull, with a whiff of expertise but no real boldness, with conscience but not too much credibility, with a little public profile but no actual power' (1993a: 334). Since 1958, he suggested, the chamber had 'worked its way back from the margins of political life' (1992: 259); but its ability to influence either Conservative or Labour governments was very limited. When Labour entered power in 1997 with a commitment to remove the hereditary peers, some claimed that this would further weaken the already feeble chamber. Perhaps understandably, such concerns were expressed by Conservatives in particular. Viscount Cranborne, as the party's leader in the Lords, claimed of Tony Blair that 'once he's got rid of the hereditaries, he'll be absolutely delighted not to put anything in their stead. And that's very bad for parliament. It gives the government absolute power' (quoted in Mitchell 1999: 145).[2] Rationally, it did seem to make sense that removing hundreds of Conservative legislators would strengthen the Labour government's position. A *Times* editorial remarked on the eve of reform that '[i]t has been widely assumed, not least by ministers, that a House of Lords in which the hereditary peers, predominantly associated with the Conservative Party, are a relatively minor presence will prove less inconvenient than the one that is shortly to be banished'.[3] But any government hopes to this effect proved to be unfounded, despite Blair's large number of Labour appointments and his failure to proceed with a second stage of reform. Instead, the hereditaries' departure, and the resulting change in party balance, gave the chamber a new confidence with which to challenge the government. The consequences for British politics are significant, as further discussed later in this chapter.

The House of Lords and contrasts with the House of Commons

Before addressing this most central point, however, it is useful to consider the question of the Lords' ethos and distinctiveness from the Commons. There are important differences in the two chambers' membership, organization and behaviour. Some of these are longstanding, and others relatively new. Some are very clear-cut, while others are far less well-defined, and consequently more disputed.

Clearly the routes into the two chambers are entirely different. MPs are elected, and thus have an accountability both to their local parties and voters in their constituencies. To remain in parliament, they face re-election at least every five years. Members of the Lords are in contrast appointed for life. This has profound consequences both for who joins the chamber and how they behave once they arrive. The effect is clearest in terms of age. At the 2010 election, 128 people aged under 40 entered the Commons (admittedly, an unusually high number); in contrast, in the preceding 11 years just three people this youthful had been appointed to the Lords. Most peers arrive following significant professional experience outside parliament. This, combined with their freedom from re-election or reappointment, their more advanced age, and relative lack of ministerial ambition, make them less subject than MPs to pressures from party whips. Explicit votes against the party line are fairly unusual, but elderly peers and those with outside professional work have credible reasons not to attend, and deliberate abstention is evidently common. The chamber thus depends far more on goodwill than does the Commons.

Two frequent claims made about peers—that they are 'more expert', and 'less party political' than MPs—contain some truth, but the picture is not straightforward. First, it is important to note that many 'expert' peers are party-aligned. Famous names such as Robert Winston, Alan Sugar, P D James, and Sebastian Coe all sit on the party benches, alongside numerous others from academia, the arts, science and business. The highest concentration of 'experts' may be on the Crossbenches, where a record of achievement outside politics is paramount in gaining a seat, but this group has no monopoly on expertise. In addition, many on the party benches can be described as experts in politics itself, following years of service in the Commons, often including ministerial high office. Thus, Lords debates benefit from a combination of specialist technical knowledge and mature political judgement. Whether this exceeds the expertise of the Commons is a sensitive and ultimately contestable point. Few MPs have reached such high professional positions before entering parliament. On the other hand, they develop a different form of specialism, complementary to that of peers, through their local representative roles. MPs' constant exposure to citizens, through party campaigning, constituency correspondence and advice surgeries, gives them insight into both public opinion and policy as experienced on the ground. As a result, the two chambers enjoy significant complementarity.

The 'less partisan' nature of the Lords—also often cited—is connected to many of the factors already mentioned. Party peers' lack of an electoral mandate and relative freedom from the whip give them a greater liberty than MPs to listen to reasoned arguments, and to resist 'populist' policies. But the Lords' less partisan ethos crucially depends on the presence of the Crossbenchers, who remain completely free to express their own opinions, and can be influential on party peers (and other Crossbenchers) when speaking from positions of known expertise. Their presence creates an environment where debate must be very different to that in the Commons, and ministers have to adopt a far more conciliatory tone. The Lords still remains a partisan assembly, where the three main parties' positions are the primary determinant in the outcome of votes. But these positions must take party peers' concerns into account, while the chamber's overall party mix adds to the need for less adversarial and more reasoned approaches. In the Commons the government can usually depend on its majority, while in the Lords it must win support (or at least acquiescence) from members of other groups. In addition there is no presumption, as in the Commons, that time is spent by default on government business, and 'self regulation' leaves the Lord Speaker relatively powerless to control debate.[4] All of this contributes to a far less certain environment, where relationships must remain cordial. Ministers piloting legislation have to listen carefully to peers, and question time can be challenging, while committees highlight important technical and constitutional matters that are often overlooked by MPs. In general, the chamber focuses more on detail and less on the 'big picture' of politics than the Commons, though showdowns over major policies are always a risk, and help condition ministers' behaviour.

The House of Lords and contemporary British politics

So the Lords is now a very different institution to the largely hereditary chamber that existed pre-1999. It is no longer a body of wealth and privilege, but instead comprises largely of individuals appointed after distinguished professional careers. Today, membership is far more balanced demographically, but crucially also in party terms. Indeed, the chamber reflects how people vote in general elections more proportionally than does the House of Commons. All of this has given peers a new confidence, and created an environment where policy has to be carefully negotiated.

A central focus of this book has been the policy impact of the contemporary House of Lords, which the material in previous chapters indicated is considerable. This is most visible through government defeats, which have been numerous since 1999. Defeats are mostly non-trivial, and many concern major aspects of policy (though complete rejection of government bills remains rare). Despite the Commons' formal ability to overturn defeats, and if necessary to pass legislation without the Lords' consent under the Parliament Acts, around half are wholly or largely accepted by the Commons.

Defeats provide a backdrop for the more extensive policy negotiation that goes on between government and the Lords day-to-day. Preparation of legislation has become increasingly elaborate, following introduction of Lords 'handling strategies' when Labour was in government. Once bills are introduced, ministers engage in significant behind-the-scenes consultation with peers, not only from their own party (as occurs in the Commons) but also routinely with Crossbenchers and the opposition frontbench. In order to avoid defeat, or unnecessary legislative delay, significant concessions may then be given, usually through government amendments. The case studies in Chapter 7 suggest that the majority of amendments moved by ministers in the Lords that have any policy substance result from pressure by non-government peers. These amount to hundreds of legislative changes per year. But the chamber also has a far less measurable influence, which may actually be more important. The knowledge inside Whitehall that government can easily be defeated in the chamber, and must defend its policies to an audience including numerous subject specialists and experienced policy-makers, shapes how policy is prepared. Scholars frequently note how a legislature's main impact generally comes not through public confrontation, but through 'anticipated reactions' (e.g. Krehbiel 1992; Loewenberg and Patterson 1979; Mezey 1979; Norton 1993). As Blondel (1970: 78) put it, a legislature's 'reactive' work is visible, but its less observable 'preventative' influence will usually be greater.

If the Lords has a significant policy impact, of both a reactive and a preventative kind, it is important to understand which groups this makes the government responsive to, and on what policy matters. This is determined by the balance of the chamber's membership, and voting patterns of different groups, but also by other factors such as the focus of its specialist committees. At the level of raw voting strength we know that the Liberal Democrats became pivotal post-1999: had they continued to support Labour in the division lobbies (as occurred initially) Lords defeats during 1999–2010 would have been rare. But the Liberal Democrats increasingly found common cause with the Conservatives (and many Crossbenchers) on constitutional and civil liberties matters, in particular—resulting in many of Tony Blair's initiatives being blocked or watered down. By now, there is no novelty in claiming that the Liberal Democrats hold a position of influence: they obviously achieved this through entering coalition government in 2012. But the third party's influence had already been established through the House of Lords, and is thus quasi-permanent. Once the Lib Dems entered government, Lords dynamics changed significantly. The Labour opposition could still inflict government defeats, but only with support from sufficient independent peers. Crossbenchers became more active, and more frequently led on hostile amendments, in order to maximize support around the chamber. This new dynamic—like the previous power shift towards the third party—has so far gone largely unnoticed outside the Lords.

One interesting counterfactual is to consider what would have happened had the Conservatives won an outright Commons majority in 2010, and formed a single party government. The Liberal Democrats would have retained their pivotal position in the Lords, and almost certainly joined forces with Labour to defeat controversial policies on matters such as NHS reform and benefit cuts. For the first time in modern politics a Conservative government would have faced resistance from a centre-left dominated House of Lords. Had this occurred, it would have made abundantly clear how much the dynamics of parliament and party politics have changed. One reason that the effects of the 1999 reform have not been more widely noted is that the Lords always historically challenged Labour governments. Post-1999 it continued to do so. But any single party government now faces that same challenge. A Conservative administration attempting to introduce a 21st-century poll tax would almost certainly be prevented from doing so by the Lords.[5] Ill-thought-through legislation is no longer tolerated by peers, as the coalition discovered over its Public Bodies Bill (see Chapter 7). The Lords not only provides an effective access point for outside groups, but also now amplifies Commons backbench dissent rather than being a forum through which Conservative governments can suppress it.

In short, there are now significant checks on executive policy-making through the Lords—which marks an important change from the late 20th century. Britain can no longer be considered to have, as Bogdanor (1997: 119) suggested prior to reform, 'in effect a unicameral system of government'. Its bicameralism is no longer 'extremely feeble' (Sartori 1994: 188). Since 1999, bicameralism at Westminster has been revived. And this has important consequences for how we view power relations in the British political system. The old 'Westminster model' was based on a strong central executive with a Commons majority, facing few checks and balances. As indicated in Chapter 1, there has been much academic debate on whether power is actually more dispersed than this characterization implied. But even following Labour's post-1997 programme of constitutional reform, attention has focused on sites of negotiation outside Westminster itself. This book instead suggests that power has shifted at the heart of Westminster. The revival of bicameralism marks a clear shift on one of Lijphart's (1984, 1999) 10 indicators of 'consensus' versus 'majoritarian' democracy, and creates a new 'institutional veto player' in Tsebelis' (2002) terms. But the chamber's effectiveness also results from its inclusion of various 'partisan veto players' (Tsebelis 2002) or, to borrow another term more suited to a body where many members are non-partisan, various groups of 'pivotal voters' (Krehbiel 1998). The 1999 reform therefore both strengthened the Lords as an institution, and made Britain more plural in partisan terms. Although a strict application of Lijphart's theory has difficulty recognizing this (see Flinders 2005), the revival of bicameralism at Westminster brings Britain closer to the consensus model. Its effect is less transformative than the adoption of proportional voting for the Commons would be, given the chamber's secondary and unelected status. But while the primary chamber retains its traditional makeup (albeit now housing a coalition government), Westminster majoritarianism has been moderated by establishment of a relatively proportional second chamber.

A suggestion that the House of Lords has become a stronger force in British politics might appear at first glance to imply that power has shifted away from the House of Commons. But as the preceding chapters demonstrated, the true picture is more complex than that. Bicameralism should not be considered a zero-sum game, where one legislative chamber necessarily gets stronger at the expense of the other. As Anthony King (1976) noted many years ago, the pivotal voters in the Commons are ultimately the government's own backbench MPs, on whom it depends for both its legislation and its continuance in office. If this group solidly backs a policy that peers oppose, the government can generally hold firm. In contrast, when the pivotal voters in the Lords join resistance to policies on which government backbench MPs have doubts, ministers will often respond to combined pressure from the two chambers. In the decades since King first made his observation, the Commons has changed considerably (Cowley 2006; Flinders and Kelso 2011; Norton 2005; Russell 2011; Ryle 2005). Backbenchers have become more prepared to openly express their dissent through casting rebel votes, which alone makes ministers in the Commons more risk averse. In addition, MPs are far better resourced, Commons select committees have significantly expanded and grown in strength, and recent innovations such as election of these committees' members and the establishment of a 'Backbench Business Committee' have further boosted MPs' sense of independence. A more assertive Lords therefore complements an already more assertive and professional House of Commons. The two chambers, with their very different and complementary memberships, have created a stronger parliament overall.

The House of Lords and legitimacy

An ever-present controversy concerns the 'legitimacy' of the House of Lords. As shown in Chapter 9, legitimacy is a disputed concept, both in debates about the Lords and more widely among scholars of politics. The moral legitimacy of the unelected chamber remains contestable, but surveys of political elites and the public, and newspaper coverage, demonstrate that the Lords is perceived as legitimate in certain respects. The presence of non-partisan figures and 'experts' in the chamber, its reputation for reasoned argument, and its occasional challenges to government policy, all find significant support. Such views nonetheless co-exist with a widespread belief that those sitting in (both chambers of) parliament should be elected, and a recognition that the chamber lacks the 'democratic legitimacy' that election would bring.

Perceptions of legitimacy are central to how bicameralism works in Britain, and indeed (as discussed later) elsewhere. They explained why the pre-1999 chamber was weak, and help account for its greater assertiveness post-1999. A sense that the chamber was 'more legitimate' resulted from the eviction of members who had attained their seats by accident of birth, but also from the chamber's greater representativeness in party terms. The Liberal Democrats, from their new position of strength in the Lords, and critical of the 'first past the post' electoral system for the Commons, used this last factor (as seen in Chapter 4) to claim a new right for the unelected chamber to contribute to the policy process.

Nonetheless, there are clear limits on how far such claims can be pressed. MPs enjoy an electoral mandate, and the government has the legitimacy that comes with maintaining their confidence. Meanwhile the Lords exists under the constant threat of reform. This combination of factors continues to generate considerable caution in how peers use their powers. Conventions governing the relationship between the two chambers have come under some pressure since 1999, but largely survived. Centrally, the respect for Commons primacy on manifesto policies, and more pragmatically on matters where the government enjoys clear popular support, remains. Peers are now more prepared to question policies that are ill-thought-through, occasionally to reject knee-jerk populism, and to stick up for unpopular minorities when MPs may be unable to do so. Yet the opposition parties in the Lords, even when enjoying the ability to win votes in the chamber, have not pushed MPs further than they are prepared to bear. We saw from survey responses in Chapter 9 that 86% of peers in 2007 believed the chamber's 'confidence to demand policy change' had increased post-reform. Among those appointed to the chamber since 2009, 99% agree that 'it is important that the House of Lords should sometimes ask the government to think again'.[6] Nonetheless, 95% of peers agreed that 'the Commons must remain as the primary chamber'.[7] If MPs are determined, the democratic claim of the Commons can ultimately win.

It has perhaps been to the advantage of the Lords that we live in an age of scepticism about elected politicians. In recent decades public affiliation to political parties has weakened, not only in Britain but in other advanced democracies (Dalton 2004; Dalton and Wattenburg 2000; Stoker 2006). Declining trust in politicians' ability to take difficult decisions has created a trend of 'depoliticization', where responsibilities are delegated to arm's-length bodies, technocrats and 'experts' (Flinders 2012; Hay 2007; Vibert 2007). Like the power of transnational governmental bodies, or the role of unelected judges in political decision-making, these developments raise difficult questions about public accountability and legitimacy. But they do make the House of Lords' gradual evolution into a chamber of professional and political expertise seem fitting to the age. How public opinion in the UK develops as we adjust to the new role of the Lords, and how the tensions in such arrangements are ultimately resolved, may hold important broader lessons.

The House of Lords and legislative bicameralism

Britain, with the longest-existing such system in the world, has over the centuries significantly influenced how bicameralism is understood. The gradual separation of representatives of different 'estates' into distinct chambers of the English parliament informed the writing of early theorists such as Montesquieu (1689–1755), whose celebration of 'mixed government' influenced constitution-making in the US and other states. More recently, the *de facto* weakness of the late 20th century House of Lords has informed comparative theories of modern government (e.g. Lijphart 1984, 1999; Sartori 1994; Tsebelis 2002). Given the changes in the 21st-century House of Lords, it is therefore appropriate to revisit such theories to consider what can be learnt. Lessons may be drawn in four main areas, the first three of which relate to the three key dimensions of bicameralism.

- The most important concerns legitimacy: a dimension often previously omitted from comparative theories (Russell 2013). Lijphart's treatment of bicameralism recognized that the Lords' weakness in the 1990s resulted from its lack of legitimacy, and assumed that this derived from its unelected basis. He concluded that '[s]econd chambers that are not directly elected lack the democratic legitimacy, and hence the real political influence, that popular election confers' (1999: 206). But while the Lords' unelected basis partly explained its timidity, subsequent events suggest that a more subtle interpretation was required. Meanwhile, legitimacy concerns are raised about many other national second chambers, including those with a democratic basis, while others that are not directly elected (such as the German *Bundesrat*) exert significant power. Hence, legitimacy matters to bicameralism, but does not entirely lie where Lijphart assumed. The contributing factors for the Lords were indicated earlier; they relate to a combination of input, output and procedural factors. In any bicameral system, two chambers will function best together if they can both claim some kind of legitimacy, while at the same time remaining distinct. In an age of disillusionment with elected politicians, there are many and complex reasons why a second chamber may—or indeed may not—find sufficient public support.

- With respect to the better-established composition dimension, the lesson from the Lords echoes earlier conclusions of others (Druckman and Thies 2002; Tsebelis 2002), that while distinctiveness between the two chambers is important, in modern democracies it is generally partisan distinctiveness that matters most. Lijphart's theory instead put emphasis on differences in territorial representation between the two chambers. The recent silencing of the previously-powerful Australian Senate when John Howard's government briefly held a majority there during 2005–08 demonstrates how territorial differences can be eclipsed by ties of party loyalty (Russell 2013). With respect to the UK, Lijphart (1984) emphasized the class distinctions between the chambers, which could even lead to an expectation that removing the hereditaries would weaken the Lords by making it more similar to the Commons. But changes to its party balance, which created new groups of pivotal voters, were far more important. In fact, the Lords and the Australian Senate now share important similarities, as relatively proportional assemblies which sit alongside, and moderate the decisions of, majoritarian lower chambers historically dominated by single party governments. Despite their backgrounds as classic examples of the elite and territorial models of bicameralism respectively, both might now best be seen as examples of a *partisan model* of bicameralism, where two chambers are purposefully designed to reflect competing party majorities. Whether elected or appointed, this can provide both complementarity of membership, and a viable competing legitimacy, to allow bicameralism to function effectively.

- With respect to formal power, the post-1999 Lords also provides support for the conclusions of previous scholars who argued that a second chamber can exert significant influence even when lacking a veto power (e.g. Money and Tsebelis 1992; Tsebelis and Money 1997). The Lords' prior weakness may have led some (particularly US scholars who view an absolute legislative veto as the norm) to assume that its powers were ineffective. But the chamber's primary weakness was its lack of legitimacy, not its lack of power. In fact (as Chapter 3 shows), the majority of national second chambers are subordinate to their respective first chambers. As shown in the rest of the book, the Lords possesses adequate formal power to make the executive and first chamber think again. The year-long delay power in the Parliament Acts is substantial, and is something that governments will generally want to avoid. But there are many other important reasons to submit to the demands of a second chamber.

This leads to a fourth and more tentative lesson for comparative scholars, already identified earlier: that bicameralism need not function as a zero-sum game. Recent British experience shows that an assertive second chamber can empower pivotal voters in the first chamber, enhancing that chamber's influence as well as its own. If the pivotal voters in both chambers can find common cause, the effect of their combined pressure becomes hard for government to resist. The extent to which this dynamic depended on particular British circumstances—most obviously the relative caution of unelected peers and the relative willingness of government backbench MPs to rebel—is difficult to know. The detailed dynamics of intercameral relations elsewhere have been relatively little explored. This would be a fruitful area for future comparative research.

Finally, comparative experience of bicameralism also offers important lessons for the future of the Lords, as discussed in Chapter 3. It reminds us that questions about second chamber legitimacy, and pressures for reform, are not limited to Britain. Should such reform proceed, overseas bicameral legislatures also demonstrate that the Lords is not as unique as some might think, and that retaining features such as long terms of office, a membership renewed in parts and at least some unelected members, would be consistent with practice in many other contemporary states. This could also be beneficial in managing future arguments between the chambers, allowing the Commons to claim greater legitimacy and therefore to retain its primacy.

Even a fully elected replacement for the Lords would inevitably have its legitimacy questioned, but disputes would essentially centre on the merits of different electoral systems. There is no certainty that in such a dispute the Commons' first past the post system would win.

The House of Lords and its future

This leads to the final question, of what future lies ahead for the House of Lords. The chamber has changed substantially since 1999; but it remains controversial, and exists under the constant threat of reform. The two obvious paths of development lead either to a major Lords reform, as promised by successive governments over the last 100 years, or to continued gradual evolution. Evolution, in turn, might either weaken or further strengthen the Lords.

The prospects for 'wholesale' reform are not promising, as discussed in Chapter 10. Developments under Labour suggested that there was in fact no model of reformed membership that could command majority support: a minority elected chamber was seen as insufficiently democratic, while a majority elected one raised concerns about loss of expertise and independence, and the appropriate balance of power between the two chambers. To achieve support among MPs for a majority-elected outcome, a reform package would probably have to include some reduction in the chamber's powers. But a powers-and-composition reform package would be complex and inevitably attract much criticism. It might thus fare even worse than recent attempts to reform the chamber's composition alone. At the 2015 general election it seems unlikely that the Conservative manifesto will reiterate the party's 2010 commitment to a majority elected chamber, and while Labour may retain such a pledge the party remains very split. Even a future Lib-Lab deal on this would probably fail. The most viable option for reform therefore seems to be further gradual change, as occurred throughout the 20th century. A menu of possible proposals was set out in Chapter 10. Even small changes will be difficult to achieve, as these can be criticized for being overly conservative, and for propping up the status quo. But if the realistic choice is between no change or some minor improvements, the latter is clearly the more desirable. Furthermore, this book has shown how reforms initially seen as inadequate temporary stopgaps can have major effects. Further small changes could turn out to incrementally boost the chamber's effectiveness and its public image. Indeed, even tiny symbolic changes could help.

The primary risk facing the chamber as things stand is that a prime minister floods it with appointees in a way that either neuters opposition, or renders it too large to function. Hence, introducing formal, or even informal, limits on prime ministerial patronage is a priority in terms of next incremental reforms. But any prime minister swamping the Lords would be taking a major political risk, and would face a media backlash as well as a fierce backlash from the chamber itself. The Lords may yet seek to put new political obstacles in a Prime Minister's way, for example, by passing resolutions that set out a size cap or a proportionality formula. These would have no binding legal force, but their political influence could be significant, and might help to establish new conventions.

The likelihood is, therefore, that the Lords continues to incrementally grow in strength, with or without further large-scale reform. In most years a handful of peers die, new ones are added, and each new intake brings greater expectations of what they should contribute, and what they can achieve. The organization on all of the chamber's benches continues to become more professional and effective. Conventions governing appointments to the chamber are also gradually changing. The bestowal of honorific peerages has already largely ended, and what is left of 'automaticity' (for example, regarding retiring military chiefs) seems likely to eventually cease. Sensitivities over the chamber's size may likewise see the Prime Minister's 'resignation' and 'dissolution' honours lists quietly discontinued, or at least scaled back. Every new peer now faces an expectation of active attendance, so the chamber's image as a 'retirement home' may therefore fade. At the same time, greater pressures for diversity seem likely. Plaid Cymru has only recently gained seats, and other parties such as the Greens and SNP have a good claim for representation in what is now basically a proportional chamber. Both the Appointments Commission and the parties are under increasing scrutiny regarding gender, ethnic, regional, and professional diversity among those who they pick as peers.

A more diverse and vibrant membership is likely to generate further pressure for organizational change. Some conventions may come under increasing strain: the arguments over financial privilege on the coalition's Welfare Reform Bill (see Chapter 6) could augur things to come. In particular, a return to single party government in the Commons—especially if this is a Conservative government—is likely to bring greater clashes with the Lords. The ability of the third party (and minor parties) to join forces with Labour and Crossbench independents to block Conservative policies has not yet been fully tested. In the extreme, a future single party government might even feel tempted (as has occurred, for example, in Japan) to build an 'outsized' coalition in order to strengthen its position in the second chamber. Pressure to appoint more ministers from the Lords is possible, and media focus on the chamber may grow. Increased attention from interest groups could also put peers' limited resources under ever greater strain.

All of this will ultimately be conditioned by unpredictable future political events. But whatever happens, one thing seems certain: the House of Lords will continue to be a controversial institution. It is a second chamber, after all. Its primary purpose is to question the decisions of an elected chamber, the House of Commons. If it didn't do so, it wouldn't be doing its job. Whether elected or appointed, strong or weak, its role will therefore always be disputed. In a sense, that is what it is for.

Notes

1. *Sunday Times* rich list 2012: <http://www.features.thesundaytimes.co.uk/richlist/2012/live/> (accessed 14 November 2012).
2. For further such doom-laden predictions, see quotations in Russell (2010: 867–8).
3. 25 October 1999.
4. The starkest recent example of this was on 14 January 2013, when peers voted to halt the coalition's planned revision of constituency boundaries for the House of Commons. This had previously been legislated for in the Parliamentary Voting System and Constituencies Act 2011 (and subjected to fierce opposition by Labour: see Chapter 7). But an amendment was later tabled to the Electoral Registration and Administration Bill to prevent the changes, and supported by Liberal Democrat peers (in open retaliation to the way that Conservative MPs had voted on Lords reform). The amendment had been formally judged as 'inadmissible' by the Clerk of the Parliaments, on the basis that it was 'not relevant to the bill'. But peers chose to vote on it anyway. In the Commons, the Speaker would not have permitted debate on such an amendment. However, when the bill did return to the Commons for ping-pong, MPs chose to support the Lords' position. In both chambers Conservative members (front and backbench) voted to keep the boundary change while Liberal Democrats (front and backbench) voted with Labour to scrap it, splitting the coalition.
5. The policy did appear in the Conservatives' 1987 general election manifesto, but in sufficiently broad terms to potentially allow a great deal of negotiation over detail. The manifesto stated that the party would 'reform local government finance to strengthen local democracy and accountability' and 'abolish the unfair domestic rating system and replace rates with a fairer Community Charge' (quoted in Butler, Adonis and Travers 1994: 105).
6. New peers' survey. n = 76. The only dissenting new entrant responded 'neither' to this question, on a five-point Likert scale; 72% 'strongly' agreed.
7. 2007 survey. n = 374.

Bibliography

Adelman, P. (1985), 'House of Lords: The Peers Versus the People', *History Today*, 35(2), [<http://www.historytoday.com/paul-adelman/house-lords-peers-versus-people>].

Adonis, A. (1993), *Making Aristocracy Work: The Peerage and the Political System in Britain, 1884–1914* (Oxford: Clarendon).

Anderson, G. (2007), *Federalism: An Introduction* (Oxford: Oxford University Press).

Archbishop of York (1953), 'The Lords Spiritual', *Parliamentary Affairs*, 7(1), 96–101.

Aristotle (1995 [*c.*330BC]), *Politics* (Oxford: Clarendon).

Arter, D. (1985), 'The Nordic Parliaments: Patterns of Legislative Influence', *West European Politics*, 8(1), 55–70.

Bagehot, W. (2001 [1867]), *The English Constitution* (Oxford: Oxford University Press).

Bailey, S. D. (1953), 'Life Peerages', *Parliamentary Affairs*, 7(1), 109–20.

Baird, V. A. (2001), 'Building Institutional Legitimacy: The Role of Procedural Justice', *Political Research Quarterly*, 54(2), 333–54.

Baldwin, N. (1985), 'Behavioural Changes: A New Professionalism and a More Independent House' in P. Norton, ed, *Parliament in the 1980s* (Oxford: Basil Blackwell).

—— (1993), 'The Membership of the House of Lords' in D. Shell & D. Beamish, eds, *The House of Lords at Work* (Oxford: Clarendon).

—— (1995), 'The House of Lords and the Labour Government 1974–79', *Journal of Legislative Studies*, 1(2), 218–42.

Ballinger, C. (2012), *The House of Lords 1911–2011: A Century of Non-Reform* (Oxford: Hart).

Barker, R. S. (1990), *Political Legitimacy and the State* (Oxford: Clarendon).

Beck, T., Glarke, G., Groff, A., Keefer, P. and Walsh, P. (2001), 'New Tools in Comparative Political Economy: The Database of Political Institutions', *World Bank Economic Review*, 15(1), 165–76.

Beckett, J. V. and Jones, C. (1989), 'Introduction: The Peerage and the House of Lords in the Seventeenth and Eighteenth Centuries' in C. Jones, ed, *A Pillar of the Constitution: The House of Lords in British Politics, 1640–1784* (London: Hambledon).

Beetham, D. (1991), *The Legitimation of Power* (New York: Palgrave).

—— and Lord, C. (1998), *Legitimacy and the EU* (Essex: Addison-Wesley Longman).

Bennion, F. A. R. (2008), *Statutory Interpretation: A Code* (London: LexisNexis).

Benton, M. and Russell, M. (2012), 'Assessing the Impact of Parliamentary Oversight Committees: The Select Committees in the British House of Commons', *Parliamentary Affairs*, online early.

Bevir, M. (2008), 'The Westminster Model, Governance and Judicial Reform', *Parliamentary Affairs*, 61(4), 559–77.

Bingle, P. (2012), 'Fertile Territory: The House of Lords is Vulnerable to the Influence of Lobbyists', *New Statesman*, 16 July, 12.

Blondel, J. (1970), 'Legislative Behaviour: Some Steps Towards a Cross-National Measurement', *Government and Opposition*, 5(1), 67–85.

Bochel, H. and Defty, A. (2010), 'A Question of Expertise: The House of Lords and Welfare Policy', *Parliamentary Affairs*, 63(1), 66–84.

Bodansky, D. (1999), 'The Legitimacy of International Governance: A Coming Challenge for International Environmental Law?', *American Journal of International Law*, 93(3), 596–624.

Bogdanor, V. (1997), *Power to the People: A Guide to Constitutional Reform* (London: Victor Gollancz).

—— (2009), *The New British Constitution* (Oxford: Hart Publishing).

Brocklehurst, A. (2008), *Peerage Creations, 1958–2008 (LLN 2008/019)* (London: House of Lords Library).

—— and Kelly, R. (2012), *Peerage Creations since 1997 (LLN 2012/023)* (London: House of Lords Library).

Bromhead, P. A. (1958), *The House of Lords and Contemporary Politics, 1911–1957* (London: Routledge & Kegan Paul).

Bryce, J. (1918), *Report of the Conference on Reform of the Second Chamber—Letter from Viscount Bryce to the Prime Minister (Cd 9038)* (London: HMSO).

Buchanan, J. M. G. and Tullock, G. (1962), *The Calculus of Consent: Logical Foundations of Constitutional Democracy* (Ann Arbor, MI: University of Michigan Press).

Butler, D., Adonis, A. and Travers, T. (1994), *Failure in British Government: The Politics of the Poll Tax* (Oxford: Oxford University Press).

Cabinet Office (1999), *Modernising Parliament: Reforming the House of Lords* (London: The Stationery Office).

—— (2007), *The House of Lords: Reform* (London: The Stationery Office).

—— (2011), *House of Lords Reform Draft Bill* (London: The Stationery Office).

—— (2012), Guide to Making Legislation (June 2012), [<http://www.cabinetoffice.gov.uk/sites/default/files/resources/Guide-to-Making-Legislation_0.pdf>, accessed 9 November 2012].

Cannadine, D. (1992), *The Decline and Fall of the British Aristocracy* (London: Papermac).

CaSE (2012), *House of Lords Reform and Expertise* (London: Campaign for Science and Engineering).

Chong, D. and Druckman, J. N. (2007), 'Framing Theory', *Annual Review of Political Science*, 10(1), 103–26.

Clarke, C. and Purvis, M. (2010), *House of Lords Reform 1997–2010: A Chronology (LLN 2010/015)* (London: House of Lords Library).
Constitution Committee (2010), *Public Bodies Bill (Sixth Report of Session 2010–11)* (London: House of Lords).
Constitution Unit (2010), 'Lords Reforms: Large and Small', *Monitor*, 44, 2.
Cook, R. (2003), *The Point of Departure* (London: Simon and Schuster).
Cooper, C. (2012), 'Heir Not Apparent: Douglas Hailsham, the Role of the House of Lords, and the Succession to the Conservative Leadership 1928–31', *Parliamentary History*, 31(2), 206–29.
Cowley, P. (2002), *Revolts and Rebellions: Parliamentary Voting Under Blair* (London: Politico's).
—— (2005), *The Rebels: How Blair Mislaid His Majority* (London: Politico's).
—— (2006), 'Making Parliament Matter?' in P. Dunleavy, R. Heffernan, P. Cowley & C. Hay, eds, *Developments in British Politics 8* (Basingstoke: Palgrave Macmillan).
—— (forthcoming), 'In the Brown Stuff? Labour Backbench Dissent Under Gordon Brown, 2007–2010', *Contemporary British History*.
—— and Norton, P. (1999), 'Rebels and rebellions: Conservative MPs in the 1992 Parliament', *British Journal of Politics and International Relations*, 1(1), 84–105.
—— and Stuart, M. (2008), 'A Rebellious Decade: Backbench Rebellions Under Tony Blair, 1997-2007', in M. Beech and S. Lee, eds, *Ten Years of New Labour* (Basingstoke: Palgrave Macmillan).
—— —— (2012a), *The Bumper Book of Coalition Rebellions* (Nottingham: University of Nottingham).
—— —— (2012b), 'Four Records Down, a Fifth Avoided', *Ballots & Bullets*, [<http://nottspolitics.org/2012/07/11/four-records-down-a-fifth-avoided/>, accessed 11 July 2012].
Cracknell, R. (2012), *Ethnic Minorities in Politics, Government and Public Life (SN/SG/1156)* (London: House of Commons Library).
Crewe, E. (2005), *Lords of Parliament: Manners, Rituals and Politics* (Manchester: Manchester University Press).
Cruse, I. (2012), *Public Attitudes Towards the House of Lords and House of Lords Reform (LLN 2012/006)* (London: House of Lords Library).
Dalton, R. J. (2004), *Democratic Challenges, Democratic Choices: The Erosion of Political Support in Advanced Industrial Democracies* (Oxford: Oxford University Press).
—— and Wattenburg, M. P., eds, (2000), *Parties without Partisans: Political Change in Advanced Industrial Democracies* (Oxford: Oxford University Press).
Department for Constitutional Affairs (2003), *Constitutional Reform: Next Steps for the House of Lords* (London: The Stationery Office).
Deschouwer, K. (2009), *The Politics of Belgium: Governing a Divided Society* (Basingstoke: Palgrave).
Dorey, P. (2006), '1949, 1969, 1999: The Labour Party and House of Lords Reform', *Parliamentary Affairs*, 59(4), 599–620.

—— (2008), 'Stumbling Through "Stage Two": New Labour and House of Lords Reform', *British Politics*, 3(1), 22–44.

—— and Kelso, A. (2011), *House of Lords Reform since 1911: Must the Lords Go?* (Basingstoke: Palgrave).

Drewry, G., ed (1985), *The New Select Committees: A Study of the 1979 Reforms* (Oxford: Clarendon).

—— and Brock, J. (1993), 'Government Legislation: An Overview' in D. Shell & D. Beamish, eds, *The House of Lords at Work: A Study Based on the 1988–1989 Session* (Oxford: Clarendon).

Druckman, J. N., Martin, L. W. and Thies, M. F. (2005), 'Influence without Confidence: Upper Chambers and Government Formation', *Legislative Studies Quarterly*, 30(4), 529–48.

—— and Thies, M. F. (2002), 'The Importance of Concurrence: The Impact of Bicameralism on Government Formation and Duration', *American Journal of Political Science*, 46(4), 760–71.

Dryzek, J. S. and Dunleavy, P. (2009), *Theories of the Democratic State* (Basingstoke: Palgrave).

Dunleavy, P. (1995), 'Policy Disasters: Explaining the UK's Record', *Public Policy and Administration*, 10(2), 52–70.

Dymond, G. (2009), *The Appellate Jurisdiction of the House of Lords (LLN 2009/010)* (London: House of Lords Library).

European Union Committee (2010), *Annual Report 2010 (Third Report of Session 2010–11)* (London: House of Lords).

European Union Committee (2012), *Report on 2010–12 (First Report of Session 2012–13)* (London: House of Lords).

Feldman, D. (2002), 'Parliamentary Scrutiny of Legislation and Human Rights', *Public Law*, 323–48.

—— (2004), 'The Impact of Human Rights on the UK Legislative Process', *Statute Law Review*, 25(2), 91–115.

Fielding, S. (2003), *The Labour Party: Continuity and Change in the Making of 'New' Labour* (Basingstoke: Palgrave).

Flinders, M. (2005), 'Majoritarian Democracy in Britain: New Labour and the Constitution', *West European Politics*, 28(1), 61–93.

—— (2009), *Democratic Drift: Majoritarian Modification and Democratic Anomie in the United Kingdom* (Oxford: Oxford University Press).

—— (2012), *Defending Politics: Why Democracy Matters in the 21st Century* (Oxford: Oxford University Press).

—— and Curry, D. (2007), 'Bi-constitutionality: Unravelling New Labour's Constitutional Orientations', *Parliamentary Affairs*, 61(1), 99–121.

—— and Kelso, A. (2011), 'Mind the Gap: Political Analysis, Public Expectations and the Parliamentary Decline Thesis', *The British Journal of Politics & International Relations*, 13(2), 249–68.

Franks, C. E. S. (1999), 'Not Dead Yet, But Should it Be Resurrected? The Canadian Senate' in S. C. Patterson & A. Mughan, eds, *Senates: Bicameralism in the Contemporary World* (Columbus: Ohio State University Press).

—— (2003), 'The Canadian Senate in Modern Times' in S. Joyal, ed, *Protecting Canadian Democracy: The Senate You Never Knew* (Montreal: McGill-Queen's University Press).

Friedrich, C. J. (1937), *Constitutional Government and Politics* (New York: Harper and Brothers).

Gallie, W. B. (1956), 'Essentially Contested Concepts', *Proceedings of the Aristotelian Society*, 56, 167–98.

Gibson, J. L. and Caldeira, G. A. (1995), 'The Legitimacy of Transnational Legal Institutions: Compliance, Support, and the European Court of Justice', *American Journal of Political Science*, 39(2), 459–89.

—— —— (2003), 'Defenders of Democracy? Legitimacy, Popular Acceptance, and the South African Constitutional Court', *The Journal of Politics*, 65(1), 1–30.

—— —— and Baird, V. A. (1998), 'On the Legitimacy of National High Courts', *The American Political Science Review*, 92(2), 343–58.

—— —— and Spence, L. K. (2003a), 'Measuring Attitudes toward the United States Supreme Court', *American Journal of Political Science*, 47(2), 354–67.

—— —— —— (2003b), 'The Supreme Court and the US Presidential Election of 2000: Wounds, Self-Inflicted or Otherwise?', *British Journal of Political Science*, 33(4), 535–56.

Goodman, V. M. R. (1953), 'Appellate Jurisdiction', *Parliamentary Affairs*, 7(1), 77–87.

Goot, M. (1999), 'Whose Mandate? Policy Promises, Strong Bicameralism and Polled Opinion', *Australian Journal of Political Science*, 34(3), 327–52.

Grant, W. (2000), *Pressure Groups and British Politics* (Basingstoke: Palgrave).

Grantham, C. (1993), 'Select Committees' in D. Shell & D. Beamish, eds, *The House of Lords at Work* (Oxford: Clarendon).

Graves, M. A. R. (1985), *The Tudor Parliaments: Crown, Lords and Commons, 1485–1603* (London: Longman).

—— (1987), *Elizabethan Parliaments 1559–1601* (London: Longman).

—— (1990), *Early Tudor Parliaments 1485–1558* (London: Longman).

Griffith, J. A. G. (1974), *Parliamentary Scrutiny of Government Bills* (London: Allen and Unwin).

Grosskopf, A. and Mondak, J. J. (1998), 'Do Attitudes Toward Specific Supreme Court Decisions Matter? The Impact of Webster and Texas v Johnson on Public Confidence in the Supreme Court', *Political Research Quarterly*, 51(3), 633–54.

Hansard Society (2008), *Law in the Making: Influence and Change in the Legislative Process* (London: Hansard Society).

Harriss, G. L. (1981), 'The Formation of Parliament, 1272–1377' in R. G. Davies & J. H. Denton, eds, *The English Parliament in the Middle Ages* (Manchester: Manchester University Press).

Hawes, D. (1993), *Power on the Back Benches? The Growth of Select Committee Influence* (Bristol: SAUS).

Hay, C. (2007), *Why We Hate Politics* (Cambridge: Polity).

Hazell, R. (2004), 'Who is the Guardian of Legal Values in the Legislative Process: Parliament or the Executive?', *Public Law*, 495–500.

—— (2008), 'Conclusion: Where will the Westminster Model End Up?' in R. Hazell, ed, *Constitutional Futures Revisited: Britain's Constitution to 2020* (Basingstoke: Palgrave Macmillan).

Heller, W. B. (1997), 'Bicameralism and Budget Deficits: The Effect of Parliamentary Structure on Government Spending', *Legislative Studies Quarterly*, 22(4), 485–516.

Henderson, J. (2011), *The Constitution of the Russian Federation: A Contextual Analysis* (Oxford: Hart).

Hennessy, P. (2011), 'On Joining the Constitution', *The Political Quarterly*, 82(2), 165–8.

Hibbing, J. R. and Theiss-Morse, E. (1995), *Congress as Public Enemy: Public Attitudes Toward American Political Institutions* (Cambridge: Cambridge University Press).

Hiebert, J. L. (2006), 'Parliament and the Human Rights Act: Can the JCHR help Facilitate a Culture of Rights?', *International Journal of Constitutional Law*, 4(1), 1–38.

Hindmoor, A., Larkin, P. and Kennon, A. (2009), 'Assessing the Influence of Select Committees in the UK: The Education and Skills Committee, 1997–2005', *Journal of Legislative Studies*, 15(1), 71–89.

Hiroi, T. (2008), 'The Dynamics of Lawmaking in a Bicameral Legislature: The Case of Brazil', *Comparative Political Studies*, 41(12), 1583–606.

HM Government (2010), *The Coalition: Our Programme for Government* (London: The Stationery Office).

Hoekstra, V. J. (1995), 'The Supreme Court and Opinion Change', *American Politics Research*, 23(1), 109–29.

Holt, J. C. (1981), 'The Prehistory of Parliament' in R. G. Davies & J. H. Denton, eds, *The English Parliament in the Middle Ages* (Manchester: Manchester University Press).

House of Commons (2010), *Sessional Returns (Session 2008–09)* (London: House of Commons).

House of Lords (2010), *Companion to the Standing Orders and Guide to the Proceedings of the House of Lords* (London: House of Lords).

—— (2012), *Statistics on Business and Membership (Session 2010–12)* (London: House of Lords).

House of Lords Appointments Commission (2011), *Annual Report (April 2010 to September 2011)* (London: House of Lords Appointments Commission).

House of Lords Information Office (2010), *The Work of the House of Lords (2008–09)* (London: House of Lords).

Hunt, M., Hooper, H. and Yowell, P. (2012), *Parliaments and Human Rights: Redressing the Democratic Deficit* (London: AHRC).

Hurrelmann, A., Schneider, S. and Steffek, J. (2007), 'Conclusion: Legitimacy—Making Sense of an Essentially Contested Concept' in A. Hurrelmann, S. Schneider & J. Steffek, eds, *Legitimacy in an Age of Global Politics* (Basingstoke: Palgrave).

Information Committee (2009), *Are the Lords Listening? Creating Connections Between People and Parliament (First Report of Session 2008–09, Volume II)* (London: House of Lords).

Israel, J. I. (1998), *The Dutch Republic: Its Rise, Greatness and Fall, 1477–1806* (Oxford: Clarendon).

Jenkins, R. (1999), *Mr Balfour's Poodle: Peers vs People* (London: Papermac).

Jennings, I. (1957), *Parliament* (Cambridge: Cambridge University Press).

Johnston, R. and Pattie, C. (2011), 'Parties and Crossbenchers Voting in the Post-2010 House of Lords: The Example of the Parliamentary Voting System and Constituencies Bill', *British Politics*, 6(4), 430–52.

Joint Committee on Conventions (2006a), *Conventions of the UK Parliament (Report of Session 2005–06, Volume I)* (London: House of Commons and House of Lords).

—— (2006b), *Conventions of the UK Parliament (Report of Session 2005–06, Volume II)* (London: House of Commons and House of Lords).

Joint Committee on House of Lords Reform (2002), *House of Lords Reform (First Report of Session 2002–03)* (London: House of Commons and House of Lords).

Joint Committee on Human Rights (2006), *The Committee's Future Working Practices (23rd Report of Session 2005–06)* (London: House of Commons and House of Lords).

Joint Committee on the Draft House of Lords Reform Bill (2012a), *Draft House of Lords Reform Bill (Report of Session 2010–12, Volume I)* (London: House of Commons and House of Lords).

—— (2012b), *Draft House of Lords Reform Bill (Report of Session 2010–12, Volume II)* (London: House of Commons and House of Lords).

Jones, D. L. (2009), 'The Judicial Role of the House of Lords Before 1870' in L. Blom-Cooper, B. Dickson & G. Drewry, eds, *The Judicial House of Lords 1876–2009* (Oxford: Oxford University Press).

Juberias, C. F. (1999), 'A House in Search of a Role: The Senado of Spain' in S. C. Patterson & A. Mughan, eds, *Senates: Bicameralism in the Contemporary World* (Columbus: Ohio State University Press).

Judge, D. (1993), *The Parliamentary State* (London: Sage).

Kelly, R. (2011), *Short Money (SN/PC/1663)* (London: House of Commons Library).

Kelso, A. (2006), 'Reforming the House of Lords: Navigating Representation, Democracy and Legitimacy at Westminster', *Parliamentary Affairs*, 59(4), 563–81.

—— (2009), *Parliamentary Reform at Westminster* (Manchester: Manchester University Press).

——(2011), 'Stages and Muddles: The House of Lords Act 1999', *Parliamentary History*, 30(1), 101–13.

Ketterer, J. P. (2001), 'From One Chamber to Two: The Case of Morocco', *Journal of Legislative Studies*, 7(1), 135–50.

King, A. (1976), 'Modes of Executive–Legislative Relations: Great Britain, France and West Germany', *Legislative Studies Quarterly*, 1(1), 11–36.

——(2007), *The British Constitution* (Oxford: Oxford University Press).

Kingdom, J. (2003), *Government and Politics in Britain: An Introduction* (Cambridge: Polity).

Klug, F. and Wildbore, H. (2007), 'Breaking New Ground: The Joint Committee on Human Rights and the Role of Parliament in Human Rights Compliance', *European Human Rights Law Review*, 2007(3), 231–50.

Krehbiel, K. (1992), *Information and Legislative Organization* (Ann Arbor, MI: University of Michigan Press).

——(1998), *Pivotal Politics: A Theory of U.S. Lawmaking* (Chicago: University of Chicago Press).

Kreppel, A. (1999), 'What Affects the European Parliament's Legislative Influence? An Analysis of the Success of EP Amendments', *Journal of Common Market Studies*, 37(3), 521–37.

Labour Party (1999), *Reforming the House of Lords for the New Millennium* (London: Labour Party).

Large, D. (1986), 'The Decline of the "Party of the Crown" and the Rise of Parties in the House of Lords, 1783–1837' in C. Jones & D. L. Jones, eds, *Peers, Politics and Power* (London: Hambledon).

Leader's Group on Members Leaving the House (2011), *Members Leaving the House (Report of Session 2010–11)* (London: House of Lords).

Leader's Group on Working Practices (2011), *Report of the Leader's Group on Working Practices (Report of Session 2010–12)* (London: House of Lords).

Lester, A. (2002), 'Parliamentary Scrutiny of Legislation Under the Human Rights Act 1998', *European Human Rights Law Review*, 2002(4), 432–51.

Levitsky, S. and Murillo, M. V. (2009), 'Variation in Institutional Strength', *Annual Review of Political Science*, 12(1), 115–33.

Levmore, S. (1992), 'Bicameralism: When Are Two Decisions Better Than One?', *International Review of Law and Economics*, 12(2), 145–62.

Liaison Committee (2012), *Review of Select Committee Activity and Proposals for New Committee Activity (Third Report of Session 2010–12)* (London: House of Lords).

Lijphart, A. (1984), *Democracies: Patterns of Majoritarian and Consensus Government in Twenty-One Countries* (New Haven: Yale University Press).

——(1992), *Parliamentary versus Presidential Government* (Oxford: Oxford University Press).

——(1999), *Patterns of Democracy: Government Forms and Performance in Thirty-Six Countries* (New Haven: Yale University Press).

Lipset, S. M. (1959), 'Some Social Requisites of Democracy: Economic Development and Political Legitimacy', *The American Political Science Review*, 53(1), 69–105.

Loewenberg, G. (2008), 'The Contribution of Comparative Research to Measuring the Policy Preferences of Legislators', *Legislative Studies Quarterly*, 33(4), 501–10.

—— and Patterson, S. C. (1979), *Comparing Legislatures* (Lanham: University Press of America).

Longley, L. D. and Olson, D. M., eds, (1991), *Two into One: The Politics and Processes of National Legislative Cameral Change* (Boulder: Westview Press).

Lord Chancellor's Department (2001), *The House of Lords—Completing the Reform* (London: The Stationery Office).

MacCaffrey, W. T. (1965), 'England: The Crown and the New Aristocracy, 1540–1600', *Past & Present*, 30(1), 52–64.

Maddicott, J. R. (2010), *The Origins of the English Parliament, 924–1327* (Oxford: Oxford University Press).

Majone, G. (1998), 'Europe's "Democratic Deficit": The Question of Standards', *European Law Journal*, 4(1), 5–28.

Marriott, J. A. R. (1910), *Second Chambers: An Inductive Study in Political Science* (Oxford: Clarendon).

Massicotte, L. (2001), 'Legislative Unicameralism: A Global Survey and a Few Case Studies', *Journal of Legislative Studies*, 7(1), 151–70.

Matthew, H. C. G. (2004; online edn 2011), 'Gladstone, William Ewart (1809–1898)' *Oxford Dictionary of National Biography* (Oxford: Oxford University Press), [<http://www.oxforddnb.com/view/article/10787>, accessed 2 May 2012].

Maurer, A. (2003), 'The Legislative Powers and Impact of the European Parliament', *Journal of Common Market Studies*, 41(2), 227–47.

Mayes, C. R. (1957), 'The Sale of Peerages in Early Stuart England', *The Journal of Modern History*, 29(1), 21–37.

McCahill, M. W. (1978), *Order and Equipoise: The Peerage and the House of Lords, 1783–1806* (London: Royal Historical Society).

McGann, A. (2006), 'Social Choice and Comparing Legislatures: Constitutional versus Institutional Constraints', *Journal of Legislative Studies*, 12(4), 443–61.

McLean, I. (2010a), 'The Bishops' 1909 Moment', *Public Policy Research*, 16(4), 232–4.

—— (2010b), *What's Wrong with the British Constitution?* (Oxford: Oxford University Press).

—— Spirling, A. and Russell, M. (2003), 'None of the Above: The UK House of Commons Votes on Reforming the House of Lords', *The Political Quarterly*, 74(3), 298–310.

Menon, A. and Weatherill, S. (2008), 'Transitional Legitimacy in a Globalising World: How the European Union Rescues its States', *West European Politics*, 31(3), 397–416.

Merits of Statutory Instruments Committee (2012), *The Work of the Committee in Session 2010–12 (60th Report of Session 2010–12)* (London: House of Lords).

Mezey, M. L. (1979), *Comparative Legislatures* (Durham, NC: Duke University Press).

Miers, D. and Brock, J. (1993), 'Government Legislation: Case-Studies' in D. Shell & D. Beamish, eds, *The House of Lords at Work: A Study Based on the 1988–1989 Session* (Oxford: Clarendon).

Miller, G. J., Hammond, T. H. and Kile, C. (1996), 'Bicameralism and the Core: An Experimental Test', *Legislative Studies Quarterly*, 21(1), 83–103.

Miller, H. (1982), 'Lords and Commons: Relations Between The Two Houses of Parliament, 1509–1558', *Parliamentary History*, 1(1), 13–24.

Ministry of Justice (2008), *An Elected Second Chamber: Further Reform of the House of Lords* (London: The Stationery Office).

Minkin, L. (1980), *The Labour Party Conference: A Study in the Politics of Intra-Party Democracy* (Manchester: Manchester University Press).

Mitchell, A. (1999), *Farewell My Lords* (London: Politico's).

Mondak, J. J. (1994), 'Policy Legitimacy and the Supreme Court: The Sources and Contexts of Legitimation', *Political Research Quarterly*, 47(3), 675–92.

Money, J. and Tsebelis, G. (1992), 'Cicero's Puzzle: Upper House Power in Comparative Perspective', *International Political Science Review*, 13(1), 25–43.

Morgan, J. P. (1975), *The House of Lords and the Labour Government 1964–1970* (London: Oxford University Press).

Morris, R. M., ed (2009), *Church and State in 21st Century Britain: The Future of Church Establishment* (Basingstoke: Palgrave).

Morrison, H. (1964), *Government and Parliament: A Survey from the Inside* (London: Oxford University Press).

Mughan, A. and Patterson, S. C. (1999), 'Senates: A Comparative Perspective' in S. C. Patterson & A. Mughan, eds, *Senates: Bicameralism in the Contemporary World* (Columbus: Ohio State University Press).

Mullin, C. (2011), *A Walk-On Part: Diaries 1994–1999* (London: Profile).

Nelson, T. E., Oxley, Z. M. and Clawson, R. A. (1997), 'Toward a Psychology of Framing Effects', *Political Behavior*, 19(3), 221–46.

Newson, N. (2010), *House of Lords: Reform of Working Practices, 2000–2010 (LLN 2010/017)* (London: House of Lords Library).

—— and Purvis, M. (2012), *Delegated Legislation in the House of Lords since 2000 (LLN 2012/012)* (London: House of Lords Library).

Norton, P. (1993), *Does Parliament Matter?* (New York; London: Harvester Wheatsheaf).

—— (2003), 'Cohesion without Discipline: Party Voting in the House of Lords', *Journal of Legislative Studies*, 9(4), 57–72.

—— (2004), 'How Many Bicameral Legislatures Are There?', *Journal of Legislative Studies*, 10(4), 1–9.

—— (2005), *Parliament in British Politics* (Basingstoke: Palgrave).

Nye, J. (2004), *Soft Power: The Means to Success in World Politics* (New York: Public Affairs).

——(2008), 'Public Diplomacy and Soft Power', *The Annals of the American Academy of Political and Social Science*, 616(1), 94–109.

Page, E. C. (2001), *Governing By Numbers: Delegated Legislation and Everyday Policy-Making* (Oxford: Hart).

Paley, R. and Seaward, P. (2010), *Honour, Interest and Power: An Illustrated History of the House of Lords, 1660–1715* (Woodbridge: Boydell Press).

Papadopoulos, Y. and Warin, P. (2007), 'Are Innovative, Participatory and Deliberative Procedures in Policy Making Democratic and Effective?', *European Journal of Political Research*, 46(4), 445–72.

Patterson, S. C. and Mughan, A. (1999), 'Senates and the Theory of Bicameralism' in S. C. Patterson & A. Mughan, eds, *Senates: Bicameralism in the Contemporary World* (Columbus: Ohio State University Press).

Patzelt, W. J. (1999), 'The Very Federal House: The German Bundesrat' in S. C. Patterson & A. Mughan, eds, *Senates: Bicameralism in the Contemporary World* (Columbus: Ohio State University Press).

Peacey, J. (2012), 'The House of Lords and the "Other House", 1640–60' in C. Jones, ed, *A Short History of Parliament: England, Great Britain, the United Kingdom, Ireland and Scotland* (Woodbridge: Boydell Press).

Perceval, R. W. (1953), 'The Origin and Development of the House of Lords', *Parliamentary Affairs*, 7(1), 33–48.

Pike, L. O. (1894), *A Constitutional History of the House of Lords* (London: Macmillan).

Pitkin, H. (1967), *The Concept of Representation* (London: University of California Press).

Powell, J. E. and Wallis, K. (1968), *The House of Lords in the Middle Ages: A History of the English House of Lords to 1540* (London: Weidenfeld & Nicolson).

Procedure Committee (2012), *Grand Committees, Questions for Written Answer (11th Report of Session 2010–12)* (London: House of Lords).

Public Administration Select Committee (2002), *The Second Chamber: Continuing the Reform (Fifth Report of Session 2001–02)* (London: House of Commons).

——(2006), *Propriety and Honours: Interim Findings (Fourth Report of Session 2005–06)* (London: House of Commons).

——(2007), *Propriety and Peerages (Second Report of Session 2007–08)* (London: House of Commons).

Pumphrey, R. E. (1959), 'The Introduction of Industrialists into the British Peerage: A Study in Adaptation of a Social Institution', *The American Historical Review*, 65(1), 1–16.

Purvis, M. (2012), *House of Lords: Party and Group Strengths and Voting (LLN 2012/026)* (London: House of Lords Library).

Rhodes, R. A. W. (1988), *Beyond Westminster and Whitehall: The Sub-Central Governments of Britain* (London: Unwin Hyman).

—— and Marsh, D., eds, (1992), *Policy Networks in British Government* (Oxford: Clarendon).

Rice, S. A. (1925), 'The Behaviour of Legislative Groups', *Political Science Quarterly*, 40, 60–72.

Richard, I. and Welfare, D. (1999), *Unfinished Business: Reforming the House of Lords* (London: Vintage).

Richards, G. C. (1928), 'The Creations of Peers Recommended by the Younger Pitt', *The American Historical Review*, 34(1), 47–54.

Richardson, J. J. and Jordan, A. G. (1979), *Governing Under Pressure: The Policy Process in a Post-Parliamentary Democracy* (Oxford: Martin Robertson).

Riker, W. H. (1992), 'The Justification of Bicameralism', *International Political Science Review*, 13(1), 101–16.

Rogers, J. R. (2001), 'An Informational Rationale for Congruent Bicameralism', *Journal of Theoretical Politics*, 13(2), 123–52.

Rowse, A. L. (1933), 'The House of Lords and Legislation', *The Political Quarterly*, 4(3), 385–402.

Royal Commission on the Reform of the House of Lords (2000), *A House for the Future* (London: The Stationery Office).

Royall, J. (2012), 'Noble Opposition: Scrutiny in the Lords'. Speech to the Centre for Opposition Studies, London, 9 February 2012.

Rush, M. (2001), 'Socio-Economic Composition and Pay and Resources in Second Chambers', *Journal of Legislative Studies*, 7(1), 27–38.

—— and Jones, D. L. (1993), 'Services and Facilities' in D. Shell & D. Beamish, eds, *The House of Lords at Work* (Oxford: Clarendon).

Rushbrook, S. (2012), *Lord Steel of Aikwood's Private Member's Bills on House of Lords Reform (LLN 2012/017)* (London: House of Lords Library).

Russell, M. (1999), *Second Chambers: Resolving Deadlock* (London: Constitution Unit).

—— (2000), *Reforming the House of Lords: Lessons from Overseas* (Oxford: Oxford University Press).

—— (2001a), 'Responsibilities of Second Chambers: Constitutional and Human Rights Safeguards', *Journal of Legislative Studies*, 7(1), 61–76.

—— (2001b), 'The Territorial Role of Second Chambers', *Journal of Legislative Studies*, 7(1), 105–18.

—— (2005), *Building New Labour: The Politics of Party Organisation* (Basingstoke: Palgrave).

—— (2009), 'House of Lords Reform: Are We Nearly There Yet?', *The Political Quarterly*, 80(1), 119–25.

—— (2010), 'A Stronger Second Chamber? Assessing the Impact of House of Lords Reform in 1999, and the Lessons for Bicameralism', *Political Studies*, 58(5), 866–85.

Russell, M. (2011), '"Never Allow a Crisis to go to Waste": The Wright Committee Reforms to Strengthen the House of Commons', *Parliamentary Affairs*, 64(4), 612–33.

——(2012a), 'Elected Second Chambers and Their Powers: An International Survey', *The Political Quarterly*, 83(1), 117–29.

——(2012b), 'Parliamentary Party Cohesion: Some Explanations from Psychology', *Party Politics*, online early.

——(2013), 'Rethinking Bicameral Strength: A Three-Dimensional Approach', *Journal of Legislative Studies*, 19(3).

——Adonis, A., Allen, G., Boothroyd, B., Butler, R., Dean, B., Dholakia, N., D'Souza, F., Forsyth, M., Hazell, R., Jay, M., Mackay, J., Norton, P., Shell, D., Steel, D., Stevenson, D., Williams, S., Woolf, H. and Wright, T. (2011), *House Full: Time to Get a Grip on Lords Appointments* (London: Constitution Unit).

——and Benton, M. (2010), *Analysis of Existing Data on the Breadth of Expertise and Experience in the House of Lords: Report to the House of Lords Appointments Commission* (London: Constitution Unit).

————(2011), *Selective Influence: The Policy Impact of House of Commons Select Committees* (London: Constitution Unit).

——and Bradbury, J. (2007), 'The Constituency Work of Scottish and Welsh MPs: Adjusting to Devolution', *Regional & Federal Studies*, 17(1), 97–116.

——and Sandford, M. (2002), 'Why Are Second Chambers So Difficult to Reform?', *Journal of Legislative Studies*, 8(3), 79–89.

——and Sciara, M. (2007), 'Why Does the Government Get Defeated in the House of Lords? The Lords, The Party System and British Politics', *British Politics*, 2(3), 299–322.

————(2008), 'The Policy Impact of Defeats in the House of Lords', *British Journal of Politics and International Relations*, 10(4), 571–89.

————(2009), 'Independent Parliamentarians En Masse: The Changing Nature and Role of the "Crossbenchers" in the House of Lords', *Parliamentary Affairs*, 62(1), 32–52.

Ryle, M. (2005), 'Forty Years on and a Future Agenda' in P. Giddings, ed, *The Future of Parliament: Issues for a New Century* (Basingstoke: Palgrave).

Sandford, M. (2012), *Parliamentary Questions: Recent Issues (SN/PC/04148)* (London: House of Commons Library).

Sartori, G. (1994), *Comparative Constitutional Engineering: An Inquiry into Structures, Incentives and Outcomes* (London: Macmillan).

Saward, M. (1992), *Co-optive Politics and State Legitimacy* (Aldershot: Dartmouth).

Schmidt, V. A. (2013), 'Democracy and Legitimacy in the European Union Revisited: Input, Output *and* "Throughput"', *Political Studies*, 61(1), 2–22.

Select Committee on the Assisted Dying for the Terminally Ill Bill (2005), *Assisted Dying for the Terminally Ill Bill* (London: House of Lords).

Select Committee on the Speakership of the House (2005), *The Speakership of the House of Lords (Report of Session 2005–06)* (London: House of Lords).

Seyd, B. (1998), *Rebalancing the Lords: The Numbers*, Briefing 18 (London: Constitution Unit).

——(1999), *A Transitional House of Lords: The Numbers*, Briefing 45 (London: Constitution Unit).

Seyd, P. (1987), *The Rise and Fall of the Labour Left* (London: St Martin's Press).

Shell, D. (1985), 'The House of Lords and the Thatcher Government', *Parliamentary Affairs*, 38(1), 16–32.

—— (1992), *The House of Lords* (Hemel Hempstead: Harvester Wheatsheaf).

—— (1993a), 'Conclusion' in D. Shell & D. Beamish, eds, *The House of Lords at Work* (Oxford: Clarendon).

—— (1993b), 'The European Communities Committee' in D. Shell & D. Beamish, eds, *The House of Lords at Work* (Oxford: Clarendon).

—— (1999), 'To Revise and Deliberate: The British House of Lords' in S. C. Patterson & A. Mughan, eds, *Senates: Bicameralism in the Contemporary World* (Columbus: Ohio State University Press).

—— (2000), 'Labour and the House of Lords: A Case Study in Constitutional Reform', *Parliamentary Affairs*, 53(2), 290–310.

—— (2001), 'The History of Bicameralism', *Journal of Legislative Studies*, 7(1), 5–18.

—— (2007), *The House of Lords* (Manchester: Manchester University Press).

—— and Beamish, D., eds, (1993), *The House of Lords at Work* (Oxford: Clarendon).

Shephard, M. and Cairney, P. (2005), 'The Impact of the Scottish Parliament in Amending Executive Legislation', *Political Studies*, 53(2), 303–19.

Shugart, M. (2006), 'Comparative Executive-Legislative Relations' in R. A. W. Rhodes, S. A. Binder & B. A. Rockman, eds, *The Oxford Handbook of Political Institutions* (Oxford: Oxford University Press).

Smith, E. A. (1992), *The House of Lords in British Politics and Society 1815–1911* (New York: Longman).

Smith, P. (2004; online edn. 2011), 'Cecil, Robert Arthur Talbot Gascoyne-, third marquess of Salisbury (1830–1903)', *Oxford Dictionary of National Biography* (Oxford: Oxford University Press), [<http://www.oxforddnb.com/view/article/32339>, accessed 25 April 2012].

Smith, P. (2009), *The Senate of the Fifth French Republic* (Basingstoke: Palgrave).

Snow, V. F. (1963), 'The Evolution of Proctorial Representation in Medieval England', *The American Journal of Legal History*, 7(4), 319–39.

St George, C. F. L. (1953), 'The Composition of the House of Lords', *Parliamentary Affairs*, 7(1), 60–7.

Stoker, G. (2006), *Why Politics Matters: Making Democracy Work* (Basingstoke: Palgrave).

Strathclyde, T. (1999), 'Redefining the Boundaries Between the Two Houses'. Speech to Politeia, London, 30 December 1999.

Swatland, A. (1996), *The House of Lords in the Reign of Charles II* (Cambridge: Cambridge University Press).

Takayanagi, M. (2008), 'A Changing House: The Life Peerages Act 1958', *Parliamentary History*, 27(3), 380–92.

Tordoff, L. (2005), 'The Role of Select Committees in the House of Lords' in N. Baldwin, ed, *Parliament in the 21st Century* (London: Politico's).

Torrance, M. (2012), *Select Committees in the House of Lords (LLN 2012/031)* (London: House of Lords Library).

Tsebelis, G. (2002), *Veto Players: How Political Institutions Work* (Princeton: Princeton University Press).

—— and Money, J. (1997), *Bicameralism* (Cambridge: Cambridge University Press).

Turberville, A. S. (1927), *The House of Lords in the XVIIIth Century* (Oxford: Clarendon).

—— (1958), *The House of Lords in the Age of Reform, 1784–1837* (London: Faber & Faber).

Tyler, P., Clarke, K., Cook, R., Wright, T. and Young, G. (2005), *Reforming the House of Lords: Breaking the Deadlock* (London: Constitution Unit).

Tyler, T. R. and Rasinski, K. (1991), 'Procedural Justice, Institutional Legitimacy, and the Acceptance of Unpopular US Supreme Court Decisions: A Reply to Gibson', *Law and Society Review*, 25(3), 621–9.

Tyrie, A. and Young, G. (2009), *An Elected Second Chamber: A Conservative View* (London: Constitution Unit).

Uhr, J. (1997), 'Parliament' in B. Galligan, I. Mcallister & J. Ravenhill, eds, *New Developments in Australian Politics* (Melbourne: Macmillan Education).

Vibert, F. (2007), *The Rise of the Unelected: Democracy and the New Separation of Powers* (Cambridge: Cambridge University Press).

Vollmer, P. M. (2011), *Financial Support for Members of the House of Lords (LLN 2011/039)* (London: House of Lords Library).

—— (2012), *Work of the House of Lords: Statistics (LLN 2012/009)* (London: House of Lords Library).

Walters, R. (2003), 'The House of Lords' in V. Bogdanor, ed, *The British Constitution in the Twentieth Century* (Oxford: Oxford University Press).

Webb, P. (2000), *The Modern British Party System* (London: Sage).

Weber, M. (1957), *The Theory of Social and Economic Organization* (Glencoe, Ill.: Free Press).

Weston, C. C. (1986), 'Salisbury and the Lords, 1868–1895' in C. Jones & D. L. Jones, eds, *Peers, Politics and Power* (London: Hambledon).

—— (1995), *The House of Lords and Ideological Politics: Lord Salisbury's Referendal Theory and the Conservative Party, 1846–1922* (Philadelphia: American Philosophical Society).

Wheeler-Booth, M. (2001), 'Procedure: A Case Study of the House of Lords', *Journal of Legislative Studies*, 7(1), 77–92.

Yong, B. (2012), 'The Coalition in Parliament' in R. Hazell & B. Yong, eds, *The Politics of Coalition: How the Conservative-Liberal Democrat Government Works* (Oxford: Hart).

—— and Hazell, R. (2011), *Putting Goats Amongst the Wolves: Appointing Ministers from Outside Parliament* (London: Constitution Unit).

Index of Names

Index

The manufacturer's authorised representative in the EU for product safety is Oxford University Press España S.A. of El Parque Empresarial San Fernando de Henares, Avenida de Castilla, 2 - 28830 Madrid (www.oup.es/en or product.safety@oup.com). OUP España S.A. also acts as importer into Spain of products made by the manufacturer.
Printed and bound by CPI Group (UK) Ltd, Croydon, CR0 4YY
14/09/2026
02216304-0009